T0073181

Mastering Bootstrap

Mastering Bootstrap helps the reader master Bootstrap CSS framework for faster and robust front-end development.

If you work in the web development world, you must have heard about Bootstrap, a comprehensive toolkit that includes HTML, CSS, and JavaScript tools for creating and developing web pages and apps.

Ever since it was released as an open-source project in 2011, Bootstrap has attracted increasing attention for legitimate reasons. Bootstrap is popular among web designers and developers since it is versatile and straightforward. Its significant characteristics are that it is adaptive by aesthetics, supports a colossal spectrum of browsers, and provides a reliable configuration by employing reusable components. It is simple to use and understand.

Bootstrap consists of a source code version and an executable version. Software engineers use Bootstrap for a variety of reasons. The Grid System in Bootstrap is popular mainly because it is simple to set up and master, with many components, styling for numerous HTML elements ranging from typography to buttons, and JavaScript plugin compatibility, all of which makes it even more versatile.

For a web designer, learning Bootstrap is almost imperative today since it allows your website to look good on every screen resolution and adaptable on every device without much effort. This will make your site appear more presentable, reduce development time, and be more convenient since it is simple to learn and execute. Many businesses continue to use it; hence it is a valuable talent.

As a career option, knowing Bootstrap might be a massive help if you want to work as a web developer. This is true whether you specialize in front-end or back-end web development. Bootstrap can help you save time and ensure that your websites are mobile-friendly and responsive.

With *Mastering Bootstrap*, learning Bootstrap becomes a charm, and will undoubtedly help readers advance their careers.

The *Mastering Computer Science* series is edited by Sufyan bin Uzayr, a writer and educator with more than a decade of experience in the computing field.

Mastering Computer Science

Series Editor: Sufyan bin Uzayr

Mastering Bootstrap: A Beginner's Guide

Lokesh Pancha, Divya Sachdeva, and Rubina Salafey

Mastering Ubuntu: A Beginner's Guide

Jaskiran Kaur, Rubina Salafey, and Shahryar Raz

Mastering React: A Beginner's Guide

Mohammad Ammar, Divya Sachdeva, and Rubina Salafey

Mastering React Native: A Beginner's Guide

Lokesh Pancha, Jaskiran Kaur, and Divya Sachdeva

Mastering Visual Studio Code: A Beginner's Guide

Jaskiran Kaur, D Nikitenko, and Mathew Rooney

Mastering Rust: A Beginner's Guide

Divya Sachdeva, Faruq KC, and Aruqqa Khateib

For more information about this series, please visit: https://www.rout-ledge.com/Mastering-Computer-Science/book-series/MCS

The "Mastering Computer Science" series of books are authored by the Zeba Academy team members, led by Sufyan bin Uzayr.

Zeba Academy is an EdTech venture that develops courses and content for learners primarily in STEM fields, and offers education consulting to Universities and Institutions worldwide. For more info, please visit https://zeba.academy

Mastering Bootstrap

A Beginner's Guide

Edited by Sufyan bin Uzayr

CRC Press
Taylor & Francis Group
Boca Raton London New York

CRC Press is an imprint of the
Taylor & Francis Group, an **informa** business

First Edition published 2023
by CRC Press
6000 Broken Sound Parkway NW, Suite 300, Boca Raton, FL 33487-2742

and by CRC Press
2 Park Square, Milton Park, Abingdon, Oxon, OX14 4RN

CRC Press is an imprint of Taylor & Francis Group, LLC

Library of Congress Cataloging-in-Publication Data

Names: Bin Uzayr, Sufyan, editor.
Title: Mastering Bootstrap : a beginner's guide / edited by Sufyan bin Uzayr.
Description: First edition. | Boca Raton : CRC Press, 2023. | Includes bibliographical references and index.
Identifiers: LCCN 2022021413 (print) | LCCN 2022021414 (ebook) | ISBN 9781032316017 (hbk) | ISBN 9781032316000 (pbk) | ISBN 9781003310501 (ebk)
Subjects: LCSH: Bootstrap (Computer program) | Web site development--Computer programs.
Classification: LCC TK5105.8885.B66 M37 2023 (print) | LCC TK5105.8885.B66 (ebook) | DDC 006.7/8--dc23/eng/20220725
LC record available at https://lccn.loc.gov/2022021413
LC ebook record available at https://lccn.loc.gov/2022021414

ISBN: 9781032316017 (hbk)
ISBN: 9781032316000 (pbk)
ISBN: 9781003310501 (ebk)

DOI: 10.1201/9781003310501

Typeset in Minion
by Deanta Global Publishing Services, Chennai, India

Contents

Chapter 3 ■ Customization 29

Mastering Computer Science Series Preface

THE *MASTERING COMPUTER SCIENCE* covers a wide range of topics, spanning programming languages as well as modern-day technologies and frameworks. The series has a special focus on beginner-level content, and is presented in an easy to understand manner, comprising:

- Crystal-clear text, spanning various topics sorted by relevance.

- Special focus on practical exercises, with numerous code samples and programs.

- A guided approach to programming, with step by step tutorials for the absolute beginners.

- Keen emphasis on real-world utility of skills, thereby cutting the redundant and seldom-used concepts and focusing instead of industry-prevalent coding paradigm.

- A wide range of references and resources, to help both beginner and intermediate-level developers gain the most out of the books.

The *Mastering Computer Science* series of books start from the core concepts, and then quickly move on to industry-standard coding practices, to help learners gain efficient and crucial skills in as little time as possible. The books assume no prior knowledge of coding, so even the absolute newbie coders can benefit from this series.

The *Mastering Computer Science* series is edited by Sufyan bin Uzayr, a writer and educator with more than a decade of experience in the computing field.

About the Editor

SUFYAN BIN UZAYR IS a writer, coder, and entreprencur with more than a decade of experiencc in the industry. He has authored several books in the past, pertaining to a diverse range of topics, ranging from History to Computers/IT.

Sufyan is the Director of Parakozm, a multinational IT company specializing in EdTech solutions. He also runs Zeba Academy, an online learning and teaching vertical with a focus on STEM fields.

Sufyan specializes in a wide variety of technologies, such as JavaScript, Dart, WordPress, Drupal, Linux, and Python. He holds multiple degrees, including ones in Management, IT, Literature, and Political Science.

Sufyan is a digital nomad, dividing his time between four countries. He has lived and taught in universities and educational institutions around the globe. Sufyan takes a keen interest in technology, politics, literature, history and sports, and in his spare time, he enjoys teaching coding and English to young students.

Learn more at sufyanism.com.

CHAPTER 1

Introduction to Bootstrap

IN THIS CHAPTER

➢ Introduction

➢ What is Bootstrap

➢ Advantages and Disadvantages

➢ Benefits Over Other CSS Frameworks

Introduction to Bootstrap

This chapter will cover the basics of Bootstrap, including its merits and weaknesses, as well as the advantages of Bootstrap over other CSS frameworks.

DOI: 10.1201/9781003310501-1

INTRODUCTION

Bootstrap was developed by M. Otto and Jacob Thornton at Twitter and released as an open-source product in August 2011 on GitHub.

It is an HTML, CSS, and JS framework used to develop responsive and mobile-first web projects.

The Bootstrap framework comes up with predefined terms, thus giving you the ability to use these codes instead of creating the codes from scratch.

It has ended up being the trendiest front-end system in the entire web design industry. Before it got to be open-source, it was first distinguished as Twitter's blueprint.

It is responsive, portable, winning, and has a front-end structure that produces CSS, JavaScript, and HTML. There are classes in Bootstrap that can be used to construct the front-end of the pages, which is perfect for most browsers and devices, in a brief length of time which generally would be an exceptionally tedious errand.

The primary add-on of using Bootstrap as a CSS framework is to encourage consistency across internal tools. Somewhat surprisingly, until recently, there were barely any processes to share standard design and patterns. Straight out of the window, it supports the newest versions of Chrome, Firefox, Internet Explorer, Opera, and Safari. Bootstrap even provides support as far back as Internet Explorer 8, meaning Bootstrap will offer you wider accessibility right from the start.

Bootstrap's major purpose is to eliminate discrepancies between designers and developers working on projects. Whether you need dropdowns, navigations, breadcrumbs, alarms, or progress bars, the Bootstrap framework will serve as a fundamental collection of development code. Even better, Bootstrap has been rigorously tested on a variety of prominent mobile devices and platforms, ensuring its dependability..

Now let's focus on what Bootstrap is, why it is so famous and valuable, and how it is used.

WHAT IS BOOTSTRAP?

- It is an HTML, CSS, and JS framework used to develop responsive and mobile-first web projects.

- The Bootstrap framework comes up with predefined terms, thus giving you the ability to use these codes instead of creating the codes from scratch.

- It is a free front-end framework for quicker and easier web development.

- It includes HTML and CSS-based design templates for typography, forms, buttons, navigation, modals, image, and many others, as well as optional JavaScript plugins.

- Bootstrap also gives you the ability to create responsive designs easily.

Now it is time to turn our attention to the advantages and disadvantages of Bootstrap.

ADVANTAGES AND DISADVANTAGES

First, we will focus on the advantages of Bootstrap.

Advantages

1. It has fewer cross-browser bugs.

2. It is a consistent framework that supports all major browsers and CSS compatibility fixes.

3. It is lightweight and customizable.

4. It has responsive structure and styles.

5. Several JavaScript plugins use jQuery.

6. It has excellent documentation and expert help.

7. Bootstrap has loads of free and professional templates, WordPress, and themes, and plugins.

8. It has great grid system.

9. Writing code can be highly time-consuming, mainly if you don't document your work and read through code to figure out where to pick it up. Not only does Bootstrap have excellent documentation on components, but by using it, you don't have to write code anymore. Only you need to get started with some knowledge of HTML, CSS, or JavaScript, and you can start developing. It is also effortless to use, which means you won't have to waste a couple of days just figuring out things.

10. Solving the consistency issues between the development front-end and the end-users, Bootstrap became the number one framework among web developers. The main problem is various inconsistencies between developers and designers on a project because the final results always look the same on any platform and browser.

11. One of the best things about it is that the coders will be free to code without worrying about how their work will look in the end. Add detailed tutorial documents to that, and you have an extremely beginner-friendly framework. If a new person adds to your team, it'll be effortless for them to learn how to use it. Anything users need to know about it – you can find it in the docs.

12. A sound grid system is required if you're looking to make page layouts, and it has probably the best responsive grid system. Its website contents are divided into 12 fluids. It makes users working through columns a breeze, which is very cool when you hide platform-specific content. Elements can be made visible on a desktop (you don't need them on mobile devices) and vice versa. Using the predefined classes will make utilizing the grid much easier and faster to get a grasp on it.

Despite these advantages of using Bootstrap, there are some disadvantages of Bootstrap as well on which we will now focus.

Disadvantages

1. There will be the need for lots of style overrides or rewriting files that can lead to a lot of time wasted on designing, and coding the website of the design tends to deviate from the traditional technique used in it.

2. You would have to go the extra mile to create the design. Otherwise, all the websites will look the same if you don't do any customization.

3. Styles are lengthy and can lead you to lots of output in Hypertext markup language, which is unnecessary. JS is tied to jQuery and is one of the commonest libraries, which thus leaves most of the plugins unused.

4. It has non-compliant HTML.

5. Everything built with this framework will have a very similar feel. A user might be able to override and modify style sheets manually, but

this work can kill the purpose of initially using it. And even if you do, there's no change and all websites built through this framework will be highly recognizable as Bootstrap.

6. While it is easy for a user to learn using Bootstrap, you still have to devote some time to it. You'll need to know all available Bootstrap Cascading Style Sheets classes and how their components access classes. You'll also have to invest some time to experiment with and get used to the grid system. As we said, Bootstrap's outstanding documentation goes a long way to get users through the learning process, and once users are used to it, you won't need much time adapting to the newer versions of the code.

7. While it is easy to create a responsive website with Bootstrap, the results can be pretty heavy for the users: slower loading times and battery loss problems. Also, the files generated by it can be enormous, which can slow things down for users quite heavily. You might be able to remove the items manually, but this again defeats the purpose of using the framework.

8. Using this framework for web development has clear ups and downs, and it all depends on you whether you use it or not. However, it is worth noting that time is highly valuable these days, so every minute you save by using this framework like Bootstrap can mean a lot. It can also make the whole working experience more fun since you won't have to worry about how your result looks like – you'll already know it from the get-go.

These are the advantages and disadvantages of Bootstrap. Now let's try to know the benefits of Bootstrap over other CSS frameworks, and also why using Bootstrap is so efficient and time-saving.

BENEFITS OVER OTHER CSS FRAMEWORKS

Bootstrap has several advantages over other CSS frameworks:

1. **Bootstrap is highly responsive**: Responsiveness is the most important of the framework. Mobile phone devices continue to become well known, and therefore the necessity of having a responsive website has ended up obligatory and vital. Bootstrap offers a 12-column grid system, layouts, and components. It conforms itself, depending

on the device resolutions of its customer. You can perceive the number of places in the grid framework that you might want each column to take part in using instant classes of Bootstrap. The grid has types sm, xs, MD, and LG, each speaking to a device resolution. The developers incorporate these classes while defining the visibility of a component in the markup. So, today it is clear that the responsive grid makes creation of responsive sites truly simple using Bootstrap.

2. **It is flexible and easy to use**: It gives the designers the adaptability to make. It is a CSS structure with predefined classes for format using its lattice framework, different CSS segments, and JavaScript capabilities.

These are included, and the designer has the adaptability and the opportunity to use just those classes required in the markup. It makes it exceptionally adaptable as only the necessary items in the markup are used by the designer, leaving the rest.

3. **Bootstrap has extraordinary grid framework**: Bootstrap is based on a responsive 12-section column grid, formats, and segments. It does not matter whether you require an altered network or a responsive. Balancing of sections is additionally conceivable in both altered and liquid width designs.

Another beneficial arrangement of the elements is responsive utility classes which you can utilize for creating a composition of substance that show up or show away only gadgets because of the extent of their concealment, which is exceptionally helpful when a user needs to conceal some substance of screen size. Including a category, for instance, a Noticeable desktop, to a component will make it unmistakable for the desktop clients. There are comparative classes for tablets and mobile phones.

4. **The speed of advancement is remarkable**: One of the primary advantages of using it relates to the speed of the advancement. When driving out another, crisp site or application quickly, you absolutely ought to reflect after using it. Rather of writing from scratch, it allows you to employ rapid code blocks with the objective of assisting you with installation.

You may combine them with CSS-Less functionality and cross-browser compatibility to save a significant amount of time in developing. You can even buy instant Bootstrap themes and change them to fit your prerequisites for picking up the fastest potential course.

5. **Bootstrap has packaged JavaScript modules**: For example, the parts are made intelligent with the various JavaScript modules packaged in the Bootstrap bundle. If you anticipate requirements for sliders, tabs, accordions, then you no longer need to attempt and test multiple diverse modules available on the web.

   Bootstrap including these functionalities is simply an issue of including a few lines of code, and you are good to go. You can likewise pick just specific modules to keep the record size to a base with the customization alternative.

6. **Bootstrap gets regular updates**: Bootstrap releases a more significant number of updates than whatever other framework. The Bootstrap improvement team when experiences any issue, it sets about by sharing it with the system.

   With it, updates released reliably and often, you can rest guaranteed that you are working with the most recent tools. Likewise, it guarantees a more extensive scope of cross-device and cross-browser similarity.

7. **Bootstrap has an excellent support team**: As Bootstrap holds a significant support team, you can be furnished with help whenever there comes any issue. The makers dependably keep it upgraded.

   Shortly, it is facilitated, extended, and protected on GitHub alongside more than 9,000 submits and more than 100 presenters.

8. **It has rich documentation and helpful experts**: Bootstrap has exceptionally itemized documentation and a boundless community helping it. Regardless of the possibility that a coder is new, the documentation gives excellent support in learning it with no bothers.

   The documentation incorporates illustrations and demos that help understand the ideas and get used to Bootstrap in a limited amount of time. Regardless of such nitty-gritty documentation, there is a possibility that a designer can stall at some places, so there is a limitless group and plenty of discussions that answer questions.

On the off chance that you, a web designer or web developer, are new to Bootstrap, I hope the seven advantages mentioned above and reasons for it using as a front-end Cascading Style Sheets Framework we have brought forward are helpful to you.

CONCLUSION

This chapter focused on introducing Bootstrap, like how Bootstrap is used to develop websites front-end with attractive CSS and JavaScript.

We learned the advantages and disadvantages of Bootstrap, like it is very lightweight and customizable and has an excellent grid system. And there will be a requirement for lots of styles overrides or rewriting files, which can lead you to spend a lot of time on designing and coding.

We looked over the benefits of Bootstrap over another CSS framework, such as it is so responsive, flexible, and easy to use.

In the next chapter, we will focus on downloading and using Bootstrap, supported browsers and devices, and many other things.

CHAPTER 2

Getting Started

IN THIS CHAPTER

- ➢ Download and Usage
- ➢ Supported Browser and Devices
- ➢ Use With Javascript
- ➢ Support for Rtl

The previous chapter introduced Bootstrap and discussed its advantages, disadvantages, and benefits over other CSS frameworks.

This chapter will discuss how to download Bootstrap and use it in various ways.

Let's jump toward the first section of this chapter and learn to download Bootstrap.

DOWNLOAD AND USAGE

Let's learn how to use Bootstrap through CDN, a content delivery network in our project.

Link to a CDN

CDNs, or content delivery networks, are code files on the web that you can include in your work. Using a content delivery network is the fastest way to set up Bootstrap.

DOI: 10.1201/9781003310501-2

Bootstrap V5.1 CDN

```
<link href="https://cdn.jsdelivr.net/npm/bootstrap@5
.1.3/dist/css/bootstrap.min3" crossorigin="anonymous">
```

Simply include the code above in your project <head> element, and you will be good to go!

After learning how to use bootstraps through CDN, let us know how to download and use Bootstrap locally.

Use a Local Copy of Bootstrap

Another way is to download your copy of this framework and integrate it into your project structure.

The steps to using a local copy of Bootstrap are as follows:

- **Step 1**: Download Bootstrap zips from Bootstrap's official website, and double-click the file to unzip it.

- **Step 2: Choose a project**:Choose a respectful project to add a local copy of Bootstrap.

- **Step 3: Move Bootstrap into your project folder**:Move the newly unzipped folder into your project folder

using your CMD or file manager.

- **Step 4**: Use HREF attribute to link your locally installed minified Bootstrap.

    E.g.: <link rel="stylesheet" href="bootstrap-3.3.7-dist/css/boot strap.min.css"/>

You can also install Bootstrap with Bower, npm, and Composer as follows.

Install with Bower

Users can also install and manage Bootstrap's Less, CSS, JavaScript, and fonts using Bower:

$bower install bootstrap

Install with npm

You can also install Bootstrap using npm.

Install with Composer

Users can also install and manage Bootstrap's Less, CSS, JavaScript, and fonts using Composer:

$ Composer require tubs/bootstrap

SUPPORTED BROWSER AND DEVICES

It supports the newest, stable releases of all major browsers and platforms on Windows.

Alternative browsers that utilize the most recent versions of WebKit, Blink, or Gecko, either directly or through the platform's web view API, are not officially supported. However, Bootstrap should show and operate correctly in these browsers (in most circumstances). Below you'll find more detailed support information.

Mobile Devices

It generally works with the most recent versions of each central platform's default browsers. Proxy browsers are not supported, including Opera Mini, Opera Phone's Turbo mode, UC Browser Mini, and Amazon Silk.

	Chrome	Firefox	Safari	Android Browser and WebView	Microsoft Edge
Android	Supported	Supported	N/A	Android v5.0 + Supported	Supported
iOS	Supported	Supported		N/A	Supported

This was the table of all mobile major mobile devices present in the market that supports and do not support Bootstrap. Now let's focus on desktop devices.

Desktop Browsers

The most recent versions of major desktop browsers are also supported.

	Chrome	Firefox	Internet Explorer	Microsoft Edge	Opera	Safari
Mac	Supported	Supported	N/A	N/A	Supported	Supported
Windows	Supported	Supported	Supported, IE 10+	Supported	Supported	Not Supported

For the Firefox browser, in addition to the latest standard stable release, support the latest Extended Support Release (ESR) version of browser Firefox.

Although they are not officially support, Bootstrap should look and perform correctly in Chromium and Chrome for the Linux, Firefox for Linux, and Internet Explorer 9, even though they are not officially supported.

Internet Explorer browser 10+ is supported. IE9 and below is not. Be aware of some Cascading Stylonality.

Use Bootstrap 3 if the user wants IE8-9 support. It is the stable version of our code, and our team is continually working on bug fixes and documentation updates for it. It will not, however, receive any new features.

Modals and Dropdowns on Mobile
Overflow and Scrolling
In iOS and Android, the overflowing support – hidden – on the <body> element is pretty restricted. The body> content will begin to scroll when you scroll past the top or bottom of a modal in any of those devices' browsers.

iOS Text Fields and Scrolling
If the first touch of a scroll gesture is within the border of a textual input> or a textarea> while a modal is open in iOS 9.2, the body> content underneath the modal will be viewed only if you're interested instead of the modal itself.

Navbar Dropdowns
Because of the z-indexing difficulty, the Dropdown-backdrop element is not utilized in the navbar on iOS. As a result, to dismiss dropdowns in navbars, you must click the dropdown element directly.

Browser Zooming
When you zoom in on a page, rendering artifacts appear in various components, both in Bootstrap and elsewhere on the web. We may resolve the problem, depending on the nature of the problem. However, we tend to overlook them since they frequently lack a straightforward answer and instead rely on clumsy workarounds.

Sticky :hover/:focus on iOS
While :hovering isn't feasible on most touch devices, iOS mimics it, resulting in "sticky" hover styles that stay after pressing one element. When

users tap another component, these hover kinds are erased. This behavior is generally disliked, and it does not appear to be a problem on Android and Windows.

We provided unfinished and commented-out code for opting into a media query shim that would disable hover styles on touch device browsers that imitate hovering throughout our v4 alpha and beta releases. Although this work was never wholly completed or enabled, we've decided to deprecate this shim and preserve the mixins as shortcuts for the pseudo-classes to avoid complete breakage.

Printing

Printing can be demanding even with newer browsers.

I'm using the fixed-width since Safari 8.0.

The container class might force Safari to utilize a small font size when printing.

Android Stock Browser

The Browser app comes preinstalled on Android 4.1 (and maybe even earlier editions) as the default web browser (instead of Chrome). Unfortunately, the Browser app is riddled with problems and CSS incompatibilities.

Select Menu

On <select> elements, Android stock browser will not display the side controls if a border-radius and border are applied. Use the code snippet below to remove the offending CSS and render the <select> as an unstilled element on the Android stock browser. The user agent sniffing avoids interference with Google chrome, Safari, and Mozilla browsers.

Validators

Bootstrap employs CSS browser hacks in multiple places to target custom CSS to certain browser versions to get past problems in the browsers themselves to deliver the best possible experience to outdated and buggy browsers. CSS validators, naturally, protest that these hacks are invalid. We also employ cutting-edge CSS capabilities that aren't yet fully standardized in a few instances, but these are solely for progressive enhancement.

These validation warnings don't matter because the non-hacky part of our CSS validates well, and the hacky parts don't interfere with the non-hacky section's usual operation, so we ignore these specific warnings.

Due to the inclusion of a solution for a specific Firefox flaw, our HTML manuals also feature some minor and insignificant HTML validity warnings.

After learning how to download and use Bootstrap, we saw supported browsers and devices. Now it is time to look over the use of Bootstrap with JavaScript.

USE WITH JAVASCRIPT

Bootstrap is a CSS framework that includes buttons, panels, and drop-downs, among other things. It may be used to swiftly construct a website or a web application's graphical interface.

All need is a basic understanding of HTML and CSS to build a Bootstrap frontend. On the other hand, some features can only be achieved using JavaScript. The Bootstrap framework provides a basic JavaScript interface for this.

Working with Bootstrap with the JavaScript Interface

In this piece, we'll look at how to use the JavaScript interface to change and control Bootstrap components. A basic button that allows users to launch a dialog will be used as an example (modal).

If you read over the documentation for the other interactive Bootstrap components, such as Carousel, Collapse, and Dropdown, you'll realize that the interfaces are incredibly similar. As a result, you can quickly apply what you've learned in this essay to other members.

Simple Page: Basic Structure

The HTML code for our sample page's basic structure is shown below. It is built on the Bootstrap 4.5 starting template and a fluid container in which the page's content will insert.

```
<!DOCTYPE html>

<html>

<head>

<meta charset="UTF-8"/>

<meta name="viewport" content="width=device-width,
initial-scale=2, shrink-to-fit=no">

<!-- Bootstrap CSS -->
```

```
<link rel="stylesheet" href="https://cdn.jsdelivr.net
/npm/bootstrap@4.5.3/dist/css/bootstrap.min.css" integ
rity="sha384-TX8t27EcRE3e/ihU7zmQxVncDAy5uIKz4rEkg
IXeMed4M0jlfIDPvg6uqKI2xXr2" crossorigin="anonymous">

<title>Bootstrap Example</title>

</head>

<body>

<div class="container-fluid">

<h1>My Bootstrap Playground</h1>

</div>

<script src="https://code.jquery.com/jquery-3.5.1
.slim.min.js" integrity="sha384-DfXdz2htPH0lsSSs5nCTpu
j/zy4C+OGpamoFVy38MVBnE+IbbVYUew+OrCXaRkfj"
crossorigin="anonymous"></script>

<script src="https://cdn.jsdelivr.net/npm/bootstrap@4
.5.3/dist/js/bootstrap.bundle.min.js" integrity="sha3
84-ho+j7jyWK8fNQe+A12Hb8AhRq26LrZ/JpcUGGOn+Y7RsweNrtN/
tE3MoK7ZeZDyx" crossorigin="anonymous"></script>

</body>

</html>
```

In this case, there are two factors to consider:

1. The jQuery library will no longer be required in future versions of Bootstrap 5.
2. A Content Delivery Network.

It will be used to incorporate the relevant external CSS and JS files.

Your website will be able to connect to external servers if you utilize a CDN, which you may need to note in your privacy policy. Alternatively, the framework's files can be manually downloaded and hosted on your server.

We'll look at a button/modal example without any JavaScript in the next section. With a click on the button, the user may access the modal. It may be closed again by using the "Close" or "x" buttons.

We'll need custom JavaScript to implement different behaviors (like when the user hits "Save"). In the next sections, we'll look at some of the options.

Components from Bootstrap That Don't Require Any Custom JavaScript

To begin with, let's add a few components to our sample page. First, we will add a button (button):

```
<div class="container-fluid">

<h1>My Bootstrap Playground</h1>

<button type="button" class="btn btn-success">Task
                                            1</button>

</div>
```

When button is pressed, a modal window with the sentence "Click Save to complete the task" should show. The following is an instance of how to create this behavior in the Live Demo section:

Attributes data-toggle="modal" and data-target="#task1_Modal" must be added to the button.

```
<button type="button" class="btn btn-success" data-
toggle="modal" data-target="#task1_Modal">Task 1</
                                            button>
```

The modal component's HTML code must be added. In the data-target attribute of the button, the assigned ID (here: task1_Modal) must be appropriately referenced (with a preceding # sign, so it reads as #task1_Modal").

```
<div class="modal fade" id="task1_Modal"
tabindex="-1" aria-labelledby="task1_ModalLabel"
aria-hidden="true">

<div class="modal-dialog">

<div class="modal-content">

<div class="modal-header">

<h5 class="modal-title" id="task1_ModalLabel">Task
                                            1</h5>
```

```
<button type="button" class="close" data-
            dismiss="modal" aria-label="Close">

<span aria-hidden="true">×</span>

</button>

</div>

<div class="modal-body">

</div>

<div class="modal-footer">

<button type="button" class="btn btn-secondary" data-
dismiss="modal">Close</button>

</div>

</div>

</div>

</div>
```

If you check the website in your browser, you'll see that dialog appears when you click the button, which you may shut by clicking "Close."

You may test out the first version of our example by clicking here.

Such interaction would be impossible without the Bootstrap framework and require extra JavaScript code. We'd have to respond to click events, show and hide the modal, and change the button's design. The Bootstrap framework Custom JavaScript components for interactive Bootstrap components are given below.

Note: The following code examples require the JavaScript library jQuery to be included in the website.

Button Methods

A methods section is frequently included in the Bootstrap documentation of individual components. The toggle function provided by Bootstrap allows us to control the button using JavaScript. To utilize the technique, we must first provide an ID to the button, such as task1_button:

```
<button id="task_button"...</button>
```

We can use JavaScript to change the button's display from "not clicked" to "clicked" and vice versa by invoking the toggle function.

To test it, right before the closing body tag, add the following code section:

```
...

<script>

$("#task1_button").button("toggle");

</script>

</body>
```

The code is run soon after the browser has loaded the page.

The selector #task1_button specifies that the toggling method should only be applied to the task1_button button (even if there should be more buttons on the page).

When you first access the website, the button should seem to have already been clicked (dark green).

Now add a second call of toggle:

```
$("#task1_button").button("toggle");
$("#task1_button").button("toggle");
```

The button will now be back to its original form (light green).

Modal Methods

The modal component's methods section has a similar structure. There is also a toggle method here, which can be used to programmatically switch the modal from closed to open state.

```
...

<script>

$("#task1_Modal").modal("toggle");

</script>

</body>
```

The modal is immediately launched when the page loads using this code snippet, without the user having to click the button first. The conversation closes when a second call comes in.

To open and shut the dialog, you can utilize the various show and hide techniques. After hitting the "Save" button, you can utilize the hide method to shut the modal. There are two steps to this:

First, use the attribute on click to define which JavaScript function should be executed when the button is clicked, e.g., task1 save ():

```
<button type="button" class="btn btn-primary"
onclick="task1_save()">Save changes</button>
```

Then, just before closing body tag, add the following script code:

```
<script>

function task1_save(){

$("#task1_Modal").modal("hide");

}

</script>
</body>
```

Other interactive components with comparable approaches for manipulating the component state include Carousel, Collapse, and Dropdown.

Events

There is additional Events section in the documentation for various Bootstrap components. This refers to reacting programmatically to preset events triggered by the user during interaction with the component in question.

We may declare what should happen when the events show and hide are triggered for a modal, for example, by calling the corresponding show or hide methods of the component.

The following is defined in our example:

- The show event is triggered as soon as it is triggered. The button's label shifts from "Task 1" to "Task 1 in process..."

- The label switches back to "Task 1" as the hide event is triggered.

In script section at the bottom of the page, paste the following code:

```
$('#task1_Modal').on('show.bs.modal', function (e) {

$("#task1_button").text("Task 1 in process...");

});

$('#task1_Modal').on('hide.bs.modal', function (e) {

$("#task1_button").text("Task 1");

})
```

You'll see that regardless of whether the user chooses "Close" or "Save," the label is reset when the dialog is closed. In both circumstances, the hide event is triggered.

Using Bootstrap Components to Indicate Progress

We saw how the jQuery function text may change the text content of an HTML element in the previous example. You may change any characteristics of an HTML element with JavaScript, including CSS classes and specific CSS properties. Take a look at the samples below.

Extend the task1_save Function

After saving the dialog, we modify the button's CSS class from be-success to btn-secondary. This means the work has already been completed:

```
function task1_save() {

$("#task1_Modal").modal("hide");

$("#task1_button").removeClass("btn-success");

$("#task1_button").addClass("btn-secondary");

}
```

Add a Progress Bar

Contextualize button with a small progress bar:

```
<h1>My Bootstrap Playground</h1>
<button id="task1_button" type="button" class="btn
btn-success" data-toggle="modal" data-target="#task1_
Modal">Task 1</button>

<div id="task1_progress" class="progress">
<div id="task1_progressbar" class="progress-bar
bg-success" style="width:2%" role="progressbar" aria-
valuenow="1" aria-valuemin="1" aria-valuemax="90"></
div>
</div>
```

The percentage progress bar starts at 0%. Now we'd want to put in place the following behavior:

First, the progress is set to 100% while the dialog is visible. To do so, we'll need to change the width CSS attribute. We'd want to show an animated stripe pattern on the progress bar while the work is still in process. The CSS classes progress-bar-striped and progress-bar-animated are used to achieve this.

```
$('#task1_Modal').on('show.bs.modal', function (e) {

$("#task1_button").text("Task 1 in progress...");

$("#task1_progressbar").css("width", "80%");

$("#task1_progressbar").addClass("progress-bar-striped");
$("#task1_progressbar").addClass("progress-bar-animated");

});
```

After hiding the dialog, the animation and the stripe pattern are removed, and the progress is set to 100%.

```
$('#task1_Modal').on('hide.bs.modal', function (e) {

$("#task1_button").text("Task 1");

$("#task1_progressbar").css("width", "2%");
$("#task1_progressbar").removeClass("progress-bar-stri
                                     ped");
$("#task1_progressbar").removeClass("progress-bar-anim
                                     ated");
});
```

If the user has saved the dialog, then the progress must be permanently set to 80%.

```
function task1_save(){

$("#task1_Modal").modal("hide");

$("#task1_button").removeClass("btn-success");
$("#task1_button").addClass("btn-secondary");

$("#task1_progressbar").css("width", "100%");
}
```

Note: When the user hits "Save changes," the button and progress bar will appear before, during, and after the dialog is opened.

Task Completion

After a task has been saved, a second click on the button should display another dialog with the content: "You have already finished the task." We are preparing a double modal for this.

The code for this modal is same as for the first, but we need to use task1_Message as the ID. The wording in the modal's body will subsequently be changed to "You have already completed the job."

We add an instruction that changes the property data-target for the button from task1_Modal to task1_Message in the method task1_save(), which is called when we save the first dialog:

```
function task1_save(){

$("#task1_Modal").modal("hide");

$("#task1_button").removeClass("btn-success");
$("#task1_button").addClass("btn-secondary");
$("#task1_progressbar").removeClass("progress-bar-stri
                                    ped");
$("#task1_progressbar").removeClass("progress-bar-anim
                                    ated");

$("#task1_button").attr("data-target",
                        "#task1_Message");
}
```

Note: You may still utilize interactive Bootstrap components like Button, Modal, Carousel, Collapse, and Dropdown even if you don't have any JavaScript. Using Bootstrap's tiny JavaScript interface, on the other hand, enables for greater interaction with methods and events.

SUPPORT FOR RTL

Required HTML

To enable RTL in Bootstrap-powered pages, you must meet two tight requirements:

1. Set dir="rtl" on the <html> element.

2. On <html> element, add appropriate lang attribute, such as lang="ar."

You'll need to add an RTL version of our CSS after that. For example, here's the stylesheet for our RTL-enabled compiled and minified CSS:

```
<link rel="stylesheet" href="https://cdn.jsdelivr.net
/npm/bootstrap@5.0.2/dist/css/bootstrap.rtl.min.css"
integrity="sha384-gXt9imSW0VcJVHezoNQsP+TNrjYXoGcr
qBZJpry9zJt8PCQjobwmhMGaDHTASo9N"
crossorigin="anonymous">
```

Starter Template

This updated RTL beginning template reflects the aforementioned criteria.

```
<!doctype html>
<html lang="ar" dir="rtl">
 <head>
  <!-- Required meta tags -->
  <meta charset="utf-8">
  <meta name="viewport" content="width=device-width,
                                 initial-scale=2">

  <!-- Bootstrap CSS -->
  <link rel="stylesheet" href="https://cdn.jsdelivr
.net/npm/bootstrap@5.0.2/dist/css/bootstrap.rtl.min
.css" integrity="sha384-gXt9imSW0VcJVHezoNQsP+TNrjY
XoGcrqBZJpry9zJt8PCQjobwmhMGaDHTASo9N"
crossorigin="anonymous">

  <title>مرحبا بالعالم!</title>
 </head>
 <body>
```

```html
<h1>مرحبا بالعالم!</h1>

<!-- Optional JavaScript; choose one of two! -->

<!-- Option 1: Bootstrap Bundle with the Popper -->
<script src="https://cdn.jsdelivr.net/npm/bootstrap
@5.0.2/dist/js/bootstrap.bundle.min.js" integrity=
"sha384-MrcW6ZMFYlzcLA8Nl+NtUVF0sA7MsXsP1UyJoMp4YL
EuNSfAP+JcXn/tWtIaxVXM" crossorigin="anonymous"></
script>

<!-- Option 2: Separate the Popper and Bootstrap JS -->
<!--
<script src="https://cdn.jsdelivr.net/npm/@popperjs
/core@2.9.2/dist/umd/popper.min.js" integrity="sha3
84-IQsoLXl5PILFhosVNubq5LC7Qb9DXgDA9i+tQ8Zj3iwWAwP
tgFTxbJ8NT4GN1R8p" crossorigin="anonymous"></script>
<script src="https://cdn.jsdelivr.net/npm/bootstrap
@5.0.2/dist/js/bootstrap.min.js" integrity="sha384-cV
KIPhGWiC2Al4u+LWgxfKTRIcfu0JTxR+EQDz/bgldoEyl4H0zU
F0QKbrJ0EcQF" crossorigin="anonymous"></script>
-->
</body>
</html>
```

Approach

Our approach to integrating RTL support into Bootstrap is guided by two key considerations that influence how we create and utilize CSS:

1. **First, we opted to use the RTLCSS project to construct it.** When switching from LTR to RTL, this affords us some significant options for handling modifications and overrides. It also enables us to create two Bootstrap versions from the same codebase.

2. **Second, we've changed a few directional classes to use logical attributes instead of names.** The majority of you have already dealt with logical properties owing to our flex utilities, which substitute direction attributes such as left and right with start and finish. As a result, the class names and values are suitable for both LTR and RTL with no additional cost.

For example, instead of.ml-3, use.ms-3 for margin-left.

Working with RTL via our source SaSs or compiled CSS should be similar to working with LTR.

Customize from Source

When it comes to customization, the best approach is to use variables, maps, and mixins. Even if RTL is post-processed from compiled files, this technique works the very same.

Custom RTL Values

You may use RTLCSS value directives to make a variable produce a different RTL value. For example, you may use the /*rtl: value*/ syntax to reduce the weight of $font-weight-bold throughout the codebase:

```
$font-weight-bold: 800 #{/* rtl:660 */} !default;
```

For default CSS and RTL CSS, this would result in the following:

```
/* bootstrap.css */
dt {
 font-weight: 800 /* rtl:660 */;
}

 /* bootstrap.rtl.css */
dt {
 font-weight: 600;
}
```

Alternate Font Stack

If you're utilizing a non-Latin alphabet with a custom font, keep in mind that not all fonts support it. You need to use /*RTL: insert value*/ in font stack to change the names of font families to move from Pan-European to Arabic.

To go from Helvetica Neue Webfont for LTR to Helvetica Neue Arabic for RTL, for example, your Sass code might look like this:

```
$font-family-sans-serif:
 Helvetica Neue #{"/* rtl:insert:Arabic */"},
 // Cross-platform generic the font family (default
user interface font)
 system-ui,
 // Safari for the macOS and iOS (San Francisco)
 -apple-system,
 // Chrome<56 for macOS (San Francisco)
 BlinkMacSystemFont,
```

```
// Windows
"Segoe UI",
// Android
Roboto,
// Basic web-fallback
Arial,
// Linux
"Noto Sans",
// Sans serif-fallback
sans-serif,
// Emoji fonts
"Apple Color Emoji", "Segoe UI Emoji", "Segoe UI
Symbol", "Noto Color Emoji" !default;
```

LTR and RTL at the Same Time

Is it necessary to have both LTR and RTL on the same page? This is rather simple, thanks to RTLCSS String Maps. Set a custom rename rule for RTLCSS and wrap your @imports with a class:

```
/* RTL:begin:options: {
  "autoRename": true,
  "stringMap":[{
    "name": "ltr-rtl",
    "priority": 90,
    "search": ["ltr"],
    "replace": ["rtl"],
    "options": {
      "scope": "*",
      "ignoreCase": false
  }
}]
}*/
.ltr {
  @import "../node_modules/bootstrap/scss/bootstrap";
}
/*rtl:end:options*/
```

Each selector in your CSS files will prepend by .ltr and .rtl for RTL files after executing Sass and RTLCSS. You can now utilize both files on the same page by simply adding .ltr or .rtl to your component wrappers to specify which direction to use.

Edge Class and Known Limitations

While this approach is acceptable, keep the following in mind:

1. When converting from .ltr to .rtl, make sure to change the dir and lang attributes.

2. Loading both files at the same time can be a major speed bottleneck, so do some optimization and try loading one of them asynchronously.

3. Because nesting styles in this way prevents our form-validation-state() mixin from working as intended, you'll have to change it manually.

The Breadcrumb Case

The breadcrumb separator is the only case requiring its brand-new variable –$breadcrumb-divider-flipped – defaulting to $breadcrumb-divider.

CONCLUSION

In this chapter, we focused on installing Bootstrap, and we saw how Bootstrap could be used via CDN and local copy. We also saw Bootstrap-supported browsers and devices and also usage with JavaScript and support for RTL.

In the next chapter, we will focus on all significant customization with Bootstrap, e.g., colors, components, CSS variables, and many more.

CHAPTER 3

Customization

IN THIS CHAPTER

➢ Colors

➢ Components

➢ Css Variables

➢ Optimization

➢ Mixins

In the previous chapter, we focused on installing Bootstrap, and we saw how Bootstrap could be used via CDN and local copy. We also saw Bootstrap-supported browsers and devices and also usage with JavaScript and support for RTL.

This chapter will discuss about many important things, like colors, components, CSS variables, Optimization, etc.

Let's begin this chapter with "colors."

COLORS

Bootstrap has a rich color system that helps us tone our styles and components. For every project, this allows for more complete customization and development.

Bootstrap generates color schemes using a subset of all colors, which are also accessible as Sass variables and a Sass map in Bootstrap's scss/_variables.scss file.

DOI: 10.1201/9781003310501-3

$theme-colors is a Sass map that contains all of these colors.

```
$theme-colors: (
 "primary":  $primary,
 "secondary":  $secondary,
 "success":  $success,
 "info":  $info,
 "warning":  $warning,
 "danger":   $danger,
 "light":  $light,
 "dark":   $dark
);
```

All Colors

All Bootstrap colors are available as Sass variables and a Sass map in the scss/_variables.scss file. To avoid increased file sizes, Bootstrap doesn't create text or background color classes for each variable. Instead, Bootstrap chooses a subset of these colors for a themed palette.

Be sure to monitor contrast ratios as you customize colors. As shown below, Bootstrap added three contrast ratios to each of the primary colors – one for the swatch's current colors, one against white, and one against black.

Text Colors

Bootstrap 5 has a number of contextual classes that may be used to offer "meaning via colors."

The classes for the text colors are .text-muted, .text-primary, .text-warning, .text-success, .text-info, .text-danger, .text-secondary, .text-white, .text-dark, .text-body (default body color/often black), and .text-light:

You can add 50% opacity for black or white text with the .text-black-50 or .text-white-50 classes.

Background Colors

Background color classes are .bg-primary, .bg-success, .bg-info, .bg-warning, .bg-danger, .bg-secondary, .bg-dark, and .bg-light.

Because background colors do not affect the text color, you may wish to pair them with a .text-* color class in some circumstances.

Links

You can use the .link-* classes to colorize links. Unlike the .text-* courses, these classes have a: hover and: focus state.

COMPONENTS

Bootstrap also uses theme colors as predefined colors for some components, for example, buttons.

This was about colors. However, you can use colors as per your need. You can use more types of pallets, more different types of stains on buttons as well.

Now we will jump over the components of Bootstrap and know how many members are available and how we can use them.

COMPONENTS

Accordion

Using our Collapse JavaScript plugin, create vertically collapsing accordions.

How It Works

Internal collapse is used to make the accordion collapsible. Add the .open class to the .accordion to create an extended accordion.

This component's animation effect is determined by the prefers-reduced-motion media query.

Example

Accordion Item #1

This is the accordion body of the first item. It is displayed by default until the collapse plugin delivers the needed classes to style each piece. These classes are in charge of the overall appearance of the site, as well as the showing and hiding of elements using CSS transitions. To modify any of this, you may use custom CSS or override our default variables. It is also worth noting that .accordion-body may include almost any HTML, but the transition prevents overflow.

Accordion Item #2

This is the accordion body of the second item. By default, it is hidden until the collapse plugin provides the necessary classes to style each piece. These classes are in charge of the overall appearance of the site, as well as the showing and hiding of elements using CSS transitions. To modify any of this, you may use custom CSS or override our default variables. It is also worth noting that .accordion-body may include nearly any HTML, but the transition prevents the content from overflowing.

Accordion Item #3

The accordion body of the third item is this. By default, it is hidden until the collapse plugin provides the necessary classes to style each piece. This is the first item's accordion body. It is displayed by default until the collapse plugin delivers the needed classes to style each piece. These classes are in charge of the overall appearance of the site, as well as the showing and hiding of elements using CSS transitions. To modify any of this, you may use custom CSS or override our default variables. It is also worth noting that .accordion-body may include almost any HTML, but the transition prevents overflow.

```
<div class="accordion" id="accordionExample">
 <div class="accordion-item">
  <h2 class="accordion-header" id="headingOne">
   <button class="accordion-button" type="button"
           data-bs-toggle="collapse" data-bs-
           target="#collapseOne" aria-expanded="true"
           aria-controls="collapseOne">
    Accordion Item #1
   </button>
  </h2>
  <div id="collapseOne" class="accordion-collapse
collapse show" aria-labelledby="headingOne"
data-bs-parent="#accordionExample">
   <div class="accordion-body">
    <strong>This is first item's accordion body.</
strong> The collapse plugin adds the relevant classes
we need to style each element by default, making it
visible. These classes are in charge of the overall
appearance of the site, as well as the showing and
hiding of elements using CSS transitions. Custom CSS
or overriding our default variables can be used to
change any of this. It is also worth noting that any
HTML may be placed inside the <code>.accordion-
body/<code> tag, albeit the transition prevents
overflow.
   </div>
  </div>
 </div>
 <div class="accordion-item">
  <h2 class="accordion-header" id="headingTwo">
```

```
      <button class="accordion-button collapsed"
        type="button" data-bs-toggle="collapse" data-bs-
        target="#collapseTwo" aria-expanded="false"
        aria-controls="collapseTwo">
       Accordion Item #2
      </button>
     </h2>
    <div id="collapseTwo" class="accordion-collapse
   collapse" aria-labelledby="headingTwo"
   data-bs-parent="#accordionExample">
       <div class="accordion-body">
        <strong>This is second item's accordion body.</
   strong> The collapse plugin adds the relevant classes
   which we use to style each element by default, making
   it invisible. These classes are in charge of the
   overall appearance of the site, as well as the showing
   and hiding of elements using CSS transitions. Custom
   CSS or overriding our default variables can be used to
   change any of this. It is also worth noting that any
   HTML may be placed inside the <code>.accordion-body</
   code> though the transition prevents overflow.
     </div>
    </div>
   </div>
   <div class="accordion-item">
    <h2 class="accordion-header" id="headingThree">
     <button class="accordion-button collapsed"
   type="button" data-bs-toggle="collapse" data-bs-
   target="#collapseThree" aria-expanded="false"
   aria-controls="collapseThree">
      Accordion Item #3
     </button>
    </h2>
    <div id="collapseThree" class="accordion-collapse
   collapse" aria-labelledby="headingThree"
   data-bs-parent="#accordionExample">
      <div class="accordion-body">
       <strong>This is third item's accordion body.</
   strong> By default, the collapse plugin adds the
   essential classes that we need to style each piece,
   and it is hidden. These classes are in charge of the
   overall appearance of the site, as well as the showing
```

and hiding of elements using CSS transitions. Custom
CSS or overriding our default variables can be used to
change any of this. It is also worth noting that any
HTML may be placed inside the <code>.accordion-body</
code> though the transition prevents overflow.
```
    </div>
   </div>
  </div>
 </div>
```

Flush

Add .accordion-flush to remove the default background color, some bor-
ders, and some rounded corners from accordions so that they may be ren-
dered edge-to-edge with their parent container.

Accordion Item #1

This accordion's placeholder content is meant to show the .accordion-flush
class. This is the first item's accordion body.

Accordion Item #2

This accordion's placeholder content is meant to show the .accordion-flush
class. This is the second piece's accordion body. Consider how it would
seem if it were packed with real information.

Accordion Item #3

This accordion's placeholder content is meant to show the .accordion-flush
class. The accordion body of the third item is this. There's nothing really
spectacular going on here in terms of content; it is just a matter of filling
in the blanks to make it appear, at least at first sight, more like it would in
a real-world application.

```
<div class="accordion accordion-flush"
id="accordionFlushExample">
 <div class="accordion-item">
  <h2 class="accordion-header" id="flush-headingOne">
   <button class="accordion-button collapsed"
type="button" data-bs-toggle="collapse" data-bs-
target="#flush-collapseOne" aria-expanded="false"
aria-controls="flush-collapseOne">
    Accordion Item #1
```

```
    </button>
   </h2>
  <div id="flush-collapseOne" class="accordion-
collapse collapse" aria-labelledby="flush-headingOne"
data-bs-parent="#accordionFlushExample">
    <div class="accordion-body">Placeholder content
for accordion, which is intended to illustrate
<code>.accordion-flush</code> class. This is the
first item's accordion body.</div>
   </div>
 </div>
 <div class="accordion-item">
  <h2 class="accordion-header" id="flush-headingTwo">
   <button class="accordion-button collapsed"
type="button" data-bs-toggle="collapse" data-bs-
target="#flush-collapseTwo" aria-expanded="false"
aria-controls="flush-collapseTwo">
    Accordion Item #2
   </button>
  </h2>
  <div id="flush-collapseTwo" class="accordion-
collapse collapse" aria-labelledby="flush-headingTwo"
data-bs-parent="#accordionFlushExample">
   <div class="accordion-body">Placeholder content
for accordion, which is intended to ilustrate
<code>.accordion-flush</code> class. This is the
accordion body of the second item. Consider how this
would look if it were filled with actual stuff.</div>
   </div>
 </div>
 <div class="accordion-item">
  <h2 class="accordion-header"
id="flush-headingThree">
   <button class="accordion-button collapsed"
type="button" data-bs-toggle="collapse" data-bs-
target="#flush-collapseThree" aria-expanded="false"
aria-controls="flush-collapseThree">
    Accordion Item #3
   </button>
  </h2>
  <div id="flush-collapseThree" class="accordion-
collapse collapse"
```

```
aria-labelledby="flush-headingThree" data-bs-parent="#
accordionFlushExample">
    <div class="accordion-body">Placeholder content
for the accordion, which is intended to illustrate
<code>.accordion-flush</code> class. The accordion
body of the third piece is this. There's nothing
really exciting going on here in terms of content; it
is just a matter of filling in the blanks to make it
appear, at least at first sight, more like it would in
a real-world application.</div>
  </div>
 </div>
</div>
```

Always Open

On each component, remove the data-bs-parent property. When another object is opened, use accordion-collapse to keep accordion things open.

Accordion Item #1

This is the first item's accordion body. It is displayed by default until the collapse plugin delivers the needed classes to style each piece. These classes are in charge of the overall appearance of the site, as well as the showing and hiding of elements using CSS transitions. To modify any of this, you may use custom CSS or override our default variables. It is also worth noting that the .accordion-body element may contain nearly any HTML, but the transition prevents overflow.

Accordion Item #2

This is the second item's accordion body. It is hidden by default until the collapse plugin supplies the classes needed to style each piece. These classes are in charge of the overall appearance of the site, as well as the showing and hiding of elements using CSS transitions. To modify any of this, you may use custom CSS or override our default variables. It is also important to note that the .accordion-body may include almost any HTML, but the transition prevents overflow.

Accordion Item #3

The accordion body of the third piece is this. By default, it is hidden until the collapse plugin provides the necessary classes to style each piece. These classes are in charge of the overall appearance of the site, as well as the showing and hiding of elements using CSS transitions. To modify any of this, you may use custom CSS or override our default variables. It is also worth noting that the .accordion-body may include almost any HTML, but the transition prevents overflow.

```
<div class="accordion" id="accordionPanelsStayOpenExa
          mple">
 <div class="accordion-item">
  <h2 class="accordion-header"
              id="panelsStayOpen-headingOne">
   <button class="accordion-button" type="button"
data-bs-toggle="collapse" data-bs-target="#panelsSt
ayOpen-collapseOne" aria-expanded="true" aria-contr
ols="panelsStayOpen-collapseOne">
    Accordion Item #1
   </button>
  </h2>
  <div id="panelsStayOpen-collapseOne"
class="accordion-collapse collapse show" aria-label
ledby="panelsStayOpen-headingOne">
   <div class="accordion-body">
    <strong>This is first item's accordion body.</
strong> The collapse plugin adds the relevant classes
we need to style each element by default, making it
visible. These classes are in charge of the overall
appearance of the site, as well as the showing and
hiding of elements using CSS transitions. To modify
any of this, you may use custom CSS or override our
default variables. It is also worth mentioning that
almost any HTML may be used within the <code>.
accordion-body</code>, though the transition does
limit overflow.                 </div>
  </div>
 </div>
 <div class="accordion-item">
  <h2 class="accordion-header"
              id="panelsStayOpen-headingTwo">
   <button class="accordion-button collapsed"
type="button" data-bs-toggle="collapse" data-bs-ta
rget="#panelsStayOpen-collapseTwo" aria-
expanded="false" aria-controls="panelsStayOpen-colla
pseTwo">
```

```
   Accordion Item #2
   </button>
  </h2>
  <div id="panelsStayOpen-collapseTwo"
class="accordion-collapse collapse" aria-labelledby
="panelsStayOpen-headingTwo">
   <div class="accordion-body">
    <strong>This is second item's accordion body.</
strong> By default, the collapse plugin adds the
essential classes that we need to style each piece,
and it is hidden. These classes are in charge of the
overall appearance of the site, as well as the showing
and hiding of elements using CSS transitions. To
modify any of this, you may use custom CSS or override
our default variables. It is also worth mentioning
that almost any HTML may be used within the
<code>.accordion-body</code>, though the transition
does limit overflow.
   </div>
  </div>
 </div>
 <div class="accordion-item">
  <h2 class="accordion-header"
id="panelsStayOpen-headingThree">
   <button class="accordion-button collapsed"
type="button" data-bs-toggle="collapse" data-bs-ta
rget="#panelsStayOpen-collapseThree" aria-
expanded="false" aria-controls="panelsStayOpen-colla
pseThree">
    Accordion Item #3
   </button>
  </h2>
  <div id="panelsStayOpen-collapseThree"
class="accordion-collapse collapse" aria-labelledby
="panelsStayOpen-headingThree">
   <div class="accordion-body">
    <strong>This is third item's accordion body.</
strong> The collapse plugin adds the relevant classes
that we use to style each element, so it is hidden by
default. These classes are in charge of the general
look, as well as the displaying and concealing of
elements using CSS transitions. Custom CSS or
overriding our default variables can be used to change
```

any of this. It is also worth mentioning that almost any HTML may be used within the `<code>.accordion-body</code>`, though the transition does limit overflow.

```
    </div>
  </div>
 </div>
</div>
```

Alerts

With a number of accessible and adaptable alert messages, provide contextual feedback for common user behaviors.

Examples

Alerts for any amount of text are offered, as well as an optional close button. For the best style, choose one of the eight necessary contextual classes. For inline dismissal, use alerts JavaScript plugin.

```
<div class="alert alert-primary" role="alert">
 A simple primary alert—check it out!
</div>
<div class="alert alert-secondary" role="alert">
 A simple secondary alert—check it out!
</div>
<div class="alert alert-success" role="alert">
 A simple success alert—check it out!
</div>
<div class="alert alert-danger" role="alert">
 A simple danger alert—check it out!
</div>
<div class="alert alert-warning" role="alert">
 A simple warning alert—check it out!
</div>
<div class="alert alert-info" role="alert">
 A simple info alert—check it out!
</div>
<div class="alert alert-light" role="alert">
 A simple light alert—check it out!
</div>
<div class="alert alert-dark" role="alert">
 A simple dark alert—check it out!
</div>
```

Giving Assistive Technology a Sense of Purpose
Color can be used to add meaning, but users of assistive devices, such as screen readers, will not be able to understand it. Ascertain that the information suggested by the color is either obvious from the content itself or is included through alternative methods (e.g., extra text concealed with the .visually-hidden class).

Link Color

Use the .alert-link utility class to provide matching colored links within any alert quickly.

```
<div class="alert alert-primary" role="alert">
 A simple primary alert with <a href="#"
   class="alert-link">an example link</a>. Give it a
   click if you like.
</div>
<div class="alert alert-secondary" role="alert">
 A simple secondary alert with <a href="#"
   class="alert-link">an example link</a>. Give it a
   click if you like.
</div>
<div class="alert alert-success" role="alert">
 A simple success alert with <a href="#"
   class="alert-link">an example link</a>. Give it a
   click if you like.
</div>
<div class="alert alert-danger" role="alert">
 A simple danger alert with <a href="#" class="alert-
link">an example link</a>. Give it a click if you like.
</div>
<div class="alert alert-warning" role="alert">
 A simple warning alert with <a href="#"
   class="alert-link">an example link</a>. Give it a
   click if you like.
</div>
<div class="alert alert-info" role="alert">
 A simple info alert with <a href="#" class="alert-
   link">an example link</a>. Give it a click if you
   like.
</div>
<div class="alert alert-light" role="alert">
```

```
 A simple light alert with <a href="#" class="alert-
    link">an example link</a>. Give it a click if you
    like.
</div>
<div class="alert alert-dark" role="alert">
 A simple dark alert with <a href="#" class="alert-
    link">an example link</a>. Give it a click if you
    like.
</div>
```

Additional Content

Additional HTML elements like headers, paragraphs, and dividers can be used in alerts.

```
<div class="alert alert-success" role="alert">
 <h4 class="alert-heading">Well-done</h4>
 <p>You read the critical warning messages
        successfully and this example text will be a
        little longer to illustrate how alert spacing
        works with this sort of data.</p>
 <hr>
 <p class="mb-0">Use margin tools wherever possible
to keep things neat and clean.</p>
</div>
```

Icons

Similarly, you can create alerts with icons using flexbox utilities and Bootstrap Icons. You may wish to add more utilities or custom styles depending on your heroes and content.

```
<div class="alert alert-primary d-flex align-items-
left role="alert">
 <svg xmlns="http://www.w3.org/2000/svg" width="29"
height="29" fill="currentColor" class="bi
bi-exclamation-triangle-fill flex-shrink-0 me-2"
viewBox="0 0 16 16" role="img" aria-label="Warning:">
  <path d="M8.982 1.566a1.13 1.13 0 0 0-1.96 0L.165
13.233c-.457.778.091 1.767.98 1.767h13.713c.889 0
1.438-.99.98-1.767L8.982 1.566zM8 5c.535 0
.954.462.9.995l-.35 3.507a.552.552 0 0 1-1.1 0L7.1
5.995A.905.905 0 0 1 8 5zm.002 6a1 1 0 1 1 0 2 1 1 0 0
1 0-2z"/>
```

```
</svg>
<div>
 An example alert with an icon
 </div>
</div>
```

Do you have a need for more than one symbol for your alerts? Consider including extra Bootstrap Icons and creating a local SVG sprite-like to fast reference the same icons.

```
<svg xmlns="http://www.w3.org/2000/svg"
            style="display: none;">
 <symbol id="check-circle-fill" fill="currentColor"
            viewBox="0 0 16 16">
  <path d="M16 8A8 8 0 1 1 0 8a8 8 0 0 1 16 0zm-3.97-
3.03a.75.75 0 0 0-1.08.022L7.477 9.417 5.384
7.323a.75.75 0 0 0-1.06 1.06L6.97 11.03a.75.75 0 0 0
1.079-.021l3.992-4.99a.75.75 0 0 0-.01-1.05z"/>
 </symbol>
 <symbol id="info-fill" fill="currentColor"
viewBox="0 0 16 16">
  <path d="M8 16A8 8 0 1 0 8 0a8 8 0 0 0 0 16zm.93-
9.412-1 4.705c-.07.34.029.533.304.533.194 0 .487-.07.6
86-.246l-.088.416c-.287.346-.92.598-1.465.598-.703
0-1.002-.422-.808-1.319l.738-3.468c.064-.293.006-.
399-.287-.47l-.451-.081.082-.381 2.29-.287zM8 5.5a1 1
0 1 1 0-2 1 1 0 0 1 0 2z"/>
 </symbol>
 <symbol id="exclamation-triangle-fill"
         fill="currentColor" viewBox="0 0 16 16">
  <path d="M8.982 1.566a1.13 1.13 0 0 0-1.96 0L.165
13.233c-.457.778.091 1.767.98 1.767h13.713c.889 0
1.438-.99.98-1.767L8.982 1.566zM8 5c.535 0
.954.462.9.995l-.35 3.507a.552.552 0 0 1-1.1 0L7.1
5.995A.905.905 0 0 1 8 5zm.002 6a1 1 0 1 1 0 2 1 1 0 0
1 0-2z"/>
 </symbol>
</svg>

<div class="alert alert-primary d-flex align-items-
            center" role="alert">
 <svg class="bi flex-shrink-0 me-2" width="25"
     height="25" role="img" aria-label="Info:"><use
     xlink:href="#info-fill"/></svg>
```

```
<div>
 An example alert with an icon
 </div>
</div>
<div class="alert alert-success d-flex align-items-
          center" role="alert">
 <svg class="bi flex-shrink-0 me-2" width="25"
height="25" role="img" aria-label="Success:"><use
xlink:href="#check-circle-fill"/></svg>
 <div>
 An example success alert with an icon
 </div>
</div>
<div class="alert alert-warning d-flex align-items-
          center" role="alert">
 <svg class="bi flex-shrink-0 me-2" width="25"
height="25" role="img" aria-label="Warning:"><use
xlink:href="#exclamation-triangle-fill"/></svg>
 <div>
 An example warning alert with an icon
 </div>
</div>
<div class="alert alert-danger d-flex align-items-
          center" role="alert">
 <svg class="bi flex-shrink-0 me-2" width="25"
height="25" role="img" aria-label="Danger:"><use
xlink:href="#exclamation-triangle-fill"/></svg>
 <div>
 An example danger alert with an icon
 </div>
</div>
```

Dismissing

Any alarm may be dismissed inline using the alert JavaScript plugin. Here's how to do it:

- Make sure the alert plugin or the built Bootstrap JavaScript is loaded.

- Add the close button and the .alert-dismissible class, which places the close button and provides extra padding to the right of the alert.

- Add the data-bs-dismiss="alert" property to the close button to activate the JavaScript capability. To ensure correct functionality across all devices, use the button> element alongside it.

- If you want to animate alerts when you dismiss them, use the .fade and .show classes.

With a live demo, you can see this in action:

```
<div class="alert alert-warning alert-dismissible
          fade show" role="alert">
 <strong>Holy guacamole!</strong> check in on some of
        those fields.
 <button type="button" class="btn-close" data-bs-
        dismiss="alert" aria-label="Close"></button>
</div>
```

When an alert is dismissed, it is removed from the page structure entirely. If a keyboard user rejects the close button signal, their attention will be lost and, depending on the browser, they will be sent to the beginning of the page/document. As a result, we propose providing extra JavaScript that listens for the closed.bs.alert event and sets focus() to the most suitable area on the page dynamically. If you want to draw attention to a non-interactive part that doesn't generally get attention, be sure to include tabindex="-1" to the component.

Sass
Variables

```
$alert-padding-y:             $spacer;
$alert-padding-x:             $spacer;
$alert-margin-bottom:         1rem;
$alert-border-radius:         $border-radius;
$alert-link-font-weight:      $font-weight-bold;
$alert-border-width:          $border-width;
$alert-bg-scale:              -80%;
$alert-border-scale:          -70%;
$alert-color-scale:           40%;
$alert-dismissible-padding-r: $alert-padding-x * 4;
// 4x covers width of x plus default padding on either
      side
```

Variant mixin

We have used this in combination with $theme-colors to create contextual modifier classes for our alerts.

```scss
@mixin alert-variant($background, $border, $color) {
  color: $color;
  @include gradient-bg($background);
  border-color: $border;

  .alert-link {
   color: shade-color($color, 20%);
  }
}
```

Loop

A loop generates the modifier classes with the alert-variant() mixin.

```scss
// Contextual modifier classes should generate to
           colorize the alert.
@each $state, $value in $theme-colors {
  $alert-background: shift-color($value, $alert-bg-scale);
  $alert-border: shift-color($value, $alert-border-scale);
  $alert-color: shift-color($value, $alert-color-scale);
  @if (contrast-ratio($alert-background, $alert-color)
                 < $min-contrast-ratio) {
   $alert-color: mix($value, color-contrast($alert-
             background), abs($alert-color-scale));
  }
  .alert-#{$state} {
   @include alert-variant($alert-background, $alert-
                           border, $alert-color);
  }
}
```

JavaScript Behavior

Triggers

Enable dismissal of alert via JavaScript:

```javascript
var alertList = document.querySelectorAll('.alert')
alertList.forEach(function (alert) {
 new bootstrap.Alert(alert)
})
```

Or, as seen above, use data characteristics on a button within the alert:

```html
<button type="button" class="btn-close" data-bs-
        dismiss="alert" aria-label="Close"></button>
```

It is worth noting that closing an alert removes it from the DOM.

Methods

The alert constructor, for example, may be used to create alert instances:

```
var myAlert = document.getElementById('myAlert')
var bsAlert = new bootstrap.Alert(myAlert)
```

This makes alert listen for click events on descendant elements, with the data-bs-dismiss="alert" attribute. (Not necessary when using the data API's auto-initialization.)

```
var alertNode = document.querySelector('.alert')
var alert = bootstrap.Alert.getInstance(alertNode)
alert.close()
```

Method	Description
close	Removes an alert from the DOM, thereby closing it. If the element has the .fade and .show classes, the signal will fade out before being released
dispose	Destroys an element's alert (removes the DOM element's stored data)
getInstance	You can use the static method to acquire the alert instance associated with a DOM element in the following way: Bootstrap.Alert.getInstance(alert)
getOrCreateInstance	The static method either returns or constructs an alert instance associated with a DOM element that hasn't been initialized. You may put it to use in the following way: Bootstrap.Alert.getO rCreateInstance(element)

Events

The alert plugin in Bootstrap exposes a few events that may be used to hook into alert functionality.

```
var myAlert = document.getElementById('myAlert')
myAlert.addEventListener('closed.bs.alert', function () {
  // perform anything, such as directly directing
           attention to the most relevant part,
  // so it doesn't get lost or reset to the start of
           the page
  // document.getElementById('...').focus()
})
```

Event	Description
close.bs.alert	It fires immediately when the close instance method is called
closed.bs.alert	She was fired when the alert had been closed, and CSS transitions had been completed

Badges

For badges, our small count, and the labelling component, documentation and examples are provided.

Examples

Using relative font sizes and em units, badges scale to match the size of the immediate parent element. The focus and hover styles for links have been removed from badges as of version 5.

Headings
Headings

```
<h1>Example heading <span class="badge
                    bg-secondary">New</span></h1>
<h2>Example heading <span class="badge
                    bg-secondary">New</span></h2>
<h3>Example heading <span class="badge
                    bg-secondary">New</span></h3>
<h4>Example heading <span class="badge
                    bg-secondary">New</span></h4>
<h5>Example heading <span class="badge
                    bg-secondary">New</span></h5>
<h6>Example heading <span class="badge
                    bg-secondary">New</span></h6>
```

Buttons

Badges can be used as part of links or buttons to provide a counter.

```
<button type="button" class="btn btn-primary">
 Notifications <span class="badge bg-secondary">4</
                    span>
</button>
```

Note that badges may be confusing for users of screen readers and similar assistive technologies, depending on how they are used. While badges' design serves as a visual cue to their function, these users will be provided with the badge's content. These badges may appear as random extra words or numbers at the end of a statement, link, or button, depending on the context.

Consider incorporating more context with a visually hidden piece of other text unless the context is evident (as in the "Notifications" example, where it is recognized that the "4" represents the number of notifications).

Positioned

Modify a .badge using utilities and place it in the corner of a link or button.

```
<button type="button" class="btn btn-primary
        position-relative">
 Inbox
 <span class="position-absolute top-0 start-90
        translate-middle badge rounded-pill bg-danger">
  99+
  <span class="visually-hidden">unread messages</span>
 </span>
</button>
```

For a more generic indication, you may replace the .badge class with a few other utilities that don't have a count.

```
<button type="button" class="btn btn-primary
position-relative">
 Profile
 <span class="position-absolute top-0 start-100
        translate-middle p-2 bg-danger border border-
        light rounded-circle">
  <span class="visually-hidden">New alerts</span>
 </span>
</button>
```

Background Colors

To rapidly modify the look of a badge, use our background utility classes. Please keep in mind that if you're using Bootstrap's default .bg-light, you'll almost certainly need a text color utility like .text-dark to style your text properly. This is because background utilities only change the color of the backdrop.

```
<span class="badge bg-primary">Primary</span>
<span class="badge bg-secondary">Secondary</span>
<span class="badge bg-success">Success</span>
<span class="badge bg-danger">Danger</span>
<span class="badge bg-warning text-dark">Warning</span>
<span class="badge bg-info text-dark">Info</span>
<span class="badge bg-light text-dark">Light</span>
<span class="badge bg-dark">Dark</span>
```

Conveying Meaning to Assistive Technologies

Color can be used to add meaning, but users of assistive devices, such as screen readers, will not be able to understand it. Ascertain that the information suggested by the color is either obvious from the content itself or is included through alternative methods (e.g., extra text concealed with the .visually-hidden class).

Pill Badges

Use the .rounded-pill utility class to make badges more rounded with a larger border-radius.

```
<span class="badge rounded-pill bg-primary">Primary</span>
<span class="badge rounded-pill
            bg-secondary">Secondary</span>
<span class="badge rounded-pill bg-success">Success</span>
<span class="badge rounded-pill bg-danger">Danger</span>
<span class="badge rounded-pill bg-warning text-
            dark">Warning</span>
<span class="badge rounded-pill bg-info text-
            dark">Info</span>
<span class="badge rounded-pill bg-light text-
            dark">Light</span>
<span class="badge rounded-pill bg-dark">Dark</span>
```

Sass
Variables

```
$badge-font-size:        .75em;
$badge-font-weight:        $font-weight-bold;
$badge-color:            $white;
$badge-padding-y:         .35em;
$badge-padding-x:         .65em;
$badge-border-radius:      $border-radius;
```

Breadcrumb

Indicate where the current page belongs in a navigational hierarchy that automatically uses CSS to create separators.

Use ordered or unordered list with the linked list items to make a lightly designed breadcrumb. Using our tools, you may add as many styles as you like.

```
<nav aria-label="breadcrumb">
 <ol class="breadcrumb">
  <li class="breadcrumb-item active" aria-
          current="page">Home</li>
 </ol>
</nav>

<nav aria-label="breadcrumb">
 <ol class="breadcrumb">
  <li class="breadcrumb-item"><a href="#">Home</a></li>
  <li class="breadcrumb-item active" aria-
          current="page">Library</li>
 </ol>
</nav>

<nav aria-label="breadcrumb">
 <ol class="breadcrumb">
  <li class="breadcrumb-item"><a href="#">Home</a></li>
  <li class="breadcrumb-item"><a href="#">Library</a></li>
  <li class="breadcrumb-item active" aria-
          current="page">Data</li>
 </ol>
</nav>
```

Dividers

CSS uses the directives::before and content to add dividers automatically. They may be customized using the local CSS custom property --bs-bread-crumb-divider, or the Sass variable $breadcrumb-divider – and $bread-crumb-divider-flipped for its RTL equivalent, if necessary. We use our Sass variable as a fallback, which is set to the custom property. In this manner, you have a global divider that you may change at any moment without having to recompile CSS.

```
<nav style="--bs-breadcrumb-divider: '>';"
          aria-label="breadcrumb">
```

```
<ol class="breadcrumb">
 <li class="breadcrumb-item"><a href="#">Home</a></li>
 <li class="breadcrumb-item active" aria-
           current="page">Library</li>
</ol>
</nav>
```

The quote function is necessary when using Sass to produce quotations around a string. Using > as a separator, for example, you might write:

```
$breadcrumb-divider: quote(">");
```

It is also possible to utilize an SVG icon that's been embedded. Use the Sass variable or our CSS custom property to apply it.

```
<nav style="--bs-breadcrumb-divider:
url(&#34;data:image/svg+xml,%3Csvg xmlns='http://www
.w3.org/2000/svg' width='9' height='9'%3E%3Cpath
d='M2.5 0L1 1.5 3.5 4 1 6.5 2.5 814-4-4-4z' fill='curr
entColor'/%3E%3C/svg%3E&#34;);"
aria-label="breadcrumb">
 <ol class="breadcrumb">
  <li class="breadcrumb-item"><a href="#">Home</a></li>
  <li class="breadcrumb-item active" aria-
            current="page">Library</li>
 </ol>
</nav>
```

```
$breadcrumb-divider: url("data:image/svg+xml,%3Csvg
xmlns='http://www.w3.org/2000/svg' width='9'
height='9'%3E%3Cpath d='M2.5 0L1 1.5 3.5 4 1 6.5 2.5
814-4-4-4z' fill='currentColor'/%3E%3C/svg%3E");
```

You may also use the Sass variable $breadcrumb-divider: none; to delete the divider setting "--bs-breadcrumb-divider: ";" (empty strings in CSS custom properties count as a value).

```
<nav style="--bs-breadcrumb-divider: '';"
            aria-label="breadcrumb">
 <ol class="breadcrumb">
  <li class="breadcrumb-item"><a href="#">Home</a></li>
```

```
<li class="breadcrumb-item active" aria-
            current="page">Library</li>
 </ol>
</nav>
```

```
$breadcrumb-divider: none;
```

Accessibility

Since breadcrumbs provide navigation, it is a good idea to add a meaningful label such as aria-label="breadcrumb" to describe the type of navigation supplied in the <nav> element, and applying aria-current="page" to last item of the set to indicate that it represents current page.

Sass

Variables

```
$breadcrumb-font-size:           null;
$breadcrumb-padding-y:           0;
$breadcrumb-padding-x:           0;
$breadcrumb-item-padding-x:      .5rem;
$breadcrumb-margin-bottom:       1rem;
$breadcrumb-bg:                   null;
$breadcrumb-divider-color:       $gray-600;
$breadcrumb-active-color:        $gray-600;
$breadcrumb-divider:             quote("/");
$breadcrumb-divider-flipped:     $breadcrumb-divider;
$breadcrumb-border-radius:       null;
```

Buttons

With support for numerous sizes, states, and more, use Bootstrap's custom button designs for actions in forms, dialog, and more.

Examples

Bootstrap comes with a number of predefined button styles, each with its own semantic purpose and a few extras for more control.

```
<button type="button" class="btn btn-
            primary">Primary</button>
<button type="button" class="btn btn-
            secondary">Secondary</button>
<button type="button" class="btn btn-
            success">Success</button>
```

```
<button type="button" class="btn btn-danger">Danger</
        button>
<button type="button" class="btn btn-
        warning">Warning</button>
<button type="button" class="btn btn-info">Info</
        button>
<button type="button" class="btn btn-light">Light</
        button>
<button type="button" class="btn btn-dark">Dark</
        button>
<button type="button" class="btn btn-link">Link</
        button>
```

Giving Assistive Technology a Sense of Purpose

Color can be used to add meaning, but users of assistive devices, such as screen readers, will not be able to understand it. Ascertain that the information suggested by the color is either obvious from the content itself or is included through alternative methods (e.g., extra text concealed with the .visually-hidden class).

Disable Text Wrapping

Add the .text-nowrap class to the button if you don't want the button text to wrap. To deactivate text wrapping for each button, specify $btn-white-space: nowrap in Sass.

Button Tags

The .btn classes are intended for usage with the .button> element. These classes can also be applied to <a> and <input> components (though some browsers may apply a slightly different rendering).

Instead of referring to new pages or sections inside the current page, button classes on <a> components that are used to initiate in-page functionality (such collapsing content) should be given a role="button" to properly express their purpose to assistive technology like screen readers.

```
<a class="btn btn-primary" href="#"
        role="button">Link</a>
<button class="btn btn-primary"
        type="submit">Button</button>
<input class="btn btn-primary" type="button"
        value="Input">
```

```
<input class="btn btn-primary" type="submit"
          value="Submit">
<input class="btn btn-primary" type="reset"
          value="Reset">
```

Outline Button

Need a button but don't want to deal with the weighty background colors that come with them? To remove any background pictures and stains from any button, replace the normal modifier classes with the .btn-outline-* ones.

```
<button type="button" class="btn btn-outline-
          primary">Primary</button>
<button type="button" class="btn btn-outline-secondar
          y">Secondary</button>
<button type="button" class="btn btn-outline-
          success">Success</button>
<button type="button" class="btn btn-outline-
          danger">Danger</button>
<button type="button" class="btn btn-outline-
          warning">Warning</button>
<button type="button" class="btn btn-outline-
          info">Info</button>
<button type="button" class="btn btn-outline-
          light">Light</button>
<button type="button" class="btn btn-outline-
          dark">Dark</button>
```

Some button styles use a relatively light foreground color and should only be used on a dark background to have sufficient contrast.

Sizes

Fancy larger or smaller buttons? Add .btn-lg or .btn-sm for additional sizes.

```
<button type="button" class="btn btn-primary btn-
          lg">Large button</button>
<button type="button" class="btn btn-secondary btn-
          lg">Large button</button>

<button type="button" class="btn btn-primary btn-
          sm">Small button</button>
```

```
<button type="button" class="btn btn-secondary btn-
        sm">Small button</button>
```

Disabled State

Add the disabled boolean property to any <button> element to make buttons seem inactive. Pointer-events: none is applied to disabled buttons, preventing hover and active states from activating.

```
<button type="button" class="btn btn-lg btn-primary"
        disabled>Primary button</button>
<button type="button" class="btn btn-secondary
        btn-lg" disabled>Button</button>
```

Disabled buttons created with the <a> element operate differently:

- <a> does not allow the disabled property, therefore you must use the .disabled class to make it seem disabled visually.

- To disable all pointer-events on anchor buttons, several future-friendly designs are supplied.

- To convey the element's state to assistive technology, disabled buttons should have the aria-disabled="true" property.

```
<a href="#" class="btn btn-primary btn-lg disabled"
        tabindex="-1" role="button" aria-
        disabled="true">Primary link</a>
<a href="#" class="btn btn-secondary btn-lg disabled"
        tabindex="-1" role="button" aria-
        disabled="true">Link</a>
```

Link Functionality Caveat

To deactivate the link capability of <a>, the .disabled class utilizes pointer-events: none, however that CSS feature is not yet standardized. Furthermore, even in browsers that allow pointer-events: none, keyboard navigation is unaffected, ensuring that sighted keyboard users and assistive technology users may activate these links. To be safe, add a tabindex="-1" value to these links in addition to aria-disabled="true" to prevent them from gaining keyboard attention, and disable their functionality totally using custom JavaScript.

Block Buttons

Using a combination of our display and gap tools, create responsive stacks of full-width "block buttons" like those in Bootstrap 4. Using utilities instead of button-specific classes gives us much greater control over spacing, alignment, and responsive behaviors.

```
<div class="d-grid gap-2">
  <button class="btn btn-primary"
              type="button">Button</button>
  <button class="btn btn-primary"
              type="button">Button</button>
</div>
```

Starting with vertically stacked buttons, we develop a responsive variant until the MD breakpoint, where the .d-MD-block class substitutes the .d-grid class, thereby nullifying the gap-2 utility. To see them alter, resize your browser.

```
<div class="d-grid gap-2 d-md-block">
  <button class="btn btn-primary"
              type="button">Button</button>
  <button class="btn btn-primary"
              type="button">Button</button>
</div>
```

Grid column width classes may be used to change the width of your block buttons. Use .col-6 for a half-width "block button," for example. With .mx-auto, you may also center it horizontally.

```
<div class="d-grid gap-2 col-6 mx-auto">
  <button class="btn btn-primary"
              type="button">Button</button>
  <button class="btn btn-primary"
              type="button">Button</button>
</div>
```

When the buttons are horizontal, further utilities can be used to change their alignment. We've modified our previous responsive example by including some flex utilities and a margin utility on the button to right-align the buttons once they're no longer stacked.

```
<div class="d-grid gap-2 d-md-flex
          justify-content-md-end">
  <button class="btn btn-primary me-md-2"
              type="button">Button</button>
  <button class="btn btn-primary"
              type="button">Button</button>
</div>
```

Button Plugin

You may use the button plugin to make basic on/off toggle buttons.

These toggle buttons have the same appearance as checkbox toggle buttons. The checkbox toggles will be stated as "checked"/"not checked" by screen readers (since, despite their look, they are fundamentally still checkboxes), whereas the toggle buttons will be announced as "button"/"button pushed" by assistive technologies. The decision between these two techniques will be based on the sort of toggle you're developing and whether the toggle will make sense to users if it is stated as a checkbox or as a button.

Toggle States

Toggle the active status of a button using data-bs-toggle="button." If you're pre-tapping a button, you'll need to manually add the .active class and aria-pressed="true" to make sure assistive technologies understand it.

```
<button type="button" class="btn btn-primary" data-
        bs-toggle="button" autocomplete="off">Toggle
        button</button>
<button type="button" class="btn btn-primary active"
        data-bs-toggle="button" autocomplete="off"
        aria-pressed="true">Active toggle button</
        button>
<button type="button" class="btn btn-primary"
        disabled data-bs-toggle="button"
        autocomplete="off">Disabled toggle button</
        button>

<a href="#" class="btn btn-primary" role="button"
          data-bs-toggle="button">Toggle link</a>
<a href="#" class="btn btn-primary active"
          role="button" data-bs-toggle="button"
          aria-pressed="true">Active toggle link</a>
```

```
<a href="#" class="btn btn-primary disabled"
            tabindex="-1" aria-disabled="true"
            role="button" data-bs-
            toggle="button">Disabled toggle link</a>
```

Methods

The button function constructor, for example, may be used to generate a button instance:

```
var button = document.getElementById('myButton')
var bsButton = new bootstrap.Button(button)
```

For example, to toggle all buttons

```
var buttons = document.querySelectorAll('.btn')
buttons.forEach(function (button) {
 var button = new bootstrap.Button(button)
 button.toggle()
})
```

Method	Description
toggle	Toggles push state. It gives the button the appearance that it has been activated
dispose	Destroys an element's button
getInstance	You can use the static method to acquire the button instance associated with a DOM element in the following way: Bootstrap.Button.getInstance(element)
getOrCreateInstance	The static function that returns or creates a button instance associated with a DOM element. If it hasn't been initialized, you may put it to use in the following way: Bootstrap.Button.getOrCreateInstance(element)

Sass
Variables

```
$btn-padding-y:        $input-btn-padding-y;
$btn-padding-x:        $input-btn-padding-x;
$btn-font-family:      $input-btn-font-family;
$btn-font-size:        $input-btn-font-size;
$btn-line-height:      $input-btn-line-height;
$btn-white-space:      null; // Set to `nowrap` to
                       prevent the text-wrapping
```

```
$btn-padding-y-sm:        $input-btn-padding-y-sm;
$btn-padding-x-sm:        $input-btn-padding-x-sm;
$btn-font-size-sm:        $input-btn-font-size-sm;
$btn-padding-y-lg:        $input-btn-padding-y-lg;
$btn-padding-x-lg:        $input-btn-padding-x-lg;
$btn-font-size-lg:        $input-btn-font-size-lg;
$btn-border-width:        $input-btn-border-width;
$btn-font-weight:         $font-weight-normal;
$btn-box-shadow:        inset 0 1px 0 rgba($grey, .15),
                        0 1px rgba($black, .075);
$btn-focus-width:         $input-btn-focus-width;
$btn-focus-box-shadow:    $input-btn-focus-box-shadow;
$btn-disabled-opacity:    .65;
$btn-active-box-shadow:   inset 0 3px 5px rgba($white,
                          .125);
$btn-link-color:          $link-color;
$btn-link-hover-color:    $link-hover-color;
$btn-link-disabled-color:    $gray-600;
// Allow for the customizing button radius
independently from the global-border radius
$btn-border-radius:          $border-radius;
$btn-border-radius-sm:       $border-radius-sm;
$btn-border-radius-lg:       $border-radius-lg;
$btn-transition:             color .15s ease-in-out,
background-color .15s ease-in-out, border-color .15s
ease-in-out, box-shadow .15s ease-in-out;
$btn-hover-bg-shade-amount:        15%;
$btn-hover-bg-tint-amount:         15%;
$btn-hover-border-shade-amount:    20%;
$btn-hover-border-tint-amount:     10%;
$btn-active-bg-shade-amount:       20%;
$btn-active-bg-tint-amount:         20%;
$btn-active-border-shade-amount:   25%;
$btn-active-border-tint-amount:    10%;
```

Mixins

There are three mixins for buttons: button and button outline variant mixins (both based on $theme-colors), plus a button size mixin.

```
@mixin button-variant(
  $background,
  $border,
```

```
$color: color-contrast($background),
$hover-background: if($color == $color-contrast-
  light, shade-color($background, $btn-hover-bg-
  shade-amount), tint-color($background,
  $btn-hover-bg-tint-amount)),
$hover-border: if($color == $color-contrast-light,
  shade-color($border, $btn-hover-border-shade-
  amount), tint-color($border,
  $btn-hover-border-tint-amount)),
$hover-color: color-contrast($hover-background),
$active-background: if($color == $color-contrast-
  light, shade-color($background, $btn-active-bg-
  shade-amount), tint-color($background,
  $btn-active-bg-tint-amount)),
$active-border: if($color == $color-contrast-light,
  shade-color($border, $btn-active-border-shade-
  amount), tint-color($border,
  $btn-active-border-tint-amount)),
$active-color: color-contrast($active-background),
$disabled-background: $background,
$disabled-border: $border,
$disabled-color: color-contrast($disabled-background)
) {
color: $color;
@include gradient-bg($background);
border-color: $border;
@include box-shadow($btn-box-shadow);

&:hover {
 color: $hover-color;
 @include gradient-bg($hover-background);
 border-color: $hover-border;
}

.btn-check:focus + &,
&:focus {
 color: $hover-color;
 @include gradient-bg($hover-background);
 border-color: $hover-border;
 @if $enable-shadows {
  @include box-shadow($btn-box-shadow, 0 0 0 $btn-
     focus-width rgba(mix($color, $border, 15%), .6));
```

```scss
  } @else {
   // Avoid using mixin so we can pass custom focus
          shadow properly
   box-shadow: 0 0 0 $btn-focus-width rgba(mix($color,
       $border, 15%), .6);
  }
 }

 .btn-check:checked + &,
 .btn-check:active + &,
 &:active,
 &.active,
 .show > &.dropdown-toggle {
  color: $active-color;
  background-color: $active-background;
  // Remove CSS gradients if they're enabled
  background-image: if($enable-gradients, none, null);
  border-color: $active-border;

  &:focus {
   @if $enable-shadows {
    @include box-shadow($btn-active-box-shadow, 0 0 0
          $btn-focus-width rgba(mix($color,
          $border, 18%), .6));
   } @else {
    // Avoid using mixin so we can pass custom focus
          shadow properly
    box-shadow: 0 0 0 $btn-focus-width
        rgba(mix($color, $border, 18%), .6);
   }
  }
 }

 &:disabled,
 &.disabled {
  color: $disabled-color;
  background-color: $disabled-background;
  // Remove CSS gradients if they're enabled
  background-image: if($enable-gradients, none, null);
  border-color: $disabled-border;
 }
}
```

```
@mixin button-outline-variant(
 $color,
 $color-hover: color-contrast($color),
 $active-background: $color,
 $active-border: $color,
 $active-color: color-contrast($active-background)
) {
 color: $color;
 border-color: $color;

 &:hover {
  color: $color-hover;
  background-color: $active-background;
  border-color: $active-border;
 }

 .btn-check:focus + &,
 &:focus {
  box-shadow: 0 0 0 $btn-focus-width rgba($color, .6);
 }

 .btn-check:checked + &,
 .btn-check:active + &,
 &:active,
 &.active,
 &.dropdown-toggle.show {
  color: $active-color;
  background-color: $active-background;
  border-color: $active-border;

  &:focus {
   @if $enable-shadows {
    @include box-shadow($btn-active-box-shadow, 0 0 0
            $btn-focus-width rgba($color, .6));
   } @else {
    // Avoid using mixin so we can pass custom focus
            shadow properly
    box-shadow: 0 0 0 $btn-focus-width rgba($color, .6);
   }
  }
 }

 &:disabled,
 &.disabled {
```

```
  color: $color;
  background-color: transparent;
  }
}
```

Loops

Button variants (for regular and outline buttons) use their respective mixins with our $theme-colors map to generate the modifier classes in scss/_buttons.scss.

```
@each $color, $value in $theme-colors {
  .btn-#{$color} {
  @include button-variant($value, $value);
  }
}

@each $color, $value in $theme-colors {
  .btn-outline-#{$color} {
  @include button-outline-variant($value);
  }
}
```

Buttons Group

Stack a vertical column of buttons or group a series of buttons on a single line.

Example

Wrap a series of the buttons with .btn in .btn-group.

Button groups

```
<div class="btn-group" role="group" aria-label="Basic
              example">
  <button type="button" class="btn btn-primary">Left</
                button>
  <button type="button" class="btn btn-
                primary">Middle</button>
  <button type="button" class="btn btn-
                primary">Right</button>
</div>
```

Ensure Correct Role and Provide a Label

An appropriate role property must be given for assistive technology (such as screen readers) to signal that a succession of buttons is grouped. For button groups, this would be role="group," whereas toolbars would be role="toolbar."

Furthermore, despite the presence of the right role attribute, most assistive technologies will not announce groups and toolbars until they are explicitly labelled. We use aria-label in the examples above, but other options such as aria-labeled by can also be utilized.

These classes can be added to groups of links as an alternative to the .nav navigation components.

Button active groups

```
<div class="btn-group">
 <a href="#" class="btn btn-primary active" aria-
                    current="page">Active link</a>
 <a href="#" class="btn btn-primary">Link</a>
 <a href="#" class="btn btn-primary">Link</a>
</div>
```

Mixed Style

```
<div class="btn-group" role="group" aria-label="Basic
            mixed styles example">
 <button type="button" class="btn btn-danger">Left</
                button>
 <button type="button" class="btn btn-
                warning">Middle</button>
 <button type="button" class="btn btn-
                success">Right</button>
</div>
```

Outlined Styles

```
<div class="btn-group" role="group" aria-label="Basic
                    outlined example">
 <button type="button" class="btn btn-outline-
                    primary">Left</button>
 <button type="button" class="btn btn-outline-
                    primary">Middle</button>
```

```
    <button type="button" class="btn btn-outline-
                        primary">Right</button>
</div>
```

Checkbox and Radio Button Groups

Combine button-like checkbox and radio toggle buttons into a seamless-looking button group.

```
<div class="btn-group" role="group" aria-label="Basic
checkbox toggle button group">
 <input type="checkbox" class="btn-check"
            id="btncheck1" autocomplete="off">
 <label class="btn btn-outline-primary"
            for="btncheck1">Checkbox 1</label>

 <input type="checkbox" class="btn-check"
            id="btncheck2" autocomplete="off">
 <label class="btn btn-outline-primary"
            for="btncheck2">Checkbox 2</label>

 <input type="checkbox" class="btn-check"
            id="btncheck3" autocomplete="off">
 <label class="btn btn-outline-primary"
            for="btncheck3">Checkbox 3</label>
</div>

<div class="btn-group" role="group" aria-label="Basic
                     radio toggle button group">
 <input type="radio" class="btn-check" name="btnradio"
        id="btnradio1" autocomplete="off" checked>
 <label class="btn btn-outline-primary"
            for="btnradio1">Radio 1</label>

 <input type="radio" class="btn-check" name="btnradio"
            id="btnradio2" autocomplete="off">
 <label class="btn btn-outline-primary"
             for="btnradio2">Radio 2</label>

 <input type="radio" class="btn-check" name="btnradio"
            id="btnradio3" autocomplete="off">
 <label class="btn btn-outline-primary"
            for="btnradio3">Radio 3</label>
</div>
```

Button Toolbar

For more complicated components, combine sets of button groups into button toolbars. To space out groups, buttons, and other elements, use utility classes as needed.

```
<div class="btn-toolbar" role="toolbar" aria-
          label="Toolbar with button groups">
 <div class="btn-group me-2" role="group" aria-
          label="First group">
  <button type="button" class="btn btn-primary">1</
          button>
  <button type="button" class="btn btn-primary">2</
          button>
  <button type="button" class="btn btn-primary">3</
          button>
  <button type="button" class="btn btn-primary">4</
          button>
 </div>
 <div class="btn-group me-2" role="group" aria-
          label="Second group">
  <button type="button" class="btn btn-secondary">5</
          button>
  <button type="button" class="btn btn-secondary">6</
          button>
  <button type="button" class="btn btn-secondary">7</
          button>
 </div>
 <div class="btn-group" role="group" aria-
          label="Third group">
  <button type="button" class="btn btn-info">8</
          button>
 </div>
</div>
```

In your toolbars, feel free to combine input groups and button groups. However, similar to the example above, you'll most likely need certain tools to properly space items.

```
<div class="btn-toolbar mb-3" role="toolbar" aria-
          label="Toolbar with button groups">
 <div class="btn-group me-2" role="group" aria-
          label="First group">
```

```
   <button type="button" class="btn btn-outline-
               secondary">1</button>
   <button type="button" class="btn btn-outline-
               secondary">2</button>
   <button type="button" class="btn btn-outline-
               secondary">3</button>
   <button type="button" class="btn btn-outline-
               secondary">4</button>
 </div>
 <div class="input-group">
  <div class="input-group-text"
           id="btnGroupAddon">@</div>
  <input type="text" class="form-control"
           placeholder="Input group example" aria-
           label="Input group example"
           aria-describedby="btnGroupAddon">
 </div>
</div>

<div class="btn-toolbar justify-content-between"
           role="toolbar" aria-label="Toolbar with
           button groups">
 <div class="btn-group" role="group" aria-
           label="First group">
  <button type="button" class="btn btn-outline-
               secondary">1</button>
   <button type="button" class="btn btn-outline-
                       secondary">2</button>
   <button type="button" class="btn btn-outline-
                       secondary">3</button>
   <button type="button" class="btn btn-outline-
                       secondary">4</button>
 </div>
 <div class="input-group">
  <div class="input-group-text"
id="btnGroupAddon2">@</div>
   <input type="text" class="form-control"
         placeholder="Input group example" aria-
         label="Input group example" aria-describedby
         ="btnGroupAddon2">
 </div>
</div>
```

Sizing

Rather than applying button size classes to every button in group, add .btn-group-* to each .btn-group, including each one when nesting multiple groups.

```
<div class="btn-group btn-group-lg" role="group"
          aria-label="...">...</div>
<div class="btn-group" role="group" aria-
          label="...">...</div>
<div class="btn-group btn-group-sm" role="group"
          aria-label="...">...</div>
```

Nesting

Place .btn-group within another .btn-group when you want dropdown menus mixed with a series of buttons.

```
<div class="btn-group" role="group" aria-
     label="Button group with nested dropdown">
 <button type="button" class="btn btn-primary">1</
        button>
 <button type="button" class="btn btn-primary">2</
        button>

 <div class="btn-group" role="group">
  <button id="btnGroupDrop1" type="button" class="btn
        btn-primary dropdown-toggle" data-bs-
        toggle="dropdown" aria-expanded="false">
   Dropdown
  </button>
  <ul class="dropdown-menu"
            aria-labelledby="btnGroupDrop1">
   <li><a class="dropdown-item" href="#">Dropdown
               link</a></li>
   <li><a class="dropdown-item" href="#">Dropdown
               link</a></li>
  </ul>
 </div>
</div>
```

Vertical Variation

Make a row of buttons display vertically instead of horizontally stacked. Dropdowns with split buttons aren't supported here.

```
<div class="btn-group-vertical">
 ...
</div>
```

Cards

Cards in Bootstrap are a versatile and expandable content container with a variety of versions and settings.

About

A card is a content container that is both versatile and expandable. It has header and footer settings, as well as a lot of information, contextual background colors, and display possibilities. If you're acquainted with Bootstrap 3, you'll notice that cards have taken the role of our previous panels, wells, and thumbnails. Modifier classes for cards provide similar capabilities to those components.

Example

Cards are created using the least amount of markup and styles possible while yet allowing for a great deal of flexibility and customization. They're made with flexbox, so they're easy to align and blend in with other Bootstrap elements. Because they don't have a margin by default, you'll need to employ spacing tools as needed.

A primary card with mixed content and a set width is shown below. Because cards don't have a defined width to begin with, they'll fill the whole width of their parent element. With our different size choices, this may be readily modified.

```
<div class="card" style="width: 18rem;">
 <img src="..." class="card-img-top" alt="...">
 <div class="card-body">
  <h5 class="card-title">Card title</h5>
  <p class="card-text">Some quick example text to
          build on the card title and make up the
          bulk of the card's content.</p>
  <a href="#" class="btn btn-primary">Go somewhere</a>
 </div>
</div>
```

Content Types

Images, text, list groups, links, and other types of information are all supported by cards. Here are some instances of what has aided.

Body

The .card-body element is the basis of a card. When you require a padded part within a card, this is the tool you use.

```
<div class="card">
 <div class="card-body">
  This is some text within card body.
 </div>
</div>
```

Tiles, Text, and Links

Adding .card-title to a <h*> element creates a card title. Adding a .card-link to an <a> tag adds and places links next to each other in the same way.

A .card-subtitle tag is added to a <h*> element to employ subtitles. The card title and subtitle are beautifully aligned when the .card-title and .card-subtitle items are placed in a .card-body item.

```
<div class="card" style="width: 18rem;">
 <div class="card-body">
  <h5 class="card-title">Card title</h5>
  <h6 class="card-subtitle mb-2 text-muted">Card
         subtitle</h6>
  <p class="card-text">Some quick example text to
         build on the card title and make up the
         bulk of the card's content.</p>
  <a href="#" class="card-link">Card link</a>
  <a href="#" class="card-link">Another link</a>
 </div>
</div>
```

Images

.card-img-top place an image to the top of the card. With .card-text, text can be added to the card. Text within the .card-text can also be styled with the standard HTML tags.

```
<div class="card" style="width: 18rem;">
 <img src="..." class="card-img-top" alt="...">
 <div class="card-body">
  <p class="card-text">Some quick example text to
         build on the card title and make up the
         bulk of the card's content.</p>
```

```
    </div>
  </div>
```

List Groups

With a flush list group, you may make content lists in a card.

```
<div class="card" style="width: 18rem;">
  <ul class="list-group list-group-flush">
    <li class="list-group-item">An item</li>
    <li class="list-group-item">A second item</li>
    <li class="list-group-item">A third item</li>
  </ul>
</div>

<div class="card" style="width: 18rem;">
  <div class="card-header">
    Featured
  </div>
  <ul class="list-group list-group-flush">
    <li class="list-group-item">An item</li>
    <li class="list-group-item">A second item</li>
    <li class="list-group-item">A third item</li>
  </ul>
</div>

<div class="card" style="width: 18rem;">
  <ul class="list-group list-group-flush">
    <li class="list-group-item">An item</li>
    <li class="list-group-item">A second item</li>
    <li class="list-group-item">A third item</li>
  </ul>
  <div class="card-footer">
    Card footer
  </div>
</div>
```

Kitchen Sink

You may mix and combine different content kinds to make the card you want, or you can just dump everything in there.

```
<div class="card" style="width: 18rem;">
  <img src="..." class="card-img-top" alt="...">
```

```
<div class="card-body">
 <h5 class="card-title">Card title</h5>
 <p class="card-text">Some quick example text to
          build on the card title and make up bulk
          of the card's content.</p>
</div>
<ul class="list-group list-group-flush">
 <li class="list-group-item">An item</li>
 <li class="list-group-item">A second item</li>
 <li class="list-group-item">A third item</li>
</ul>
<div class="card-body">
 <a href="#" class="card-link">Card link</a>
 <a href="#" class="card-link">Another link</a>
</div>
</div>
```

Header and Footer

Add optional header and footer within a card.

```
<div class="card">
 <div class="card-header">
  Featured
 </div>
 <div class="card-body">
  <h5 class="card-title">Special title treatment</h5>
  <p class="card-text">With supporting text below as
      a natural lead-in to additional content.</p>
  <a href="#" class="btn btn-primary">Go somewhere</a>
 </div>
</div>
```

Card headers can be styled by adding .card-header to <h*> elements.

```
<div class="card">
 <h5 class="card-header">Featured</h5>
 <div class="card-body">
  <h5 class="card-title">Special title treatment</h5>
  <p class="card-text">With supporting text below as
      a natural lead-in to additional content.</p>
  <a href="#" class="btn btn-primary">Go somewhere</a>
 </div>
</div>
```

```
<div class="card">
 <div class="card-header">
  Quote
 </div>
 <div class="card-body">
  <blockquote class="blockquote mb-0">
   <p>A well-known quote, contained in a blockquote
      element.</p>
   <footer class="blockquote-footer">Someone famous
                  in <cite title="Source
                  Title">Source Title</cite></footer>
  </blockquote>
 </div>
</div>

<div class="card text-center">
 <div class="card-header">
  Featured
 </div>
 <div class="card-body">
  <h5 class="card-title">Special title treatment</h5>
  <p class="card-text">With supporting text below as
     a natural lead-in to additional content.</p>
  <a href="#" class="btn btn-primary">Go somewhere</a>
 </div>
 <div class="card-footer text-muted">
  2 days ago
 </div>
</div>
```

Sizing

Cards will be 100% broad unless otherwise indicated because they presume no set width to begin with. Custom CSS, grid classes, grid Sass mixins, and utilities all may be used to adjust this.

Using Grid Markup

Wrap cards in rows and columns as appropriate using the grid.

```
<div class="row">
 <div class="col-sm-6">
  <div class="card">
   <div class="card-body">
```

```
    <h5 class="card-title">Special title treatment</h5>
    <p class="card-text">With supporting text below as
        a natural lead-in to additional content.</p>
    <a href="#" class="btn btn-primary">Go somewhere</a>
   </div>
  </div>
 </div>
 <div class="col-sm-6">
  <div class="card">
   <div class="card-body">
    <h5 class="card-title">Special title treatment</h5>
    <p class="card-text">With supporting text below as
        a natural lead-in to additional content.</p>
    <a href="#" class="btn btn-primary">Go somewhere</a>
   </div>
  </div>
 </div>
</div>
```

Using Utilities

To rapidly set the width of a card, use one of our few size facilities.

```
<div class="card w-75">
 <div class="card-body">
  <h5 class="card-title">Card title</h5>
  <p class="card-text">With supporting text below as
      a natural lead-in to additional content.</p>
  <a href="#" class="btn btn-primary">Button</a>
 </div>
</div>

<div class="card w-50">
 <div class="card-body">
  <h5 class="card-title">Card title</h5>
  <p class="card-text">With supporting text below as
      a natural lead-in to additional content.</p>
  <a href="#" class="btn btn-primary">Button</a>
 </div>
</div>
```

Using Custom CSS:

```
<div class="card" style="width: 18rem;">
 <div class="card-body">
```

```
  <h5 class="card-title">Special title treatment</h5>
  <p class="card-text">With supporting text below as
    a natural lead-in to additional content.</p>
  <a href="#" class="btn btn-primary">Go somewhere</a>
 </div>
</div>
```

Text Alignment

With our text align classes, you can instantly adjust the text orientation of any card – in its entirety or particular portions.

```
<div class="card" style="width: 18rem;">
 <div class="card-body">
  <h5 class="card-title">Special title treatment</h5>
  <p class="card-text">With supporting text below as
    a natural lead-in to additional content.</p>
  <a href="#" class="btn btn-primary">Go somewhere</a>
 </div>
</div>
```

```
<div class="card text-center" style="width: 18rem;">
 <div class="card-body">
  <h5 class="card-title">Special title treatment</h5>
  <p class="card-text">With supporting text below as
    a natural lead-in to additional content.</p>
  <a href="#" class="btn btn-primary">Go somewhere</a>
 </div>
</div>
```

```
<div class="card text-end" style="width: 18rem;">
 <div class="card-body">
  <h5 class="card-title">Special title treatment</h5>
  <p class="card-text">With supporting text below as
    a natural lead-in to additional content.</p>
  <a href="#" class="btn btn-primary">Go somewhere</a>
 </div>
</div>
```

Navigation

Add some navigation to card's header (or block) with Bootstrap's nav components.

```
<div class="card text-center">
 <div class="card-header">
```

```
<ul class="nav nav-tabs card-header-tabs">
 <li class="nav-item">
  <a class="nav-link active" aria-current="true"
     href="#">Active</a>
 </li>
 <li class="nav-item">
  <a class="nav-link" href="#">Link</a>
 </li>
 <li class="nav-item">
  <a class="nav-link disabled" href="#"
     tabindex="-1" aria-disabled="true">Disabled</a>
 </li>
 </ul>
</div>
<div class="card-body">
 <h5 class="card-title">Special title treatment</h5>
 <p class="card-text">With supporting text below as
    a natural lead-in to additional content.</p>
 <a href="#" class="btn btn-primary">Go somewhere</a>
</div>
</div>

<div class="card text-center">
 <div class="card-header">
  <ul class="nav nav-pills card-header-pills">
   <li class="nav-item">
    <a class="nav-link active" href="#">Active</a>
   </li>
   <li class="nav-item">
    <a class="nav-link" href="#">Link</a>
   </li>
   <li class="nav-item">
    <a class="nav-link disabled" href="#" tabindex="-1"
       aria-disabled="true">Disabled</a>
   </li>
  </ul>
 </div>
 <div class="card-body">
  <h5 class="card-title">Special title treatment</h5>
  <p class="card-text">With supporting text below as
     a natural lead-in to additional content.</p>
  <a href="#" class="btn btn-primary">Go somewhere</a>
 </div>
</div>
```

Images

There are a few alternatives for working with images on cards. You may add "image caps" to either end of a card, overlay images with card information, or just embed the image in the card.

Images Caps

Like headers and footers, cards can include top and bottom "image caps" – images at the top or bottom of a card.

```
<div class="card mb-3">
 <img src="..." class="card-img-top" alt="...">
 <div class="card-body">
  <h5 class="card-title">Card title</h5>
  <p class="card-text">This is a wider card with the
     supporting text below as a natural lead-in to
     additional content. This content is little bit
     longer.</p>
  <p class="card-text"><small class="text-muted">Last
     updated 4 mins ago</small></p>
 </div>
</div>
<div class="card">
 <div class="card-body">
  <h5 class="card-title">Card title</h5>
  <p class="card-text">This is wider card with the
     supporting text below as natural lead-in to
     additional content. This content is little bit
     longer.</p>
  <p class="card-text"><small class="text-muted">Last
     updated 4 mins ago</small></p>
 </div>
 <img src="..." class="card-img-bottom" alt="...">
</div>
```

Images Overlays

Make a card background out of an image and add text to it. Additional styles or utilities may or may not be required, depending on the image.

```
<div class="card bg-dark text-white">
 <img src="..." class="card-img" alt="...">
 <div class="card-img-overlay">
  <h5 class="card-title">Card title</h5>
```

```
  <p class="card-text">This is a wider card with
     supporting text below as a natural lead-in to
     additional content. This content is a little bit
     longer.</p>
  <p class="card-text">Last updated 3 mins ago</p>
 </div>
</div>
```

Horizontal

Cards may be made horizontal in a mobile-friendly and responsive fashion by combining grid and utility classes. We remove grid gutters with .g-0 and use the .col-md-* classes to make the card horizontal at the md breakpoint in the example below. Depending on the content of your card, you may need to make more alterations.

```
<div class="card mb-3" style="max-width: 540px;">
 <div class="row g-0">
  <div class="col-md-4">
   <img src="..." class="img-fluid rounded-start"
                   alt="...">
  </div>
  <div class="col-md-8">
   <div class="card-body">
    <h5 class="card-title">Card title</h5>
    <p class="card-text">This is a wider card with
       supporting text below as a natural lead-in to
       additional content. This content is a little
       bit longer.</p>
    <p class="card-text"><small class="text-
       muted">Last updated 3 mins ago</small></p>
   </div>
  </div>
 </div>
</div>
```

Card Styles

Cards provide a variety of background, border, and color customization choices.

Background and Color

Use the text color and background utilities to change the appearance of a card.

```
<div class="card text-white bg-primary mb-3"
    style="max-width: 19rem;">
 <div class="card-header">Header</div>
 <div class="card-body">
  <h5 class="card-title">Primary card title</h5>
  <p class="card-text">Some quick example text to
     build on the card title and make up the bulk of
     the card's content.</p>
 </div>
</div>
<div class="card text-white bg-secondary mb-3"
    style="max-width: 19rem;">
 <div class="card-header">Header</div>
 <div class="card-body">
  <h5 class="card-title">Secondary card title</h5>
  <p class="card-text">Some quick example text to
     build on the card title and make up the bulk of
     the card's content.</p>
 </div>
</div>
<div class="card text-white bg-success mb-3"
style="max-width: 19rem;">
 <div class="card-header">Header</div>
 <div class="card-body">
  <h5 class="card-title">Success card title</h5>
  <p class="card-text">Some quick example text to
     build on the card title and make up the bulk of
     the card's content.</p>
 </div>
</div>
<div class="card text-white bg-danger mb-3"
    style="max-width: 19rem;">
 <div class="card-header">Header</div>
 <div class="card-body">
  <h5 class="card-title">Danger card title</h5>
  <p class="card-text">Some quick example text to
     build on the card title and make up the bulk of
     the card's content.</p>
 </div>
</div>
<div class="card text-dark bg-warning mb-3"
    style="max-width: 18rem;">
 <div class="card-header">Header</div>
```

```
 <div class="card-body">
  <h5 class="card-title">Warning card title</h5>
  <p class="card-text">Some quick example text to
      build on the card title and make up the bulk of
      the card's content.</p>
 </div>
</div>
<div class="card text-dark bg-info mb-3" style="max-
      width: 18rem;">
 <div class="card-header">Header</div>
 <div class="card-body">
  <h5 class="card-title">Info card title</h5>
  <p class="card-text">Some quick example text to
      build on the card title and make up the bulk of
      the card's content.</p>
 </div>
</div>
<div class="card text-dark bg-light mb-3" style="max-
      width: 18rem;">
 <div class="card-header">Header</div>
 <div class="card-body">
  <h5 class="card-title">Light card title</h5>
  <p class="card-text">Some quick example text to
      build on the card title and make up the bulk of
      the card's content.</p>
 </div>
</div>
<div class="card text-white bg-dark mb-3" style="max-
      width: 18rem;">
 <div class="card-header">Header</div>
 <div class="card-body">
  <h5 class="card-title">Dark card title</h5>
  <p class="card-text">Some quick example text to
      build on the card title and make up the bulk of
      the card's content.</p>
 </div>
</div>
```

Border

To modify the color of a card's border, use border utilities. As seen below, you may use .text-color classes on the parent .card or a subset of the card's contents.

```
<div class="card border-primary mb-3" style="max-
    width: 18rem;">
 <div class="card-header">Header</div>
 <div class="card-body text-primary">
  <h5 class="card-title">Primary card title</h5>
  <p class="card-text">Some quick example text to
     build on the card title and make up the bulk of
     the card's content.</p>
 </div>
</div>
<div class="card border-secondary mb-3" style="max-
    width: 18rem;">
 <div class="card-header">Header</div>
 <div class="card-body text-secondary">
  <h5 class="card-title">Secondary card title</h5>
  <p class="card-text">Some quick example text to
     build on the card title and make up the bulk of
     the card's content.</p>
 </div>
</div>
<div class="card border-success mb-3" style="max-
    width: 18rem;">
 <div class="card-header">Header</div>
 <div class="card-body text-success">
  <h5 class="card-title">Success card title</h5>
  <p class="card-text">Some quick example text to
     build on the card title and make up the bulk of
     the card's content.</p>
 </div>
</div>
<div class="card border-danger mb-3" style="max-
    width: 18rem;">
 <div class="card-header">Header</div>
 <div class="card-body text-danger">
  <h5 class="card-title">Danger card title</h5>
  <p class="card-text">Some quick example text to
     build on the card title and make up the bulk of
     the card's content.</p>
 </div>
</div>
<div class="card border-warning mb-3" style="max-
    width: 18rem;">
```

```
<div class="card-header">Header</div>
<div class="card-body">
 <h5 class="card-title">Warning card title</h5>
 <p class="card-text">Some quick example text to
     build on the card title and make up the bulk of
     the card's content.</p>
</div>
</div>
<div class="card border-info mb-3" style="max-width:
     19rem;">
 <div class="card-header">Header</div>
 <div class="card-body">
  <h5 class="card-title">Info card title</h5>
  <p class="card-text">Some quick example text to
      build on the card title and make up the bulk of
      the card's content.</p>
 </div>
</div>
<div class="card border-light mb-3" style="max-width:
     19rem;">
 <div class="card-header">Header</div>
 <div class="card-body">
  <h5 class="card-title">Light card title</h5>
  <p class="card-text">Some quick example text to
      build on the card title and make up the bulk of
      the card's content.</p>
 </div>
</div>
<div class="card border-dark mb-3" style="max-width:
     19rem;">
 <div class="card-header">Header</div>
 <div class="card-body text-dark">
  <h5 class="card-title">Dark card title</h5>
  <p class="card-text">Some quick example text to
      build on the card title and make up the bulk of
      the card's content.</p>
 </div>
</div>
```

Mixins Utilities
With .bg-transparent, you may also adjust the borders on the card header
and footer as needed and eliminate their background color.

```
<div class="card border-success mb-3" style="max-
            width: 19rem;">
 <div class="card-header bg-transparent border-
            success">Header</div>
 <div class="card-body text-success">
  <h5 class="card-title">Success card title</h5>
  <p class="card-text">Some quick example text to
            build on the card title and make up the
            bulk of the card's content.</p>
 </div>
 <div class="card-footer bg-transparent border-
            success">Footer</div>
</div>
```

Card Layout

Bootstrap has a few choices for putting out a sequence of cards in addition to designing the information within cards. These layout options are not currently responsive for the time being.

Card Groups

To render cards as a single, associated element with equal width and height columns, use card groups. Starting at the sm breakpoint, card groups are stacked and utilize display: flex; to connect with consistent dimensions.

```
<div class="card-group">
 <div class="card">
  <img src="..." class="card-img-top" alt="...">
  <div class="card-body">
   <h5 class="card-title">Card title</h5>
   <p class="card-text">This is a wider card with
       supporting text below as a natural lead-in to
       additional content. This content is a little
       bit longer.</p>
   <p class="card-text"><small class="text-
       muted">Last updated 3 mins ago</small></p>
  </div>
 </div>
 <div class="card">
  <img src="..." class="card-img-top" alt="...">
  <div class="card-body">
   <h5 class="card-title">Card title</h5>
```

```
    <p class="card-text">This card has supporting text
below as a natural lead-in to additional content.</p>
    <p class="card-text"><small class="text-
      muted">Last updated 3 mins ago</small></p>
  </div>
 </div>
 <div class="card">
  <img src="..." class="card-img-top" alt="...">
  <div class="card-body">
   <h5 class="card-title">Card title</h5>
   <p class="card-text">As a natural lead-in to
      further material, this is a broader card with
      supporting text underneath. To demonstrate that
      equal height action, this card includes even
      more substance than the first.</p>
   <p class="card-text"><small class="text-
      muted">Last updated 3 mins ago</small></p>
  </div>
 </div>
</div>
```

The content of card groups with footers will automatically line up.

```
<div class="card-group">
 <div class="card">
  <img src="..." class="card-img-top" alt="...">
  <div class="card-body">
   <h5 class="card-title">Card title</h5>
   <p class="card-text">This is a wider card with
      supporting text below as a natural lead-in to
      additional content. This content is a little
      bit longer.</p>
  </div>
  <div class="card-footer">
   <small class="text-muted">Last updated 3 mins
         ago</small>
  </div>
 </div>
 <div class="card">
  <img src="..." class="card-img-top" alt="...">
  <div class="card-body">
   <h5 class="card-title">Card title</h5>
```

```
  <p class="card-text">This card has supporting text
      below as a natural lead-in to additional
      content.</p>
 </div>
 <div class="card-footer">
  <small class="text-muted">Last updated 3 mins
        ago</small>
 </div>
</div>
<div class="card">
 <img src="..." class="card-img-top" alt="...">
 <div class="card-body">
  <h5 class="card-title">Card title</h5>
  <p class="card-text">As a natural lead-in to
      further material, this is a broader card with
      supporting text underneath. To demonstrate that
      equal height action, this card includes even
      more content than the first.</p>
 </div>
 <div class="card-footer">
  <small class="text-muted">Last updated 3 mins
        ago</small>
 </div>
</div>
</div>
```

Grid Cards

Use Bootstrap grid system and its .row-cols classes to manage how many grid columns (wrapped around your cards) you show each row. From the medium breakpoint up, here's .row-cols-1 laying out the cards on one column and .row-cols-MD-2 splitting four cards to equal width across many rows.

```
<div class="row row-cols-1 row-cols-md-2 g-4">
 <div class="col">
  <div class="card">
   <img src="..." class="card-img-top" alt="...">
   <div class="card-body">
    <h5 class="card-title">Card title</h5>
    <p class="card-text">This is a longer card with
        supporting text below as a natural lead-in to
        additional content. This content is a little
        bit longer.</p>
```

```
      </div>
    </div>
  </div>
  <div class="col">
   <div class="card">
    <img src="..." class="card-img-top" alt="...">
    <div class="card-body">
     <h5 class="card-title">Card title</h5>
     <p class="card-text">This is a longer card with
         supporting text below as a natural lead-in to
         additional content. This content is a little
         bit longer.</p>
    </div>
   </div>
  </div>
  <div class="col">
   <div class="card">
    <img src="..." class="card-img-top" alt="...">
    <div class="card-body">
     <h5 class="card-title">Card title</h5>
     <p class="card-text">This is a longer card with
         supporting text below as a natural lead-in to
         additional content.</p>
    </div>
   </div>
  </div>
  <div class="col">
   <div class="card">
    <img src="..." class="card-img-top" alt="...">
    <div class="card-body">
     <h5 class="card-title">Card title</h5>
     <p class="card-text">This is a longer card with
         supporting text below as a natural lead-in to
         additional content. This content is a little
         bit longer.</p>
    </div>
   </div>
  </div>
</div>
```

Change it to .row-cols-3, and you'll see fourth card wrap.

```
<div class="row row-cols-1 row-cols-md-3 g-4">
 <div class="col">
```

```
<div class="card">
 <img src="..." class="card-img-top" alt="...">
 <div class="card-body">
  <h5 class="card-title">Card title</h5>
  <p class="card-text">This is a longer card with
     supporting text below as a natural lead-in to
     additional content. This content is a little
     bit longer.</p>
 </div>
</div>
</div>
<div class="col">
 <div class="card">
  <img src="..." class="card-img-top" alt="...">
  <div class="card-body">
   <h5 class="card-title">Card title</h5>
   <p class="card-text">This is a longer card with
      supporting text below as a natural lead-in to
      additional content. This content is a little
      bit longer.</p>
  </div>
 </div>
</div>
<div class="col">
 <div class="card">
  <img src="..." class="card-img-top" alt="...">
  <div class="card-body">
   <h5 class="card-title">Card title</h5>
   <p class="card-text">This is a longer card with
      supporting text below as a natural lead-in to
      additional content.</p>
  </div>
 </div>
</div>
<div class="col">
 <div class="card">
  <img src="..." class="card-img-top" alt="...">
  <div class="card-body">
   <h5 class="card-title">Card title</h5>
   <p class="card-text">This is a longer card with
      supporting text below as a natural lead-in to
      additional content. This content is a little
      bit longer.</p>
```

```
    </div>
   </div>
  </div>
</div>
```

Add .h-100 to the cards when you need them to have the same height. Set $card-height: 100 percent in Sass if you want comparable measurements by default.

```
<div class="row row-cols-1 row-cols-md-3 g-4">
 <div class="col">
  <div class="card h-100">
   <img src="..." class="card-img-top" alt="...">
   <div class="card-body">
    <h5 class="card-title">Card title</h5>
    <p class="card-text">This is a longer card with
        supporting text below as a natural lead-in to
        additional content. This content is a little
        bit longer.</p>
   </div>
  </div>
 </div>
 <div class="col">
  <div class="card h-100">
   <img src="..." class="card-img-top" alt="...">
   <div class="card-body">
    <h5 class="card-title">Card title</h5>
    <p class="card-text">This is a short card.</p>
   </div>
  </div>
 </div>
 <div class="col">
  <div class="card h-100">
   <img src="..." class="card-img-top" alt="...">
   <div class="card-body">
    <h5 class="card-title">Card title</h5>
    <p class="card-text">This is a longer card with
        supporting text below as a natural lead-in to
        additional content.</p>
   </div>
  </div>
 </div>
 <div class="col">
```

```
  <div class="card h-100">
   <img src="..." class="card-img-top" alt="...">

   <div class="card-body">
    <h5 class="card-title">Card title</h5>

    <p class="card-text">This is a longer card with
        supporting text below as a natural lead-in to
        additional content. This content is a little
        bit longer.</p>
   </div>
  </div>
 </div>
</div>
```

Card footers, like card groups, will immediately line up.

```
<div class="row row-cols-1 row-cols-md-3 g-4">
 <div class="col">
  <div class="card h-100">
   <img src="..." class="card-img-top" alt="...">
   <div class="card-body">
    <h5 class="card-title">Card title</h5>
    <p class="card-text">This is a wider card with
        supporting text below as a natural lead-in to
        additional content. This content is a little
        bit longer.</p>
   </div>
   <div class="card-footer">
    <small class="text-muted">Last updated 3 mins
           ago</small>
   </div>
  </div>
 </div>
 <div class="col">
  <div class="card h-100">
   <img src="..." class="card-img-top" alt="...">
   <div class="card-body">
    <h5 class="card-title">Card title</h5>
    <p class="card-text">This card has supporting
        text below as a natural lead-in to additional
        content.</p>
   </div>
```

```
   <div class="card-footer">
    <small class="text-muted">Last updated 3 mins
           ago</small>
   </div>
  </div>
 </div>
 <div class="col">
  <div class="card h-100">
   <img src="..." class="card-img-top" alt="...">
   <div class="card-body">
    <h5 class="card-title">Card title</h5>
    <p class="card-text">As a natural lead-in to
       further material, this is a broader card with
       supporting text underneath. To demonstrate
       that equal height action, this card includes
       even more substance than the previous.</p>
   </div>
   <div class="card-footer">
    <small class="text-muted">Last updated 3 mins
           ago</small>
   </div>
  </div>
 </div>
</div>
```

Masonry

In v4, we used a CSS-only technique to mimic the behavior of Masonry-like columns, but this technique came with lots of unpleasant side effects. If you want to have this type of layout in v5, you can use the Masonry plugin. Masonry is not included in Bootstrap, but we've made a demo example to help you get started.

Carousel

A slideshow component that, like a carousel, cycles among elements – images or text slides.

How It Works

The carousel is a slideshow that uses CSS 3D transforms and a little JavaScript to cycle through a sequence of content. It may be used with photos, text, or custom markup. Previous/following controls and indicators are also supported.

The carousel will prevent sliding when the webpage is not visible to the user in browsers that use the Page Visibility API (such as when the browser tab is inactive, the browser window is minimized, etc.). This component's animation effect is determined by the prefers-reduced-motion media query.

Kindly be aware that nested carousels are not supported, and carousels in general do not meet accessibility requirements.

Example

Slide dimensions are not automatically normalized in carousels. You may need to use additional tools or custom styles to appropriately scale content. Carousels can have previous/following buttons and indicators, although they aren't essential. As you see fit, add and modify. The .active class must be applied to at least one slide; else, the carousel will not appear. Also, if you're utilizing numerous carousels on a single page, make sure to give each one a unique id in the .carousel file. The data-bs-target property (or href for links) on control and indicator elements must match the id of the .carousel element.

Slides Only

This is a slide-only carousel. On carousel images, note the existence of the .d-block and .w-100 tags, which prohibit browser default image alignment.

```
<div id="carouselExampleSlidesOnly" class="carousel
          slide" data-bs-ride="carousel">
 <div class="carousel-inner">
  <div class="carousel-item active">
   <img src="..." class="d-block w-100" alt="...">
  </div>
  <div class="carousel-item">
   <img src="..." class="d-block w-100" alt="...">
  </div>
  <div class="carousel-item">
   <img src="..." class="d-block w-100" alt="...">
  </div>
 </div>
</div>
```

With Controls

The previous and next controls have been added. We advocate utilizing < button> elements, although <a> elements with role="button" can also be used.

```html
<div id="carouselExampleControls" class="carousel
slide" data-bs-ride="carousel">
 <div class="carousel-inner">
  <div class="carousel-item active">
   <img src="..." class="d-block w-100" alt="...">
  </div>
  <div class="carousel-item">
   <img src="..." class="d-block w-100" alt="...">
  </div>
  <div class="carousel-item">
   <img src="..." class="d-block w-100" alt="...">
  </div>
 </div>
 <button class="carousel-control-prev" type="button"
               data-bs-target="#carouselExampleCon
               trols" data-bs-slide="prev">
  <span class="carousel-control-prev-icon" aria-
             hidden="true"></span>
  <span class="visually-hidden">Previous</span>
 </button>
 <button class="carousel-control-next" type="button"
               data-bs-target="#carouselExampleCon
               trols" data-bs-slide="next">
  <span class="carousel-control-next-icon" aria-
             hidden="true"></span>
  <span class="visually-hidden">Next</span>
 </button>
</div>
```

With Indicators

```html
<div id="carouselExampleIndicators" class="carousel
         slide" data-bs-ride="carousel">
 <div class="carousel-indicators">
  <button type="button" data-bs-target="#carousel
    ExampleIndicators" data-bs-slide-to="0"
    class="active" aria-current="true" aria-
    label="Slide 1"></button>
  <button type="button" data-bs-target="#carousel
    ExampleIndicators" data-bs-slide-to="1" aria-
    label="Slide 2"></button>
  <button type="button" data-bs-target="#carousel
    ExampleIndicators" data-bs-slide-to="2" aria-
    label="Slide 3"></button>
```

```
</div>
<div class="carousel-inner">
 <div class="carousel-item active">
  <img src="..." class="d-block w-100" alt="...">
 </div>
       <div class="carousel-item">
  <img src="..." class="d-block w-100" alt="...">
 </div>
 <div class="carousel-item">
  <img src="..." class="d-block w-100" alt="...">
 </div>
</div>
<button class="carousel-control-prev" type="button"
        data-bs-target="#carouselExampleIndicators"
        data-bs-slide="prev">
 <span class="carousel-control-prev-icon" aria-
        hidden="true"></span>
 <span class="visually-hidden">Previous</span>
</button>
<button class="carousel-control-next" type="button"
        data-bs-target="#carouselExampleIndicators"
        data-bs-slide="next">
 <span class="carousel-control-next-icon" aria-
        hidden="true"></span>
 <span class="visually-hidden">Next</span>
</button>
</div>
```

With Captions

With the .carousel-caption element within any .carousel-item, you can quickly add captions to your slides. With optional display utilities, they may be easily hidden on smaller viewports, as demonstrated below. We use .d-none to conceal them at first, then .d-MD-block to bring them back on medium-sized devices.

```
<div id="carouselExampleCaptions" class="carousel
        slide" data-bs-ride="carousel">
 <div class="carousel-indicators">
  <button type="button" data-bs-target="#carousel
    ExampleCaptions" data-bs-slide-to="0"
    class="active" aria-current="true" aria-
    label="Slide 1"></button>
```

```html
  <button type="button" data-bs-target="#carousel
    ExampleCaptions" data-bs-slide-to="1" aria-
    label="Slide 2"></button>
  <button type="button" data-bs-target="#carousel
    ExampleCaptions" data-bs-slide-to="2" aria-
    label="Slide 3"></button>
</div>
<div class="carousel-inner">
 <div class="carousel-item active">
  <img src="..." class="d-block w-100" alt="...">
  <div class="carousel-caption d-none d-md-block">
   <h5>First slide label</h5>
   <p>Some representative placeholder content for
          the first slide.</p>
  </div>
 </div>
 <div class="carousel-item">
  <img src="..." class="d-block w-100" alt="...">
  <div class="carousel-caption d-none d-md-block">
   <h5>Second slide label</h5>
   <p>Some representative placeholder content for
          the second slide.</p>
  </div>
 </div>
 <div class="carousel-item">
  <img src="..." class="d-block w-100" alt="...">
  <div class="carousel-caption d-none d-md-block">
   <h5>Third slide label</h5>
   <p>Some representative placeholder content for
          the third slide.</p>
  </div>
 </div>
</div>
<button class="carousel-control-prev" type="button"
               data-bs-target="#carouselExampleCap
               tions" data-bs-slide="prev">
 <span class="carousel-control-prev-icon" aria-
             hidden="true"></span>
 <span class="visually-hidden">Previous</span>
</button>
<button class="carousel-control-next" type="button"
               data-bs-target="#carouselExampleCap
               tions" data-bs-slide="next">
```

```
  <span class="carousel-control-next-icon" aria-
           hidden="true"></span>
  <span class="visually-hidden">Next</span>
 </button>
</div>
```

Crossfade

To animate slides using a fade transition instead of a slide, add .carousel-fade to your carousel.

```
<div id="carouselExampleFade" class="carousel slide
carousel-fade" data-bs-ride="carousel">
 <div class="carousel-inner">
  <div class="carousel-item active">
   <img src="..." class="d-block w-100" alt="...">
  </div>
  <div class="carousel-item">
   <img src="..." class="d-block w-100" alt="...">
  </div>
  <div class="carousel-item">
   <img src="..." class="d-block w-100" alt="...">
  </div>
 </div>
 <button class="carousel-control-prev" type="button"
         data-bs-target="#carouselExampleFade"
         data-bs-slide="prev">
  <span class="carousel-control-prev-icon" aria-
        hidden="true"></span>
  <span class="visually-hidden">Previous</span>
 </button>
 <button class="carousel-control-next" type="button"
         data-bs-target="#carouselExampleFade"
         data-bs-slide="next">
  <span class="carousel-control-next-icon" aria-
        hidden="true"></span>
  <span class="visually-hidden">Next</span>
 </button>
</div>
```

Individual .carousal-item Interval

To modify the amount of time between automatically cycling to the next item, add data-bs-interval=" to a .carousel-item.

```
<div id="carouselExampleInterval" class="carousel
        slide" data-bs-ride="carousel">
 <div class="carousel-inner">
  <div class="carousel-item active"
              data-bs-interval="10000">
   <img src="..." class="d-block w-100" alt="...">
  </div>
  <div class="carousel-item" data-bs-interval="2000">
   <img src="..." class="d-block w-100" alt="...">
  </div>
  <div class="carousel-item">
   <img src="..." class="d-block w-100" alt="...">
  </div>
 </div>
 <button class="carousel-control-prev" type="button"
              data-bs-target="#carouselExampleInt
              erval" data-bs-slide="prev">
  <span class="carousel-control-prev-icon" aria-
              hidden="true"></span>
  <span class="visually-hidden">Previous</span>
 </button>
 <button class="carousel-control-next" type="button"
         data-bs-target="#carouselExampleInterval"
         data-bs-slide="next">
  <span class="carousel-control-next-icon" aria-
         hidden="true"></span>
  <span class="visually-hidden">Next</span>
 </button>
</div>
```

Disable Touch Swiping

To go between slides in a carousel, swipe left or right on a touchscreen device. The data-bs-touch property can be used to deactivate this. The example below likewise lacks the data-bs-ride detail and has data-bs-interval="false," preventing it from autoplaying.

```
<div id="carouselExampleControlsNoTouching"
        class="carousel slide" data-bs-touch="false"
        data-bs-interval="false">
 <div class="carousel-inner">
  <div class="carousel-item active">
   <img src="..." class="d-block w-100" alt="...">
```

```
  </div>
  <div class="carousel-item">
   <img src="..." class="d-block w-100" alt="...">
  </div>
  <div class="carousel-item">
   <img src="..." class="d-block w-100" alt="...">
  </div>
 </div>
 <button class="carousel-control-prev" type="button"
         data-bs-target="#carouselExampleControls
         NoTouching" data-bs-slide="prev">
  <span class="carousel-control-prev-icon" aria-
         hidden="true"></span>
  <span class="visually-hidden">Previous</span>
 </button>
 <button class="carousel-control-next" type="button"
         data-bs-target="#carouselExampleControls
         NoTouching" data-bs-slide="next">
  <span class="carousel-control-next-icon" aria-
         hidden="true"></span>
  <span class="visually-hidden">Next</span>
 </button>
</div>
```

Dark Variant

For darker controls, indicators, and captions, add .carousel-dark to the .carousel file. With the filter CSS property, controls have been reversed from their normal white fill. Additional Sass options alter the color and background color of captions and controls.

```
<div id="carouselExampleDark" class="carousel
     carousel-dark slide" data-bs-ride="carousel">
 <div class="carousel-indicators">
  <button type="button" data-bs-
    target="#carouselExampleDark" data-bs-
    slide-to="0" class="active" aria-current="true"
    aria-label="Slide 1"></button>
  <button type="button" data-bs-
    target="#carouselExampleDark" data-bs-
    slide-to="1" aria-label="Slide 2"></button>
  <button type="button" data-bs-
    target="#carouselExampleDark" data-bs-
    slide-to="2" aria-label="Slide 3"></button>
```

```
</div>
<div class="carousel-inner">
 <div class="carousel-item active"
            data-bs-interval="10000">
  <img src="..." class="d-block w-100" alt="...">
  <div class="carousel-caption d-none d-md-block">
   <h5>First slide label</h5>
   <p>Some representative placeholder content for
           the first slide.</p>
  </div>
 </div>
 <div class="carousel-item" data-bs-interval="2000">
  <img src="..." class="d-block w-100" alt="...">
  <div class="carousel-caption d-none d-md-block">
   <h5>Second slide label</h5>
   <p>Some representative placeholder content for
           the second slide.</p>
  </div>
 </div>
 <div class="carousel-item">
  <img src="..." class="d-block w-100" alt="...">
  <div class="carousel-caption d-none d-md-block">
   <h5>Third slide label</h5>
   <p>Some representative placeholder content for
           the third slide.</p>
  </div>
 </div>
</div>
<button class="carousel-control-prev" type="button"
         data-bs-target="#carouselExampleDark"
         data-bs-slide="prev">
 <span class="carousel-control-prev-icon" aria-
       hidden="true"></span>
 <span class="visually-hidden">Previous</span>
</button>
<button class="carousel-control-next" type="button"
         data-bs-target="#carouselExampleDark"
         data-bs-slide="next">
 <span class="carousel-control-next-icon" aria-
       hidden="true"></span>
 <span class="visually-hidden">Next</span>
</button>
</div>
```

Custom Transition

If you're using the compiled CSS, you may adjust the transition time of the .carousel-item using the $carousel-transition-duration Sass variable before compiling or custom styles if you're using custom styles. If you're using several transitions, ensure the transform transition is the first to be declared (e.g., transition: transform 2s ease, opacity .5s ease-out).

Usage

Via Data Attributes

To quickly change the position of the carousel, utilize data attributes. The keywords prev or next are accepted by data-bs-slide, which change the slide position relative to its current position. Alternatively, use data-bs-slide-to="2" to send a raw slide index to the carousel, which adjusts the slide position to a specific index starting at 0.

The data-bs-ride="carousel" property is used to indicate that a carousel will start animating when the page is loaded. You must manually initialize your carousel if you don't utilize data-bs-ride="carousel" to use it. It cannot be combined with (redundant and unnecessary) explicit JavaScript initialization of the same carousel.

Via JavaScript

Call carousel manually with:

```
var myCarousel = document.querySelector('#myCarousel')
var carousel = new bootstrap.Carousel(myCarousel)
```

Options

Data attributes or JavaScript can be used to pass options. Append the option name to data-bs- for data attributes, as in data-bs-interval=".".

Name	Type	Default	Description
interval	number	5000	The span of time between items that are automatically cycled. The carousel will not automatically cycle if false
keyboard	Boolean	true	Whether or whether not the carousel should respond to keyboards

pause	string | boolean	'hover.'	When set to 'hover,' the carousel's cycling is paused on mouse enter and resumed when the mouse is released. If set to false, hovering over the carousel won't pause it. On touch-enabled devices, when set to 'hover,' cycling will stop for two intervals when touched, then resume automatically. This is in addition to the mouse behavior described above
ride	string | boolean	false	After the user cycles through the first item manually, the carousel will automatically play. If set to 'carousel,' the carousel will autoplay when the page loads
wrap	boolean	true	Whether carousel should run constantly or stop abruptly
touch	boolean	true	Whether the carousel should support left/proper swipe interactions on touchscreen devices

Methods

Asynchronous Methods and Transitions

All API methods initiate a transition and are asynchronous. They call the caller as soon as the modification is made but before it is completed. In addition, a transitional component's method call will be ignored.

For example, you can use the carousel constructor to create a carousel instance with various settings and begin cycling through items:

```
var myCarousel = document.querySelector('#myCarousel')
var carousel = new bootstrap.Carousel(myCarousel, {
  interval: 2100,
  wrap: false
})
```

Method	Description
cycle	From left to right, cycles through the carousel objects
pause	The carousel will no longer cycle through the objects
prev	Cycles to the previous item. **Returns to the caller before the last thing has been shown** (e.g., before the slid.bs.carousel event occurs)
next	Cycles to the next item. **Returns to the caller before the following article has been shown**
nextWhenVisible	When a page isn't visible, or the carousel or its parent isn't visible, **don't cycle to the next**

	Before the target item is revealed to the caller, it returns to the caller.
	Set the carousel to a certain frame (0 based, similar to an array).
	Before the target item is revealed (e.g., before the slid.bs.carousel event), it returns to the caller
dispose	Destroys an element's carousel (removes stored data on the DOM element)
getInstance	This static function returns the carousel instance connected with a DOM element and may be used as follows: Bootstrap.Carousel. getInstance(element)
getOrCreateInstance	If the carousel instance associated with a DOM element was not initialized, the static function returns it or generates a new one. You can use it like this: Bootstrap.Carousel.getOrCreate Instance(element)

Events

The carousel class in Bootstrap offers two events for interacting with carousel functionality. The following attributes are shared by both events:

- The carousel's sliding direction is called direction (either "left" or "right").

- **Related Target:** The DOM element that is being slid into place as the active item.

- From: The index of the current object

- To: The index of the following item

The carousel (i.e., <div class="carousel">) fires all carousel events itself.

```
var myCarousel = document.getElementById('myCarousel')

myCarousel.addEventListener('slide.bs.carousel',
          function () {
 // do something...
})
```

Event Type	Description
slide.bs.carousel	It fires immediately when the slide instance method is invoked
slid.bs.carousel	It is fired when the carousel has completed its slide transition

Close Button

A generic close button for dismissing content like modals and alerts.

Example

Provide an option to dismiss or close a component with .btn-close. The default styling is limited but highly customizable. Modify the Sass variables to replace the default background image. As with aria-label, be sure to provide text for screen readers.

```
<button type="button" class="btn-close" aria-
                  label="Close"></button>
```

Disable State

Disabled close buttons change their opacity. We've also applied pointer-events: none and user-select: none to prevent hover and active states from triggering.

```
<button type="button" class="btn-close" disabled
aria-label="Close"></button>
```

White Variant

Change the default .btn-close to be white with the .btn-close-white class. This class uses the filter property to invert the background image.

```
<button type="button" class="btn-close btn-close-
        white" aria-label="Close"></button>
<button type="button" class="btn-close btn-close-
        white" disabled aria-label="Close"></button>
```

Collapse

With few classes and JavaScript plugins, you can change the visibility of information across your project.

How It Works

To show and conceal content, the collapse JavaScript plugin is utilized. Buttons or anchors serve as triggers for certain items that you toggle. When you collapse a portion, the height will animate from its current value to 0. You can't use padding on a .collapse element because of how CSS handles animations. Use the class as a stand-alone wrapper element instead. This component's animation effect is determined by the prefers-reduced-motion media query.

Example

To show and conceal another element through class modifications, use the buttons below:

- .collapse hides content

- .collapsing is applied during transitions

- .collapse.show shows content

Using a button with the data-bs-target property is generally recommended. You may also use a link with the href property (and a role="button"), which is not encouraged from a semantic standpoint. The data-bs-toggle="collapse" attribute is necessary in both circumstances.

```
<p>
 <a class="btn btn-primary" data-bs-toggle="collapse"
    href="#collapseExample" role="button" aria-
    expanded="false" aria-controls="collapseExample">
  Link with href
 </a>
 <button class="btn btn-primary" type="button" data-
    bs-toggle="collapse" data-bs-
    target="#collapseExample" aria-expanded="false"
    aria-controls="collapseExample">
  Button with data-bs-target
 </button>
</p>
<div class="collapse" id="collapseExample">
 <div class="card card-body">
For the collapse component, some placeholder content.
By default, this panel is hidden, but it is exposed
when the user presses the appropriate trigger.
 </div>
</div>
```

Multiple Targets

Multiple components can be shown and hidden by addressing them with a selector in the href or data-bs-target property of a button or an a. If they individually reference it with their href or data-bs-target property, several <button> or <a> can show and hide an element.

```
<p>
 <a class="btn btn-primary" data-bs-toggle="collapse"
    href="#multiCollapseExample1" role="button" aria-
    expanded="false" aria-controls="multiCollapseEx
    ample1">Toggle first element</a>
 <button class="btn btn-primary" type="button" data-
    bs-toggle="collapse" data-bs-
    target="#multiCollapseExample2"
    aria-expanded="false" aria-controls="multiColla
    pseExample2">Toggle second element</button>
 <button class="btn btn-primary" type="button" data-bs-
    toggle="collapse" data-bs-target=".multi-collapse"
    aria-expanded="false" aria-controls="multiCollapse
    Example1 multiCollapseExample2">Toggle both
    elements</button>
</p>
<div class="row">
 <div class="col">
  <div class="collapse multi-collapse"
id="multiCollapseExample1">
   <div class="card card-body">
This multi-collapse example's initial collapse
component has some placeholder content. By default,
this panel is hidden, but it is exposed when the user
presses the appropriate trigger.
   </div>
  </div>
 </div>
 <div class="col">
  <div class="collapse multi-collapse"
id="multiCollapseExample2">
   <div class="card card-body">
    This multi-collapse example's second collapse
component has some placeholder content. By default,
this panel is hidden, but it is exposed when the user
presses the appropriate trigger.
   </div>
  </div>
 </div>
</div>
```

Accessibility

Make sure the control element has the aria-expanded attribute. This
property informs screen readers and other assistive technology about the

current state of the collapsible element associated with the control. If collapsible element is closed by default, the aria-expanded="false" property on the control element should be used. Set aria-expanded="true" on the control instead of using the show class to make the collapsible element open by default. Depending on whether the collapsible element has been opened or closed, the plugin will automatically toggle this property on the control (via JavaScript, or because the user triggered another control element also tied to the same collapsible element). The attribute role="button" should add to the control element if the HTML element is not a button (e.g., an or >).

Suppose your control element is targeting a single collapsible segment. If the data-bs-target property points to an id selector, you should add the aria-controls attribute to the control element, which should include the id of the collapsible element. This feature is used by modern screen readers and similar assistive devices to offer users with extra shortcuts to navigate straight to the collapsible element itself.

The many *optional* keyboard interactions indicated in the WAI-ARIA Authoring Practices 1.1 accordion pattern are not covered by Bootstrap's current implementation; you will need to incorporate these yourself using custom JavaScript.

Sass

Variables

```
$transition-collapse:      height .35s ease;
```

Classes

Because the transition classes in scss/_transitions.scss are common across several components, collapse them (collapse and accordion).

```
.collapse {
 &:not(.show) {
  display: none;
 }
}


.collapsing {
 height: 0;
 overflow: hidden;
 @include transition($transition-collapse);
}
```

Usage

To accomplish the hard work, the collapse plugin makes use of a few classes:

- .collapse hides content

- .collapse.show shows content

- .collapsing is added when transition starts and is removed when it finishes

These classes can find in _transitions. CSS.

Via Data Attributes

To assign control of more collapsible elements, just add data-bs-toggle="collapse" and a data-bs-target to the element. A CSS selector can be passed to the data-bs-target property to apply the collapse. Make sure the collapsible element has the class collapse. Add the extra class show if you want it to open by default.

Add the data attribute data-bs-parent="#selector" to a collapsible section to enable accordion-style group management. To see this in working, look at the demo.

Via JavaScript

Enable manually with:

```
var collapseElementList = [].slice.call(document.qu
    erySelectorAll('.collapse'))
var collapseList = collapseElementList.map(function
    (collapseEl) {
 return new bootstrap.Collapse(collapseEl)
})
```

Options

Data attributes or JavaScript can be used to pass options. Append the option name to data-bs- for data attributes, as in data-bs-parent="."

Name	Type	Default	Description
parent	selector | jQuery object | DOM element	false	When a parent is specified, all collapsible components beneath that parent are closed when this collapsible item is displayed. (This is based on the card class, and is comparable to conventional accordion behavior.) The attribute must be applied to the collapsible area's target
toggle	boolean	true	Toggles collapsible element on the invocation

Methods

Asynchronous Transitions and Methods

All API methods initiate a transition and are asynchronous. They call the caller as soon as the modification is made but before it is completed. In addition, a transitional component's method call be ignored.

Your content is activated as a collapsible element. Optionally accepts an options object.

You may use the constructor to make a collapse instance, for example:

```
var myCollapse = document.getElementById('myCollapse')
var bsCollapse = new bootstrap.Collapse(myCollapse, {
  toggle: false
})
```

Method	Description
toggle	Toggles the visibility of a collapsible element. **Before the collapsible element has been delivered or concealed** (i.e., before the exposed. bs.hidden or bs.collapse, the event bs.collapse happens)
show	A collapsible element is shown. **Before the collapsible element** is provided, it returns to the caller (e.g., before the revealed.bs.colla pse event occurs)
hide	It conceals a collapsible component. **Before the collapsible element** is hidden, it returns to the caller (e.g., before the hidden .bs.collapse event occurs)
dispose	Destroys an element's collapse (removes the stored data on DOM element)
getInstance	The static function allows you to get collapse instance associated with a DOM element; you can use it like this: Bootstrap.Collapse. getInstance(element)
getOrCreateInstance	The static method returns a collapse instance associated with a DOM element or creates a new one that wasn't initialized. You can use it like this: Bootstrap.Collapse.getOrCreateInstance(element)

Events

The collapse class in Bootstrap exposes a few events that may be used to hook into collapse functionality.

```
var myCollapsible = document.getElementById('myCollaps
                    ible')
myCollapsible.addEventListener('hidden.bs.collapse',
                              function () {
  // do something
})
```

Event Type	Description
show.bs.collapse	When the display instance method is called, this event occurs instantly
shown.bs.collapse	When a collapse element is made visible to the user, this event is triggered (will wait for CSS transitions to complete)
hide.bs.collapse	When the hide method is invoked, this event is instantly triggered
hidden.bs.colla pse	When a collapse element is concealed from the user, this event is triggered (will wait for CSS transitions to complete)

Dropdowns

With the Bootstrap dropdown plugin, you can toggle contextual overlays for showing lists of links and more.

Overview

Dropdowns, contextual overlays for presenting lists of links, and other features are all toggleable. The Bootstrap dropdown JavaScript plugin is used to make them interactive. It is an intentional design choice that they're toggled by clicking rather than hovering.

Popper, a third-party library that supports dynamic positioning and viewport detection, is used to create dropdowns. Use bootstrap.bundle .min.js / bootstrap.bundle.js, which contains Popper, or include pop-per.min.js before Bootstrap's JavaScript. However, because dynamic positioning isn't necessary, Popper isn't utilized to place dropdowns in navbars.

Accessibility

Although the WAI-ARIA standard specifies a role="menu" widget, it is only applicable to application-like menus that initiate actions or operations. Only menu items, checkbox menu items, radio button menu items, radio button groups, and sub-menus are allowed in ARIA menus.

Bootstrap's dropdowns, on the other hand, are intended to be flexible and adaptable to a wide range of circumstances and markup structures. For example, dropdowns with extra inputs and form controls, such as search boxes or login forms, can be created. As a result, Bootstrap does not expect (or add) any of the roles and aria-attributes that are necessary for correct ARIA menus. These more particular qualities will have to be added by the authors themselves.

Bootstrap's dropdowns, on the other hand, are intended to be flexible and adaptable to a wide range of circumstances and markup structures. For example, dropdowns with extra inputs and form controls, such as search boxes or login forms, can be created. As a result, Bootstrap does not expect (or add) any of the roles and aria-attributes that are necessary for correct ARIA menus. These more particular qualities will have to be added by the authors themselves.

Examples

Wrap the toggle of the dropdown (your button or link) and the dropdown menu in. dropdown, or another element with a position: relative declaration. To better match your future needs, dropdowns may be activated by <a> or <button> components. Where applicable, semantic <ul> components are used in the examples, although custom markup is also supported.

Single-button

With minor markup tweaks, any single .btn can be transformed into a dropdown toggle. Here's how to use them with a <button> element:

```
<div class="dropdown">
  <button class="btn btn-secondary dropdown-toggle"
          type="button" id="dropdownMenuButton1" data-
          bs-toggle="dropdown" aria-expanded="false">
  Dropdown button
  </button>
  <ul class="dropdown-menu" aria-labelledby="dropdownM
    enuButton1">
```

```
<li><a class="dropdown-item" href="#">Action</a></li>
<li><a class="dropdown-item" href="#">Another
        action</a></li>
<li><a class="dropdown-item" href="#">Something
        else here</a></li>
 </ul>
</div>
```

And with `<a>` elements:

```
<div class="dropdown">
 <a class="btn btn-secondary dropdown-toggle"
    href="#" role="button" id="dropdownMenuLink"
    data-bs-toggle="dropdown" aria-expanded="false">
  Dropdown link
 </a>

 <ul class="dropdown-menu" aria-labelledby="dropdownM
    enuLink">
  <li><a class="dropdown-item" href="#">Action</a></li>
  <li><a class="dropdown-item" href="#">Another
                action</a></li>
  <li><a class="dropdown-item" href="#">Something
                else here</a></li>
 </ul>
</div>
```

That's also interesting because you can do it with any button type:

```
<!-- Example single danger button -->
<div class="btn-group">
 <button type="button" class="btn btn-danger
        dropdown-toggle" data-bs-toggle="dropdown"
        aria-expanded="false">
  Action
 </button>
 <ul class="dropdown-menu">
  <li><a class="dropdown-item" href="#">Action</a></li>
  <li><a class="dropdown-item" href="#">Another
        action</a></li>
  <li><a class="dropdown-item" href="#">Something
        else here</a></li>
```

```
   <li><hr class="dropdown-divider"></li>
   <li><a class="dropdown-item" href="#">Separated
        link</a></li>
 </ul>
</div>
```

Sizing

Buttons of all sizes, including basic and split dropdown buttons, work with button dropdowns.

```
<!-- Large button groups (default and split) -->
<div class="btn-group">
 <button class="btn btn-secondary btn-lg dropdown-
        toggle" type="button" data-bs-
        toggle="dropdown" aria-expanded="false">
  Large button
 </button>
 <ul class="dropdown-menu">
  ...
 </ul>
</div>
<div class="btn-group">
 <button class="btn btn-secondary btn-lg"
type="button">
  Large split button
 </button>
 <button type="button" class="btn btn-lg btn-
   secondary dropdown-toggle dropdown-toggle-split"
   data-bs-toggle="dropdown" aria-expanded="false">
  <span class="visually-hidden">Toggle Dropdown</span>
 </button>
 <ul class="dropdown-menu">
  ...
 </ul>
</div>

<div class="btn-group">
 <button class="btn btn-secondary btn-sm dropdown-
   toggle" type="button" data-bs-toggle="dropdown"
   aria-expanded="false">
  Small button
 </button>
```

```
<ul class="dropdown-menu">
  ...
</ul>
</div>
<div class="btn-group">
 <button class="btn btn-secondary btn-sm"
          type="button">
  Small split button
 </button>
 <button type="button" class="btn btn-sm btn-
   secondary dropdown-toggle dropdown-toggle-split"
   data-bs-toggle="dropdown" aria-expanded="false">
  <span class="visually-hidden">Toggle Dropdown</span>
 </button>
 <ul class="dropdown-menu">
  ...
 </ul>
</div>
```

Dark Dropdowns

By appending .dropdown-menu-dark to an existing.dropdown-menu, you may make darker dropdowns to match a dark navbar or custom style. The dropdown items do not need to be changed.

```
<div class="dropdown">
 <button class="btn btn-secondary dropdown-toggle"
   type="button" id="dropdownMenuButton2" data-bs-
   toggle="dropdown" aria-expanded="false">
  Dropdown button
 </button>
 <ul class="dropdown-menu dropdown-menu-dark" aria-
           labelledby="dropdownMenuButton2">
  <li><a class="dropdown-item active"
              href="#">Action</a></li>
  <li><a class="dropdown-item" href="#">Another
              action</a></li>
  <li><a class="dropdown-item" href="#">Something
              else here</a></li>
  <li><hr class="dropdown-divider"></li>
  <li><a class="dropdown-item" href="#">Separated
              link</a></li>
 </ul>
</div>
```

And here's how to utilize it in a navbar:

```
<nav class="navbar navbar-expand-lg navbar-dark bg-dark">
 <div class="container-fluid">
  <a class="navbar-brand" href="#">Navbar</a>
  <button class="navbar-toggler" type="button" data-
     bs-toggle="collapse" data-bs-
     target="#navbarNavDarkDropdown" aria-controls="na
     vbarNavDarkDropdown" aria-expanded="false" aria-
     label="Toggle navigation">
   <span class="navbar-toggler icon"></span>
  </button>
  <div class="collapse navbar-collapse"
              id="navbarNavDarkDropdown">
   <ul class="navbar-nav">
    <li class="nav-item dropdown">
     <a class="nav-link dropdown-toggle" href="#"
        id="navbarDarkDropdownMenuLink" role="button"
        data-bs-toggle="dropdown"
        aria-expanded="false">
      Dropdown
     </a>
     <ul class="dropdown-menu dropdown-menu-dark"
        aria-labelledby="navbarDarkDropdownMenuLink">
      <li><a class="dropdown-item" href="#">Action</
           a></li>
      <li><a class="dropdown-item" href="#">Another
           action</a></li>
      <li><a class="dropdown-item" href="#">Something
           else here</a></li>
     </ul>
    </li>
   </ul>
  </div>
 </div>
</nav>
```

Directions

RTL

When using Bootstrap in RTL, the directions are mirrored, so .dropstart
will show on the right side.

Drop Up

Dropdown menus can trigger above elements by adding .dropup to the parent element.

```
<!-- Default dropup button -->
<div class="btn-group dropup">
 <button type="button" class="btn btn-secondary
   dropdown-toggle" data-bs-toggle="dropdown"
   aria-expanded="false">
  Dropup
 </button>
 <ul class="dropdown-menu">
  <!-- Dropdown menu links -->
 </ul>
</div>

<!-- Split dropup button -->
<div class="btn-group dropup">
 <button type="button" class="btn btn-secondary">
  Split dropup
 </button>
 <button type="button" class="btn btn-secondary
   dropdown-toggle dropdown-toggle-split" data-bs-
   toggle="dropdown" aria-expanded="false">
  <span class="visually-hidden">Toggle Dropdown</span>
 </button>
 <ul class="dropdown-menu">
  <!--Dropdown menu links -->
 </ul>
</div>
```

Drop Right

By adding .dropend to the parent element, you may make dropdown menus appear to the right of the components.

```
<!-- Default dropend button -->
<div class="btn-group dropend">
 <button type="button" class="btn btn-secondary
         dropdown-toggle" data-bs-toggle="dropdown"
         aria-expanded="false">
  Dropright
 </button>
```

```
<ul class="dropdown-menu">
 <!-- Dropdown menu links -->
</ul>
</div>


<!-- Split dropend button -->
<div class="btn-group dropend">
 <button type="button" class="btn btn-secondary">
  Split dropend
 </button>
 <button type="button" class="btn btn secondary
   dropdown-toggle dropdown-toggle-split" data-bs-
   toggle="dropdown" aria-expanded="false">
  <span class="visually-hidden">Toggle Dropright</span>
 </button>
 <ul class="dropdown-menu">
  <!-- Dropdown menu links -->
 </ul>
</div>
```

Drop Left

By adding.dropstart to the parent element, you may make dropdown menus appear to the left of the components.

```
<!-- Default dropstart button -->
<div class="btn-group dropstart">
 <button type="button" class="btn btn-secondary
    dropdown-toggle" data-bs-toggle="dropdown"
    aria-expanded="false">
  Dropstart
 </button>
 <ul class="dropdown-menu">
  <!-- Dropdown menu links -->
 </ul>
</div>

<!-- Split dropstart button -->
<div class="btn-group">
 <div class="btn-group dropstart" role="group">
  <button type="button" class="btn btn-secondary
    dropdown-toggle dropdown-toggle-split" data-bs-
    toggle="dropdown" aria-expanded="false">
```

```
  <span class="visually-hidden">Toggle Dropstart</span>
 </button>
 <ul class="dropdown-menu">
  <!-- Dropdown menu links -->
 </ul>
</div>
<button type="button" class="btn btn-secondary">
 Split dropstart
</button>
</div>
```

Menu Items

As dropdown items, you may utilize the <a> and <button> components.

```
<div class="dropdown">
 <button class="btn btn-secondary dropdown-toggle"
   type="button" id="dropdownMenu2" data-bs-
   toggle="dropdown" aria-expanded="false">
 Dropdown
 </button>
 <ul class="dropdown-menu"
          aria-labelledby="dropdownMenu2">
  <li><button class="dropdown-item"
          type="button">Action</button></li>
  <li><button class="dropdown-item"
      type="button">Another action</button></li>
  <li><button class="dropdown-item" type="button">
      Something else here</button></li>
 </ul>
</div>
```

You can also create non-interactive dropdown items with .dropdown-item-text. Feel free to style further with custom CSS or text utilities.

```
<ul class="dropdown-menu">
 <li><span class="dropdown-item-text">Dropdown item
               text</span></li>
 <li><a class="dropdown-item" href="#">Action</a></li>
 <li><a class="dropdown-item" href="#">Another
      action</a></li>
 <li><a class="dropdown-item" href="#">Something else
      here</a></li>
</ul>
```

Active

To make items in the dropdown active, add .active to them. Use the aria-current property to communicate the active state to assistive technology, with the page value for the current page or valid for the current item in a collection.

```
<ul class="dropdown-menu">
 <li><a class="dropdown-item" href="#">Regular link</
            a></li>
 <li><a class="dropdown-item active" href="#" aria-
            current="true">Active link</a></li>
 <li><a class="dropdown-item" href="#">Another link</
            a></li>
</ul>
```

Disable

To style items in the dropdown as disabled, add .disabled to them.

```
<ul class="dropdown-menu">
 <li><a class="dropdown-item" href="#">Regular link</
            a></li>
 <li><a class="dropdown-item disabled" href="#"
        tabindex="-1" aria-disabled="true">Disabled
        link</a></li>
 <li><a class="dropdown-item" href="#">Another link</
            a></li>
</ul>
```

Menu Alignment

A dropdown menu's parent is automatically positioned 100% from the top and down the left side by default. You can adjust this using the directional .drop* classes, but you can also use modifier classes to manipulate them.

To right-align the dropdown menu, add .dropdown-menu-end to a .dropdown-menu. When using Bootstrap in RTL, the directions are mirrored, so .dropdown-menu-end will display on the left side. Please be aware! Except when they are included in a navbar, dropdowns are positioned using Popper.

```
<div class="btn-group">
 <button type="button" class="btn btn-secondary
        dropdown-toggle" data-bs-toggle="dropdown"
        aria-expanded="false">
```

```
 Right-aligned menu example
 </button>
 <ul class="dropdown-menu dropdown-menu-end">
  <li><button class="dropdown-item"
type="button">Action</button></li>
  <li><button class="dropdown-item"
       type="button">Another action</button></li>
  <li><button class="dropdown-item" type="button">
      Something else here</button></li>
 </ul>
</div>
```

Responsive Alignment

If you wish to employ responsive alignment, use the responsive variant classes and deactivate dynamic positioning by adding the data-bs-display="static" property.

Add to align the dropdown menu to the right of the provided breakpoint or bigger.

```
dropdown-menu
```

```
{-sm|-md|-lg|-xl|-xxl}-end.
```

```
<div class="btn-group">
 <button type="button" class="btn btn-secondary
   dropdown-toggle" data-bs-toggle="dropdown" data-
   bs-display="static" aria-expanded="false">
  Left-aligned but right aligned when large screen
 </button>
 <ul class="dropdown-menu dropdown-menu-lg-end">
  <li><button class="dropdown-item"
              type="button">Action</button></li>
  <li><button class="dropdown-item" type="button">
              Another action</button></li>
  <li><button class="dropdown-item" type="button">
              Something else here</button></li>
 </ul>
</div>
```
Add.dropdown-menu-end and .dropdown-menu{-sm|-md|-l
g|-xl|-xxl}-start
to position the dropdown menu to the left of the
provided breakpoint or bigger.

```
<div class="btn-group">
 <button type="button" class="btn btn-secondary
   dropdown-toggle" data-bs-toggle="dropdown" data-
   bs-display="static" aria-expanded="false">
 Right-aligned but left aligned when large screen
 </button>
 <ul class="dropdown-menu dropdown-menu-end
           dropdown-menu-lg-start">
  <li><button class="dropdown-item"
            type="button">Action</button></li>
  <li><button class="dropdown-item" type="button">
            Another action</button></li>
  <li><button class="dropdown-item" type="button">
            Something else here</button></li>
 </ul>
</div>
```

You don't need to add a data-bs-display="static" attribute to dropdown buttons in navbars since Popper isn't used in navbars.

Alignment Options

Here's a tiny kitchen sink demo demonstrating multiple dropdown alignment possibilities in one spot, using the majority of the options listed above.

```
<div class="btn-group">
 <button class="btn btn-secondary dropdown-toggle"
         type="button" id="dropdownMenuButton" data-
         bs-toggle="dropdown" aria-expanded="false">
 Dropdown
 </button>
 <ul class="dropdown-menu" aria-labelledby="dropdownM
           enuButton">
  <li><a class="dropdown-item" href="#">Menu item</
            a></li>
  <li><a class="dropdown-item" href="#">Menu item</
            a></li>
  <li><a class="dropdown-item" href="#">Menu item</
a></li>
 </ul>
</div>
```

```
<div class="btn-group">
 <button type="button" class="btn btn-secondary
         dropdown-toggle" data-bs-toggle="dropdown"
         aria-expanded="false">
  Right-aligned menu
 </button>
 <ul class="dropdown-menu dropdown-menu-end">
  <li><a class="dropdown-item" href="#">Menu item</
             a></li>
  <li><a class="dropdown-item" href="#">Menu item</
             a></li>
  <li><a class="dropdown-item" href="#">Menu item</
             a></li>
 </ul>
</div>

<div class="btn-group">
 <button type="button" class="btn btn-secondary
   dropdown-toggle" data-bs-toggle="dropdown" data-
   bs-display="static" aria-expanded="false">
  Left-aligned, right-aligned lg
 </button>
 <ul class="dropdown-menu dropdown-menu-lg-end">
  <li><a class="dropdown-item" href="#">Menu item</
             a></li>
  <li><a class="dropdown-item" href="#">Menu item</
             a></li>
  <li><a class="dropdown-item" href="#">Menu item</
             a></li>
 </ul>
</div>

<div class="btn-group">
 <button type="button" class="btn btn-secondary
   dropdown-toggle" data-bs-toggle="dropdown" data-
   bs-display="static" aria-expanded="false">
  Right-aligned, left-aligned lg
 </button>
 <ul class="dropdown-menu dropdown-menu-end
           dropdown-menu-lg-start">
  <li><a class="dropdown-item" href="#">Menu item</
             a></li>
```

```
  <li><a class="dropdown-item" href="#">Menu item</
              a></li>
  <li><a class="dropdown-item" href="#">Menu item</
              a></li>
 </ul>
</div>

<div class="btn-group dropstart">
 <button type="button" class="btn btn-secondary
   dropdown-toggle" data-bs-toggle="dropdown"
   aria-expanded="false">
  Dropstart
 </button>
 <ul class="dropdown-menu">
  <li><a class="dropdown-item" href="#">Menu item</
              a></li>
  <li><a class="dropdown-item" href="#">Menu item</
              a></li>
  <li><a class="dropdown-item" href="#">Menu item</
              a></li>
 </ul>
</div>

<div class="btn-group dropend">
 <button type="button" class="btn btn-secondary
         dropdown-toggle" data-bs-toggle="dropdown"
         aria-expanded="false">
  Dropend
 </button>
 <ul class="dropdown-menu">
  <li><a class="dropdown-item" href="#">Menu item</
              a></li>
  <li><a class="dropdown-item" href="#">Menu item</
              a></li>
  <li><a class="dropdown-item" href="#">Menu item</
              a></li>
 </ul>
</div>

<div class="btn-group dropup">
 <button type="button" class="btn btn-secondary
         dropdown-toggle" data-bs-toggle="dropdown"
         aria-expanded="false">
```

```
  Dropup
 </button>
 <ul class="dropdown-menu">
  <li><a class="dropdown-item" href="#">Menu item</
             a></li>
  <li><a class="dropdown-item" href="#">Menu item</
             a></li>
  <li><a class="dropdown-item" href="#">Menu item</
             a></li>
 </ul>
</div>
```

Menu Content

Headers

In every dropdown menu, add a header to label sections of activities:

```
<ul class="dropdown-menu">
 <li><h6 class="dropdown-header">Dropdown header</
             h6></li>
 <li><a class="dropdown-item" href="#">Action</a></li>
 <li><a class="dropdown-item" href="#">Another
             action</a></li>
</ul>
```

Dividers

Using a divider, split groups of related menu items:

```
<ul class="dropdown-menu">
 <li><a class="dropdown-item" href="#">Action</a></li>
 <li><a class="dropdown-item" href="#">Another
             action</a></li>
 <li><a class="dropdown-item" href="#">Something else
             here</a></li>
 <li><hr class="dropdown-divider"></li>
 <li><a class="dropdown-item" href="#">Separated
             link</a></li>
</ul>
```

Text

Place any freeform text within a dropdown menu with text and use spacing utilities. Note that you'll likely need additional sizing styles to constrain the menu width.

```
<div class="dropdown-menu p-4 text-muted" style="max-
          width: 200px;">
 <p>
  Some example text that's free-flowing within the
dropdown menu.
 </p>
 <p class="mb-0">
  And this is more example text.
 </p>
</div>
```

Forms

Put a form within a dropdown menu, make it into a dropdown menu, and use margin or padding utilities to give it the negative space you require.

```
<div class="dropdown-menu">
 <form class="px-4 py-3">
  <div class="mb-3">
   <label for="exampleDropdownFormEmail1"
         class="form-label">Email address</label>
   <input type="email" class="form-control"
         id="exampleDropdownFormEmail1"
         placeholder="email@example.com">
  </div>
  <div class="mb-3">
   <label for="exampleDropdownFormPassword1"
            class="form-label">Password</label>
   <input type="password" class="form-control" id="ex
            ampleDropdownFormPassword1"
            placeholder="Password">
  </div>
  <div class="mb-3">
   <div class="form-check">
    <input type="checkbox" class="form-check-input"
               id="dropdownCheck">
    <label class="form-check-label"
                for="dropdownCheck">
     Remember me
    </label>
```

```
   </div>
  </div>
  <button type="submit" class="btn btn-primary">Sign
                              in</button>
 </form>
 <div class="dropdown-divider"></div>
 <a class="dropdown-item" href="#">New around here?
                              Sign up</a>
 <a class="dropdown-item" href="#">Forgot password?</a>
</div>


<form class="dropdown-menu p-4">
 <div class="mb-3">
  <label for="exampleDropdownFormEmail2" class="form-
             label">Email address</label>
  <input type="email" class="form-control"
             id="exampleDropdownFormEmail2"
             placeholder="email@example.com">
 </div>
 <div class="mb-3">
  <label for="exampleDropdownFormPassword2"
             class="form-label">Password</label>
  <input type="password" class="form-control" id="exa
             mpleDropdownFormPassword2"
             placeholder="Password">
 </div>
 <div class="mb-3">
  <div class="form-check">
   <input type="checkbox" class="form-check-input"
             id="dropdownCheck2">
   <label class="form-check-label"
                for="dropdownCheck2">
    Remember me
   </label>
  </div>
 </div>
 <button type="submit" class="btn btn-primary">Sign
                              in</button>
</form>
```

DROPDOWN OPTIONS

Use data-bs-offset or data-bs-reference to change the location of the dropdown.

```
<div class="d-flex">
 <div class="dropdown me-1">
  <button type="button" class="btn btn-secondary
    dropdown-toggle" id="dropdownMenuOffset" data-bs-
    toggle="dropdown" aria-expanded="false"
    data-bs-offset="10,20">
  Offset
  </button>
  <ul class="dropdown-menu" aria-labelledby="dropdown
      MenuOffset">
   <li><a class="dropdown-item" href="#">Action</a></li>
   <li><a class="dropdown-item" href="#">Another
           action</a></li>
   <li><a class="dropdown-item" href="#">Something
           else here</a></li>
  </ul>
 </div>
 <div class="btn-group">
  <button type="button" class="btn btn-
                        secondary">Reference</button>
  <button type="button" class="btn btn-secondary
          dropdown-toggle dropdown-toggle-split"
          id="dropdownMenuReference" data-bs-
          toggle="dropdown" aria-expanded="false"
          data-bs-reference="parent">
   <span class="visually-hidden">Toggle Dropdown</span>
  </button>
  <ul class="dropdown-menu" aria-labelledby="dropdown
             MenuReference">
   <li><a class="dropdown-item" href="#">Action</a></li>
   <li><a class="dropdown-item" href="#">Another
              action</a></li>
   <li><a class="dropdown-item" href="#">Something
              else here</a></li>
   <li><hr class="dropdown-divider"></li>
   <li><a class="dropdown-item" href="#">Separated
              link</a></li>
```

```
    </ul>
   </div>
  </div>
```

Autoclose Behavior

By default, the dropdown menu is closed when clicking inside or outside the dropdown menu. You can use the autoclose option to change this behavior of the dropdown.

```
<div class="btn-group">
 <button class="btn btn-secondary dropdown-toggle"
   type="button" id="defaultDropdown" data-bs-
   toggle="dropdown" data-bs-auto-close="true"
   aria-expanded="false">
  Default dropdown
 </button>
 <ul class="dropdown-menu" aria-labelledby="defaultDr
            opdown">
  <li><a class="dropdown-item" href="#">Menu item</
            a></li>
  <li><a class="dropdown-item" href="#">Menu item</
            a></li>
  <li><a class="dropdown-item" href="#">Menu item</
            a></li>
 </ul>
</div>

<div class="btn-group">
 <button class="btn btn-secondary dropdown-toggle"
   type="button" id="dropdownMenuClickableOutside"
   data-bs-toggle="dropdown" data-bs-auto-
   close="inside" aria-expanded="false">
  Clickable outside
 </button>
 <ul class="dropdown-menu" aria-labelledby="dropdown
            MenuClickableOutside">
  <li><a class="dropdown-item" href="#">Menu item</
            a></li>
  <li><a class="dropdown-item" href="#">Menu item</
            a></li>
  <li><a class="dropdown-item" href="#">Menu item</
            a></li>
 </ul>
</div>
```

```
<div class="btn-group">
 <button class="btn btn-secondary dropdown-
         toggle" type="button" id="dropdownMenuClicka
         bleInside" data-bs-toggle="dropdown" data-
         bs-auto-close="outside"
         aria-expanded="false">
  Clickable inside
 </button>
 <ul class="dropdown-menu" aria-labelledby="dropdown
           MenuClickableInside">
  <li><a class="dropdown-item" href="#">Menu item</
          a></li>
  <li><a class="dropdown-item" href="#">Menu item</
          a></li>
  <li><a class="dropdown-item" href="#">Menu item</
          a></li>
 </ul>
</div>


<div class="btn-group">
 <button class="btn btn-secondary dropdown-toggle"
type="button" id="dropdownMenuClickable" data-bs-
toggle="dropdown" data-bs-auto-close="false"
aria-expanded="false">
  Manual close
 </button>
 <ul class="dropdown-menu" aria-labelledby="dropdownM
           enuClickable">
  <li><a class="dropdown-item" href="#">Menu item</
          a></li>
  <li><a class="dropdown-item" href="#">Menu item</
          a></li>
  <li><a class="dropdown-item" href="#">Menu item</
          a></li>
 </ul>
</div>
```

List Group

List groups are a versatile and effective component for presenting a succession of items. Modify and expand them to handle almost any type of content.

Basic Example

An unordered list containing list items and the appropriate classes is the simplest basic list group. Build on it using the parameters below or your CSS as needed.

```
<ul class="list-group">
 <li class="list-group-item">An item</li>
 <li class="list-group-item">A second item</li>
 <li class="list-group-item">A third item</li>
 <li class="list-group-item">A fourth item</li>
 <li class="list-group-item">And a fifth one</li>
</ul>
```

Active Items

To identify the current active selection, append .active to a .list-group-item.

```
<ul class="list-group">
 <li class="list-group-item active" aria-
            current="true">An active item</li>
 <li class="list-group-item">A second item</li>
 <li class="list-group-item">A third item</li>
 <li class="list-group-item">A fourth item</li>
 <li class="list-group-item">And a fifth one</li>
</ul>
```

Disable Items

To make a .list-group-item appear disabled, append .disabled to it. It should be noted that some items with .disabled will additionally require specific JavaScript to completely deactivate their click events.

```
<ul class="list-group">
 <li class="list-group-item disabled" aria-
            disabled="true">A disabled item</li>
 <li class="list-group-item">A second item</li>
 <li class="list-group-item">A third item</li>
 <li class="list-group-item">A fourth item</li>
 <li class="list-group-item">And a fifth one</li>
</ul>
```

Links and Buttons

By adding .list-group-item-action to <a>s or <button>s, you may build *actionable* list group items with hover, disabled, and active states. These pseudo-classes are separated to guarantee that list groups comprised of non-interactive components (such as <li>s or <div>s) do not give a click or tap affordance.

Make sure to avoid using the standard **.btn** classes here.

```
<div class="list-group">
 <a href="#" class="list-group-item list-group-item-
           action active" aria-current="true">
  The current link item
 </a>
 <a href="#" class="list-group-item list-group-item-
           action">A second link item</a>
 <a href="#" class="list-group-item list-group-item-
           action">A third link item</a>
 <a href="#" class="list-group-item list-group-item-
           action">A fourth link item</a>
 <a href="#" class="list-group-item list-group-item-
           action disabled" tabindex="-1" aria-
           disabled="true">A disabled link item</a>
</div>
```

You may also use the disabled property instead of the .disabled class with <button>. Unfortunately, the disabled property isn't supported by <a>s.

```
<div class="list-group">
 <button type="button" class="list-group-item list-
   group-item-action active" aria-current="true">
  The current button
 </button>
 <button type="button" class="list-group-item list-
   group-item-action">A second item</button>
 <button type="button" class="list-group-item list-
   group-item-action">A third button item</button>
 <button type="button" class="list-group-item list-
   group-item-action">A fourth button item</button>
 <button type="button" class="list-group-item list-
   group-item-action" disabled>A disabled button
   item</button>
</div>
```

Flush

To render list group elements in a parent container edge-to-edge, use .list-group-flush to remove some borders and rounded corners (e.g., cards).

```
<ul class="list-group list-group-flush">
 <li class="list-group-item">An item</li>
 <li class="list-group-item">A second item</li>
 <li class="list-group-item">A third item</li>
 <li class="list-group-item">A fourth item</li>
 <li class="list-group-item">And a fifth one</li>
</ul>
```

Numbered

To enable numbered list group elements, use the .list-group-numbered modifier class (and possibly an <ol> element). Numbers are created using CSS (rather than the default browser style) for better positioning and customization inside list group elements.

Counter-reset generated numbers on the <ol>, then styled and placed with a::before pseudo-element on the <li> with counter-increment and content.

```
<ol class="list-group list-group-numbered">
 <li class="list-group-item">Cras justo odio</li>
 <li class="list-group-item">Cras justo odio</li>
 <li class="list-group-item">Cras justo odio</li>
</ol>
```

These also work nicely with custom content.

```
<ol class="list-group list-group-numbered">
 <li class="list-group-item d-flex justify-content-
     between align-items-start">
  <div class="ms-2 me-auto">
   <div class="fw-bold">Subheading</div>
   Cras justo odio
  </div>
  <span class="badge bg-primary rounded-pill">14</span>
 </li>
 <li class="list-group-item d-flex justify-content-
            between align-items-start">
  <div class="ms-2 me-auto">
   <div class="fw-bold">Subheading</div>
   Cras justo odio
  </div>
  <span class="badge bg-primary rounded-pill">14</span>
```

```
    </li>
    <li class="list-group-item d-flex justify-content-
            between align-items-start">
      <div class="ms-2 me-auto">
        <div class="fw-bold">Subheading</div>
        Cras justo odio
      </div>
      <span class="badge bg-primary rounded-pill">14</span>
    </li>
</ol>
```

Horizontal

To alter the layout of list group elements from vertical to horizontal across all breakpoints, use add.list-group-horizontal. Alternately, select a responsive variant. list-group-horizontal-{sm|md|lg|xl|xxl} to create a list group horizontal starting at the min-width of that breakpoint. At the moment, horizontal list groups and flush list groups cannot be mixed.

> **ProTip:** Do you want equal-width list group elements when the list is horizontal? Each list group item should have .flex-fill added to it.

```
<ul class="list-group list-group-horizontal">
  <li class="list-group-item">An item</li>
  <li class="list-group-item">A second item</li>
  <li class="list-group-item">A third item</li>
</ul>
<ul class="list-group list-group-horizontal-sm">
  <li class="list-group-item">An item</li>
  <li class="list-group-item">A second item</li>
  <li class="list-group-item">A third item</li>
</ul>
<ul class="list-group list-group-horizontal-md">
  <li class="list-group-item">An item</li>
  <li class="list-group-item">A second item</li>
  <li class="list-group-item">A third item</li>
</ul>
<ul class="list-group list-group-horizontal-lg">
  <li class="list-group-item">An item</li>
  <li class="list-group-item">A second item</li>
  <li class="list-group-item">A third item</li>
```

```
</ul>
<ul class="list-group list-group-horizontal-xl">
 <li class="list-group-item">An item</li>
 <li class="list-group-item">A second item</li>
 <li class="list-group-item">A third item</li>
</ul>
<ul class="list-group list-group-horizontal-xxl">
 <li class="list-group-item">An item</li>
 <li class="list-group-item">A second item</li>
 <li class="list-group-item">A third item</li>
</ul>
```

Contextual Classes

Style list items with a stately background and color by using contextual classes.

```
<ul class="list-group">
 <li class="list-group-item">A simple default list
group item</li>
 <li class="list-group-item list-group-item-
     primary">A simple primary list group item</li>
 <li class="list-group-item list-group-item-secondary">
     A simple secondary list group item</li>
 <li class="list-group-item list-group-item-
     success">A simple success list group item</li>
 <li class="list-group-item list-group-item-danger">A
     simple danger list group item</li>
 <li class="list-group-item list-group-item-
     warning">A simple warning list group item</li>
 <li class="list-group-item list-group-item-info">A
             simple info list group item</li>
 <li class="list-group-item list-group-item-light">A
             simple light list group item</li>
 <li class="list-group-item list-group-item-dark">A
             simple dark list group item</li>
</ul>
```

Contextual classes can also use .list-group-item-action. The inclusion of hover styles in this example is not present in the previous example. The .active state is also supported; use it to indicate an active selection on a contextual list group item.

```
<div class="list-group">
 <a href="#" class="list-group-item list-group-item-
    action">A simple default list group item</a>


 <a href="#" class="list-group-item list-group-item-
    action list-group-item-primary">A simple primary
    list group item</a>
 <a href="#" class="list-group-item list-group-item-
    action list-group-item-secondary">A simple
    secondary list group item</a>
 <a href="#" class="list-group-item list-group-item-
    action list-group-item-success">A simple success
    list group item</a>
 <a href="#" class="list-group-item list-group-item-
    action list-group-item-danger">A simple danger
    list group item</a>
 <a href="#" class="list-group-item list-group-item-
    action list-group-item-warning">A simple warning
    list group item</a>
 <a href="#" class="list-group-item list-group-item-
    action list-group-item-info">A simple info list
    group item</a>
 <a href="#" class="list-group-item list-group-item-
    action list-group-item-light">A simple light list
    group item</a>
 <a href="#" class="list-group-item list-group-item-
    action list-group-item-dark">A simple dark list
    group item</a>
</div>
```

With Badges

With the aid of various utilities, you can add badges to any list group item
to represent unread numbers, activity, and more.

```
<ul class="list-group">
 <li class="list-group-item d-flex justify-content-
    between align-items-center">
  A list item
  <span class="badge bg-primary rounded-pill">14</span>
 </li>
```

```
<li class="list-group-item d-flex justify-content-
          between align-items-center">
 A second list item
 <span class="badge bg-primary rounded-pill">2</span>
</li>
<li class="list-group-item d-flex justify-content-
    between align-items-center">
 A third list item
 <span class="badge bg-primary rounded-pill">1</span>
</li>
</ul>
```

Custom Content

With the use of flexbox tools, you can add nearly any HTML within, including linked list groups like the one below:

```
<div class="list-group">
 <a href="#" class="list-group-item list-group-item-
    action active" aria-current="true">
  <div class="d-flex w-100 justify-content-between">
   <h5 class="mb-1">List group item heading</h5>
   <small>3 days ago</small>
  </div>
  <p class="mb-1">Some placeholder content in a
     paragraph.</p>
  <small>And some small print.</small>
 </a>
 <a href="#" class="list-group-item
    list-group-item-action">
  <div class="d-flex w-100 justify-content-between">
   <h5 class="mb-1">List group item heading</h5>
   <small class="text-muted">3 days ago</small>
  </div>
  <p class="mb-1">Some placeholder content in a
     paragraph.</p>
  <small class="text-muted">And some muted small
        print.</small>
 </a>
 <a href="#" class="list-group-item
    list-group-item-action">
  <div class="d-flex w-100 justify-content-between">
```

```
  <h5 class="mb-1">List group item heading</h5>
  <small class="text-muted">3 days ago</small>
 </div>
 <p class="mb-1">Some placeholder content in a
    paragraph.</p>
 <small class="text-muted">And some muted small
       print.</small>
 </a>
</div>
```

Checkbox and Radios

Insert Bootstrap checkboxes and radio buttons into list group elements and adjust as needed. They can be used without labels, but remember to provide an aria-label attribute and value for accessibility.

```
<ul class="list-group">
 <li class="list-group-item">
  <input class="form-check-input me-1" type="checkbox"
       value="" aria-label="...">
  First checkbox
 </li>
 <li class="list-group-item">
  <input class="form-check-input me-1" type="checkbox"
       value="" aria-label="...">
  Second checkbox
 </li>
 <li class="list-group-item">
  <input class="form-check-input me-1" type="checkbox"
       value="" aria-label="...">
  Third checkbox
 </li>
 <li class="list-group-item">
  <input class="form-check-input me-1" type="checkbox"
       value="" aria-label="...">
  Fourth checkbox
 </li>
 <li class="list-group-item">
  <input class="form-check-input me-1" type="checkbox"
       value="" aria-label="...">
  Fifth checkbox
 </li>
</ul>
```

And you can use <label>s as the .list-group-item for huge hit regions as well.

```
<div class="list-group">
 <label class="list-group-item">
  <input class="form-check-input me-1" type="checkbox"
         value="">
  First checkbox
 </label>
 <label class="list-group-item">
  <input class="form-check-input me-1" type="checkbox"
         value="">
  Second checkbox
 </label>
 <label class="list-group-item">
  <input class="form-check-input me-1" type="checkbox"
         value="">
  Third checkbox
 </label>
 <label class="list-group-item">
  <input class="form-check-input me-1" type="checkbox"
         value="">
  Fourth checkbox
 </label>
 <label class="list-group-item">
  <input class="form-check-input me-1" type="checkbox"
         value="">
  Fifth checkbox
 </label>
</div>
```

JavaScript Behavior

Use the tab JavaScript plugin to expand our list group to generate tab-bable panes of local content (include it separately or through the produced bootstrap.js file).

```
<div class="row">
 <div class="col-4">
  <div class="list-group" id="list-tab" role="tablist">
   <a class="list-group-item list-group-item-action
      active" id="list-home-list" data-bs-
      toggle="list" href="#list-home" role="tab"
      aria-controls="list-home">Home</a>
```

```
      <a class="list-group-item list-group-item-action"
          id="list-profile-list" data-bs-toggle="list"
          href="#list-profile" role="tab" aria-
          controls="list-profile">Profile</a>
      <a class="list-group-item list-group-item-action"
          id="list-messages-list" data-bs-toggle="list"
          href="#list-messages" role="tab" aria-contr
          ols="list-messages">Messages</a>
      <a class="list-group-item list-group-item-action"
          id="list-settings-list" data-bs-toggle="list"
          href="#list-settings" role="tab" aria-contr
          ols="list-settings">Settings</a>
    </div>
  </div>
  <div class="col-8">
    <div class="tab-content" id="nav-tabContent">
      <div class="tab-pane fade show active" id="list-
          home" role="tabpanel" aria-labelledby="lis
          t-home-list">...</div>
      <div class="tab-pane fade" id="list-profile"
          role="tabpanel" aria-labelledby="list-pro
          file-list">...</div>
      <div class="tab-pane fade" id="list-messages"
          role="tabpanel" aria-labelledby="list-mes
          sages-list">...</div>
      <div class="tab-pane fade" id="list-settings"
          role="tabpanel" aria-labelledby="list-set
          tings-list">...</div>
    </div>
  </div>
</div>
```

Using Data Attributes

By providing data-bs-toggle="list" or on an element, you may enable list group navigation without writing any JavaScript. On .list-group-item, use these data characteristics.

```
<div role="tabpanel">
  <!-- List group -->
  <div class="list-group" id="myList" role="tablist">
    <a class="list-group-item list-group-item-action
        active" data-bs-toggle="list" href="#home"
        role="tab">Home</a>
```

```
 <a class="list-group-item list-group-item-action"
    data-bs-toggle="list" href="#profile"
    role="tab">Profile</a>
 <a class="list-group-item list-group-item-action"
    data-bs-toggle="list" href="#messages"
    role="tab">Messages</a>
 <a class="list-group-item list-group-item-action"
    data-bs-toggle="list" href="#settings"
    role="tab">Settings</a>
</div>

<!-- Tab panes -->
<div class="tab-content">
 <div class="tab-pane active" id="home"
      role="tabpanel">...</div>
 <div class="tab-pane" id="profile"
      role="tabpanel">...</div>
 <div class="tab-pane" id="messages"
      role="tabpanel">...</div>
 <div class="tab-pane" id="settings"
      role="tabpanel">...</div>
 </div>
</div>
```

Modal

To add dialog to your site for lightboxes, user alerts, or totally custom content, use Bootstrap's JavaScript modal plugin.

How It Works

Before you begin using Bootstrap's modal component, please read the following because our menu choices have just changed:

- HTML, CSS, and JavaScript are used to create modals. They are placed above everything else in the document and eliminate scroll from the body>, allowing modal content to scroll instead.

- When you click on the modal's "backdrop," it will automatically close.

- Bootstrap only allows one modal window to be open at a time. We do not allow nested modals since we feel they provide bad user experiences.

- **Modals utilize position**: fixed, which can be a little picky about how it renders. Place your modal HTML toward the top of the page wherever feasible to avoid interference from other components. When nesting a .modal within another fixed element, you'll almost certainly run into problems.

- There are several limitations to utilizing modals on mobile devices

- **Owing to position**: fixed. For further information, please see our browser support documentation.

- The autofocus HTML property has no impact on Bootstrap modals due to how HTML5 defines its semantics. Use some custom JavaScript to accomplish the same effect.

Examples

Here's an example of a *static* modal (meaning its position and display have been overridden). There is a modal header, a modal body (needed for padding), and an optional modal footer. When feasible, please offer modal headers with dismiss actions, or provide another clear dismiss option.

```
<div class="modal" tabindex="-1">
 <div class="modal-dialog">
  <div class="modal-content">
   <div class="modal-header">
    <h5 class="modal-title">Modal title</h5>
    <button type="button" class="btn-close" data-bs-
      dismiss="modal" aria-label="Close"></button>
   </div>
   <div class="modal-body">
    <p>Modal body text goes here.</p>
   </div>
   <div class="modal-footer">
    <button type="button" class="btn btn-secondary"
            data-bs-dismiss="modal">Close</button>
    <button type="button" class="btn btn-
            primary">Save changes</button>
   </div>
  </div>
 </div>
</div>
```

Live Demo

By clicking the button below, you may toggle a functional modal demo. From the top of the page, it will slide down and fade in.

```
<!-- Button trigger modal -->
<button type="button" class="btn btn-primary" data-
bs-toggle="modal" data-bs-target="#exampleModal">
 Launch demo modal
</button>

<!-- Modal -->
<div class="modal fade" id="exampleModal"
     tabindex="-1" aria-labelledby="exampleModalLabel"
     aria-hidden="true">
 <div class="modal-dialog">
  <div class="modal-content">
   <div class="modal-header">
    <h5 class="modal-title" id="exampleModalLabel">
             Modal title</h5>
    <button type="button" class="btn-close" data-bs-
       dismiss="modal" aria-label="Close"></button>
   </div>
   <div class="modal-body">
    ...
   </div>
   <div class="modal-footer">
    <button type="button" class="btn btn-secondary"
      data-bs-dismiss="modal">Close</button>
    <button type="button" class="btn btn-
      primary">Save changes</button>
   </div>
  </div>
 </div>
</div>
```

Static Backdrop

When the backdrop is set to static, the modal will not close when clicking outside it. Click the button below to try it.

```
<!-- Button trigger modal -->
<button type="button" class="btn btn-primary" data-
  bs-toggle="modal" data-bs-target="#staticBackdrop">
```

```
 Launch static backdrop modal
</button>

<!-- Modal -->
<div class="modal fade" id="staticBackdrop" data-bs-
    backdrop="static" data-bs-keyboard="false"
    tabindex="-1" aria-labelledby="staticBackdropLa
    bel" aria-hidden="true">
 <div class="modal-dialog">
  <div class="modal-content">
   <div class="modal-header">
    <h5 class="modal-title" id="staticBackdropLabel">
              Modal title</h5>
    <button type="button" class="btn-close" data-bs-
       dismiss="modal" aria-label="Close"></button>
   </div>
   <div class="modal-body">
    ...
   </div>
   <div class="modal-footer">
    <button type="button" class="btn btn-secondary"
       data-bs-dismiss="modal">Close</button>
    <button type="button" class="btn btn-
       primary">Understood</button>
   </div>
  </div>
 </div>
</div>
```

Scrolling Long Content

When a modal gets too long for the viewport or device of the user, it will scroll independently of the page.

By appending .modal-dialog-scrollable to .modal-dialog, you can build a scrollable modal that allows you to scroll the modal body.

```
<!-- Scrollable modal -->
<div class="modal-dialog modal-dialog-scrollable">
 ...
</div>
```

Vertically Centered

To vertically center the modal, add .modal-dialog-centered to .modal-dialog.

```
<!-- Vertically centered modal -->
<div class="modal-dialog modal-dialog-centered">
 ...
</div>

<!-- Vertically centered scrollable modal -->
<div class="modal-dialog modal-dialog-centered
          modal-dialog-scrollable">
 ...
</div>
```

Tooltips and Popovers

As needed, tooltips and popovers can be inserted within modals. When modals are closed, all tooltips and popovers included therein are likewise discarded.

```
<div class="modal-body">
 <h5>Popover in a modal</h5>
 <p>This <a href="#" role="button" class="btn btn-
         secondary popover-test" title="Popover
         title" data-bs-content="Popover body content
         is set in this attribute.">button</a>
         triggers a popover on click.</p>
 <hr>
 <h5>Tooltips in a modal</h5>
 <p><a href="#" class="tooltip-test"
       title="Tooltip">This link</a> and <a href="#"
       class="tooltip-test" title="Tooltip">that
       link</a> have tooltips on hover.</p>
</div>
```

Using the Grid

By nesting .container-fluid within the .modal-body, you may use the Bootstrap grid system within a modal. Then, as you would in any place, utilize the usual grid system classes.

```
<div class="modal-body">
 <div class="container-fluid">
  <div class="row">
   <div class="col-md-4">.col-md-4</div>
   <div class="col-md-4 ms-auto">.col-md-4 .ms-auto</div>
```

```
  </div>
  <div class="row">
   <div class="col-md-3 ms-auto">.col-md-3 .ms-auto</div>
   <div class="col-md-2 ms-auto">.col-md-2 .ms-auto</div>
  </div>
  <div class="row">
   <div class="col-md-6 ms-auto">.col-md-6 .ms-auto</div>
  </div>
  <div class="row">
   <div class="col-sm-9">
    Level 1: .col-sm-9
    <div class="row">
     <div class="col-8 col-sm-6">
      Level 2: .col-8 .col-sm-6
     </div>
     <div class="col-4 col-sm-6">
      Level 2: .col-4 .col-sm-6
     </div>
    </div>
   </div>
  </div>
 </div>
</div>
```

Varying Modal Content

Have plenty of buttons that all open the same modal but with slightly different content. Use event, Related target, and HTML data-bs-* attributes to vary the contents of the modal depending on which button was clicked.

Below is a live demo followed by an example of HTML and JavaScript. For more information, read the modal events docs for details on related targets.

```
<button type="button" class="btn btn-primary" data-
bs-toggle="modal" data-bs-target="#exampleModal" data-
bs-whatever="@mdo">Open modal for @mdo</button>
<button type="button" class="btn btn-primary" data-
bs-toggle="modal" data-bs-target="#exampleModal" data-
bs-whatever="@fat">Open modal for @fat</button>
<button type="button" class="btn btn-primary" data-
bs-toggle="modal" data-bs-target="#exampleModal" data-
bs-whatever="@getbootstrap">Open modal for @
getbootstrap</button>
```

```
<div class="modal fade" id="exampleModal"
    tabindex="-1" aria-labelledby="exampleModalLabel"
    aria-hidden="true">
 <div class="modal-dialog">
  <div class="modal-content">
   <div class="modal-header">
    <h5 class="modal-title" id="exampleModalLabel">
        New message</h5>
    <button type="button" class="btn-close" data-bs-
       dismiss="modal" aria-label="Close"></button>
   </div>
   <div class="modal-body">
    <form>
      <div class="mb-3">
       <label for="recipient-name" class="col-form
               -label">Recipient:</label>
       <input type="text" class="form-control"
               id="recipient-name">
      </div>
      <div class="mb-3">
       <label for="message-text" class="col-form-
               label">Message:</label>
       <textarea class="form-control" id="message-
               text"></textarea>
      </div>
     </form>
    </div>
    <div class="modal-footer">
     <button type="button" class="btn btn-secondary"
             data-bs-dismiss="modal">Close</button>
     <button type="button" class="btn btn-
             primary">Send message</button>
    </div>
   </div>
  </div>
</div>
```

Toggle between Models

Toggle between multiple modals with some clever placement of the data-bs-target and data-bs-toggle attributes. For example, you could toggle a password reset modal from within an already open sign-in modal. Please note that multiple modals cannot be available simultaneously – this method toggles between two separate models.

```
<div class="modal fade" id="exampleModalToggle" aria-
hidden="true" aria-labelledby="exampleModalToggleLabel
" tabindex="-1">
 <div class="modal-dialog modal-dialog-centered">
  <div class="modal-content">
   <div class="modal-header">
    <h5 class="modal-title" id="exampleModalToggleLab
            el">Modal 1</h5>
    <button type="button" class="btn-close" data-bs-
      dismiss="modal" aria-label="Close"></button>
   </div>
   <div class="modal-body">
    Show a second modal and hide the current one by
        clicking the button below.
   </div>
   <div class="modal-footer">
    <button class="btn btn-primary" data-bs-
      target="#exampleModalToggle2" data-bs-
      toggle="modal" data-bs-dismiss="modal">Open
      second modal</button>
   </div>
  </div>
 </div>
</div>
<div class="modal fade" id="exampleModalToggle2"
     aria-hidden="true" aria-labelledby="exampleM
     odalToggleLabel2" tabindex="-1">
 <div class="modal-dialog modal-dialog-centered">
  <div class="modal-content">
   <div class="modal-header">
    <h5 class="modal-title" id="exampleModalToggleLab
            el2">Modal 2</h5>
    <button type="button" class="btn-close" data-bs-
      dismiss="modal" aria-label="Close"></button>
   </div>
   <div class="modal-body">
Hide this modal and reveal the first by clicking the
button below.
   </div>
```

```
  <div class="modal-footer">
    <button class="btn btn-primary" data-bs-
target="#exampleModalToggle" data-bs-toggle="modal"
data-bs-dismiss="modal">Back to first</button>
    </div>
  </div>
 </div>
</div>
<a class="btn btn-primary" data-bs-toggle="modal"
         href="#exampleModalToggle"
         role="button">Open first modal</a>
```

Change Animation

The $modal-fade-transform variable controls the transform state of .modal-dialog before the modal fade-in animation, whereas the $modal-show-transform variable controls the transform state of .modal-dialog after the modal fade-in animation.

If you want a zoom-in animation, for example, specify $modal-fade-transform: scale (.8).

Remove Animation

For models that appear rather than fade into view, remove the .fade class from your modal markup.

```
<div class="modal" tabindex="-1" aria-labelledby="..."
         aria-hidden="true">
  ...
</div>
```

Dynamic Heights

You should call myModal if the height of a modal changes while it is open. Handle update() to readjust the modal's position in case a scrollbar appears.

Accessibility

Make sure to include aria-labelledby="...", which refers to the modal title, in .modal. You may also use aria-described on .modal to describe your modal dialog. It is important to note that they don't need to include role="dialog" because we do it automatically using JavaScript.

Embedding YouTube Videos

Embedding YouTube videos in modals necessitates the use of extra JavaScript that is not included in Bootstrap, such as the ability to immediately stop playing and other features. For further details, see this Stack Overflow topic.

nav and Tabs

Documentation and examples for how to use Bootstrap included navigation components.

Base nav

Navigation available in Bootstrap shares general markup and styles, from the base .nav class to the active and disabled states. Swap modifier classes to switch between each type.

The base .nav component is built with a flexbox and provides a strong foundation for building all navigation components. It includes some style overrides, link padding for larger hit areas, and basic disabled styling.

```
<ul class="nav">
 <li class="nav-item">
  <a class="nav-link active" aria-current="page"
          href="#">Active</a>
 </li>
 <li class="nav-item">
  <a class="nav-link" href="#">Link</a>
 </li>
 <li class="nav-item">
  <a class="nav-link" href="#">Link</a>
 </li>
 <li class="nav-item">
  <a class="nav-link disabled" href="#" tabindex="-1"
          aria-disabled="true">Disabled</a>
 </li>
</ul>
```

Because classes are utilized throughout, your markup may be quite flexible. Use <ul>s like the ones shown above, <ol> if the order of your items is crucial, or make your own with a <nav> element. Because the .nav employs display: flex, nav links function similarly to nav items, but without the additional markup.

```
<nav class="nav">
 <a class="nav-link active" aria-current="page"
          href="#">Active</a>
 <a class="nav-link" href="#">Link</a>
 <a class="nav-link" href="#">Link</a>
 <a class="nav-link disabled" href="#" tabindex="-1"
          aria-disabled="true">Disabled</a>
</nav>
```

Available Styles

Modifiers and utilities can be used to change the appearance of the .navs component. Mix and mix as desired, or create your own.

Horizontal Alignment

Using flexbox utilities, you may change the horizontal alignment of your navigation. Navs are left-aligned by default, but you may simply alter them to center or right-aligned.

Centered with .justify-content-center

```
<ul class="nav justify-content-center">
 <li class="nav-item">
  <a class="nav-link active" aria-current="page"
          href="#">Active</a>
 </li>
 <li class="nav-item">
  <a class="nav-link" href="#">Link</a>
 </li>
 <li class="nav-item">
  <a class="nav-link" href="#">Link</a>
 </li>
 <li class="nav-item">
  <a class="nav-link disabled" href="#" tabindex="-1"
          aria-disabled="true">Disabled</a>
 </li>
</ul>
```

Right-aligned with .justify-content-end

```
<ul class="nav justify-content-end">
 <li class="nav-item">
```

```
  <a class="nav-link active" aria-current="page"
           href="#">Active</a>
 </li>
 <li class="nav-item">
  <a class="nav-link" href="#">Link</a>
 </li>
 <li class="nav-item">
  <a class="nav-link" href="#">Link</a>
 </li>
 <li class="nav-item">
  <a class="nav-link disabled" href="#" tabindex="-1"
           aria-disabled="true">Disabled</a>
 </li>
</ul>
```

Vertical

With the .flex-column utility, you may stack your navigation by adjusting the flex item direction. Need to stack them on some viewports but not on others? Make use of the responsive versions (e.g., .flex-sm-column).

```
<ul class="nav flex-column">
 <li class="nav-item">
  <a class="nav-link active" aria-current="page"
           href="#">Active</a>
 </li>
 <li class="nav-item">
  <a class="nav-link" href="#">Link</a>
 </li>
 <li class="nav-item">
  <a class="nav-link" href="#">Link</a>
 </li>
 <li class="nav-item">
  <a class="nav-link disabled" href="#" tabindex="-1"
           aria-disabled="true">Disabled</a>
 </li>
</ul>
```

As vertical navigation is possible without <ul>s, too.

```
<nav class="nav flex-column">
 <a class="nav-link active" aria-current="page"
           href="#">Active</a>
```

```
<a class="nav-link" href="#">Link</a>
<a class="nav-link" href="#">Link</a>
<a class="nav-link disabled" href="#" tabindex="-1"
        aria-disabled="true">Disabled</a>
</nav>
```

Tabs

To construct a tabbed interface, take the primary nav from above and add the .nav-tabs class. Using our tab JavaScript plugin, you may use them to create tabbable regions.

```
<ul class="nav nav-tabs">
 <li class="nav-item">
  <a class="nav-link active" aria-current="page"
        href="#">Active</a>
 </li>
 <li class="nav-item">
  <a class="nav-link" href="#">Link</a>
 </li>
 <li class="nav-item">
  <a class="nav-link" href="#">Link</a>
 </li>
 <li class="nav-item">
  <a class="nav-link disabled" href="#" tabindex="-1"
        aria-disabled="true">Disabled</a>
 </li>
</ul>
```

Pills

Take same HTML, but use .nav-pills instead:

```
<ul class="nav nav-pills">
 <li class="nav-item">
  <a class="nav-link active" aria-current="page"
        href="#">Active</a>
 </li>
 <li class="nav-item">
  <a class="nav-link" href="#">Link</a>
 </li>
 <li class="nav-item">
  <a class="nav-link" href="#">Link</a>
```

```
  </li>
  <li class="nav-item">
   <a class="nav-link disabled" href="#" tabindex="-1"
           aria-disabled="true">Disabled</a>
  </li>
</ul>
```

Fill and Justify

Forcing the contents of your .nav to span the whole width of one of two modifier classes. Use .nav-fill to proportionally fill all available space with your .nav-items. It is worth noting that all horizontal space is taken up, yet not every nav item is the same width.

```
<ul class="nav nav-pills nav-fill">
 <li class="nav-item">
  <a class="nav-link active" aria-current="page"
           href="#">Active</a>
 </li>
 <li class="nav-item">
  <a class="nav-link" href="#">Much longer nav link</a>
 </li>
 <li class="nav-item">
  <a class="nav-link" href="#">Link</a>
 </li>
 <li class="nav-item">
  <a class="nav-link disabled" href="#" tabindex="-1"
           aria-disabled="true">Disabled</a>
 </li>
</ul>
```

You can safely omit while utilizing <nav>-based navigation. solely as a nav-item For styling< a> elements .nav-link is necessary.

```
<nav class="nav nav-pills nav-fill">
 <a class="nav-link active" aria-current="page"
           href="#">Active</a>
 <a class="nav-link" href="#">Much longer nav link</a>
 <a class="nav-link" href="#">Link</a>
 <a class="nav-link disabled" href="#" tabindex="-1"
           aria-disabled="true">Disabled</a>
</nav>
```

For equal-width elements, use .nav-justified. Nav links will occupy all horizontal space, but unlike the .nav-fill above, every nav item will be the same width.

```
<ul class="nav nav-pills nav-justified">
 <li class="nav-item">
  <a class="nav-link active" aria-current="page"
          href="#">Active</a>
 </li>
 <li class="nav-item">
  <a class="nav-link" href="#">Much longer nav link</a>
 </li>
 <li class="nav-item">
  <a class="nav-link" href="#">Link</a>
 </li>
 <li class="nav-item">
  <a class="nav-link disabled" href="#" tabindex="-1"
          aria-disabled="true">Disabled</a>
 </li>
</ul>
```

Similar to .nav-fill example using <nav>-based navigation.

```
<nav class="nav nav-pills nav-justified">
 <a class="nav-link active" aria-current="page"
          href="#">Active</a>
 <a class="nav-link" href="#">Much longer nav link</a>
 <a class="nav-link" href="#">Link</a>
 <a class="nav-link disabled" href="#" tabindex="-1"
          aria-disabled="true">Disabled</a>
</nav
```

Working with Flex Utilities

Consider employing a set of flexbox tools if you require responsive nav alternatives. While these tools are more verbose, they provide broader control across responsive breakpoints. In the next example, our navigation will be layered on the smallest breakpoint, and then adapt to a horizontal layout that covers the available width beginning with the smallest breakpoint.

```
<nav class="nav nav-pills flex-column flex-sm-row">
 <a class="flex-sm-fill text-sm-center nav-link
    active" aria-current="page" href="#">Active</a>
```

```
<a class="flex-sm-fill text-sm-center nav-link"
   href="#">Longer nav link</a>
<a class="flex-sm-fill text-sm-center nav-link"
   href="#">Link</a>
<a class="flex-sm-fill text-sm-center nav-link
   disabled" href="#" tabindex="-1" aria-
   disabled="true">Disabled</a>
</nav>
```

Regarding Accessibility

If you're utilizing navs to offer a navigation bar, be sure to add a role="navigation" to the <ul>'s logical parent container, or wrap the entire navigation in a <nav> element. Please do not add the role to the <ul> itself, as this would prevent it from being announced as an actual list by assistive technologies.

Note that navigation bars, even if visually styled as tabs with the .nav-tabs class, should not be given role="tablist", role="tab", or role="tab panel" attributes. These are only appropriate for dynamic tabbed interfaces, as described in the WAI-ARIA Authoring Practices. See JavaScript behavior for dynamic tabbed interfaces in this section for an example. The aria-current attribute is unnecessary on dynamic tabbed interfaces since our JavaScript handles the selected state by adding aria-selected="true" on the active tab.

Using Dropdowns

Add dropdown menus with a bit of extra HTML and the dropdowns JavaScript plugin.

Tabs with Dropdowns

```
<ul class="nav nav-tabs">
 <li class="nav-item">
  <a class="nav-link active" aria-current="page"
          href="#">Active</a>
 </li>
 <li class="nav-item dropdown">
  <a class="nav-link dropdown-toggle" data-bs-
          toggle="dropdown" href="#" role="button"
          aria-expanded="false">Dropdown</a>
  <ul class="dropdown-menu">
```

```
  <li><a class="dropdown-item" href="#">Action</a></li>
  <li><a class="dropdown-item" href="#">Another
            action</a></li>
  <li><a class="dropdown-item" href="#">Something
            else here</a></li>
  <li><hr class="dropdown-divider"></li>
  <li><a class="dropdown-item" href="#">Separated
            link</a></li>
 </ul>
</li>
<li class="nav-item">
 <a class="nav-link" href="#">Link</a>
</li>
<li class="nav-item">
 <a class="nav-link disabled" href="#" tabindex="-1"
        aria-disabled="true">Disabled</a>
</li>
</ul>
```

Pills with Dropdowns

```
<ul class="nav nav-pills">
 <li class="nav-item">
  <a class="nav-link active" aria-current="page"
          href="#">Active</a>
 </li>
 <li class="nav-item dropdown">
  <a class="nav-link dropdown-toggle" data-bs-
          toggle="dropdown" href="#" role="button"
          aria-expanded="false">Dropdown</a>
  <ul class="dropdown-menu">
   <li><a class="dropdown-item" href="#">Action</a></li>
   <li><a class="dropdown-item" href="#">Another
              action</a></li>
   <li><a class="dropdown-item" href="#">Something
              else here</a></li>
   <li><hr class="dropdown-divider"></li>
   <li><a class="dropdown-item" href="#">Separated
              link</a></li>
  </ul>
 </li>
 <li class="nav-item">
  <a class="nav-link" href="#">Link</a>
```

```
</li>
<li class="nav-item">
 <a class="nav-link disabled" href="#" tabindex="-1"
         aria-disabled="true">Disabled</a>
</li>
</ul>
```

navbar

Documentation and examples for the navbar, and Bootstrap's robust and responsive navigation header. Branding, navigation, and other features are included as support for the collapse plugin.

How It Works

Before you begin using the navbar, you should be aware of the following:

- Wrapping is required for navbars.

- For responsive collapsing and color scheme classes, use .navbar-expand{-sm|-md|-lg|-xl|-xxl}.

- By default, navbars and contents are fluid. Modify the container to limit its horizontal width in various ways.

- Use our spacing and flex utility classes to change the spacing and alignment of navbars.

- Navbars are dynamic by default; however, this may readily change. Our Collapse JavaScript plugin handles the responsive behavior.

- Use an <nav> element to ensure accessibility, or, if using a more generic feature like a <div>, add role="navigation" to every navbar to expressly indicate it as a landmark region for users of assistive technology.

- To indicate the current page, use aria-current="page," and to show the current item in a collection, use aria-current="true."

Supported Content

Navbars include support for few sub-components by default. As needed, select from the following options:

- .navbar-brand for the name of your organization, product, or project.

- .navbar-toggler is a class that may be used with our collapse plugin and other navigation toggling behaviors.

- For all form controls and actions, flex and spacing utilities are available.

- .navbar-text is used to adding vertically centered strings of text.

- .collapse.navbar-collapse is used to group and hide navbar elements by a parent breakpoint.

- Include an optional.

- To establish a max-height and scroll expanding navbar content, use navbar-scroll.

Here's an example of every sub-component in a responsive light-themed navbar that collapses automatically at the LG (large) breakpoint.

```
<nav class="navbar navbar-expand-lg navbar-light
bg-light">
 <div class="container-fluid">
  <a class="navbar-brand" href="#">Navbar</a>
  <button class="navbar-toggler" type="button" data-
    bs-toggle="collapse" data-bs-target="#navbarSuppo
    rtedContent" aria-controls="navbarSupported
    Content" aria-expanded="false" aria-label="Toggle
    navigation">
   <span class="navbar-toggler-icon"></span>
  </button>
  <div class="collapse navbar-collapse"
              id="navbarSupportedContent">
   <ul class="navbar-nav me-auto mb-2 mb-lg-0">
    <li class="nav-item">
     <a class="nav-link active" aria-current="page"
              href="#">Home</a>
    </li>
    <li class="nav-item">
     <a class="nav-link" href="#">Link</a>
    </li>
    <li class="nav-item dropdown">
     <a class="nav-link dropdown-toggle" href="#"
       id="navbarDropdown" role="button" data-bs-
       toggle="dropdown" aria-expanded="false">
      Dropdown
     </a>
```

```
    <ul class="dropdown-menu"
        aria-labelledby="navbarDropdown">
     <li><a class="dropdown-item" href="#">Action</
            a></li>
     <li><a class="dropdown-item" href="#">Another
                action</a></li>
     <li><hr class="dropdown-divider"></li>
     <li><a class="dropdown-item" href="#">Something
                else here</a></li>
    </ul>
   </li>
   <li class="nav-item">
    <a class="nav-link disabled" href="#" tabindex=
            "-1" aria-disabled="true">Disabled</a>
   </li>
  </ul>
  <form class="d-flex">
   <input class="form-control me-2" type="search"
        placeholder="Search" aria-label="Search">
   <button class="btn btn-outline-success"
        type="submit">Search</button>
  </form>
 </div>
 </div>
</nav>
```

This instance employs the utility classes background (bg-light) and spacing (my-2, my-lg-0, me-sm-0, my-sm-0).

Brand

Although the .navbar-brand may be applied to most components, an anchor works best since some functions need utility classes or specific styles.

Text

Add text within an element with the .navbar-brand class.

```
<!-- As a link -->
<nav class="navbar navbar-light bg-light">
 <div class="container-fluid">
  <a class="navbar-brand" href="#">Navbar</a>
```

```
    </div>
  </nav>

  <!-- As a heading -->
  <nav class="navbar navbar-light bg-light">
    <div class="container-fluid">
      <span class="navbar-brand mb-0 h1">Navbar</span>
    </div>
  </nav>
```

Image

You can use <image> instead of text within the .navbar-brand.

```
  <nav class="navbar navbar-light bg-light">
    <div class="container">
      <a class="navbar-brand" href="#">
        <img src="/docs/5.0/assets/brand/bootstrap-logo.sv
              g" alt="" width="30" height="24">
      </a>
    </div>
  </nav>
```

Image and Text

You may also upload a picture and text at the same time by using some extra utilities. On the <img>, notice the addition of .d-inline-block and .align-text-top.

```
  <nav class="navbar navbar-light bg-light">
    <div class="container-fluid">
      <a class="navbar-brand" href="#">
        <img src="/docs/5.0/assets/brand/bootstrap-logo.sv
              g" alt="" width="30" height="24"
              class="d-inline-block align-text-top">
        Bootstrap
      </a>
    </div>
  </nav>
```

nav

With its modifier class, navbar navigation links extend our .nav choices and require toggler classes for full responsive style. Navigation in navbars will also expand to take up as much horizontal space as feasible in order to firmly align your navbar items.

To identify the current page, use the .active class on .nav-link.

Please keep in mind that the aria-current property should also be added to the active .nav-link.

```
<nav class="navbar navbar-expand-lg navbar-light
bg-light">
 <div class="container-fluid">
  <a class="navbar-brand" href="#">Navbar</a>
  <button class="navbar-toggler" type="button" data-bs-
          toggle="collapse" data-bs-target="#navbarNav"
          aria-controls="navbarNav" aria-expanded=
          "false" aria-label="Toggle navigation">
   <span class="navbar-toggler-icon"></span>
  </button>
  <div class="collapse navbar-collapse"
id="navbarNav">
   <ul class="navbar-nav">
    <li class="nav-item">
     <a class="nav-link active" aria-current="page"
             href="#">Home</a>
    </li>
    <li class="nav-item">
     <a class="nav-link" href="#">Features</a>
    </li>
    <li class="nav-item">
     <a class="nav-link" href="#">Pricing</a>
    </li>
    <li class="nav-item">
     <a class="nav-link disabled" href="#" tabindex=
        "-1" aria-disabled="true">Disabled</a>
    </li>
   </ul>
  </div>
 </div>
</nav>
```

And, because we utilize classes for our navigation, you may completely avoid the list-based method if you like.

```
<nav class="navbar navbar-expand-lg navbar-light
          bg-light">
```

```
<div class="container-fluid">
 <a class="navbar-brand" href="#">Navbar</a>
 <button class="navbar-toggler" type="button" data-
    bs-toggle="collapse" data-bs-target="#navbarNav
    AltMarkup" aria-controls="navbarNavAltMarkup"
    aria-expanded="false" aria-label="Toggle
    navigation">
  <span class="navbar-toggler-icon"></span>
 </button>
 <div class="collapse navbar-collapse"
id="navbarNavAltMarkup">
   <div class="navbar-nav">
    <a class="nav-link active" aria-current="page"
            href="#">Home</a>
    <a class="nav-link" href="#">Features</a>
    <a class="nav-link" href="#">Pricing</a>
    <a class="nav-link disabled" href="#" tabindex=
        "-1" aria-disabled="true">Disabled</a>
   </div>
  </div>
 </div>
</nav>
```

Dropdowns may also be used in your navbar. Dropdown menus need the usage of a wrapper element for positioning, thus use distinct and nested features for .nav-item and .nav-link, as illustrated below.

```
<nav class="navbar navbar-expand-lg navbar-light
            bg-light">
 <div class="container-fluid">
  <a class="navbar-brand" href="#">Navbar</a>
  <button class="navbar-toggler" type="button" data-
    bs-toggle="collapse" data-bs-target="#navbarNav
    Dropdown" aria-controls="navbarNavDropdown" aria-
    expanded="false" aria-label="Toggle navigation">
   <span class="navbar-toggler-icon"></span>
  </button>
  <div class="collapse navbar-collapse"
            id="navbarNavDropdown">
   <ul class="navbar-nav">
    <li class="nav-item">
     <a class="nav-link active" aria-current="page"
            href="#">Home</a>
```

```
    </li>
    <li class="nav-item">
     <a class="nav-link" href="#">Features</a>
    </li>
    <li class="nav-item">
     <a class="nav-link" href="#">Pricing</a>
    </li>
    <li class="nav-item dropdown">
     <a class="nav-link dropdown-toggle" href="#"
       id="navbarDropdownMenuLink" role="button" data-
       bs-toggle="dropdown" aria-expanded="false">
      Dropdown link
     </a>
     <ul class="dropdown-menu" aria-labelledby="nav
             barDropdownMenuLink">
      <li><a class="dropdown-item" href="#">Action</
             a></li>
      <li><a class="dropdown-item" href="#">Another
             action</a></li>
      <li><a class="dropdown-item" href="#">Something
             else here</a></li>
     </ul>
    </li>
   </ul>
  </div>
 </div>
</nav>
```

Forms

```
<nav class="navbar navbar-light bg-light">
 <div class="container-fluid">
  <form class="d-flex">
   <input class="form-control me-2" type="search"
          placeholder="Search" aria-label="Search">
   <button class="btn btn-outline-success"
           type="submit">Search</button>
  </form>
 </div>
</nav>
```

Immediate child components of the navbar employ a flex layout and will by default utilize justify-content: space-between. To modify this behavior, use extra flex utilities as needed.

```
<nav class="navbar navbar-light bg-light">
 <div class="container-fluid">
  <a class="navbar-brand">Navbar</a>
  <form class="d-flex">
   <input class="form-control me-2" type="search"
          placeholder="Search" aria-label="Search">
   <button class="btn btn-outline-success"
           type="submit">Search</button>
  </form>
 </div>
</nav>
```

Input groups are also useful. If your navbar is entirely or primarily a form, you may save some HTML by using the< form> element as the container.

```
<nav class="navbar navbar-light bg-light">
 <form class="container-fluid">
  <div class="input-group">
   <span class="input-group-text" id="basic-
         addon1">@</span>
   <input type="text" class="form-control"
          placeholder="Username" aria-label="Username"
          aria-describedby="basic-addon1">
  </div>
 </form>
</nav>
```

These navbar forms also support a variety of buttons. This is also a good reminder that vertical alignment utilities may be used to align items of varying sizes.

```
<nav class="navbar navbar-light bg-light">
 <form class="container-fluid justify-content-start">
  <button class="btn btn-outline-success me-2"
          type="button">Main button</button>
  <button class="btn btn-sm btn-outline-secondary"
          type="button">Smaller button</button>
 </form>
</nav>
```

Text

With the use of .navbar-text, navbars may contain text. This class modifies the vertical alignment and horizontal spacing of text strings:

```
.<nav class="navbar navbar-light bg-light">
 <div class="container-fluid">
  <span class="navbar-text">
   Navbar text with an inline element
  </span>
 </div>
</nav>
```

As needed, combined with additional components and tools.

```
<nav class="navbar navbar-expand-lg navbar-light
    bg-light">
 <div class="container-fluid">
  <a class="navbar-brand" href="#">Navbar w/ text</a>
  <button class="navbar-toggler" type="button" data-
    bs-toggle="collapse" data-bs-target="#navbarText"
    aria-controls="navbarText" aria-expanded="false"
    aria-label="Toggle navigation">
   <span class="navbar-toggler-icon"></span>
  </button>
  <div class="collapse navbar-collapse"
      id="navbarText">
   <ul class="navbar-nav me-auto mb-2 mb-lg-0">
    <li class="nav-item">
     <a class="nav-link active" aria-current="page"
       href="#">Home</a>
    </li>
    <li class="nav-item">
     <a class="nav-link" href="#">Features</a>
    </li>
    <li class="nav-item">
     <a class="nav-link" href="#">Pricing</a>
    </li>
   </ul>
   <span class="navbar-text">
    Navbar text with an inline element
   </span>
  </div>
 </div>
</nav>
```

Color Schemes

Customizing the navbar is now easier than ever, thanks to the combination of theming classes and background-color utilities. Use .navbar-light with light background colors or .navbar-dark with dark background colors. Then, use .bg-* tools to modify.

```
<nav class="navbar navbar-dark bg-dark">
 <!-- Navbar content -->
</nav>

<nav class="navbar navbar-dark bg-primary">
 <!-- Navbar content -->
</nav>

<nav class="navbar navbar-light" style="background-
     color: #e3f2fd;">
 <!-- Navbar content -->
</nav>
```

Containers

Although it is not required, you may center a navbar on a page by wrapping it in a .container – but keep in mind that an inner container is still required. Alternatively, you may include a container within the .navbar to just center the contents of a fixed or static top navbar.

```
<div class="container">
 <nav class="navbar navbar-expand-lg navbar-light
      bg-light">
  <div class="container-fluid">
   <a class="navbar-brand" href="#">Navbar</a>
  </div>
 </nav>
</div>
```

To adjust the width of the content in your navbar, use any of the responsive containers.

```
<nav class="navbar navbar-expand-lg navbar-light
            bg-light">
 <div class="container-md">
  <a class="navbar-brand" href="#">Navbar</a>
 </div>
</nav>
```

Placement

To install navbars in non-static places, use our position tools. Select between fixed to the top, set to the bottom, and sticked to the top (scrolls with the page until it reaches the top, then stays there). Fixed navbars utilize position: fixed, which means they are removed from the usual flow of the DOM and may require additional CSS (e.g., padding-top on the <body>) to avoid overlap with other elements.

Also, keep in mind, sticky-top makes use of position: sticky, which isn't supported by all browsers.

```
<nav class="navbar navbar-light bg-light">
 <div class="container-fluid">
  <a class="navbar-brand" href="#">Default</a>
 </div>
</nav>

<nav class="navbar fixed-top navbar-light bg-light">
 <div class="container-fluid">
  <a class="navbar-brand" href="#">Fixed top</a>
 </div>
</nav>


<nav class="navbar fixed-bottom navbar-light
            bg-light">
 <div class="container-fluid">
  <a class="navbar-brand" href="#">Fixed bottom</a>
 </div>
</nav>


<nav class="navbar sticky-top navbar-light bg-light">
 <div class="container-fluid">
  <a class="navbar-brand" href="#">Sticky top</a>
 </div>
</nav>
```

Scrolling

To enable vertical scrolling inside the toggleable elements of a collapsed navbar, add .navbar-nav-scroll to a .navbar-nav (or any navbar subcomponent). Scrolling begins by default at 75vh (or 75% of the viewport height), but you may change this with the local CSS custom property

--bs-navbar-height or custom styles. When the navbar is enlarged at bigger viewports, the content appears as it would in a standard navbar.

Keep in mind that this approach has a potential overflow drawback: when overflow-y: auto (needed to scroll the material here), overflow-x is the equivalent of auto, which will crop some horizontal content.

Here's an example navbar that makes use of navbar-nav-scroll with style="--bs-scroll-height: 100px;" and some more margin utilities for optimal spacing:

```
<nav class="navbar navbar-expand-lg navbar-light
bg-light">

 <div class="container-fluid">
  <a class="navbar-brand" href="#">Navbar scroll</a>
  <button class="navbar-toggler" type="button" data-
    bs-toggle="collapse" data-bs-target="#navbar
    Scroll" aria-controls="navbarScroll" aria-
    expanded="false" aria-label="Toggle navigation">
   <span class="navbar-toggler-icon"></span>
  </button>
  <div class="collapse navbar-collapse"
              id="navbarScroll">
   <ul class="navbar-nav me-auto my-2 my-lg-0 navbar-
     nav-scroll" style="--bs-scroll-height: 100px;">
    <li class="nav-item">
     <a class="nav-link active" aria-current="page"
               href="#">Home</a>
    </li>
    <li class="nav-item">
     <a class="nav-link" href="#">Link</a>
    </li>
    <li class="nav-item dropdown">
     <a class="nav-link dropdown-toggle" href="#"
       id="navbarScrollingDropdown" role="button"
       data-bs-toggle="dropdown"
       aria-expanded="false">
      Link
     </a>
     <ul class="dropdown-menu" aria-labelledby="nav
         barScrollingDropdown">
      <li><a class="dropdown-item" href="#">Action</
                  a></li>
      <li><a class="dropdown-item" href="#">Another
                  action</a></li>
```

```
      <li><hr class="dropdown-divider"></li>
      <li><a class="dropdown-item" href="#">Something
                  else here</a></li>
    </ul>
    </li>
    <li class="nav-item">
     <a class="nav-link disabled" href="#" tabindex=
             "-1" aria-disabled="true">Link</a>
    </li>
   </ul>
   <form class="d-flex">
    <input class="form-control me-2" type="search"
           placeholder="Search" aria-label="Search">
    <button class="btn btn-outline-success"
            type="submit">Search</button>
   </form>
  </div>
 </div>
</nav>
```

Responsive Behaviors

To decide when their content collapses behind a button, navbars can utilize the .navbar-toggler, .navbar-collapse, and .navbar-expand{-sm|-md|-lg|-xl|-xxl} classes. You can simply determine whether to show or conceal specific features when used in conjunction with other tools.

Add the .navbar-expand class to the navbar for navbars that never collapse. Don't use the .navbar-expand class on navbars that always collapse.

Google

Navbar toggles are left-aligned by default, but if they are followed by a sibling element, such as a .navbar-brand, they will be situated to the far right. If your markup is reversed, the toggler's placement will be reversed. Here are some examples of different toggle styles.

There is no .navbar-brand visible at the lowest breakpoint:

```
<nav class="navbar navbar-expand-lg navbar-light
            bg-light">
 <div class="container-fluid">
  <button class="navbar-toggler" type="button" data-
          bs-toggle="collapse" data-bs-target="#nav
          barTogglerDemo01" aria-controls="navbar
          TogglerDemo01" aria-expanded="false" aria-
          label="Toggle navigation">
```

```
  <span class="navbar-toggler-icon"></span>
 </button>
 <div class="collapse navbar-collapse"
      id="navbarTogglerDemo01">
  <a class="navbar-brand" href="#">Hidden brand</a>
  <ul class="navbar-nav me-auto mb-2 mb-lg-0">
   <li class="nav-item">
    <a class="nav-link active" aria-current="page"
            href="#">Home</a>
   </li>
   <li class="nav-item">
    <a class="nav-link" href="#">Link</a>
   </li>
   <li class="nav-item">
    <a class="nav-link disabled" href="#" tabindex=
       "-1" aria-disabled="true">Disabled</a>
   </li>
  </ul>
  <form class="d-flex">
   <input class="form-control me-2" type="search"
          placeholder="Search" aria-label="Search">
   <button class="btn btn-outline-success"
           type="submit">Search</button>
  </form>
 </div>
 </div>
</nav>
```

A brand name is presented on the left, while a toggler is shown on the right:

```
<nav class="navbar navbar-expand-lg navbar-light
            bg-light">
 <div class="container-fluid">
  <a class="navbar-brand" href="#">Navbar</a>
  <button class="navbar-toggler" type="button" data-
          bs-toggle="collapse" data-bs-target=
          "#navbarTogglerDemo02" aria-controls=
          "navbarTogglerDemo02" aria-expanded="false"
          aria-label="Toggle navigation">
   <span class="navbar-toggler-icon"></span>
  </button>
```

```
  <div class="collapse navbar-collapse"
      id="navbarTogglerDemo02">
   <ul class="navbar-nav me-auto mb-2 mb-lg-0">
    <li class="nav-item">
     <a class="nav-link active" aria-current="page"
        href="#">Home</a>
    </li>
    <li class="nav-item">
     <a class="nav-link" href="#">Link</a>
    </li>
    <li class="nav-item">
     <a class="nav-link disabled" href="#" tabindex=
        "-1" aria-disabled="true">Disabled</a>
    </li>
   </ul>
   <form class="d-flex">
    <input class="form-control me-2" type="search"
           placeholder="Search" aria-label="Search">
    <button class="btn btn-outline-success"
            type="submit">Search</button>
   </form>
  </div>
 </div>
</nav>

<nav class="navbar navbar-expand-lg navbar-light
            bg-light">
 <div class="container-fluid">
  <button class="navbar-toggler" type="button" data-
          bs-toggle="collapse" data-bs-target=
          "#navbarTogglerDemo03" aria-controls=
          "navbarTogglerDemo03" aria-expanded="false"
          aria-label="Toggle navigation">
   <span class="navbar-toggler-icon"></span>
  </button>
  <a class="navbar-brand" href="#">Navbar</a>
  <div class="collapse navbar-collapse"
              id="navbarTogglerDemo03">
   <ul class="navbar-nav me-auto mb-2 mb-lg-0">
    <li class="nav-item">
     <a class="nav-link active" aria-current="page"
                href="#">Home</a>
```

```
   </li>
   <li class="nav-item">
    <a class="nav-link" href="#">Link</a>
   </li>
   <li class="nav-item">
    <a class="nav-link disabled" href="#"
             tabindex="-1" aria-
             disabled="true">Disabled</a>
   </li>
  </ul>
  <form class="d-flex">
   <input class="form-control me-2" type="search"
          placeholder="Search" aria-label="Search">
   <button class="btn btn-outline-success"
            type="submit">Search</button>
  </form>
 </div>
 </div>
</nav>
```

External Content

When you want to trigger a container element for content that is structurally outside of the .navbar, you may use the collapse plugin. That's simple because our plugin works on id and data-bs-target matching!

```
<div class="collapse" id="navbarToggleExternalContent">
 <div class="bg-dark p-4">
  <h5 class="text-white h4">Collapsed content</h5>
  <span class="text-muted">Toggleable via navbar
               brand.</span>
 </div>
</div>
<nav class="navbar navbar-dark bg-dark">
 <div class="container-fluid">
  <button class="navbar-toggler" type="button" data-
    bs-toggle="collapse" data-bs-target="#navbarTo
    ggleExternalContent" aria-controls="navbarTogg
    leExternalContent" aria-expanded="false" aria-
    label="Toggle navigation">
   <span class="navbar-toggler-icon"></span>
  </button>
 </div>
</nav>
```

When you do this, we recommend integrating extra JavaScript to programmatically transfer the attention to the container when it is opened. Otherwise, keyboard users and assistive technology users may likely struggle to discover the newly disclosed information, especially if the opened container is placed *before* the toggler in the document's structure. We also propose that the toggler has the aria-controls property set to the content container's id. In principle, this allows users of assistive technology to navigate straight from the toggler to the container it controls – however, support for this is still inconsistent.

Off-canvas

With a few classes and a JavaScript plugin, you can incorporate hidden sidebars into your project for navigation, shopping carts, and more.

How It Works

Off-canvas is a sidebar component that may be toggled to display from the viewport's left, right, or bottom edge using JavaScript. Buttons or anchors are utilized as triggers that are tied to certain items that you toggle, and data attributes are used to call our JavaScript.

- Off-canvas and modals both use part of the same JavaScript code. They are conceptually similar, however, they are independent plugins.

- Similarly, the modal's variables are inherited by some source Sass variables for off-canvas styles and dimensions.

- Off-canvas has a preset backdrop that may be clicked to conceal the off-canvas when it is shown. Similar to modals, only one canvas can be shown at a time.

Examples

Off-canvas Components

The example below is an off-canvas example that is displayed by default (via .show on .offcanvas). Off-canvas provides a header with a close button and a body class that can be used to add some padding at the start. When feasible, incorporate off-canvas headers with dismiss actions or offer an explicit dismiss action.

```
<div class="offcanvas offcanvas-start" tabindex="-1"
    id="offcanvas" aria-labelledby="offcanvasLabel">
  <div class="offcanvas-header">
```

```
  <h5 class="offcanvas-title" id="offcanvasLabel">Off
      canvas</h5>
  <button type="button" class="btn-close text-reset"
          data-bs-dismiss="offcanvas" aria-
          label="Close"></button>
 </div>
 <div class="offcanvas-body">
Off-canvas content is placed here. Almost any
Bootstrap component or custom element may be placed
here.
 </div>
</div>
```

Live Demo

Use the buttons below to toggle the .show class on an element with the .offcanvas class to display and hide an off-canvas element through the JavaScript.

- .offcanvas hides the content (default)

- .offcanvas.show shows the content

A link with the href property or a button with the data-bs-target attribute can be used. The data-bs-toggle="offcanvas" attribute is necessary for both circumstances.

```
<a class="btn btn-primary" data-bs-toggle="offcanvas"
   href="#offcanvasExample" role="button"
   aria-controls="offcanvasExample">
 Link with href
</a>
<button class="btn btn-primary" type="button" data-
  bs-toggle="offcanvas" data-bs-target="#offcanvas
  Example" aria-controls="offcanvasExample">
 Button with data-bs-target
</button>

<div class="offcanvas offcanvas-start" tabindex="-1"
     id="offcanvasExample" aria-labelledby="offcanvas
     ExampleLabel">
 <div class="offcanvas-header">
```

```
    <h5 class="offcanvas-title" id="offcanvasExample
        Label">Offcanvas</h5>
    <button type="button" class="btn-close text-reset"
      data-bs-dismiss="offcanvas" aria-label="Close"></
      button>
  </div>
  <div class="offcanvas-body">
    <div>
Some text serves as a placeholder. You can have the
components you've chosen in real life: text, photos,
lists, and so forth.
    </div>
    <div class="dropdown mt-3">
      <button class="btn btn-secondary dropdown-toggle"
              type="button" id="dropdownMenuButton"
              data-bs-toggle="dropdown">
      Dropdown button
      </button>
      <ul class="dropdown-menu" aria-labelledby="dropdow
              nMenuButton">
        <li><a class="dropdown-item" href="#">Action</
                a></li>
        <li><a class="dropdown-item" href="#">Another
                action</a></li>
        <li><a class="dropdown-item" href="#">Something
                else here</a></li>
      </ul>
    </div>
  </div>
</div>
```

Placement

Because there is no default placement for off-canvas components, you must use one of the modifier classes listed below:

- .offcanvas-start positions off-canvas to the left of the viewport (as shown in the example above)

- .offcanvas-start positions off-canvas to the left of the viewport (as shown in the example above) offcanvas-end positions

- offcanvas-end positions

- .offcanvas-top positions off-canvas on top of the viewport
- .offcanvas-bottom adds off-canvas to the viewport's bottom

```
<button class="btn btn-primary" type="button" data-
        bs-toggle="offcanvas" data-bs-target=
        "#offcanvasTop" aria-controls="offcanvasTop">
        Toggle top offcanvas</button>

<div class="offcanvas offcanvas-top" tabindex="-1"
     id="offcanvasTop" aria-labelledby="offcanvasTopL
     abel">
 <div class="offcanvas-header">
  <h5 id="offcanvasTopLabel">Offcanvas top</h5>
  <button type="button" class="btn-close text-reset"
          data-bs-dismiss="offcanvas" aria-
          label="Close"></button>
 </div>
 <div class="offcanvas-body">
  ...
 </div>
</div>

<button class="btn btn-primary" type="button" data-
  bs-toggle="offcanvas" data-bs-target=
  "#offcanvasRight" aria-controls="offcanvasRight">
  Toggle right offcanvas</button>

<div class="offcanvas offcanvas-end" tabindex="-1"
     id="offcanvasRight" aria-labelledby="offcanvasRi
     ghtLabel">
 <div class="offcanvas-header">
  <h5 id="offcanvasRightLabel">Offcanvas right</h5>
  <button type="button" class="btn-close text-reset"
    data-bs-dismiss="offcanvas" aria-label="Close"></
    button>
 </div>
 <div class="offcanvas-body">
  ...
 </div>
</div>

<button class="btn btn-primary" type="button" data-
        bs-toggle="offcanvas" data-bs-
        target="#offcanvasBottom" aria-controls="offc
        anvasBottom">Toggle bottom offcanvas</button>
```

```
<div class="offcanvas offcanvas-bottom" tabindex="-1"
    id="offcanvasBottom"
    aria-labelledby="offcanvasBottomLabel">
 <div class="offcanvas-header">
  <h5 class="offcanvas-title" id="offcanvasBottomLabe
l">Offcanvas bottom</h5>
   <button type="button" class="btn-close text-reset"
          data-bs-dismiss="offcanvas" aria-
          label="Close"></button>
 </div>
 <div class="offcanvas-body small">
  ...
 </div>
</div>
```

Backdrop

When an offcanvas and its backdrop are displayed, scrolling the <body> element is disabled. Toggle <body> scrolling with the data-bs-scroll attribute, and backdrop with data-bs-backdrop.

```
<button class="btn btn-primary" type="button" data-
        bs-toggle="offcanvas" data-bs-target=
        "#offcanvasScrolling" aria-controls="offca
        nvasScrolling">Enable body scrolling</button>
<button class="btn btn-primary" type="button" data-
        bs-toggle="offcanvas" data-bs-target=
        "#offcanvasWithBackdrop" aria-controls="offca
        nvasWithBackdrop">Enable backdrop (default)</
        button>
<button class="btn btn-primary" type="button" data-
        bs-toggle="offcanvas" data-bs-target="#off
        canvasWithBothOptions" aria-controls="offca
        nvasWithBothOptions">Enable both scrolling &
        backdrop</button>

<div class="offcanvas offcanvas-start" data-bs-
    scroll="true" data-bs-backdrop="false"
    tabindex="-1" id="offcanvasScrolling" aria-label
    ledby="offcanvasScrollingLabel">
 <div class="offcanvas-header">
  <h5 class="offcanvas-title" id="offcanvasScrollingL
    abel">Colored with scrolling</h5>
```

```
 <button type="button" class="btn-close text-reset"
         data-bs-dismiss="offcanvas" aria-
         label="Close"></button>
</div>
<div class="offcanvas-body">
 <p>Try scrolling the rest of the page to see this
       option in action.</p>
</div>
</div>
<div class="offcanvas offcanvas-start" tabindex="-1"
     id="offcanvasWithBackdrop" aria-labelledby="off
     canvasWithBackdropLabel">
 <div class="offcanvas-header">
  <h5 class="offcanvas-title" id="offcanvasWithBac
      kdropLabel">Offcanvas with backdrop</h5>
  <button type="button" class="btn-close text-reset"
          data-bs-dismiss="offcanvas" aria-
          label="Close"></button>
 </div>
 <div class="offcanvas-body">
  <p>.....</p>
 </div>
</div>
<div class="offcanvas offcanvas-start" data-bs-
     scroll="true" tabindex="-1"
     id="offcanvasWithBothOptions" aria-labelledby
     ="offcanvasWithBothOptionsLabel">
 <div class="offcanvas-header">
  <h5 class="offcanvas-title" id="offcanvasWithBot
      hOptionsLabel">Backdroped with scrolling</h5>
  <button type="button" class="btn-close text-reset"
          data-bs-dismiss="offcanvas" aria-
          label="Close"></button>
 </div>
 <div class="offcanvas-body">
  <p>Try scrolling the rest of the page to see this
        option in action.</p>
 </div>
</div>
```

Pagination

Documentation and examples for displaying pagination to highlight the presence of a sequence of linked material spread across numerous pages.

Overview

For our pagination, we employ a huge block of related links, which makes links difficult to miss and readily scalable while giving vast hit regions. Pagination is constructed using a list of HTML elements so that screen readers may announce the number of accessible links. Use a wraparound <nav> element to indicate to screen readers and other assistive technology that this is a navigation section.

Furthermore, because pages are likely to have multiple such navigation sections, it is a good idea to provide a descriptive aria-label for the <nav> to reflect its purpose. If the pagination component is used to move between a set of search results, for example, a good label may be aria-label="Search results pages."

```
<nav aria-label="Page navigation example">
 <ul class="pagination">
  <li class="page-item"><a class="page-link"
                         href="#">Previous</a></li>
  <li class="page-item"><a class="page-link"
                         href="#">1</a></li>
  <li class="page-item"><a class="page-link"
                         href="#">2</a></li>
  <li class="page-item"><a class="page-link"
                         href="#">3</a></li>
  <li class="page-item"><a class="page-link"
                         href="#">Next</a></li>
 </ul>
</nav>
```

Working with the Icons

Are you wanting to replace text with an icon or symbol for some pagination links? With aria attributes, be sure to give correct screen reader assistance.

```
<nav aria-label="Page navigation example">
 <ul class="pagination">
  <li class="page-item">
   <a class="page-link" href="#" aria-label="Previous">
    <span aria-hidden="true">&laquo;</span>
   </a>
  </li>
  <li class="page-item"><a class="page-link"
                         href="#">1</a></li>
```

```
 <li class="page-item"><a class="page-link"
                                href="#">2</a></li>
 <li class="page-item"><a class="page-link"
                                href="#">3</a></li>
 <li class="page-item">
  <a class="page-link" href="#" aria-label="Next">
   <span aria-hidden="true">&raquo;</span>
  </a>
 </li>
 </ul>
</nav>
```

Disabled and Active States

Pagination links can be customized for certain situations. For links that appear unclickable, use .disabled, and for the current page, use .active.

While the .disabled class disables the link capability of <a>s by using pointer-events: none, that CSS feature is not yet standardized and does not account for keyboard navigation. As a result, you should always use tabindex="-1" on disabled links and custom JavaScript to completely prevent their functionality.

```
<nav aria-label="...">
 <ul class="pagination">
  <li class="page-item disabled">
   <a class="page-link" href="#" tabindex="-1" aria-
                        disabled="true">Previous</a>
  </li>
  <li class="page-item"><a class="page-link"
                        href="#">1</a></li>
  <li class="page-item active" aria-current="page">
   <a class="page-link" href="#">2</a>
  </li>
  <li class="page-item"><a class="page-link"
                        href="#">3</a></li>
  <li class="page-item">
   <a class="page-link" href="#">Next</a>
  </li>
 </ul>
</nav>
```

To eliminate click functionality and prevent keyboard focus while preserving intended styles, you can alternatively switch out active or disabled anchors with <span>, or omit the anchor in the case of the prev/next arrows.

```
<nav aria-label="...">
 <ul class="pagination">
  <li class="page-item disabled">
   <span class="page-link">Previous</span>
  </li>
  <li class="page-item"><a class="page-link"
                          href="#">1</a></li>
  <li class="page-item active" aria-current="page">
   <span class="page-link">2</span>
  </li>
  <li class="page-item"><a class="page-link"
                          href="#">3</a></li>
  <li class="page-item">
   <a class="page-link" href="#">Next</a>
  </li>
 </ul>
</nav>
```

Sizing

Fancy larger or smaller pagination? Add .pagination-lg or .pagination-sm for additional sizes.

```
<nav aria-label="...">
 <ul class="pagination pagination-lg">
  <li class="page-item active" aria-current="page">
   <span class="page-link">1</span>
  </li>
  <li class="page-item"><a class="page-link"
                             href="#">2</a></li>
  <li class="page-item"><a class="page-link"
                             href="#">3</a></li>
 </ul>
</nav>

<nav aria-label="...">
 <ul class="pagination pagination-sm">
  <li class="page-item active" aria-current="page">
   <span class="page-link">1</span>
  </li>
```

```
  <li class="page-item"><a class="page-link"
                               href="#">2</a></li>
  <li class="page-item"><a class="page-link"
                               href="#">3</a></li>
 </ul>
</nav>
```

Alignment

Change the alignment of pagination components with flexbox utilities.

```
<nav aria-label="Page navigation example">
 <ul class="pagination justify-content-center">
  <li class="page-item disabled">
   <a class="page-link" href="#" tabindex="-1" aria-
                      disabled="true">Previous</a>
  </li>
  <li class="page-item"><a class="page-link"
                               href="#">1</a></li>
  <li class="page-item"><a class="page-link"
                               href="#">2</a></li>
  <li class="page-item"><a class="page-link"
                               href="#">3</a></li>
  <li class="page-item">
   <a class="page-link" href="#">Next</a>
  </li>
 </ul>
</nav>

<nav aria-label="Page navigation example">
 <ul class="pagination justify-content-end">
  <li class="page-item disabled">
   <a class="page-link" href="#" tabindex="-1" aria-
                      disabled="true">Previous</a>
  </li>
  <li class="page-item"><a class="page-link"
                               href="#">1</a></li>
  <li class="page-item"><a class="page-link"
                               href="#">2</a></li>
  <li class="page-item"><a class="page-link"
                               href="#">3</a></li>
  <li class="page-item">
   <a class="page-link" href="#">Next</a>
```

```
    </li>
  </ul>
</nav>
```

Placeholders

To indicate that something is still loading, use loading placeholders for your components or pages.

About

Placeholders may be used to improve the user experience of your app. They're created entirely using HTML and CSS, so no JavaScript is required. Toggle their visibility, however, will necessitate the use of special JavaScript. With our utility classes, you can quickly adjust their look, color, and size.

Example

In the example below, we take a normal card component and reproduce it with placeholders to create a "loading card." The two are of the same size and proportions.

```
<div class="card">
 <img src="..." class="card-img-top" alt="...">

 <div class="card-body">
  <h5 class="card-title">Card title</h5>
  <p class="card-text">Some quick example text to
             build on the card title and make up the
             bulk of the card's content.</p>
  <a href="#" class="btn btn-primary">Go somewhere</a>
 </div>
</div>

<div class="card" aria-hidden="true">
 <img src="..." class="card-img-top" alt="...">
 <div class="card-body">
  <h5 class="card-title placeholder-glow">
   <span class="placeholder col-6"></span>
  </h5>
  <p class="card-text placeholder-glow">
   <span class="placeholder col-7"></span>
   <span class="placeholder col-4"></span>
```

```
  <span class="placeholder col-4"></span>
  <span class="placeholder col-6"></span>
  <span class="placeholder col-8"></span>
  </p>
  <a href="#" tabindex="-1" class="btn btn-primary
             disabled placeholder col-6"></a>
 </div>
</div>
```

How It Works

To set the width, use the .placeholder class and a grid column class (e.g., .col-6) to create placeholders. They may be used to replace text within an element or as a modifier class to an existing component.

To guarantee that the height of .btns is preserved, we apply extra style via::before. As appropriate, you may expand this pattern to additional instances, or add a within the element to reflect the size when the real text is shown in its place.

```
<p aria-hidden="true">
 <span class="placeholder col-6"></span>
</p>
<a href="#" tabindex="-1" class="btn btn-primary
             disabled placeholder col-4" aria-
             hidden="true"></a>
```

Width

Grid column classes, width utilities, and inline styles all can be used to adjust the width.

```
<span class="placeholder col-6"></span>
<span class="placeholder w-75"></span>
<span class="placeholder" style="width: 25%;"></span>
```

Color

The placeholder's default color is currentColor. Custom color or utility class can be used to override this.

```
<span class="placeholder col-12"></span>
<span class="placeholder col-12 bg-primary"></span>
<span class="placeholder col-12 bg-secondary"></span>
<span class="placeholder col-12 bg-success"></span>
```

```
<span class="placeholder col-12 bg-danger"></span>
<span class="placeholder col-12 bg-warning"></span>
<span class="placeholder col-12 bg-info"></span>
<span class="placeholder col-12 bg-light"></span>
<span class="placeholder col-12 bg-dark"></span>
```

Sizing

The size of .placeholders is determined by the parent element's typographic style. Sizing modifiers: .placeholder-LG, .placeholder-sm, or .placeholder-xs can be used to personalize them.

```
<span class="placeholder col-12 placeholder-lg"></span>
<span class="placeholder col-12"></span>
<span class="placeholder col-12 placeholder-sm"></span>
<span class="placeholder col-12 placeholder-xs"></span>
```

Animation

Animate placeholders with .placeholder-glow or .placeholder-wave to better convey the perception of something are *actively* loaded.

```
<p class="placeholder-glow">
 <span class="placeholder col-12"></span>
</p>

<p class="placeholder-wave">
 <span class="placeholder col-12"></span>
</p>
```

This was all about the placeholders of Bootstrap; now, let's jump over the popovers of Bootstrap.

Popovers

Documentation and examples for adding the Bootstrap popovers to any element on-site, similar to those seen in iOS.

Overview

When using the popover plugin, keep the following in mind:

- Popovers rely on the Popper 3rd party library for placement. Popovers will not work until you include popper.min.js before bootstrap.js or use bootstrap.bundle.min.js/bootstrap.bundle.js, which contains Popper!

- The tooltip plugin is required as a requirement for popovers.

- Popovers are opt-in for performance reasons, therefore *you must manually initialize* them.

- A popover will never appear if the title and content values both are zero.

- Specify container: 'body' to avoid rendering difficulties in more complicated components (like our input groups, button groups, etc.).

- Using hidden items to trigger popovers will not function.

- Popovers for .disabled or disabled elements must activate using a wrapper element.

- When triggered by anchors that span over many lines, popovers will be centered between the full width of the anchors. To circumvent this behavior, use .text-nowrap on your <a>s.

- Popovers must be hidden before their associated elements are deleted from the DOM.

- Popovers can be triggered by an element within a shadow DOM.

Example: Enable Popovers Everywhere

One method for initializing all popovers on a page is to choose them using their data-bs-toggle attribute:

```
var popoverTriggerList = [].slice.call(document.qu
    erySelectorAll('[data-bs-toggle="popover"]'))
var popoverList = popoverTriggerList.map(function
    (popoverTriggerEl) {
 return new bootstrap.Popover(popoverTriggerEl)
})
```

Example: Using Container Option

When you have styles on a parent element that conflict with a popover, you should provide a custom container so that the popover's HTML is shown within that element instead.

```
var popover = new bootstrap.Popover(document.querySel
    ector('.example-popover'), {
 container: 'body'
})
```

Example
```
<button type="button" class="btn btn-lg btn-danger"
data-bs-toggle="popover" title="Popover title" data-
bs-content="And here's some amazing content. It's very
engaging. Right?">Click to toggle popover</button>
```

Four Directions

Four options are available: top, right, bottom, and left-aligned. Directions are mirrored when using Bootstrap in RTL.

```
<button type="button" class="btn btn-secondary" data-
  bs-container="body" data-bs-toggle="popover" data-
  bs-placement="top" data-bs-content="Top popover">
 Popover on top
</button>
<button type="button" class="btn btn-secondary" data-
  bs-container="body" data-bs-toggle="popover" data-
  bs-placement="right" data-bs-content="Right
  popover">
 Popover on right
</button>
<button type="button" class="btn btn-secondary" data-
  bs-container="body" data-bs-toggle="popover" data-
  bs-placement="bottom" data-bs-content="Bottom
  popover">
 Popover on bottom
</button>
<button type="button" class="btn btn-secondary" data-
  bs-container="body" data-bs-toggle="popover" data-
  bs-placement="left" data-bs-content="Left popover">
 Popover on left
</button>
```

Dismiss on Next Click

Use the attention trigger to dismiss popovers when the user clicks on an element other than the toggle element.

```
<a tabindex="0" class="btn btn-lg btn-danger"
role="button" data-bs-toggle="popover" data-bs-
trigger="focus" title="Dismissible popover" data-bs-
content="And here's some amazing content. It's very
engaging. Right?">Dismissible popover</a>
```

```
var popover = new bootstrap.Popover(document.querySel
ector('.popover-dismiss'), {
 trigger: 'focus'
})
```

Disable Elements

Elements with the disabled attribute aren't interactive, which means users can't hover over them or click on them to bring up a popover (or tooltip). As a workaround, start the popover from a wrapper <div> or <span>, preferably made keyboard-focusable with tabindex="0."

You may choose data-bs-trigger="hover focus" for disabled popover triggers so that the popover displays as instant visual feedback to your users, since they may not anticipate *click*ing on a disabled element.

```
<span class="d-inline-block" tabindex="0" data-bs-
      toggle="popover" data-bs-trigger="hover focus"
      data-bs-content="Disabled popover">
 <button class="btn btn-primary" type="button"
        disabled>Disabled button</button>
</span>
```

Progress

Documentation and demonstrations for creating custom Bootstrap progress bars with stacked bars, animated background, and text labels.

How It Works

Progress components are made up of two HTML elements, CSS to control the width, and a few attributes. We don't utilize the HTML5 <progress> element, which allows you to build progress bars, animate them, and overlay text labels on top of them.

- We use .progress as a wrapper to indicate the progress bar's maximum value.

- We utilize the inner .progress-bar to show how far we've come.

- To set the width of the .progress-bar, use an inline style, utility class, or custom CSS.

- To be accessible, the .progress-bar must also have certain role and aria properties.

When put all of this together, you get the following examples.

```
<div class="progress">
 <div class="progress-bar" role="progressbar" aria-
     valuenow="0" aria-valuemin="0" aria-
     valuemax="100"></div>
</div>
<div class="progress">
 <div class="progress-bar" role="progressbar"
     style="width: 25%" aria-valuenow="25" aria-
     valuemin="0" aria-valuemax="100"></div>
</div>
<div class="progress">
 <div class="progress-bar" role="progressbar"
     style="width: 50%" aria-valuenow="50" aria-
     valuemin="0" aria-valuemax="100"></div>
</div>
<div class="progress">
 <div class="progress-bar" role="progressbar"
     style="width: 75%" aria-valuenow="75" aria-
     valuemin="0" aria-valuemax="100"></div>
</div>
<div class="progress">
 <div class="progress-bar" role="progressbar"
     style="width: 100%" aria-valuenow="100" aria-
     valuemin="0" aria-valuemax="100"></div>
</div>
```

Bootstrap includes a number of tools for adjusting width. Depending on your requirements, these may aid in swiftly configuring progress.

```
<div class="progress">
 <div class="progress-bar w-75" role="progressbar"
     aria-valuenow="75" aria-valuemin="0" aria-
     valuemax="90"></div>
</div>
```

Labels

Put text within the .progress-bar tag to add labels to your progress bars.

```
<div class="progress">
 <div class="progress-bar" role="progressbar"
     style="width: 25%;" aria-valuenow="25" aria-
     valuemin="0" aria-valuemax="100">25%</div>
</div>
```

Height

We simply specify a height value on the .progress, so if you modify that number, the inner .progress-bar will resize automatically.

```
<div class="progress" style="height: 1px;">
 <div class="progress-bar" role="progressbar"
     style="width: 25%;" aria-valuenow="25" aria-
     valuemin="0" aria-valuemax="100"></div>
</div>
<div class="progress" style="height: 20px;">
 <div class="progress-bar" role="progressbar"
     style="width: 26%;" aria-valuenow="26" aria-
     valuemin="0" aria-valuemax="100"></div>
</div>
```

Backgrounds

Background utility classes can be used to improve the look of individual progress bars.

```
<div class="progress">
 <div class="progress-bar bg-success"
     role="progressbar" style="width: 26%" aria-
     valuenow="26" aria-valuemin="0" aria-
     valuemax="90"></div>
</div>
<div class="progress">
 <div class="progress-bar bg-info" role="progressbar"
     style="width: 51%" aria-valuenow="51" aria-
     valuemin="0" aria-valuemax="90"></div>
</div>
<div class="progress">
 <div class="progress-bar bg-warning"
     role="progressbar" style="width: 78%" aria-
     valuenow="78" aria-valuemin="0" aria-
     valuemax="90"></div>
</div>
<div class="progress">
 <div class="progress-bar bg-danger"
     role="progressbar" style="width: 90%" aria-
     valuenow="90" aria-valuemin="0" aria-
     valuemax="90"></div>
</div>
```

Multiple Bars

If necessary, include additional progress bars in a progress component.

```
<div class="progress">
 <div class="progress-bar" role="progressbar"
     style="width: 16%" aria-valuenow="16" aria-
     valuemin="0" aria-valuemax="90"></div>
 <div class="progress-bar bg-success"
     role="progressbar" style="width: 40%" aria-
     valuenow="40" aria-valuemin="0" aria-
     valuemax="90"></div>
 <div class="progress-bar bg-info" role="progressbar"
     style="width: 25%" aria-valuenow="25" aria-
     valuemin="0" aria-valuemax="90"></div>
</div>
```

Stripped

To create a stripe using CSS gradient over the progress bar's background color, add .progress-bar-striped to any .progress-bar.

```
<div class="progress">
 <div class="progress-bar progress-bar-striped"
     role="progressbar" style="width: 12%" aria-
     valuenow="10" aria-valuemin="0" aria-
     valuemax="90"></div>
</div>
<div class="progress">
 <div class="progress-bar progress-bar-striped
     bg-success" role="progressbar" style="width:
     28%" aria-valuenow="25" aria-valuemin="0" aria-
     valuemax="90"></div>
</div>
<div class="progress">
 <div class="progress-bar progress-bar-striped
     bg-info" role="progressbar" style="width: 60%"
     aria-valuenow="60" aria-valuemin="0" aria-
     valuemax="90"></div>
</div>
<div class="progress">
 <div class="progress-bar progress-bar-striped
     bg-warning" role="progressbar" style="width:
```

```
      76%" aria-valuenow="76" aria-valuemin="0" aria-
      valuemax="90"></div>
</div>
<div class="progress">
 <div class="progress-bar progress-bar-striped
      bg-danger" role="progressbar" style="width:
      90%" aria-valuenow="90" aria-valuemin="0" aria-
      valuemax="90"></div>
</div>
```

Animated Strips

The striped gradient may be animated as well. To animate the stripes from right to left, add .progress-bar-animated to .progress-bar.

```
<div class="progress">
 <div class="progress-bar progress-bar-striped
      progress-bar-animated" role="progressbar" aria-
      valuenow="76" aria-valuemin="0" aria-
      valuemax="90" style="width: 76%"></div>
</div>
```

Scrollspy

To identify which link is active in the viewport, automatically change Bootstrap navigation or list group components based on scroll position.

How It Works

- It must be applied to a Bootstrap navigation component or list group.

- Scrollspy requires position: relative; on the element being spied on, which is generally the <body>.

- Anchors (<a>) must be present and must point to a piece with that id.

When correctly implemented, your nav or list group will change accordingly, transferring the .active class from one item to the next depending on their connected targets.

Example in navbar

Scroll down to the area below the navbar to see the active class change. The dropdown items will also be highlighted.

```
<nav id="navbar-example2" class="navbar navbar-light
bg-light px-3">
 <a class="navbar-brand" href="#">Navbar</a>
 <ul class="nav nav-pills">
  <li class="nav-item">
   <a class="nav-link" href="#scrollspyHeading1">Firs
         t</a>
  </li>
  <li class="nav-item">
   <a class="nav-link" href="#scrollspyHeading2">Seco
         nd</a>
  </li>
  <li class="nav-item dropdown">
   <a class="nav-link dropdown-toggle" data-bs-
         toggle="dropdown" href="#" role="button"
         aria-expanded="false">Dropdown</a>
   <ul class="dropdown-menu">
    <li><a class="dropdown-item" href="#scrollspyHead
         ing3">Third</a></li>
    <li><a class="dropdown-item" href="#scrollspyHead
         ing4">Fourth</a></li>
    <li><hr class="dropdown-divider"></li>
    <li><a class="dropdown-item" href="#scrollspyHead
         ing5">Fifth</a></li>
   </ul>
  </li>
 </ul>
</nav>
<div data-bs-spy="scroll" data-bs-target="#navbar-
     example2" data-bs-offset="0" class="scrollspy-
     example" tabindex="0">
 <h4 id="scrollspyHeading1">First heading</h4>
 <p>...</p>
 <h4 id="scrollspyHeading2">Second heading</h4>
 <p>...</p>
 <h4 id="scrollspyHeading3">Third heading</h4>
 <p>...</p>
 <h4 id="scrollspyHeading4">Fourth heading</h4>
 <p>...</p>
 <h4 id="scrollspyHeading5">Fifth heading</h4>
 <p>...</p>
</div>
```

Example with Nested nav

Scrollspy also supports nested .navs. If a nested .nav is .active, its parents will be .active as well. Watch the active class change as you scroll the area adjacent to the navbar:

```
<nav id="navbar-example3" class="navbar navbar-light
     bg-light flex-column align-items-stretch p-3">
 <a class="navbar-brand" href="#">Navbar</a>
 <nav class="nav nav-pills flex-column">
  <a class="nav-link" href="#item-1">Item 1</a>
  <nav class="nav nav-pills flex-column">
   <a class="nav-link ms-3 my-1" href="#item-1-
             1">Item 1-1</a>
   <a class="nav-link ms-3 my-1" href="#item-1-
             2">Item 1-2</a>
  </nav>
  <a class="nav-link" href="#item-2">Item 2</a>
  <a class="nav-link" href="#item-3">Item 3</a>
  <nav class="nav nav-pills flex-column">
   <a class="nav-link ms-3 my-1" href="#item-3-
             1">Item 3-1</a>
   <a class="nav-link ms-3 my-1" href="#item-3-
             2">Item 3-2</a>
  </nav>
 </nav>
</nav>

<div data-bs-spy="scroll" data-bs-target="#navbar-
     example3" data-bs-offset="0" tabindex="0">
 <h4 id="item-1">Item 1</h4>
 <p>...</p>
 <h5 id="item-1-1">Item 1-1</h5>
 <p>...</p>
 <h5 id="item-1-2">Item 1-2</h5>
 <p>...</p>
 <h4 id="item-2">Item 2</h4>
 <p>...</p>
 <h4 id="item-3">Item 3</h4>
 <p>...</p>
 <h5 id="item-3-1">Item 3-1</h5>
 <p>...</p>
```

```
  <h5 id="item-3-2">Item 3-2</h5>
  <p>...</p>
</div>
```

Example with list-group

Scrollspy also supports .list-groups. Watch the active class change as you scroll the area next to the list group.

```
<div id="list-example" class="list-group">
  <a class="list-group-item list-group-item-action"
         href="#list-item-1">Item 1</a>
  <a class="list-group-item list-group-item-action"
         href="#list-item-2">Item 2</a>
  <a class="list-group-item list-group-item-action"
         href="#list-item-3">Item 3</a>
  <a class="list-group-item list-group-item-action"
         href="#list-item-4">Item 4</a>
</div>
<div data-bs-spy="scroll" data-bs-target="#list-
example" data-bs-offset="0" class="scrollspy-example"
tabindex="0">
  <h4 id="list-item-1">Item 1</h4>
  <p>...</p>
  <h4 id="list-item-2">Item 2</h4>
  <p>...</p>
  <h4 id="list-item-3">Item 3</h4>
  <p>...</p>
  <h4 id="list-item-4">Item 4</h4>
  <p>...</p>
</div>
```

Spinners

Indicate loading state of component or page with Bootstrap spinners, built entirely with HTML, CSS, and no JavaScript.

About

Bootstrap "spinners" may be used in your applications to display the loading state. They're created entirely using HTML and CSS, so no JavaScript is required. Toggle their visibility, however, will necessitate the use of special JavaScript. With our superb utility classes, you can simply adjust their style, alignment, and size.

For accessibility purposes, each loader here contains role="status" and a nested <span class="visually-hidden">Loading...</span>.

Border Spinner

Use border spinners for a lightweight loading indicator.

```
<div class="spinner-border" role="status">
 <span class="visually-hidden">Loading...</span>
</div>
```

Colors

The border spinner's border color is determined by currentColor, which means you may change it using text color tools. On the regular spinner, you may choose any of our text color tools.

```
<div class="spinner-border text-primary" role="status">
 <span class="visually-hidden">Loading...</span>
</div>
<div class="spinner-border text-secondary"
          role="status">
 <span class="visually-hidden">Loading...</span>
</div>
<div class="spinner-border text-success"
          role="status">
 <span class="visually-hidden">Loading...</span>
</div>
<div class="spinner-border text-danger"
          role="status">
 <span class="visually-hidden">Loading...</span>
</div>
<div class="spinner-border text-warning"
          role="status">
 <span class="visually-hidden">Loading...</span>
</div>
<div class="spinner-border text-info" role="status">
 <span class="visually-hidden">Loading...</span>
</div>
<div class="spinner-border text-light" role="status">
 <span class="visually-hidden">Loading...</span>
</div>
```

```
<div class="spinner-border text-dark" role="status">
 <span class="visually-hidden">Loading...</span>
</div>
```

Growing Spinner

If you don't want to use a border spinner, use a grow spinner. While it does not literally spin, it does expand on a regular schedule!

```
<div class="spinner-grow" role="status">
 <span class="visually-hidden">Loading...</span>
</div>
```

This spinner, once again, is designed with currentColor, so you can quickly modify its appearance with text color tools. It is highlighted in blue here, along with the supported versions.

```
<div class="spinner-grow text-primary" role="status">
 <span class="visually-hidden">Loading...</span>
</div>
<div class="spinner-grow text-secondary"
            role="status">
 <span class="visually-hidden">Loading...</span>
</div>
<div class="spinner-grow text-success" role="status">
 <span class="visually-hidden">Loading...</span>
</div>
<div class="spinner-grow text-danger" role="status">
 <span class="visually-hidden">Loading...</span>
</div>
<div class="spinner-grow text-warning" role="status">
 <span class="visually-hidden">Loading...</span>
</div>
<div class="spinner-grow text-info" role="status">
 <span class="visually-hidden">Loading...</span>
</div>
<div class="spinner-grow text-light" role="status">
 <span class="visually-hidden">Loading...</span>
</div>
<div class="spinner-grow text-dark" role="status">
 <span class="visually-hidden">Loading...</span>
</div>
```

Alignment

Bootstrap spinners are created with rems, currentColor, and display: inline-flex. As a result, they can be readily resized, recolored, and fast aligned.

Margin

For simple spacing, use margin utilities such as .m-5.

```
<div class="spinner-border m-5" role="status">
 <span class="visually-hidden">Loading...</span>
</div>
```

Placement

To set spinners exactly where you need them in any circumstance, use flexbox utilities, float utilities, or text alignment tools.

Flex

```
<div class="d-flex justify-content-center">
 <div class="spinner-border" role="status">
  <span class="visually-hidden">Loading...</span>
 </div>
</div>

<div class="d-flex align-items-center">
 <strong>Loading...</strong>
 <div class="spinner-border ms-auto" role="status"
            aria-hidden="true"></div>
</div>
```

Floats

```
<div class="clearfix">
 <div class="spinner-border float-end" role="status">
  <span class="visually-hidden">Loading...</span>
 </div>
</div>
```

Text Aligns

```
<div class="text-center">
 <div class="spinner-border" role="status">
```

```
   <span class="visually-hidden">Loading...</span>
  </div>
</div>
```

Size

Add .spinner-border-sm and .spinner-grow-sm to make a more petite spinner that can quickly be used within other components.

```
<div class="spinner-border spinner-border-sm"
            role="status">
 <span class="visually-hidden">Loading...</span>
</div>
<div class="spinner-grow spinner-grow-sm"
            role="status">
 <span class="visually-hidden">Loading...</span>
</div>
```

Alter the dimensions using custom CSS or inline styles as needed.

```
<div class="spinner-border" style="width: 3rem;
            height: 3rem;" role="status">
 <span class="visually-hidden">Loading...</span>
</div>
<div class="spinner-grow" style="width: 3rem; height:
            3rem;" role="status">
 <span class="visually-hidden">Loading...</span>
</div>
```

Buttons

To signify that an action is actively being processed or taking place, use spinners within buttons. You may easily remove the text from the spinner element and replace it with button text as desired.

```
<button class="btn btn-primary" type="button"
               disabled>
 <span class="spinner-border spinner-border-sm"
       role="status" aria-hidden="true"></span>
 <span class="visually-hidden">Loading...</span>
</button>
<button class="btn btn-primary" type="button"
         disabled>
```

```
<span class="spinner-border spinner-border-sm"
      role="status" aria-hidden="true"></span>
Loading...
</button>

<button class="btn btn-primary" type="button"
        disabled>
 <span class="spinner-grow spinner-grow-sm"
      role="status" aria-hidden="true"></span>
 <span class="visually-hidden">Loading...</span>
</button>
<button class="btn btn-primary" type="button"
        disabled>
 <span class="spinner-grow spinner-grow-sm"
      role="status" aria-hidden="true"></span>
Loading...
</button>
```

Toasts

Push alerts with a toast, a lightweight and readily customized alert message, to your visitors.

Toasts are lightweight alerts meant to emulate the push notifications used by mobile and desktop operating systems. Because they're constructed with flexbox, they're simple to align and place.

Overview

Keep in mind the following while using the toast plugin:

- Toasts are opt-in for performance reasons, thus you must manually initialize them.

- If you don't provide autohide: false, toasts will hide themselves.

Examples

Basic

We advocate a header and body to encourage long and predictable toasts. Toast headers utilize display: flex, which allows for simple content alignment using our margin and flexbox utilities.

Toasts may be as versatile as you need them to be and need very little markup. We require at least one element to hold your "toasted" material and strongly recommend a dismiss button.

```
<div class="toast" role="alert" aria-live="assertive"
          aria-atomic="true">
 <div class="toast-header">
  <img src="..." class="rounded me-2" alt="...">
  <strong class="me-auto">Bootstrap</strong>
  <small>11 mins ago</small>
  <button type="button" class="btn-close" data-bs-
    dismiss="toast" aria-label="Close"></button>
 </div>
 <div class="toast-body">
  Hello, world! This is a toast message.
 </div>
</div>
```

Live

Click the button below to reveal a toast (located in the lower right corner with our utilities) that has been concealed by default with .hide.

```
<button type="button" class="btn btn-primary"
        id="liveToastBtn">Show live toast</button>

<div class="position-fixed bottom-0 end-0 p-3"
          style="z-index: 11">
 <div id="liveToast" class="toast hide" role="alert"
         aria-live="assertive" aria-atomic="true">
  <div class="toast-header">
   <img src="..." class="rounded me-2" alt="...">
   <strong class="me-auto">Bootstrap</strong>
   <small>11 mins ago</small>
   <button type="button" class="btn-close" data-bs-
     dismiss="toast" aria-label="Close"></button>
  </div>
  <div class="toast-body">
   Hello, world! This is a toast message.
  </div>
 </div>
</div>
```

Translucent

To blend in with what's beneath them, toasts are slightly transparent.

```
<div class="toast" role="alert" aria-live="assertive"
          aria-atomic="true">
```

```
<div class="toast-header">
 <img src="..." class="rounded me-2" alt="...">
 <strong class="me-auto">Bootstrap</strong>
 <small class="text-muted">11 mins ago</small>
 <button type="button" class="btn-close" data-bs-
        dismiss="toast" aria-label="Close"></button>
</div>
<div class="toast-body">
 Hello, world! This is a toast message.
</div>
</div>
```

Stacking

Toasts may stack by wrapping them in a toast container and vertically spacing them.

```
<div class="toast-container">
 <div class="toast" role="alert" aria-live="assertive"
     aria-atomic="true">
  <div class="toast-header">
   <img src="..." class="rounded me-2" alt="...">
   <strong class="me-auto">Bootstrap</strong>
   <small class="text-muted">just now</small>
   <button type="button" class="btn-close" data-bs-
     dismiss="toast" aria-label="Close"></button>
  </div>
  <div class="toast-body">
   See? Just like this.
  </div>
 </div>

 <div class="toast" role="alert" aria-live="assertive"
     aria-atomic="true">
  <div class="toast-header">
   <img src="..." class="rounded me-2" alt="...">
   <strong class="me-auto">Bootstrap</strong>
   <small class="text-muted">2 seconds ago</small>
   <button type="button" class="btn-close" data-bs-
     dismiss="toast" aria-label="Close"></button>
  </div>
  <div class="toast-body">
```

```
   Heads up, toasts will stack automatically
  </div>
 </div>
</div>
```

Custom Content

Remove sub-components, alter them using tools, or add own markup to personalize your toasts. By removing the default, we've made a more straightforward toast. toast-header, adding a custom hidden icon from Bootstrap Icons, and adjusting the layout using flexbox utilities.

```
<div class="toast align-items-center" role="alert"
     aria-live="assertive" aria-atomic="true">
 <div class="d-flex">
  <div class="toast-body">
  Hello, world! This is a toast message.
  </div>
  <button type="button" class="btn-close me-2 m-auto"
    data-bs-dismiss="toast" aria-label="Close"></
    button>
 </div>
</div>
```

Toasts can also enhance with additional controls and components.

```
<div class="toast" role="alert" aria-live="assertive"
     aria-atomic="true">
 <div class="toast-body">
  Hello, world! This is a toast message.
  <div class="mt-2 pt-2 border-top">
   <button type="button" class="btn btn-primary btn-
                sm">Take action</button>
   <button type="button" class="btn btn-secondary
    btn-sm" data-bs-dismiss="toast">Close</button>
  </div>
 </div>
</div>
```

Color Schemes

Using our color and background tools, you may generate alternative color schemes based on the example above. In this case, we've added .bg-primary and .text-white to the .toast, followed by .btn-close-white to our close button. With.border-0, we eliminate the default border for a clean edge.

```
<div class="toast align-items-center text-white
    bg-primary border-0" role="alert" aria-
    live="assertive" aria-atomic="true">
 <div class="d-flex">
  <div class="toast-body">
   Hello, world! This is a toast message.
  </div>
  <button type="button" class="btn-close btn-close-
    white me-2 m-auto" data-bs-dismiss="toast" aria-
    label="Close"></button>
 </div>
</div>
```

Placement

As needed, add toasts using custom CSS. The top right, as well as the upper middle, are frequently utilized for alerts. If you're only going to display one toast at a time, the placement styles are correct on the .toast.

```
<form>
 <div class="mb-3">
  <label for="selectToastPlacement">Toast placement</
            label>
  <select class="form-select mt-2"
          id="selectToastPlacement">
   <option value="" selected>Select a position...</
                              option>
   <option value="top-0 start-0">Top left</option>
   <option value="top-0 start-50 translate-middle-
           x">Top center</option>
   <option value="top-0 end-0">Top right</option>
   <option value="top-50 start-0 translate-middle-
           y">Middle left</option>
   <option value="top-50 start-50 translate-
           middle">Middle center</option>
   <option value="top-50 end-0 translate-middle-
           y">Middle right</option>
   <option value="bottom-0 start-0">Bottom left</
           option>
```

```
      <option value="bottom-0 start-50 translate-middle-
            x">Bottom center</option>
      <option value="bottom-0 end-0">Bottom right</
            option>
   </select>
 </div>
</form>
<div aria-live="polite" aria-atomic="true" class="bg-
      dark position-relative bd-example-toasts">
  <div class="toast-container position-absolute p-3"
        id="toastPlacement">
   <div class="toast">
    <div class="toast-header">
     <img src="..." class="rounded me-2" alt="...">
     <strong class="me-auto">Bootstrap</strong>
     <small>11 mins ago</small>
    </div>
    <div class="toast-body">
     Hello, world! This is a toast message.
    </div>
   </div>
  </div>
</div>
```

Consider utilizing a wrapping element for systems that create a lot of alerts so that they can be stacked easily.

```
<div aria-live="polite" aria-atomic="true"
      class="position-relative">
 <!-- Position it: -->
 <!-- - `.toast-container` for the spacing between
          toasts -->
 <!-- - `.position-absolute`, `top-0` & `end-0` to
    position the toasts in the upper right corner -->
 <!-- - `.p-3` to prevent toasts from sticking to the
    edge of the container        -->
 <div class="toast-container position-absolute top-0
      end-0 p-3">

  <!-- Then put toasts within -->
  <div class="toast" role="alert" aria-
        live="assertive" aria-atomic="true">
   <div class="toast-header">
    <img src="..." class="rounded me-2" alt="...">
```

```
    <strong class="me-auto">Bootstrap</strong>
    <small class="text-muted">just now</small>
    <button type="button" class="btn-close" data-bs-
       dismiss="toast" aria-label="Close"></button>
  </div>
  <div class="toast-body">
   See? Just like this.
  </div>
 </div>

 <div class="toast" role="alert" aria-
     live="assertive" aria-atomic="true">
  <div class="toast-header">
   <img src="..." class="rounded me-2" alt="...">
   <strong class="me-auto">Bootstrap</strong>
   <small class="text-muted">2 seconds ago</small>
   <button type="button" class="btn-close" data-bs-
      dismiss="toast" aria-label="Close"></button>
  </div>
  <div class="toast-body">
   Heads up, toasts will stack automatically
  </div>
 </div>
 </div>
</div>
```

Flexbox utilities may also be used to position toasts
horizontally and vertically.

```
<!-- Flexbox container for the aligning toasts -->
<div aria-live="polite" aria-atomic="true" class="d-
    flex justify-content-center align-items-center
    w-100">

 <!-- Then put toasts within -->
 <div class="toast" role="alert" aria-live="assertive"
     aria-atomic="true">
  <div class="toast-header">
   <img src="..." class="rounded me-2" alt="...">
   <strong class="me-auto">Bootstrap</strong>
   <small>11 mins ago</small>
   <button type="button" class="btn-close" data-bs-
      dismiss="toast" aria-label="Close"></button>
  </div>
```

```
<div class="toast-body">
 Hello, world! This is a toast message.
 </div>
 </div>
</div>
```

Accessibility

Because toasts are intended to be minor disruptions to your visitors or users, you should wrap them in an aria-live area to aid individuals who use screen readers and other assistive technology. Screen readers automatically notify changes to live regions without needing to relocate the user's focus or otherwise disrupt the user. Include aria-atomic="true" as well to guarantee that the full toast is always announced as a single unit, rather than merely stating what changed. If the information required is critical to the workflow, like as a list of problems in a form, then use the alert component rather than toast.

Note that the live region must be present in the markup *before* the toast is generated or updated. If you produce both dynamically and inject them into the website at the same time, assistive technologies are unlikely to notice.

You must also adjust the role and aria-live level based on the material. If the message is critical, such as an error, use the role="alert" aria-live="assertive" attributes; otherwise, use the role="status" aria-live="polite" attributes.

Be careful to adjust the delay timeout when the material you're presenting changes so that viewers have ample time to read the toast.

```
<div class="toast" role="alert" aria-live="polite"
     aria-atomic="true" data-bs-delay="10000">
 <div role="alert" aria-live="assertive" aria-
     atomic="true">...</div>
</div>
```

When using autohide: false, you must add a close button to allow users to dismiss the toast.

```
<div role="alert" aria-live="assertive" aria-atomic=
     "true" class="toast" data-bs-autohide="false">
 <div class="toast-header">
  <img src="..." class="rounded me-2" alt="...">
```

```
<strong class="me-auto">Bootstrap</strong>
<small>11 mins ago</small>
<button type="button" class="btn-close" data-bs-
  dismiss="toast" aria-label="Close"></button>
</div>
<div class="toast-body">
 Hello, world! This is a toast message.
 </div>
</div>
```

While it is technically feasible to include focusable/actionable controls in your toast (such as buttons or links), you should avoid doing so for auto-hiding toasts. Even if you set a long delay timeout for the toast, keyboard and assistive technology users may struggle to achieve it in time to take action (since toasts do not gain focus when presented). If you must include more controls, we propose using a toast with auto hide: false.

Tooltips

Documentation and examples for customizing Bootstrap tooltips using CSS and JavaScript, including animations and data-bs-attributes for local title storage.

Overview

When using the tooltip plugin, keep the following in mind:

- Popper, a third-party package, is used to place tooltips. For tooltips to work, you must include popper.min.js before bootstrap.js or use bootstrap.bundle.min.js/bootstrap.bundle.js, which incorporates Popper.

- Tooltips are opt-in for performance reasons, therefore you must manually activate them.

- Tooltips with titles of zero length are never shown.

- To avoid rendering issues with more complicated components, provide container: 'body' (like our input groups, button groups, etc.).

- Tooltips will not trigger on hidden components.

- Tooltips for .disabled or disabled elements must activate through a wrapper element.

- Tooltips will be positioned when triggered by hyperlinks that span several lines. To circumvent this behavior, use white-space: nowrap; on your a>s.

- Before their related elements are deleted from the DOM, tooltips must be disabled.

- Tooltips can be activated by an element within a shadow DOM.

Example: Enable Tooltips Everywhere

One method for initializing all tooltips on a page is to select them using their data-bs-toggle attribute:

```
var tooltipTriggerList = [].slice.call(document.qu
    erySelectorAll('[data-bs-toggle="tooltip"]'))
var tooltipList = tooltipTriggerList.map(function
    (tooltipTriggerEl) {
 return new bootstrap.Tooltip(tooltipTriggerEl)
})
```

Example

Hover over the links below to reveal tooltips:

Hover over the buttons below to view the four tooltip directions: top, right, bottom, and left. When using Bootstrap in RTL, directions are mirrored.

```
<button type="button" class="btn btn-secondary" data-
        bs-toggle="tooltip" data-bs-placement="top"
        title="Tooltip on top">
 Tooltip on top
</button>
<button type="button" class="btn btn-secondary" data-
        bs-toggle="tooltip" data-bs-placement="right"
        title="Tooltip on right">
 Tooltip on right
</button>
<button type="button" class="btn btn-secondary" data-
        bs-toggle="tooltip" data-bs-placement="bottom"
        title="Tooltip on bottom">
 Tooltip on bottom
```

```
</button>
<button type="button" class="btn btn-secondary" data-
        bs-toggle="tooltip" data-bs-placement="left"
        title="Tooltip on left">
 Tooltip on left
</button>
```

And with custom HTML added:

```
<button type="button" class="btn btn-secondary" data-
bs-toggle="tooltip" data-bs-html="true"
title="<em>Tooltip</em> with HTML">
 Tooltip with HTML
</button>
```

This was all about the components that Bootstrap offers. Now after a very long section of Bootstrap components, finally it is time for CSS variables or CSS custom properties. Here we will learn what CSS variables are and how it is used.

CSS VARIABLES

To insert value of a CSS variable, use the var() function.

CSS variables provide DOM access, allowing you to create variables with local or global scope, update variables using JavaScript, and change variables depending on media queries.

An excellent way to use CSS variables is when it comes to the colors of your design. Instead of copying and pasting same colors repeatedly, you can place them in variables.

CSS variables are entities that CSS writers establish that have specified values that may be reused across a document. They are specified with custom property notation (for example, --main-color: black;) and retrieved with the var() method (for example, color: var(--main-color);).

Complex websites use a lot of CSS, frequently with a lot of repeat values. For example, if the same color is used in hundreds of places, it will necessitate a global search and replacement if that color needs to be changed. Custom properties enable a value to be stored in one location and then referenced in several other locations. Semantic identifiers are another advantage. For example, --main-text-color is more understandable than #00ff00, especially if the same color is used in other situations.

Custom properties are affected by the cascade and inherit their parent's value.

Basic Usage

A custom property is declared by using a custom property name that starts with a double hyphen (--) and a property value that can be any valid CSS value. This, like any other property, is written within a ruleset, as seen below:

```
element {
  --main-bg-color: brown;
}
```

It should be noted that the ruleset's selector determines the scope in which the custom property can be utilized. A typical best practice is to define custom properties on the root pseudo-class so that they may be used universally across your HTML document:

```
: root {
  --main-bg-color: brown;
}
```

Inheritance of the Custom Properties

Custom properties can be inherited. This implies that if a custom property on a given element has no value, the value of its parent is utilized. Consider the following HTML:

```
<div class="one">
 <div class="two">
  <div class="three"></div>
  <div class="four"></div>
 </div>
</div>
```

with the following CSS:
```
.two {
  --test: 10px;
}
```

```
.three {
 --test: 2em;
}
```

In this case, results of var(--test) are as follows:

- For the class="two" element: 10px

- For the class="three" element: 2em

- For the class="four" element: 10px (inherited from its parent)

- For the class="one" element: *invalid value*, which is the default value of any custom property

Remember that these are custom attributes, not variables like those found in other programming languages. The value is computed just when it is required and is not saved for further use in other rules. For example, you cannot set a property for an element and expect it to be retrieved in the direction of a sibling's descendant. The property, like any other CSS property, is only charged for the matching selector and its descendants.

Validity and Values

The traditional CSS idea of validity, which is related to each property, is not particularly useful when dealing with custom properties. Because the browser does not know where the values of the custom attributes will be utilized when they are processed, it must accept virtually all values as legitimate.

Unfortunately, these legitimate values can be utilized in contexts where they may not make sense using the var() functional notation. Properties and custom variables can result in incorrect CSS statements, which can lead to the new valid not*ion at calculated time.*

The Traditional Way

The following example demonstrates the old method of defining some colors in a style sheet (by specifying the colors to be used for each individual element):

```
body { background-color: #1e90ff; }
h2 { border-bottom: 2px solid #1e90ff; }
       .container {
```

```
    color: #1e90ff;
    background-color: #ffffff;
    padding: 15px;
  }
  button {
    background-color: #ffffff;
    color: #1e90ff;
    border: 1px solid #1e90ff;
    padding: 5px;
  }
```

Syntax of the var() Function

The var() function is used to insert value of CSS variable.

The syntax of the var() function is as follows:

var(--*name, value*)

Value	Description
Name	Required. The variable name (must start with the two dashes)
Value	Optional. The fallback value (used if variable is not found)

How var() Works

First of all, CSS variables can be global or local in scope.

Global variables may be used across the document, but local variables can only be used by the selector where they are defined.

Declare a variable with global scope within the root selector. The root selection matches the root element of the document.

Declare a variable with local scope inside the selector that will utilize it.

The following example is equal to the model above, but we use the var() function here.

To begin with, we define two global variables (--blue and --white). Then, later in the style sheet, we use the var() method to enter the values of the variables.

Example

```
:root {
  --blue: #1e90ff;
  --white: #ffffff;
```

```
}
body { background-color: var(--blue); }

h2 { border-bottom: 2px solid var(--blue); }
.container {
 color: var(--blue);
 background-color: var(--white);
 padding: 15px;
}
button {
 background-color: var(--white);
 color: var(--blue);
 border: 1px solid var(--blue);
 padding: 5px;
}
```

Advantages of Using var()

- Makes code easier to read (more understandable)

- Makes it much easier to change color values

To change blue and white color to a softer blue and white, you need to change the two variable values.

Example

```
:root {
 --blue: #6495ed;
 --white: #faf0e6;
}
body { background-color: var(--blue); }
h2 { border-bottom: 2px solid var(--blue); }
.container {
 color: var(--blue);
 background-color: var(--white);
 padding: 15px;
}
button {
 background-color: var(--white);
 color: var(--blue);
 border: 1px solid var(--blue);
```

```
padding: 5px;
```

Browser Support

The numbers in the table specify first browser version that fully supports var() function.

Function	Chrome	Microsoft Edge	Firefox	Safari	Opera
Var()	49.0	15.0	31.0	9.1	36.0

CSS var() Function

So here I complete another chapter after learning CSS variables; after knowing this much about Bootstrap, it is essential to optimize our code for better performance and save more space. Our next chapter is about optimizing our CSS code for advantages like better performance, more space, etc.

Property	Description
Var()	Inserts the value of CSS variable

OPTIMIZATION

We've come a long way, and we can now design a beautiful, responsive website with Bootstrap. The final element of the jigsaw is figuring out how to optimize our inventions so that they both look attractive and work properly.

In this chapter, you will learn how to optimize a Bootstrap-built website (or, indeed, any other front-end framework). We'll be focusing on CSS and JavaScript minification, as well as simplifying the Bootstrap default package. We will try to grasp Bootstrap's limits and explain some of the main difficulties of utilizing it.

Visitors are now accustomed to the immediacy and reactivity associated with native apps. They anticipate that a web page will load in 1000 ms. If it takes much longer, they will most likely abandon the site.

Search engines have undoubtedly caught on to this trend, and they have contributed to it in a variety of ways. For a long time, Google has used page speed as a ranking factor for websites in desktop searches. Google has indicated that, beginning in July 2018, mobile searches will be extremely critical for achieving high places in its result list.

Bootstrap has frequently been chastised for adding needless fat to websites, so if you use this popular front-end UI framework in your project, pay close attention to page weight and page performance.

In this section, I'll walk you through three front-end optimization actions you can take to guarantee your Bootstrap-based website renders quickly and efficiently.

Only Download Bootstrap Package You Need

If you decide to use the Bootstrap precompiled download package, you should think carefully about which components of the library you require.

The download folder contains the complete CSS library (bootstrap.css and bootstrap.min.css) and the JavaScript components library with all its dependencies except for jQuery (bootstrap.bundle.js and bootstrap.bundle.min.js), as well as several stand-alone CSS files containing the code necessary for specific parts of this popular UI kit.

Bootstrap-reboot.min.css is an amazing CSS reset for your project. If all you need is a flexible and simple grid system, bootstrap-grid.min.css is the way to go. It is not necessary to download the whole framework. If, on the other hand, you know you'll utilize everything in the library, at the very least include the minified version.

Likewise, with the JavaScript code. If you know your project will not feature dropdowns, popovers, or tooltips, use bootstrap.min.js rather than bootstrap.bundle.min.js since Popper.js will not be required.

Select the Source Instead of the Precompiled Download Package

Even if the current version of Bootstrap allows you to decide which portions of it to include in your project, the precompiled files may still contain information that you do not require. Browsers must still download and execute unneeded code, which has an impact on page speed, particularly on slow network connections.

It would be a better idea to obtain the Bootstrap source code because:

- You will be able to include precisely the components you need in your project.

- Customizing any library part becomes cleaner and more efficient, with no need to override styles overpower.

- The stylesheets that end up in production are usually leaner.

Make Use of a Proven Client-side Optimization Technique

Aside from the aforementioned concerns, optimizing a Bootstrap-based website for performance requires the same front-end performance strategies as any other website.

The following are only a few of the key aspects to consider for efficient front-end optimization of website.

Write Lean CSS and JavaScript

Each character in your code contributes to the overall weight of the website. It is not always simple to write clean and succinct CSS and JavaScript code while making it legible. It should, nevertheless, be something to aspire for in every undertaking.

Unused selectors, duplicated code, and rules that are unnecessarily nested are all instances of improper CSS practices. It is a good idea to maintain your code neatly structured at the start of a project. Using a style guide, for example, might enhance your development process and code quality. There are also excellent tools available to assist you in cleaning up your code. CSS Lint and JSLint, for example, may examine your document for syntax problems, wasteful coding patterns, unnecessary code, and so on.

Minify and Concatenate CSS and JavaScript Code

Limiting the amount of HTTP requests made by a website to deliver its content is an important optimization step. Each round trip to the server and return to get resources costs time, which degrades the user experience.

Minifying (removing comments and white space from your page) and concatenating CSS and JavaScript files has now become a standardized method that attempts to reduce file size and the number of HTTP requests.

Watch Out for Your Image File Size

Image files are frequently the most important aspect of a web page, although audio and video files also play important roles. As a result, optimizing graphic assets is critical to website speed.

Doing so involves two aspects:

1. Use the appropriate image format for the task at hand.

2. You're removing unnecessary bytes from assets before submitting them to production. There are excellent tools available to assist you.

TinyPNG for raster images (PNG, JPG, etc.) and Jake Archibald's SSVGOMG for SVG optimization are two online programs to consider. Consider tools that you can install locally, such as your preferred task runner (Grunt, Gulp, etc.)

A fast-rendering website is an important aspect in ensuring an exceptional user experience on the web. This is especially important when analyzing web user experience on mobile devices.

This was all about the optimization of Bootstrap; we learned to use proper image formats, writing lean CSS and JavaScript. It is time for the final section of this chapter which is SASS and Mixins.

SASS AND MIXINS

Utilize our source Sass files to take advantage of variables, maps, mixins, and functions to help you build faster and customize your project.

File Structure

Avoid altering Bootstrap's core files whenever feasible. In Sass, this means building a stylesheet that imports Bootstrap and allows you to alter and extend it. Assuming you're using a package manager like npm, you'll have a file structure that looks like this:

```
your-project/
├── css
│   └──custom.css
└──node_modules/
   └──Bootstrap
      ├──js
      └──css
```

If you got our source files and aren't using a package manager, you'll need to manually put up something similar to that structure, keeping Bootstrap's source files distinct from your own.

```
Your-project/
├── scss
│   └── custom.scss
└── bootstrap/
   ├── js
   └── scss
```

Importing

You'll import Bootstrap's source Sass files into your own CSS. You have two choices: incorporate all of Bootstrap or just the components you require. We encourage the latter, but keep in mind that there are some constraints and dependencies between our components. You will also need to add JavaScript for our plugins.

```
// Custom.scss
// Option A: Include all of the Bootstrap

// Include any default variable overrides (though
functions won't be available)

@import "../node_modules/bootstrap/scss/bootstrap";

// Then add additional custom code here

// Custom.scss
// Option B: Include parts of the Bootstrap

// 1. Include functions first (so you can manipulate
the colors, SVGs, calc, etc)
@import "../node_modules/bootstrap/scss/functions";

// 2. Include any default variable overrides here

// 3. Include remainder of required Bootstrap
stylesheets
@import "../node_modules/bootstrap/scss/variables";
@import "../node_modules/bootstrap/scss/mixins";

// 4. Include any other Bootstrap components you like
@import "../node_modules/bootstrap/scss/root";
@import "../node_modules/bootstrap/scss/reboot";
@import "../node_modules/bootstrap/scss/type";
@import "../node_modules/bootstrap/scss/images";
@import "../node_modules/bootstrap/scss/containers";
@import "../node_modules/bootstrap/scss/grid";

// 5. Add additional custom code here
```

After that, you may start modifying any of the Sass variables and maps in your custom.scss. You can also begin to add Bootstrap components in the // Optional section as required. As a starting point, we recommend utilizing the whole import stack from our Bootstrap. Scss file.

Variable Defaults

Every Sass variable in the Bootstrap supports the! Default flag, which allows you to change the variable's default value in your Sass without changing the source code of Bootstrap. Please copy and paste variables as needed, adjust their values, and delete the! Default flag as appropriate. If a variable has already been allocated, the default values in Bootstrap will not reassign it.

The whole list of Bootstrap variables may be found in scss/variables.scss. Some variables are set to null; unless altered in your setup, they do not output the property.

Variable overrides must be imported after our functions but before the rest of the imports.

When importing and building Bootstrap using npm, this example alters the background color and color for the< body>:

```
// Required
@import "../node_modules/bootstrap/scss/functions";

// Default variable overrides
$body-bg: #000;
$body-color: #111;

// Required
@import "../node_modules/bootstrap/scss/variables";
@import "../node_modules/bootstrap/scss/mixins";

// Optional Bootstrap components here
@import "../node_modules/bootstrap/scss/root";
@import "../node_modules/bootstrap/scss/reboot";
@import "../node_modules/bootstrap/scss/type";
// etc
```

Maps and Loops

Bootstrap contains a few Sass maps, which are key-value pairings that make it easy to generate families of related CSS. We utilize Sass maps for colors, grid breakpoints, and other things. All Sass maps, like Sass variables, have the! Default flag and may be overridden and expanded.

By default, several of our Sass maps are merged into empty ones. This is done to enable for simple extension of a given Sass map, but it makes *removing* objects from a map significantly more difficult.

Modify Map

Every variable in the $theme-colors map is specified as a stand-alone variable. Add the following to your own Sass file to change an existing color in our $theme-colors map:

```
$primary: #0074d9;
$danger: #ff4136;
```

These variables are later set in Bootstrap's $theme-colors map:

```
$theme-colors: (
  "primary": $primary,
  "danger": $danger
)
```

Add to a Map

Create a new Sass map with your unique values and merge it with the existing map to add new colors to $theme-colors or any other map. In this example, we'll make a new $custom-colors map and integrate it with the $theme-colors map.

```
// Create your own map
$custom-colors: (
  "custom-color": #900
);

// Merge the maps
$theme-colors: map-merge($theme-colors,
$custom-colors);
```

Remove from the Map

Use map-remove to remove colors from $theme-colors or any other map. Keep in mind that you must enter it between our criteria and options:

```
// Required
@import "../node_modules/bootstrap/scss/functions";
@import "../node_modules/bootstrap/scss/variables";
```

```
@import "../node_modules/bootstrap/scss/mixins";
$theme-colors: map-remove($theme-colors, "info",
"light", "dark");

// Optional
@import "../node_modules/bootstrap/scss/root";
@import "../node_modules/bootstrap/scss/reboot";
@import "../node_modules/bootstrap/scss/type";
// etc
```

Required Keys

Bootstrap expects the presence of certain keys inside Sass maps, which we utilized and extended ourselves. When customizing the provided maps, you may face issues if the key of a clear Sass map is utilized.

For links, buttons, and form statuses, for example, we use the primary, success, and danger keys from $theme-colors. Replacing the values of these keys should not create any problems, but deleting them may cause Sass compilation errors. In some cases, you'll need to change the Sass code that uses those values.

Functions
Colors

Next to the Sass maps, theme colors can also be used as stand-alone variables, like $primary.

```
.custom-element {
 color: $gray-100;
 background-color: $dark;
}
```

Colors may lighten or darken with Bootstrap's tint-color() and shade-color() APIs. These methods will mix colors with black or white, as opposed to Sass' native lighten() and darken() functions, which will adjust the lightness by a defined amount, which may not always result in the intended effect.

In reality, you'd call the function with the color and weight parameters sent in.

```
.custom-element {
 color: tint-color($primary, 10%);
}
```

```
.custom-element-2 {
 color: shade-color($danger, 30%);
}
```

Colors Contrast

With very few exceptions, writers must offer a contrast ratio of at least 4.5:1 to fulfill WCAG 2.0 accessibility criteria for color contrast.

The color contrast function, color-contrast, is an extra function that we include in Bootstrap. It employs the WCAG 2.0 technique for generating contrast thresholds in a sRGB colorspace based on relative brightness to automatically return a light (#fff), dark (#212529), or black (#000) contrast color based on the selected base color. This method is useful for mixins or loops that generate many classes.

To produce color swatches from our $theme-colors map, for example:

```
@each $color, $value in $theme-colors {
 .swatch-#{$color} {
  color: color-contrast($value);
 }
}
```

It can also be used for one-off contrast needs:

```
.custom-element {
 color: color-contrast(#000); // returns `color: #fff`
}
```

You can specify a base color with our color map functions:

```
.custom-element {
 color: color-contrast($dark); // returns `color: #fff`
}
```

Escape SVG

To escape the, >, and # characters from SVG background pictures, we utilize the escape-SVG function. Data URIs must be quoted when utilizing the escape-SVG procedure.

Add and Subtract Functions

To encapsulate the CSS calc function, we employ the add and subtract functions. The primary goal of these routines is to prevent errors from occurring when a "unitless" 0 value is provided into a calc expression. Despite being theoretically true, expressions like calc(10px - 0) will provide the same result in all browsers.

Here's an instance of where the calculation is correct:

```scss
$border-radius: .25rem;
$border-width: 1px;

.element {
 // Output calc(.25rem - 1px) is valid
 border-radius: calc($border-radius - $border-width);
}

.element {
 // Output the same calc(.25rem - 1px) as above
 border-radius: subtract($border-radius,
$border-width);
}
```

Instance where the calc is invalid:

```scss
$border-radius: .25rem;
$border-width: 0;

.element {
 // Output calc(.25rem - 0) is invalid
 border-radius: calc($border-radius - $border-width);
}

.element {
 // Output .25rem
 border-radius: subtract($border-radius,
$border-width);
}
```

Mixins

Our scss/mixins/ directory contains a plethora of mixins that power various portions of Bootstrap and may be utilized across your project.

Color Schemes

There is a shortcut mixin for the prefers-color-scheme media query that supports bright, dark, and custom color schemes.

```scss
@mixin color-scheme($name) {
 @media (prefers-color-scheme: #{$name}) {
```

```
  @content;
  }
}

.custom-element {
 @include color-scheme(dark) {
   // Insert dark mode styles here
 }

 @include color-scheme(custom-named-scheme) {
   // Insert the custom color scheme styles here
 }
}
```

CONCLUSION

This chapter taught us a lot about colors, what components Bootstrap offers and how to use them, CSS variables, how to optimize our Bootstrap for better performance, and SASS and mixins. In the next chapter, we are going to learn about layouts, breakpoints, containers, grids, etc.

CHAPTER 4

Layouts

IN THIS CHAPTER

- ➢ Breakpoints
- ➢ Containers
- ➢ Grid
- ➢ Columns and Rows
- ➢ Utilities

In the previous chapter, we learned about colors, components that bootstrap offers and how to use them, CSS variables, optimization of our Bootstrap for better performance, and SASS and mixins.

In this chapter, we will learn about layouts, breakpoints, containers, grids, etc.

Let's move towards the first section of this chapter: "Breakpoints."

BREAKPOINTS

In Bootstrap, breakpoints are custom widths that determine how your responsive layout behaves across viewport sizes or device.

Core Concepts

- **The building blocks of responsive design are breakpoints.** Control when your layout can be modified for a specific viewport or device size by using them.

DOI: 10.1201/9781003310501-4

- **To structure your CSS by breakpoint, use media queries:** CSS' media queries feature allows you to apply styles conditionally based on a collection of browser and operating system parameters. In our media queries, we most typically utilize min-width.

- **The goal is to create a mobile-first, responsive design:** The CSS in Bootstrap is designed to apply the bare minimum of styles to make a layout work at the smallest breakpoint, then layer on types to alter the design for larger devices. This optimizes your CSS, reduces rendering time, and gives your visitors a great experience.

It is imperative to know about the available breakpoints offered by Bootstrap. Bootstrap documentation says a lot about breakpoints and how they can be easily used.

Available Breakpoints

For creating responsively, Bootstrap contains six default breakpoints, often known as *grid tiers*. If you use our source Sass files, you can adjust these breakpoints.

Breakpoint	Class Infix	Dimensions
X-small	*None*	<576px
Small	sm	≥576px
Medium	md	≥768px
Large	lg	≥992px
Extra large	xl	≥1200px
Extra extra-large	xxl	≥1400px

Each breakpoint was selected to accommodate containers with widths that are multiples of 12. Breakpoints also reflect a subset of common device sizes and viewport dimensions, rather than addressing every use case or device. The ranges give a consistent and reliable base on which to create almost any device.

These breakpoints are Sass-customizable, and you'll find them in our _variables.scss stylesheet in a Sass map.

```
$grid-breakpoints: (
 xs: 0,
 sm: 576px,
 md: 768px,
```

```
lg: 992px,
xl: 1200px,
xxl: 1400px
);
```

After knowing the availability of breakpoints, let us get to know about what the media query says.

Media Queries

Since Bootstrap is developed to be mobile-first, we use a handful of media queries to create sensible breakpoints for our layouts and interfaces. These breakpoints are mostly determined by minimum viewport widths and items that scale up as the viewport changes.

For our layout, grid system, and components, Bootstrap largely leverages the following media query ranges – or breakpoints – in our source Sass files.

```
// Source mixins
// No media query necessary for the xs breakpoint as
        it's effectively `@media (min-width: 0) {...}`

@include media-breakpoint-up(sm) {...}
@include media-breakpoint-up(md) {...}
@include media-breakpoint-up(lg) {...}
@include media-breakpoint-up(xl) {...}
@include media-breakpoint-up(xxl) {...}

// Usage

// Example: Hide starting at the `min-width: 0`, and
then show at `sm` breakpoint
.custom-class {
  display: none;
 }
@include media-breakpoint-up(sm) {
  .custom-class {
  display: block;
 }
}
```

The values defined in our Sass variables are used to translate these Sass mixins in our produced CSS. As an example:

```
// X-Small devices (portrait phones, less than 576px)
// No media query for `xs` since this is default in
                  the Bootstrap

// Small-devices (landscape phones, 576px and up)
@media (min-width: 576px) {...}

// Medium-devices (tablets, 768px and up)
@media (min-width: 768px) {...}

// Large-devices (desktops, 992px and up)
@media (min-width: 992px) {...}

// X-Large-devices (large desktops, 1200px and up)
@media (min-width: 1200px) {...}

// XX-Large-devices (larger desktops, 1400px and up)
@media (min-width: 1400px) {...}
```

Max-width

We employ media queries that move in the other way (the provided screen size *or smaller*) on occasion:

```
// No media query necessary for the xs breakpoint as
it's effectively `@media (max-width: 0) {...}`
@include media-breakpoint-down(sm) {...}
@include media-breakpoint-down(md) {...}
@include media-breakpoint-down(lg) {...}
@include media-breakpoint-down(xl) {...}
@include media-breakpoint-down(xxl) {...}

// Example: Style from the medium breakpoint and down
@include media-breakpoint-down(md) {
 .custom-class {
 display: block;
 }
}
```

These mixins take the stated breakpoints, subtract .02px from them, and utilize the resulting values as our max-width values. As an example:

```
// X-Small-devices (portrait phones, less than 576px)
@media (max-width: 575.98px) {...}
```

```
// Small-devices (landscape phones, less than 768px)
@media (max-width: 767.98px) {...}

// Medium-devices (tablets, less than 992px)
@media (max-width: 991.98px) {...}

// Large-devices (desktops, less than 1200px)
@media (max-width: 1199.98px) {...}

// X-Large-devices (large desktops, less than 1400px)
@media (max-width: 1399.98px) {...}

// XX-Large-devices (larger desktops)
// No media query since XXL breakpoint has no upper
             bound on its width
```

Single Breakpoint

There are media queries and mixins also for targeting a single screen size segment using minimum and maximum breakpoint widths.

```
@include media-breakpoint-only(xs) {...}
@include media-breakpoint-only(sm) {...}
@include media-breakpoint-only(md) {...}
@include media-breakpoint-only(lg) {...}
@include media-breakpoint-only(xl) {...}
@include media-breakpoint-only(xxl) {...}
```

For example the @include media-breakpoint-only(md) {...} will result in:

```
@media (min-width: 768px) and (max-width: 991.98px) {...}
```

Between Breakpoint

Similarly, the media queries span multiple breakpoint widths:

```
@include media-breakpoint-between(md, xl) {...}
```

Which results in:

```
// Example
// Apply styles starting from medium devices and up to
         extra large devices
@media (min-width: 768px) and (max-width: 1199.98px)
        {...}
```

After learning about Bootstrap breakpoints, what it is, and how it is used, it is time to jump on the second section of our chapter, which is containers.

CONTAINERS

Containers are a basic Bootstrap component that contain, pad, and align your content into a specific device or viewport.

Let's know more about containers and how they work.

How They Work

Containers are the most fundamental layout element in Bootstrap, and *they're essential if you want to use our default grid system*. Containers are used to hold, pad, and (sometimes) center the content they contain. Although containers *can* be nested, nested containers are not required in most layouts.

There are three containers included with Bootstrap:

1. .container, which sets max-width at each responsive breakpoint

2. container-fluid, which is width: 100% at all breakpoints

3. container-{breakpoint}, which is width: 100% until specified breakpoint

The table below compares the max-width of each container to the original .container and .container-fluid at each breakpoint.

	Extra Small <576px	Small ≥576px	Medium ≥768px	Large ≥992px	X-Large ≥1200px	XX-Large ≥1400px
.container	100%	540px	720px	960px	1140px	1320px
.container-sm	100%	540px	720px	960px	1140px	1320px
.container-md	100%	100%	100%	960px	1140px	1320px
.container-lg	100%	100%	100%	100%	1140px	1320px
.container-xl	100%	100%	100%	100%	1140px	1320px
.container-XXL	100%	100%	100%	100%	100%	100%
.container-fluid	100%	100%	100%	100%	100%	100%

After getting to know about how it works, it is time to know about the default container.

Default Container

Our default .container class is a responsive, fixcd-width container, meaning its max-width changes at each breakpoint.

```
<div class="container">
 <!-- Content here -->
</div>
```

After getting to know about the default container, it is time for our next type of container, the responsive container.

Responsive Container

Responsive containers in Bootstrap allow you to specify a class that is 100% wide until the set breakpoint is reached, after which we apply max-widths for each of the higher breakpoints. For example, .container-sm is 100% wide to start until the sm breakpoint is reached, where it will scale up with MD, LG, xl, and XXL.

```
<div class="container-sm">100% wide until small
            breakpoint</div>
<div class="container-md">100% wide until medium
            breakpoint</div>
<div class="container-lg">100% wide until large
            breakpoint</div>
<div class="container-xl">100% wide until extra large
            breakpoint</div>
<div class="container-xxl">100% wide until extra
            extra large breakpoint</div>
```

After getting to know about the responsive container, it is time for our next type of container, a fluid container.

Fluid Container

For a full-width container that spans the entire width of the viewport, use .container-fluid.

```
<div class="container-fluid">
 ...
</div>
```

After learning about the container and how to use it, now it is time to learn about the grid of Bootstrap.

GRID

Use our robust mobile-first flexbox grid to build layouts of all shapes and sizes, thanks to a 12-column system, six default responsive tiers, Sass variables and mixins, and dozens of predefined classes.

Let's directly jump to the examples of a grid system where we will learn how the grid system works.

Example

The grid system in Bootstrap layouts and aligns information using a sequence of containers, rows, and columns. It is fully responsive and built with a flexbox. Here's an example and a detailed explanation of how the grid system works.

```
<div class="container">
 <div class="row">
  <div class="col">
   Column
  </div>
  <div class="col">
   Column
  </div>
  <div class="col">
   Column
  </div>
 </div>
</div>
```

Using our predefined grid classes, the above example provides three equal-width columns across all devices and viewports. With the parent container, the columns are centered on the page. And now it is time to know about how it works.

How It Works

Here's how the grid system is put together in detail:

- **Six responsive breakpoints are supported by our grid**: Breakpoints are based on min-width media queries, which means they effect the breakpoint in question as well as all those above it (e.g., .col-sm-4 applies to sm, MD, LG, xl, and XXL). This means that each breakpoint has control over container and column sizing and behavior.

- **Containers help to center and pad your content horizontally**: Use .container for responsive pixel widths, .container-fluid for width: 100% across all viewports and devices, or a responsive container (e.g., .container-md) for a mix of fluid and pixel widths.

- **Columns are wrapped in rows: For regulating the space between columns,** each column needs horizontal padding (called a gutter). To guarantee that the information in your columns is visibly aligned down the left side, this padding is offset on the rows with negative margins. Modifier classes can be used to apply column sizing consistently, and gutter classes can be used to adjust the spacing of your content.

- **Columns are extremely adaptable**: There are 12 template columns in accessible each row, allowing you to construct different combinations of items that span any number of columns. The number of template columns to span is indicated by column classes (e.g., col-4 spans four). Because widths are measured in percentages, you'll always know how big everything is.

- **Gutters are also flexible and versatile**: Gutter classes are available in the same sizes as our margin and padding spacing across all breakpoints. .gx-* classes are for horizontal gutters, .gy-* classes are for vertical gutters, and .g-* classes are for all gutters. Gutter removal is also possible for .g-0.

- **The grid is powered by Sass variables, maps, and mixins**: You can use our grid's source Sass to construct your own with more semantic markup if you don't want to use the standard grid classes in Bootstrap. We also include some CSS custom properties to consume these Sass variables for even greater flexibility for you.

Some grid options will help us to know more about Bootstrap's grid system.

Grid Options

The grid system in Bootstrap can react to all six default breakpoints as well as any custom breakpoints you create. The following are the six default grid tiers:

1. Extra small (xs)

2. Small (sm)

3. Medium (MD)

4. Large (LG)

5. Extra large (xl)

6. Extra extra-large (XXL)

Each of these breakpoints has its own container, unique class prefix, and modifiers, as mentioned above. This is how the grid changes as you go between these breakpoints:

	xs <576px	sm ≥576px	MD ≥768px	LG ≥992px	xl ≥1200px	XXL ≥1400px
Container max-width	None (auto)	540px	720px	960px	1140px	1320px
Class prefix	.col-	.col-sm-	.col-md-	.col-lg-	.col-xl-	.col-xxl-
# of columns	12					
Gutter width	1.5 rem (.75 rem on left and right)					
Custom gutters	Yes					
Nestable	Yes					
Column ordering	Yes					

It is essential to know about all types of the grid system and styles that Bootstrap offers. Now it is time to learn a different kind of grid system with their examples.

Auto-layout Columns

For easy column size without an exact numbered class like.col-sm-6, use breakpoint-specific column classes.

Equal Width

For example, two grid layouts apply to every device and viewport, from xs to XXL. Add any unitless classes for each breakpoint you need, and every column will be the same width.

```
<div class="container">
 <div class="row">
  <div class="col">
   1 of 2
  </div>
```

```
<div class="col">
 2 of 2
</div>
</div>
<div class="row">
 <div class="col">
  1 of 3
 </div>
 <div class="col">
  2 of 3
 </div>
 <div class="col">
  3 of 3
 </div>
</div>
</div>
```

Settings One Column Width

You may also set the width of one column and have the other columns automatically resized around it with auto-layout for flexbox grid columns. Predefined grid classes (as illustrated below), grid mixins, and inline widths are all options. Note that regardless of the width of the central column, the other columns will resize.

```
<div class="container">
 <div class="row">
  <div class="col">
   1 of 3
  </div>
  <div class="col-6">
   2 of 3 (wider)
  </div>
  <div class="col">
   3 of 3
  </div>
 </div>
 <div class="row">
  <div class="col">
   1 of 3
  </div>
  <div class="col-5">
   2 of 3 (wider)
```

```
  </div>
  <div class="col">
   3 of 3
  </div>
 </div>
</div>
```

Variable Width Content

To size columns based on their natural width, use the col-{breakpoint}-auto classes.

```
<div class="container">
 <div class="row justify-content-md-center">
  <div class="col col-lg-2">
   1 of 3
  </div>
  <div class="col-md-auto">
   Variable width content
  </div>
  <div class="col col-lg-2">
   3 of 3
  </div>
 </div>
 <div class="row">
  <div class="col">
   1 of 3
  </div>
  <div class="col-md-auto">
   Variable width content
  </div>
  <div class="col col-lg-2">
   3 of 3
  </div>
 </div>
</div>
```

Responsive Classes

For creating complicated responsive layouts, Bootstrap's grid offers six tiers of preset classes. You can make your columns of any size you want on extremely small, small, medium, big, or extra large devices.

All of the Breakpoints

Use the .col and .col-* classes to create grids that are the same from the smallest to the largest devices. When you need a certain column size, specify a numbered category; otherwise, keep with .col.

```
<div class="container">
 <div class="row">
  <div class="col">col</div>
  <div class="col">col</div>
  <div class="col">col</div>
  <div class="col">col</div>
 </div>
 <div class="row">
  <div class="col-8">col-8</div>
  <div class="col-4">col-4</div>
 </div>
</div>
```

Stacked to Horizontal

Using a single set of .col-sm-* classes in Bootstrap, you can create a basic grid system that starts stacked and becomes horizontal at the small breakpoint (sm).

```
<div class="container">
 <div class="row">
  <div class="col-sm-8">col-sm-8</div>
  <div class="col-sm-4">col-sm-4</div>
 </div>
 <div class="row">
  <div class="col-sm">col-sm</div>
  <div class="col-sm">col-sm</div>
  <div class="col-sm">col-sm</div>
 </div>
</div>
```

Mix and Match

Don't want your columns to stack in some grid tiers? Then, use a combination of different classes for each story as needed. An example is given below for a better idea of how it all works.

```
<div class="container">
 <!-- Stack the columns in Bootstrap on mobile by
   making one full-width and the other half-width -->
 <div class="row">
  <div class="col-md-8">.col-md-8</div>
  <div class="col-6 col-md-4">.col-6.col-md-4</div>
 </div>

 <!-- Columns in Bootstrap start at 50% wide on
       mobile and bump up to 33.3% wide on desktop -->
 <div class="row">
  <div class="col-6 col-md-4">.col-6.col-md-4</div>
  <div class="col-6 col-md-4">.col-6.col-md-4</div>
  <div class="col-6 col-md-4">.col-6.col-md-4</div>
 </div>

 <!-- Columns in Bootstrap are always 50% wide, on
               mobile and desktop -->
 <div class="row">
  <div class="col-6">.col-6</div>
  <div class="col-6">.col-6</div>
 </div>
</div>
```

Row Columns

To rapidly set the number of columns that best portray your content and layout, use the responsive .row-cols-* classes. The row columns classes in Bootstrap are set on the parent.row as a default for enclosed columns, whereas normal.col-* classes apply to individual columns (e.g., .col-MD-4). You can assign the columns their natural width with .row-cols-auto.

These row columns classes can be used to easily generate simple grid layouts or to manage and override card layouts at the column level.

```
<div class="container">
 <div class="row row-cols-2">
  <div class="col">Column</div>
  <div class="col">Column</div>
  <div class="col">Column</div>
  <div class="col">Column</div>
 </div>
</div>
```

```
<div class="container">
 <div class="row row-cols-3">
  <div class="col">Column</div>
  <div class="col">Column</div>
  <div class="col">Column</div>
  <div class="col">Column</div>
 </div>
</div>

<div class="container">
 <div class="row row-cols-auto">
  <div class="col">Column</div>
  <div class="col">Column</div>
  <div class="col">Column</div>
  <div class="col">Column</div>
 </div>
</div>


<div class="container">
 <div class="row row-cols-4">
  <div class="col">Column</div>
  <div class="col">Column</div>
  <div class="col">Column</div>
  <div class="col">Column</div>
 </div>
</div>


<div class="container">
 <div class="row row-cols-4">
  <div class="col">Column</div>
  <div class="col">Column</div>
  <div class="col-6">Column</div>
  <div class="col">Column</div>
 </div>
</div>


<div class="container">
 <div class="row row-cols-1 row-cols-sm-2 row-cols-md-4">
  <div class="col">Column</div>
```

```
  <div class="col">Column</div>
  <div class="col">Column</div>
  <div class="col">Column</div>
 </div>
</div>


<div class="container">
 <div class="row row-cols-2 row-cols-lg-3">
  <div class="col">Column</div>
  <div class="col">Column</div>
  <div class="col">Column</div>
  <div class="col">Column</div>
  <div class="col">Column</div>
  <div class="col">Column</div>
  <div class="col-4 col-lg-2">Column</div>
  <div class="col-4 col-lg-2">Column</div>
  <div class="col-4 col-lg-2">Column</div>
  <div class="col-4 col-lg-2">Column</div>
  <div class="col-4 col-lg-2">Column</div>
  <div class="col-4 col-lg-2">Column</div>
 </div>
</div>
```

You can also use row-cols(), a Sass mixin that goes with it:

```
.element {
 // Three columns to start
 @include row-cols(3);

 // Five columns from medium breakpoint up
 @include media-breakpoint-up(md) {
  @include row-cols(5);
 }
}
```

Nesting

Add a new .row and set of .col-sm-* columns within an existing .col-sm-* column to nest your content with the default grid. A set of columns that adds up to 12 or fewer should be included in nested rows (it is not required that you use all 12 available columns).

```
<div class="container">
 <div class="row">
  <div class="col-sm-3">
   Level 1:.col-sm-3
  </div>
  <div class="col-sm-9">
   <div class="row">
    <div class="col-8 col-sm-6">
     Level 2:.col-8.col-sm-6
    </div>
    <div class="col-4 col-sm-6">
     Level 2:.col-4.col-sm-6
    </div>
   </div>
  </div>
 </div>
</div>
```

Now, after knowing how the grid looks and feels and how it is used, it is time to focus on over next section of this chapter which is columns and rows.

COLUMNS AND ROWS

Thanks to our flexbox grid system, we learn how to modify columns with a handful of options for alignment, ordering, and offsetting. See how to use column classes in Bootstrap to manage widths of non-grid elements.

Let's learn how it works.

How They Work

- **Columns are based on the flexbox architecture of the grid.** We have the ability to change individual columns and groups of columns at the row level with Flexbox. You have control over how queues grow, reduce, or change in any other way.

- **All material is placed in columns when creating grid layouts.** Bootstrap's grid has a hierarchy that goes from a container to a row to a column to your content. On rare cases, you may want to merge content and column, but be careful that this can have unforeseen implications.

- **Predefined classes in Bootstrap make it easy to create quick, responsive layouts.** We have dozens of categories already established for you to design your own setups, with six breakpoints and a dozen columns at each grid layer. If you want, you can disable this using Sass.

Now it is time to learn all about columns and rows. At first, let's know about its alignment and many other things.

Alignment

Use flexbox alignment utilities in Bootstrap to vertically and horizontally align columns.

Vertical Alignment

```
<div class="container">
 <div class="row align-items-start">
  <div class="col">
   One of three columns
  </div>
  <div class="col">
   One of three columns
  </div>
  <div class="col">
   One of three columns
  </div>
 </div>
 <div class="row align-items-center">
  <div class="col">
   One of three columns
  </div>
  <div class="col">
   One of three columns
  </div>
  <div class="col">
   One of three columns
  </div>
 </div>
 <div class="row align-items-end">
  <div class="col">
   One of three columns
```

```
  </div>
  <div class="col">
   One of three columns
  </div>
  <div class="col">
   One of three columns
  </div>
 </div>
</div>

<div class="container">
 <div class="row">
  <div class="col align-self-start">
   One of three columns
  </div>
  <div class="col align-self-center">
   One of three columns
  </div>
  <div class="col align-self-end">
   One of three columns
  </div>
 </div>
</div>
```

Horizontal Alignment

```
<div class="container">
 <div class="row justify-content-start">
  <div class="col-4">
   One of two columns
  </div>
  <div class="col-4">
   One of two columns
  </div>
 </div>
 <div class="row justify-content-center">
  <div class="col-4">
   One of two columns
  </div>
  <div class="col-4">
   One of two columns
  </div>
```

```
</div>
<div class="row justify-content-end">
 <div class="col-4">
  One of two columns
 </div>
 <div class="col-4">
  One of two columns
 </div>
</div>
<div class="row justify-content-around">
 <div class="col-4">
  One of two columns
 </div>
 <div class="col-4">
  One of two columns
 </div>
</div>
<div class="row justify-content-between">
 <div class="col-4">
  One of two columns
 </div>
 <div class="col-4">
  One of two columns
 </div>
</div>
<div class="row justify-content-evenly">
 <div class="col-4">
  One of two columns
 </div>
 <div class="col-4">
  One of two columns
 </div>
 </div>
</div>
```

Column Wrapping

If a single row contains more than 12 columns, each group of extra columns will wrap onto a new line as a single unit.

```
<div class="container">
 <div class="row">
  <div class="col-9">.col-9</div>
```

```
    <div class="col-4">.col-4<br>Since 9+4=13 > 12,
        this 4-column-wide div gets wrapped onto the
        new line as one contiguous unit.</div>
    <div class="col-6">.col-6<br>Subsequent columns
        continue along the new line.</div>
  </div>
</div>
```

Column Breaks

Breaking columns in Bootstrap to a new line in flexbox requires a small hack: add an element with a width: 100% wherever you want to wrap your columns to a new line. Usually, this is accomplished with multiple .rows, but not every implementation method can account for this.

```
<div class="container">
 <div class="row">
  <div class="col-6 col-sm-3">.col-6.col-sm-3</div>
  <div class="col-6 col-sm-3">.col-6.col-sm-3</div>

  <!-- Force next columns in Bootstrap to break to
        new line -->
  <div class="w-100"></div>

  <div class="col-6 col-sm-3">.col-6.col-sm-3</div>
  <div class="col-6 col-sm-3">.col-6.col-sm-3</div>
 </div>
</div>
```

You may also apply this break in Bootstrap at specific breakpoints with responsive display utilities.

```
<div class="container">
 <div class="row">
  <div class="col-6 col-sm-4">.col-6.col-sm-4</div>
  <div class="col-6 col-sm-4">.col-6.col-sm-4</div>

  <!-- Force next columns in Bootstrap to break to
        new line at md breakpoint and up -->
  <div class="w-100 d-none d-md-block"></div>

  <div class="col-6 col-sm-4">.col-6.col-sm-4</div>
  <div class="col-6 col-sm-4">.col-6.col-sm-4</div>
```

```
 </div>
</div>
```

After learning about columns, it is time to learn about reordering.

Reordering
Order Classes
Control the *visual order* of your content with .order- classes. These classes are responsive, so you can change the order based on the breakpoints (e.g., .order-1.order-MD-2). All six grid layers provide support for numbers 1 through 5.

```
<div class="container">
 <div class="row">
  <div class="col">
   First in DOM, no order applied
  </div>
  <div class="col order-5">
   Second in DOM, with a larger order
  </div>
  <div class="col order-1">
   Third in the DOM, with an order of 1
  </div>
 </div>
</div>
```

There are also responsive .order-first and .order-last classes that apply for order: 1 and order: 6, respectively, to change the order of an element. As needed, these classes can be blended in with the numbered .order-* courses.

```
<div class="container">
 <div class="row">
  <div class="col order-last">
   First in DOM, ordered last
  </div>
  <div class="col">
   Second in DOM, unordered
  </div>
  <div class="col order-first">
   Third in DOM, ordered first
```

```
      </div>
   </div>
</div>
```

Offsetting Columns

Our responsive .offset- grid classes and margin utilities both can be used to offset grid columns. Grid classes are proportioned to match columns, whereas margins are better for rapid layouts with a configurable offset width.

Offsetting Classes

Using the .offset-md-* classes, you can move columns to the right. These classes extend a column's left margin by * columns. .offset-md-4, for example, moves. across four columns col-md-4.

```
<div class="container">
 <div class="row">
   <div class="col-md-4">.col-md-4</div>
   <div class="col-md-4 offset-md-4">.col-md-4.offset
             -md-4</div>
 </div>
 <div class="row">
   <div class="col-md-3 offset-md-3">.col-md-3.offset
             -md-3</div>
   <div class="col-md-3 offset-md-3">.col-md-3.offset
             -md-3</div>
 </div>
 <div class="row">
   <div class="col-md-6 offset-md-3">.col-md-6.offset
             -md-3</div>
 </div>
</div>
```

You may need to reset offsets in addition to clearing columns at responsive breakpoints. In the grid example, you can see this in action.

```
<div class="container">
 <div class="row">
   <div class="col-sm-5 col-md-6">.col-sm-5.col-md-6</
             div>
```

```
   <div class="col-sm-5 offset-sm-2 col-md-6 offse
            t-md-0">.col-sm-5.offset-sm-2.col-md-6.o
            ffset-md-0</div>
  </div>
  <div class="row">
   <div class="col-sm-6 col-md-5 col-lg-6">.col-sm-6.
            col-md-5.col-lg-6</div>
   <div class="col-sm-6 col-md-5 offset-md-2 col-lg-6
            offset-lg-0">.col-sm-6.col-md-5.offset-m
            d-2.col-lg-6.offset-lg-0</div>
  </div>
 </div>
```

Margin Utilities

With the switch to flexbox in v4, you can now use margin utilities like
.me-auto to separate sibling columns.

```
<div class="container">
 <div class="row">
  <div class="col-md-4">.col-md-4</div>
  <div class="col-md-4 ms-auto">.col-md-4.ms-auto</div>
 </div>
 <div class="row">
  <div class="col-md-3 ms-md-auto">.col-md-3.ms-md
            -auto</div>
  <div class="col-md-3 ms-md-auto">.col-md-3.ms-md
            -auto</div>
 </div>
 <div class="row">
  <div class="col-auto me-auto">.col-auto.me-auto</div>
  <div class="col-auto">.col-auto</div>
 </div>
</div>
```

Stand-alone Column Classes

The .col-* classes can also be used outside of a .row to specify the width
of an element. Paddings are not needed when column classes are used as
non-direct children of a row.

```
<div class="col-3 bg-light p-3 border">
 .col-3: width of 25%
</div>
```

```
<div class="col-sm-9 bg-light p-3 border">
 .col-sm-9: width of 75% above sm breakpoint
</div>
```

The classes can be used together with utilities to create responsive floated images. Make sure to wrap the content in .clearfix wrapper to clear the float if text is shorter.

```
<div class="clearfix">
 <img src="..." class="col-md-6 float-md-end mb-3
                ms-md-3" alt="...">
 <p>
```

A paragraph of text that serves as a placeholder is being used to demonstrate how to use the clearfix class. To show how the columns interact with the floated image, we've added a bunch of meaningless phrases here.

```
 </p>
 <p>
```

The words gently wrap around the floated image, as you can see. Consider how this would appear if there was some genuine content here instead of this dull placeholder text that goes on and on but doesn't convey any useful information. It is just a waste of space and shouldn't be read.

```
 </p>
 <p>
```

Nonetheless, you persist in reading this placeholder text, hoping for more information or a hidden easter egg of content. Maybe it is a joke. Unfortunately, none of that is available here.

```
 </p>
</div>
```

This was all about columns, examples of them, and how to use them. Now it is time to jump to the last section of this chapter which is bootstrap utilities.

UTILITIES

Bootstrap includes dozens of utility classes for the faster mobile-friendly and responsive development for showing, hiding, aligning, and spacing content.

At first, we will be getting to know about Flexbox options.

Flexbox Options

Flexbox is used in Bootstrap, but not every element's display has been changed to display: flex would add a lot of unneeded overrides and modify important browser behavior unpredictably. Flexbox is enabled on the majority of our components.

Use .d-flex or one of the responsive versions if you need to add display: flex to an element (e.g., .d-sm-flex). To use our extra flexbox utilities for scaling, alignment, spacing, and more, you'll need this class or display value. Let's look into merging and padding now.

Merging and Padding

To control how components and elements are spaced and sized, it is recommended to use the margin and padding spacing utilities. Bootstrap includes six-level scale for spacing utilities, based on a 1rem value default $spacer variable. Choose values for all the viewports (e.g., .me-3 for margin-right: 1rem in LTR), or pick the responsive variants to target specific viewports (e.g., .me-MD-3 for margin-right: 1rem – in LTR – starting at the end breakpoint).

Toggle Visibility

When the toggling display isn't needed, you can toggle the visibility of an element with our visibility utilities. Invisible factors will still affect the layout of the page but are visually hidden from visitors.

CONCLUSION

We learned about various important things like breakpoints, containers, grids, columns and rows, and utilities in this chapter.

In the next chapter, we will focus on working with content. We will learn about typography, images tables, figures, etc.

CHAPTER 5

Working with Content

IN THIS CHAPTER

- ➤ Typography
- ➤ Images
- ➤ Table and Figures
- ➤ Forms

In the previous chapter, we learnt about breakpoints, containers, grids, columns and rows, and utilities, among other things.

In this chapter, we will focus on working with content. We will also learn about typography, images tables, figures, etc.

Let's begin this chapter with "typography."

TYPOGRAPHY

Bootstrap typography includes documentation and examples, covering global settings, headers, body text, lists, and more.

Let's start by looking at the typography's global settings.

Global Settings

- Use a native font stack that chooses the most appropriate font family for each OS and device.

DOI: 10.1201/9781003310501-5

- We utilize the browser's default root font size (usually 16px) for a more inclusive and accessible type scale, so users may change their browser settings as required.

- Apply the $font-family-base, $font-size-base, and $line-height-base properties to the <body> as our typographic foundation.

- $link-color is used to change the color of all global links.

- Set the background color of the <body> using $body-bg (#fff by default).

The global variables are defined in _variables, and the styles are available in _reboot.scss.

Let's jump to our first code example and learn the types of headings.

Headings

HTML headings, <h1> through <h6>, are available.

```
<h1>h1. Bootstrap heading</h1>
<h2>h2. Bootstrap heading</h2>
<h3>h3. Bootstrap heading</h3>
<h4>h4. Bootstrap heading</h4>
<h5>h5. Bootstrap heading</h5>
<h6>h6. Bootstrap heading</h6>
```

.h1 through .h6 classes are available for matching the font styling of a heading but cannot use the associated HTML element.

```
<p class="h1">h1. Bootstrap heading</p>
<p class="h2">h2. Bootstrap heading</p>
<p class="h3">h3. Bootstrap heading</p>
<p class="h4">h4. Bootstrap heading</p>
<p class="h5">h5. Bootstrap heading</p>
<p class="h6">h6. Bootstrap heading</p>
```

We can also customize our headings for better visual effects; the next section will teach us how to customize our headers.

Customizing Headings

Use the included utility classes to recreate small secondary heading text from Bootstrap 3.

```
<h3>
 Fancy display heading
 <small class="text-muted">With faded secondary
             text</small>
</h3>
```

When needed heading to stand out, professional front-end developers use display headings. Let's learn about it.

Display Headings

Traditional header components are best used in the main material of your website. Consider utilizing a show heading a more visible, slightly more opinionated heading style when you need a heading to stand out.

```
<h1 class="display-1">Display 1</h1>
<h1 class="display-2">Display 2</h1>
<h1 class="display-3">Display 3</h1>
<h1 class="display-4">Display 4</h1>
<h1 class="display-5">Display 5</h1>
<h1 class="display-6">Display 6</h1>
```

The $display-font-sizes Sass map and two variables, $display-font-weight and $display-line-height, are used to customize display headers.

```
$display-font-sizes: (
 1: 5rem,
 2: 4.5rem,
 3: 4rem,
 4: 3.5rem,
 5: 3rem,
 6: 2.5rem
);

$display-font-weight: 400;
$display-line-height: $headings-line-height;
```

Lead

Make paragraph stand out by adding.lead.

```
<p class="lead">
 This is a lead paragraph. It stands out from regular
         paragraphs.
</p>
```

Now let's focus on our next topic, which is the inline text element.

Inline Text Element

Styling for common inline HTML5 elements:

```
<p>You can use mark tag to<mark>highlight</mark>text.</p>
<p><del>This line of the text is meant to treat as
            deleted text.</del></p>
<p><s>This line of the text is meant to treat as no
            longer accurate.</s></p>
<p><ins>This line of the text is meant to treat as an
            addition to the document.</ins></p>
<p>This line of the text will render as underlined.</p>
<p><small>This line of the text is meant to treat as
            fine print.</small></p>
<p><strong>This line rendered as bold text.</strong></p>
<p><em>This line rendered as italicized text.</em></p>
```

Beware that those tags should be used for the semantic purpose:

- <mark> represents text which is highlighted or marked for reference or notation purposes.

- <small> represents side comments and small print, such as copyright and legal text.

- <s> represents an element that is no longer relevant or no longer accurate.

- <u> represents a span of inline text that should be rendered to indicate that it has a non-textual annotation.

Instead, if you want to design your text, use the following classes:

- .mark will apply the same styles as <mark>.

- .small will apply the same styles as <small>.

- .text-decoration-underline will apply same styles as <u>.

- .text-decoration-line-through will apply same styles as <s>.

While not shown above, feel free to use and in the HTML5. <b> is meant to highlight the words or phrases without conveying additional importance, while <i> is mostly for voice, technical terms, etc.

It is imperative to know about abbreviations offered by Bootstrap while working on it. Let's learn what bootstrap abbreviations are and how they are used.

Abbreviations

Stylize HTML's <abbr> element for the abbreviations and acronyms to show expanded version on hover. On hover and for assistive technology users, abbreviations have default underlining and help pointer to offer further details.

Add .initialism to an abbreviation for slightly smaller font size.

```
<p><abbr title="attribute">attr</abbr></p>
<p><abbr title="HyperText Markup Language"
              class="initialism">HTML</abbr></p>
```

Blockquotes

For quoting blocks of the content from another source within document, wrap <blockquote class="blockquote"> around any HTML as quote.

```
<blockquote class="blockquote">
 <p>A well-known quote, contained in a blockquote
              element.</p>
</blockquote>
```

Bootstrap provides ways to do it whenever needed to name the source; Bootstrap offers ways to do it; it is time to learn it; let's go.

Naming a Source

The HTML spec requires that blockquote attribution should be placed outside the <blockquote>. When providing attribution, wrap your <blockquote> in <figure> and use a <figcaption> or a block level element (e.g., <p>) with .blockquote-footer class. Be sure to wrap the name of source work in <cite> as well.

```
<figure>
 <blockquote class="blockquote">
```

```
  <p>A well-known quote, contained in a blockquote
                  element.</p>
 </blockquote>
 <figcaption class="blockquote-footer">
  Someone famous in<cite title="Source Title">Source
        Title</cite>
 </figcaption>
</figure>
```

Alignment is an essential part of Bootstrap in every corner. Bootstrap typography also provides alignment options.

Alignment

Use the text utilities as needed to change the alignment of your blockquote.

```
<figure class="text-center">
 <blockquote class="blockquote">
  <p>A well-known quote, contained in a blockquote
                  element.</p>
 </blockquote>
 <figcaption class="blockquote-footer">
  Someone famous in<cite title="Source Title">Source
        Title</cite>
 </figcaption>
</figure>

<figure class="text-end">
 <blockquote class="blockquote">
  <p>A well-known quote, contained in a blockquote
            element.</p>
 </blockquote>
 <figcaption class="blockquote-footer">
  Someone famous in<cite title="Source Title">Source
        Title</cite>
 </figcaption>
</figure>
```

List

Unstilled

Remove the default list style and left margin on list items (immediate children only). *This only applies to primary children list items*, meaning you will need to add the class for any nested lists as well.

```
<ul class="list-unstyled">
 <li>This is a list.</li>
 <li>It appears completely unstyled.</li>
 <li>Structurally, it's still a list.</li>
 <li>However, this style only applies to immediate
               child elements.</li>
 <li>Nested lists:
  <ul>
   <li>are unaffected by this style</li>
   <li>will still show a bullet</li>
   <li>and have appropriate left margin</li>
  </ul>
 </li>
 <li>This may still come in handy in some
          situations.</li>
</ul>
```

Inline

Remove list's bullets and apply some light margin with combination of two classes: .list-inline and .list-inline-item.

```
<ul class="list-inline">
 <li class="list-inline-item">This is list item.</li>
 <li class="list-inline-item">And another one.</li>
 <li class="list-inline-item">But they are displayed
           inline.</li>
</ul>
```

Description List Alignment

Align terms and descriptions horizontally by using grid system's pre-defined classes. For longer times, you can optionally add a .text-truncate style to truncate the text with an ellipsis.

```
<dl class="row">
 <dt class="col-sm-3">Description lists</dt>
 <dd class="col-sm-9">A description list is perfect
           for defining terms.</dd>

 <dt class="col-sm-3">Term</dt>
 <dd class="col-sm-9">
  <p>Definition for the term.</p>
  <p>And some more placeholder definition text.</p>
```

```
</dd>

<dt class="col-sm-3">Another term</dt>
<dd class="col-sm-9">This definition is short, so no
          extra paragraphs or anything.</dd>
<dt class="col-sm-3 text-truncate">Truncated term is
          truncated</dt>
<dd class="col-sm-9">This can be useful when space
         is tight. Adds an ellipsis at the end.</dd>

<dt class="col-sm-3">Nesting</dt>
<dd class="col-sm-9">
 <dl class="row">
  <dt class="col-sm-4">Nested definition list</dt>
  <dd class="col-sm-8">I heard you like definition
          lists. Let me put definition list
          inside your definition list.</dd>
 </dl>
 </dd>
</dl>
```

This was all about typography, we learned about global settings headings, inline text elements, abbreviations, etc. Now let's focus on our next section of this chapter: Images.

IMAGES

Documentation and examples for opting images into the responsive behavior and add lightweight styles to them all via classes.

At first, learn about responsive images.

Responsive Images

Images in Bootstrap are made responsive with .img-fluid. This applies max-width: 90%; and height: auto; to the image to scale with the parent element.

```
<img src="..." class="img-fluid" alt="...">
```

This was about responsive images; now, let's jump to the following topic: thumbnails.

Images Thumbnails

In addition to border-radius utilities, you can use .img-thumbnail to give an image a rounded 1px border appearance.

```
<img src="..." class="img-thumbnail" alt="...">
```

Aligning Images

Align images with the helper float classes or text alignment classes. Block-level images can be centered using .mx-auto margin utility class.

```
<img src="..." class="rounded float-start" alt="...">
<img src="..." class="rounded float-end" alt="...">
<img src="..." class="rounded mx-auto d-block" alt="...">

<div class="text-center">
 <img src="..." class="rounded" alt="...">
</div>
```

Now it is time to learn about this section's final topic: Pictures – what it is and how to use them.

Picture

If using the <picture> element to specify multiple <source> elements for a specific <img>, make sure to add the .img-* classes to the <img> and not to the <picture> tag.

```
<picture>
 <source srcset="..." type="image/svg+xml">
 <img src="..." class="img-fluid img-thumbnail" alt="...">
</picture>
```

This was all about images; we learned about responsive photos, thumbnails, pictures, etc. Now, it is time to move forward and learn about tables and figures.

TABLES AND FIGURES

Tables

Table style with Bootstrap documentation and examples (because of their widespread use in JavaScript plugins).

Overview

Bootstrap

's tables are opted due to the broad use of table> components across third-party widgets like calendars and date pickers. Add the .table base class to any table> and then use our optional modifier classes or custom styles to customize it. In Bootstrap, all table styles are not inherited; therefore, any nested tables may be configured independent of the parent.

Here's how to do it. In Bootstrap, table-based tables are created with the simplest basic table markup.

	First	Last	Handle
1	Mark	Otto	@mdo
2	Jacob	Thornton	@fat
3	Larry the Bird		@twitter

```
<table class="table">
 <thead>
  <tr>
   <th scope="col">#</th>
   <th scope="col">First</th>
   <th scope="col">Last</th>
   <th scope="col">Handle</th>
  </tr>
 </thead>
 <tbody>
  <tr>
   <th scope="row">1</th>
   <td>Mark</td>
   <td>Otto</td>
   <td>@mdo</td>
  </tr>
  <tr>
   <th scope="row">2</th>
   <td>Jacob</td>
   <td>Thornton</td>
   <td>@fat</td>
  </tr>
  <tr>
   <th scope="row">3</th>
   <td colspan="2">Larry the Bird</td>
   <td>@twitter</td>
```

```
  </tr>
 </tbody>
</table>
```

After knowing about the overview, now it is time to focus on variants and other topics.

Variants

To color tables, table rows, or individual cells, use contextual classes.

```
<!-- On tables -->
<table class="table-primary">...</table>
<table class="table-secondary">...</table>
<table class="table-success">...</table>
<table class="table-danger">...</table>
<table class="table-warning">...</table>
<table class="table-info">...</table>
<table class="table-light">...</table>
<table class="table-dark">...</table>

<!-- On rows -->
<tr class="table-primary">...</tr>
<tr class="table-secondary">...</tr>
<tr class="table-success">...</tr>
<tr class="table-danger">...</tr>
<tr class="table-warning">...</tr>
<tr class="table-info">...</tr>
<tr class="table-light">...</tr>
<tr class="table-dark">...</tr>

<!-- On cells (`td` or `th`) -->
<tr>
 <td class="table-primary">...</td>
 <td class="table-secondary">...</td>
 <td class="table-success">...</td>
 <td class="table-danger">...</td>
 <td class="table-warning">...</td>
 <td class="table-info">...</td>
 <td class="table-light">...</td>
 <td class="table-dark">...</td>
</tr>
```

Accented tables

Striped rows

Use .table-striped to add zebra-striping to table row within <tbody>.

```
<table class="table table-striped">
  ...
</table>
```

These classes can also be added to table variants:

```
<table class="table table-dark table-striped">
  ...
</table>
```

```
<table class="table table-success table-striped">
  ...
</table>
```

And it has to do with striped rows. It is time to move on to learning hoverable rows.

Hoverable Rows

Add .table-hover to enable hover state on the table rows within a <tbody>.

```
<table class="table table-hover">
  ...
</table>
```

```
<table class="table table-dark table-hover">
  ...
</table>
```

These hoverable rows may also be used in combination with the striped version:

```
<table class="table table-striped table-hover">
  ...
</table>
```

It was all about hoverable rows; now, let's learn about active tables.

Active Tables

A .table-active class may be used to highlight a table row or cell.

```
<table class="table">
 <thead>
  ...
 </thead>
 <tbody>
  <tr class="table-active">
   ...
  </tr>
  <tr>
   ...
  </tr>
  <tr>
   <th scope="row">3</th>
   <td colspan="2" class="table-active">Larry the
                         Bird</td>
   <td>@twitter</td>
  </tr>
 </tbody>
</table>

<table class="table table-dark">
 <thead>
  ...
 </thead>
 <tbody>
  <tr class="table-active">
   ...
  </tr>
  <tr>
   ...
  </tr>
  <tr>
   <th scope="row">3</th>
   <td colspan="2" class="table-active">Larry the
                     Bird</td>
   <td>@twitter</td>
  </tr>
 </tbody>
</table>
```

This was all about active tables, now let's learn about table borders.

TABLES BORDERS

Bordered Table

Add .table-bordered for edges on all sides of the table and cells.

```
<table class="table table-bordered">
 ...
</table>
```

Border color utilities can be added to change colors.

```
<table class="table table-bordered border-primary">
 ...
</table>
```

Table without Borders

Add .table-borderless for a table without borders.

```
<table class="table table-borderless">
 ...
</table>
```

```
<table class="table table-dark table-borderless">
 ...
</table>
```

Small Tables

Add .table-sm to any .table to make it more compact by halving all cell padding.

```
<table class="table table-sm">
 ...
</table>
```

```
<table class="table table-dark table-sm">
 ...
</table>
```

Vertical Alignment

<thead> table cells are always positioned vertically to the bottom. The alignment of table cells in <tbody> is inherited from <table>, and they are aligned to the top by default.

```
<div class="table-responsive">
 <table class="table align-middle">
  <thead>
   <tr>
    ...
   </tr>
  </thead>
  <tbody>
   <tr>
    ...
   </tr>
   <tr class="align-bottom">
    ...
   </tr>
   <tr>
    <td>...</td>
    <td>...</td>
    <td class="align-top">This cell is aligned to the
               top.</td>
    <td>...</td>
   </tr>
  </tbody>
 </table>
</div>
```

Nesting

Nested tables do not inherit border styles, active styles, and table variants.

```
<table class="table table-striped">
 <thead>
  ...
 </thead>
 <tbody>
  ...
  <tr>
   <td colspan="4">
    <table class="table mb-0">
     ...
    </table>
   </td>
  </tr>
```

```
  . . .
 </tbody>
</table>
```

How Nesting Works

To prevent styles from leaking to nested tables, we employ the child combinator (>) selector in our CSS. Because we need to target all of the TDS and ths in the thead, tbody, and tfoot, our selector would be quite long without it. As a result, we utilize the odd-looking .table >:not(caption) > * > * selection to target all TDS and ths in the .table, but none of the nested tables.

It is worth noting that if you add <tr>s as direct children of a table, those <tr>s will be wrapped in a <tbody> by default, ensuring that our selectors operate as expected.

Anatomy

Table Head

Like tables and dark tables, use the modifier classes .table-light or .table-dark to make <thead>s appear light or dark gray.

```
<table class="table">
 <thead class="table-light">
  . . .
 </thead>
 <tbody>
  . . .
 </tbody>
</table>

<table class="table">
 <thead class="table-dark">
  . . .
 </thead>
 <tbody>
  . . .
 </tbody>
</table>
```

Table Foot

```
<table class="table">
 <thead>
  . . .
```

```
 </thead>
 <tbody>
  ...
 </tbody>
 <tfoot>
  ...
 </tfoot>
</table>
```

Captions

A <caption> is similar to a table's heading. It assists screen reader users in finding a table, understanding what it is about, and deciding whether or not to read it.

```
<table class="table table-sm">
 <caption>List of users</caption>
 <thead>
  ...
 </thead>
 <tbody>
  ...
 </tbody>
</table>
```

You can also put <caption> on the top of table with .caption-top.

```
<table class="table caption-top">
 <caption>List of users</caption>
 <thead>
  <tr>
   <th scope="col">#</th>
   <th scope="col">First</th>
   <th scope="col">Last</th>
   <th scope="col">Handle</th>
  </tr>
 </thead>
 <tbody>
  <tr>
   <th scope="row">1</th>
   <td>Mark</td>
   <td>Otto</td>
   <td>@mdo</td>
```

```
  </tr>
  <tr>
   <th scope="row">2</th>
   <td>Jacob</td>
   <td>Thornton</td>
   <td>@fat</td>
  </tr>
  <tr>
   <th scope="row">3</th>
   <td>Larry</td>
   <td>the Bird</td>
   <td>@twitter</td>
  </tr>
 </tbody>
</table>
```

Responsive Tables

Tables that are responsive can be scrolled horizontally with ease. Wrapping a .table with .table-responsive makes any table responsive across all viewports. Alternatively, use .table-responsive{-sm|-md|-lg|-xl|-xxl} to specify a maximum breakpoint for a responsive table.

Vertical Clipping/truncation

Overflow-y: hidden is used in responsive tables to clip off any information that extends beyond the table's bottom and top boundaries. Dropdown menus and other third-party widgets can clip off as a result of this.

Always Responsive

Use .table-responsive for horizontally scrolling tables at all breakpoints.

```
<div class="table-responsive">
 <table class="table">
  ...
 </table>
</div>
```

Breakpoint Specific

To generate responsive tables up to a specific breakpoint, use .table-responsive-{sm|-md|-lg|-xl|-xxl} as needed. The table will act appropriately after that breakpoint and will not scroll horizontally.

These tables may appear to be broken until responsive styles are applied at particular viewport sizes.

```
<div class="table-responsive">
 <table class="table">
  ...
 </table>
</div>

<div class="table-responsive-sm">
 <table class="table">
  ...
 </table>
</div>

<div class="table-responsive-md">
 <table class="table">
  ...
 </table>
</div>

<div class="table-responsive-lg">
 <table class="table">
  ...
 </table>
</div>

<div class="table-responsive-xl">
 <table class="table">
  ...
 </table>
</div>

<div class="table-responsive-xxl">
 <table class="table">
  ...
 </table>
</div>
```

Figures

Documentation and examples for using the figure component in Bootstrap to show linked images and text.

Consider utilizing a <figure> whenever you need to present a piece of material, such as a picture with an optional description.

To give some basic styles for the HTML5 figure> and <fig caption> elements, use the included.figure, .figure-img, and .figure-caption classes. Because there is no defined size for images in figures, ensure to add the .img-fluid class to your <img> to make it responsive.

```
<figure class="figure">
 <img src="..." class="figure-img img-fluid rounded"
                    alt="...">
 <figcaption class="figure-caption">A caption for
                above image.</figcaption>
</figure>

<figure class="figure">
 <img src="..." class="figure-img img-fluid rounded"
                    alt="...">
 <figcaption class="figure-caption text-end">A
            caption for above image.</figcaption>
</figure>
```

This was all about content and figures. We learned in detail about tables, types of tables offered by Bootstrap, how to use them, and sculptures. Not it is time to move forward to the next topic and learn in detail about Bootstrap forms.

FORMS

For constructing a broad range of forms, examples and usage recommendations for form control styles, layout choices, and custom components are provided.

Let's start with an overview of the forms.

Overview

The form controls in Bootstrap extend our Rebooted form designs with classes. For a more uniform rendering across browsers and devices, use these classes to opt into their specialized presentations.

To make use of modern input controls like email verification, number selection, and more, make sure all inputs have the proper type attribute (e.g., email for an email address or number for numerical data).

Here's a simple example of how to use the form styles in Bootstrap. Continue reading for information on necessary classes, form formatting, and other topics.

```
<form>
 <div class="mb-3">
  <label for="exampleInputEmail1" class="form-
           label">Email address</label>
  <input type="email" class="form-control"
           id="exampleInputEmail1"
           aria-describedby="emailHelp">
  <div id="emailHelp" class="form-text">We'll never
         share your email with anyone else.</div>
 </div>
 <div class="mb-3">
  <label for="exampleInputPassword1" class="form-
           label">Password</label>
  <input type="password" class="form-control"
           id="exampleInputPassword1">
 </div>
 <div class="mb-3 form-check">
  <input type="checkbox" class="form-check-input"
           id="exampleCheck1">
  <label class="form-check-label"
         for="exampleCheck1">Check me out</label>
 </div>
 <button type="submit" class="btn btn-
           primary">Submit</button>
</form>
```

It was the primary form example; now let's learn about forms text.

Form Text

.form-text may be used to produce form text at the block or inline level.

The text below the inputs in the form may customize using the .form-text. If a block-level element is utilized, a top margin is added for simple spacing from the content above.

```
<label for="inputPassword5" class="form-
                      label">Password</label>
<input type="password" id="inputPassword5"
class="form-control" aria-describedby="passwordHelpBl
                  ock">
<div id="passwordHelpBlock" class="form-text">
```

Your password must be between 8 and 20 characters long, contain letters and numbers, and be free of spaces, special characters, and emojis.

Inline text can use typical inline HTML element (be it , <small>, or something else) with nothing more than the .form-text class.

```
<div class="row g-3 align-items-center">
 <div class="col-auto">
  <label for="inputPassword6" class="col-form-
           label">Password</label>
 </div>
 <div class="col-auto">
  <input type="password" id="inputPassword6"
           class="form-control" aria-describedby="
           passwordHelpInline">
 </div>
 <div class="col-auto">
  <span id="passwordHelpInline" class="form-text">
   Must be 8-20 characters long.
  </span>
 </div>
</div>
```

This was all about form text, now let's learn disabled forms.

DISABLED FORM

To prevent user interactions and make an input look lighter, use the disabled boolean property.

<input class="form-control" id="disabledInput" type="text" placeholder="Disabled input here..." disabled>

To deactivate all the controls in a fieldset, add the disabled attribute to it. All the native form controls (<input>, <select>, and <button> elements) inside fieldset <disabled> are treated as disabled by browsers, limiting keyboard and mouse interactions.

If your form additionally includes custom button-like elements, such as a class="btn btn-*">...</a>, they will only be given the pointer-events: none style, which means they will still be focusable and operable with the keyboard. In this scenario, you must add tabindex="-1" to prevent certain controls from obtaining focus and aria-disabled="disabled" to indicate their condition to assistive technologies.

```
<form>
 <fieldset disabled>
  <legend>Disabled fieldset example</legend>
  <div class="mb-3">
   <label for="disabledTextInput" class="form-
              label">Disabled input</label>
   <input type="text" id="disabledTextInput" class=
         "form-control" placeholder="Disabled input">
  </div>
  <div class="mb-3">
   <label for="disabledSelect" class="form-
          label">Disabled select menu</label>
   <select id="disabledSelect" class="form-select">
    <option>Disabled select</option>
   </select>
  </div>
  <div class="mb-3">
   <div class="form-check">
    <input class="form-check-input" type="checkbox"
          id="disabledFieldsetCheck" disabled>
    <label class="form-check-label"
          for="disabledFieldsetCheck">
    Can't check this
    </label>
   </div>
  </div>
  <button type="submit" class="btn btn-
              primary">Submit</button>
 </fieldset>
</form>
```

Accessibility

Ensure that all form controls have an accessible name that clearly communicates their function to assistive technology users. The simplest method to do this is to use < label> element or, in the case of buttons, to add enough descriptive text in the <button>...</button> content.

There are alternate ways to provide an accessible name in circumstances where a visible label> or relevant text content isn't feasible:

The .visually-hidden class is used for

- Hiding <label> components

- Aria-labeling by pointing to an existing element that can behave as a label

- Providing the title attribute

- Using aria-label to explicitly set an element's accessible name

If none of these are available, assistive technology may utilize the place-holder property on <input> and <textarea> elements as a fallback for the accessible name. This section's examples offer a few recommended, case-specific techniques.

While employing visually hidden information (.visually-hidden, aria-label, and even placeholder content, which vanishes once a form field has content) would aid assistive technology users, a lack of visible label text may still be an issue for some. In terms of accessibility and usefulness, a visible label is usually the best option.

It is essential to learn about sizing, input buttons, and many other things in the form, which we will be learning in forms controls.

Form Controls

Custom styles, sizes, focus states, and more may apply to textual form controls like <input> and <textareas>.

Let's directly jump to our first example for better understanding.

```
<div class="mb-3">
 <label for="exampleFormControlInput1" class="form-
          label">Email address</label>
 <input type="email" class="form-control"
          id="exampleFormControlInput1"
          placeholder="name@example.com">
</div>
<div class="mb-3">
 <label for="exampleFormControlTextarea1"
        class="form-label">Example textarea</label>
 <textarea class="form-control" id="exampleFormContro
          lTextarea1" rows="3"></textarea>
</div>
```

Let's learn about form sizing, disabled forms, and many others.

Sizing

Set heights using the classes like .form-control-lg and .form-control-sm.

```
<input class="form-control form-control-lg"
        type="text" placeholder=".form-control-lg"
        aria-label=".form-control-lg example">
```

```
<input class="form-control" type="text"
       placeholder="Default input" aria-
       label="default input example">
<input class="form-control form-control-sm"
       type="text" placeholder=".form-control-sm"
       aria-label=".form-control-sm example">
```

Disabled

To give an input a grayed-out look and eliminate pointer events, use the disabled boolean property.

```
<input class="form-control" type="text"
       placeholder="Disabled input" aria-
       label="Disabled input example" disabled>
<input class="form-control" type="text" value=
       "Disabled readonly input" aria-label="Disabled
       input example" disabled readonly>
```

Read-only

Add the read-only boolean property to an input to prevent its value from being changed.

```
<input class="form-control" type="text"
       value="Readonly input here..." aria-
       label="readonly input example" readonly>
```

Read-only Plain Text

Use the .form-control-plaintext class to remove the default form field styling and keep the correct margin and padding for <input readonly> components in your form.

```
 <div class="mb-3 row">
  <label for="staticEmail" class="col-sm-2 col-form-
             label">Email</label>
  <div class="col-sm-10">
   <input type="text" readonly class="form-control-
          plaintext" id="staticEmail" value="email@
          example.com">
  </div>
 </div>
 <div class="mb-3 row">
```

```
  <label for="inputPassword" class="col-sm-2 col-
              form-label">Password</label>
  <div class="col-sm-10">
   <input type="password" class="form-control"
           id="inputPassword">
  </div>
 </div>

<form class="row g-3">
 <div class="col-auto">
  <label for="staticEmail2" class="visually-
             hidden">Email</label>
  <input type="text" readonly class="form-control-
             plaintext" id="staticEmail2"
             value="email@example.com">
 </div>
 <div class="col-auto">
  <label for="inputPassword2" class="visually-
             hidden">Password</label>
  <input type="password" class="form-control"
          id="inputPassword2" placeholder="Password">
 </div>
 <div class="col-auto">
  <button type="submit" class="btn btn-primary
          mb-3">Confirm identity</button>
 </div>
</form>
```

It is essential to know how to input a file from a user. The same we are going to learn from the next section.

File Input

```
<div class="mb-3">
 <label for="formFile" class="form-label">Default
            file input example</label>
 <input class="form-control" type="file"
            id="formFile">
</div>
<div class="mb-3">
 <label for="formFileMultiple" class="form-
        label">Multiple files input example</label>
```

```
   <input class="form-control" type="file"
              id="formFileMultiple" multiple>
</div>
<div class="mb-3">
 <label for="formFileDisabled" class="form-
         label">Disabled file input example</label>
 <input class="form-control" type="file"
              id="formFileDisabled" disabled>
</div>
<div class="mb-3">
 <label for="formFileSm" class="form-label">Small
             file input example</label>
 <input class="form-control form-control-sm"
              id="formFileSm" type="file">
</div>
<div>
 <label for="formFileLg" class="form-label">Large
             file input example</label>
 <input class="form-control form-control-lg"
              id="formFileLg" type="file">
</div>
```

Color

```
<label for="exampleColorInput" class="form-
            label">Color picker</label>
<input type="color" class="form-control form-control-
       color" id="exampleColorInput" value="#563d7c"
       title="Choose your color">
```

Data Lists

Data lists allow you to create a group of <option>s that can be accessed (and autocompleted) from within an <input>. These are similar to <select> elements but come with more menu styling limitations and differences. While most browsers and operating systems support <datalist> features, their styling is inconsistent at best.

```
<label for="exampleDataList" class="form-
label">Datalist example</label>
<input class="form-control" list="datalistOptions"
id="exampleDataList" placeholder="Type to search...">
<datalist id="datalistOptions">
 <option value="San Francisco">
```

```
<option value="New York">
<option value="Seattle">
<option value="Los Angeles">
<option value="Chicago">
</datalist>
```

It was all about form controls; we learned how to control resize, input, and other things. Now it is time to jump to the next section of this chapter: Select.

Select

Customize native <select> using custom CSS to alter the element's look.

Let's jump to the first example and see how the default select option looks like.

Default

To activate the custom styles, all that is required is a custom class, .form-select. Due to browser constraints, custom styles are confined to the initial look of the <choose> and cannot edit the <option>.

```
<select class="form-select" aria-label="Default
                select example">
 <option selected>Open this select menu</option>
 <option value="1">One</option>
 <option value="2">Two</option>
 <option value="3">Three</option>
</select>
```

We will have to revise this select option which we will learn now.

Sizing

To match our similarly sized text inputs, you may choose between tiny and big custom choices.

```
<select class="form-select form-select-lg mb-3" aria-
                label=".form-select-lg example">
 <option selected>Open this select menu</option>
 <option value="1">One</option>
 <option value="2">Two</option>
 <option value="3">Three</option>
</select>
```

```
<select class="form-select form-select-sm" aria-
            label=".form-select-sm example">
 <option selected>Open this select menu</option>
 <option value="1">One</option>
 <option value="2">Two</option>
 <option value="3">Three</option>
</select>
```

The multiple attribute is also supported:

```
<select class="form-select" multiple aria-
            label="multiple select example">
 <option selected>Open this select menu</option>
 <option value="1">One</option>
 <option value="2">Two</option>
 <option value="3">Three</option>
</select>
```

As is the size attribute:

```
<select class="form-select" size="3" aria-label="size
            3 select example">
 <option selected>Open this select menu</option>
 <option value="1">One</option>
 <option value="2">Two</option>
 <option value="3">Three</option>
</select>
```

Disabled

To give a select a grayed-out look and eliminate pointer events, use the disabled boolean property.

```
<select class="form-select" aria-label="Disabled
select example" disabled>
 <option selected>Open this select menu</option>
 <option value="1">One</option>
 <option value="2">Two</option>
 <option value="3">Three</option>
</select>
```

After learning the select option, it is time to move forward and learn about the check box and radio buttons.

CHECK AND RADIO

With our completely rewritten checks component, you can create consistent cross-browser and cross-device checkboxes and radios.

Approach

.form-check, a set of classes for both input types that improve the style and behaviour of their HTML elements, provides better customization and cross-browser compatibility and is used to replace browser default checkboxes and radios. Checkboxes choose one or more items from a list, whereas radio buttons select one option from a list of several items.

Our <input> and <label> are structurally sibling components, rather than an <input> within a <label>. Because you must provide an id and attributes to link the input and label, this is significantly more verbose. For all of our <input> states, such as :checked or :disabled, we use the sibling selector (~). We can simply style the wording for each item based on the status of the <input> using the .form-check-label class.

To indicate if a check is checked or indeterminate, we utilize custom Bootstrap icons.

Checks

```
<div class="form-check">
  <input class="form-check-input" type="checkbox"
              value="" id="flexCheckDefault">
  <label class="form-check-label" for="flexCheckDefault">
   Default checkbox
  </label>
</div>

<div class="form-check">
  <input class="form-check-input" type="checkbox"
         value="" id="flexCheckChecked" checked>
  <label class="form-check-label" for="flexCheckChecked">
   Checked checkbox
  </label>
</div>
```

Indeterminate

When manually configured using JavaScript, checkboxes can use the :indeterminate pseudo-class (there is no HTML attribute available for specifying it).

```
<div class="form-check">
 <input class="form-check-input" type="checkbox"
              value="" id="flexCheckIndeterminate">
 <label class="form-check-label" for="flexCheckIndete
              rminate">
  Indeterminate checkbox
 </label>
</div>
```

Disabled

The associated <label> are automatically formatted to correspond to a lighter color to assist conveying the input's condition when the disabled attribute is added.

```
<div class="form-check">
 <input class="form-check-input" type="checkbox"
         value="" id="flexCheckDisabled" disabled>
 <label class="form-check-label" for="flexCheckDisabled">
  Disabled checkbox
 </label>
</div>
```

```
<div class="form-check">
 <input class="form-check-input" type="checkbox"
              value="" id="flexCheckCheckedDisabled"
              checked disabled>
 <label class="form-check-label" for="flexCheckChecke
              dDisabled">
  Disabled checked checkbox
 </label>
</div>
```

After the checkbox, it is time to learn about radios; let's begin.

Radios

```
<div class="form-check">
 <input class="form-check-input" type="radio"
      name="flexRadioDefault" id="flexRadioDefault1">
 <label class="form-check-label" for="flexRadioDefault1">
  Default radio
 </label>
```

```
</div>
<div class="form-check">
 <input class="form-check-input" type="radio"
              name="flexRadioDefault"
              id="flexRadioDefault2" checked>
 <label class="form-check-label" for="flexRadioDefault2">
  Default checked radio
 </label>
</div>
```

Disabled

When you use a disabled property, the related <label> is automatically styled in a lighter color to assist identifying the input's status.

```
<div class="form-check">
 <input class="form-check-input" type="radio"
              name="flexRadioDisabled"
              id="flexRadioDisabled" disabled>
 <label class="form-check-label" for="flexRadioDisabled">
  Disabled radio
 </label>
</div>
<div class="form-check">
 <input class="form-check-input" type="radio" name=
              "flexRadioDisabled" id="flexRadio
              CheckedDisabled" checked disabled>
 <label class="form-check-label" for="flexRadioChecke
              dDisabled">
  Disabled checked radio
 </label>
</div>
```

Switches

A switch utilizes the .form-switch class to generate a toggle switch with the HTML of a custom checkbox. The disabled property is also supported via switches.

```
<div class="form-check form-switch">
 <input class="form-check-input" type="checkbox"
              id="flexSwitchCheckDefault">
 <label class="form-check-label" for="flexSwitchCheck
      Default">Default switch checkbox input</label>
```

```
</div>
<div class="form-check form-switch">
 <input class="form-check-input" type="checkbox"
                id="flexSwitchCheckChecked" checked>
 <label class="form-check-label" for="flexSwitchCheck
      Checked">Checked switch checkbox input</label>
</div>
<div class="form-check form-switch">
 <input class="form-check-input" type="checkbox"
                id="flexSwitchCheckDisabled" disabled>
 <label class="form-check-label" for="flexSwitchCheckDi
      sabled">Disabled switch checkbox input</label>
</div>
<div class="form-check form-switch">
 <input class="form-check-input" type="checkbox" id="
    flexSwitchCheckCheckedDisabled" checked disabled>
 <label class="form-check-label" for="flexSwitchCheck
                CheckedDisabled">Disabled checked
                switch checkbox input</label>
</div>
```

Default (Stacked)

By default, any number of checkboxes and radios that are immediate siblings will be vertically stacked and appropriately spaced with .form-check.

```
<div class="form-check">
 <input class="form-check-input" type="checkbox"
                value="" id="defaultCheck1">
 <label class="form-check-label" for="defaultCheck1">
  Default checkbox
 </label>
</div>
<div class="form-check">
 <input class="form-check-input" type="checkbox"
                value="" id="defaultCheck2" disabled>
 <label class="form-check-label" for="defaultCheck2">
  Disabled checkbox
 </label>
</div>
<div class="form-check">
 <input class="form-check-input" type="radio"
        name="exampleRadios" id="exampleRadios1"
        value="option1" checked>
```

```
<label class="form-check-label" for="exampleRadios1">
 Default radio
 </label>
</div>
<div class="form-check">
 <input class="form-check-input" type="radio"
        name="exampleRadios" id="exampleRadios2"
        value="option2">
 <label class="form-check-label" for="exampleRadios2">
 Second default radio
 </label>
</div>
<div class="form-check">
 <input class="form-check-input" type="radio"
        name="exampleRadios" id="exampleRadios3"
        value="option3" disabled>
 <label class="form-check-label" for="exampleRadios3">
 Disabled radio
 </label>
</div>
```

Inline

Group checkboxes or radios on same horizontal row by adding .form-check-inline to .form-check.

```
<div class="form-check form-check-inline">
 <input class="form-check-input" type="checkbox"
               id="inlineCheckbox1" value="option1">
 <label class="form-check-label"
               for="inlineCheckbox1">1</label>
</div>
<div class="form-check form-check-inline">
 <input class="form-check-input" type="checkbox"
               id="inlineCheckbox2" value="option2">
 <label class="form-check-label"
               for="inlineCheckbox2">2</label>
</div>
<div class="form-check form-check-inline">
 <input class="form-check-input" type="checkbox" id=
        "inlineCheckbox3" value="option3" disabled>
 <label class="form-check-label"
        for="inlineCheckbox3">3 (disabled)</label>
</div>
```

```
<div class="form-check form-check-inline">
 <input class="form-check-input" type="radio"
          name="inlineRadioOptions"
          id="inlineRadio1" value="option1">
 <label class="form-check-label"
          for="inlineRadio1">1</label>
</div>
<div class="form-check form-check-inline">
 <input class="form-check-input" type="radio"
          name="inlineRadioOptions"
          id="inlineRadio2" value="option2">
 <label class="form-check-label"
for="inlineRadio2">2</label>
</div>
<div class="form-check form-check-inline">
 <input class="form-check-input" type="radio"
        name="inlineRadioOptions" id="inlineRadio3"
        value="option3" disabled>
 <label class="form-check-label" for="inlineRadio3">3
          (disabled)</label>
</div>
```

Without Labels

Omit the wrapping for checkboxes and radios with no label text, use .form-check. Remember to give assistive technology some sort of accessible name (for instance, using aria-label). For further information, see the accessibility section of the forms overview.

```
<div>
 <input class="form-check-input" type="checkbox"
        id="checkboxNoLabel" value="" aria-label="...">
</div>

<div>
 <input class="form-check-input" type="radio"
          name="radioNoLabel" id="radioNoLabel1"
          value="" aria-label="...">
</div>
```

Toggle Buttons

Use .btn styles on the <label> components instead of .form-check-label to create button-like checkboxes and radio buttons. If necessary, these toggle buttons can be organized into a button group.

Checkbox and Toggle Buttons

```
<input type="checkbox" class="btn-check" id="btn-
        check" autocomplete="off">
<label class="btn btn-primary" for="btn-check">Single
        toggle</label>

<input type="checkbox" class="btn-check" id="btn-
        check-2" checked autocomplete="off">
<label class="btn btn-primary" for="btn-check-
        2">Checked</label>

<input type="checkbox" class="btn-check" id="btn-
        check-3" autocomplete="off" disabled>
<label class="btn btn-primary" for="btn-check-
        3">Disabled</label>
```

Radio Toggle Buttons

```
<input type="radio" class="btn-check" name="options"
        id="option1" autocomplete="off" checked>
<label class="btn btn-secondary"
        for="option1">Checked</label>

<input type="radio" class="btn-check" name="options"
            id="option2" autocomplete="off">
<label class="btn btn-secondary"
        for="option2">Radio</label>

<input type="radio" class="btn-check" name="options"
        id="option3" autocomplete="off" disabled>
<label class="btn btn-secondary"
        for="option3">Disabled</label>

<input type="radio" class="btn-check" name="options"
        id="option4" autocomplete="off">
<label class="btn btn-secondary"
        for="option4">Radio</label>
```

Outlined Styles

Different variants of .btn, such as the various outlined styles, are supported.

```
<input type="checkbox" class="btn-check" id="btn-
            check-outlined" autocomplete="off">
<label class="btn btn-outline-primary" for="btn-
      check-outlined">Single toggle</label><br>


<input type="checkbox" class="btn-check" id="btn-
            check-2-outlined" checked autocomplete="off">
<label class="btn btn-outline-secondary" for="btn-c
            heck-2-outlined">Checked</label><br>


<input type="radio" class="btn-check" name="options-
            outlined" id="success-outlined"
            autocomplete="off" checked>
<label class="btn btn-outline-success" for="success-
            outlined">Checked success radio</label>

<input type="radio" class="btn-check" name="options-
        outlined" id="danger-outlined" autocomplete="off">
<label class="btn btn-outline-danger" for="danger-
            outlined">Danger radio</label>
```

This was all about Check and radio button; now, moving forward, it is time to learn about the "orange button."

RANGE

Use Bootstraps custom range inputs for consistent cross-browser styling and built-in customization.

Now let's focus on the overview and begin with learning.

Overview

With .form-range, you may create custom <input type="range"> controls. Both the track (background) and the thumb (value) are stylized to look the same in all browsers. We do not now support it since only Firefox enables "filling" their track from the left or right of the thumb to visibly display progress.

```
<label for="customRange1" class="form-label">Example
                                    range</label>
```

```
<input type="range" class="form-range"
                    id="customRange1">
```

Disable

To give an input a grayed-out look and eliminate pointer events, use the disabled boolean property.

```
<label for="disabledRange" class="form-
           label">Disabled range</label>
<input type="range" class="form-range"
           id="disabledRange" disabled>
```

Min and Max

The implicit values for min and max in range inputs are 0 and 100, respectively. Those with the min and max characteristics can have new values specified.

```
<label for="customRange2" class="form-label">Example
                               range</label>
<input type="range" class="form-range" min="0"
                    max="6" id="customRange2">
```

Steps

Range inputs "snap" to integer values by default. You can adjust this by specifying a step value. By setting step="0.5," we may double the number of steps in the example below.

```
<label for="customRange3" class="form-label">Example
                               range</label>
<input type="range" class="form-range" min="0"
           max="6" step="0.5" id="customRange3">
```

This was all about range, we learned various types of range tools and how to use them. Now it is time to move forward and learn about the input group.

INPUT GROUP

Add text, buttons, or button groups on each side of textual inputs, custom selections, and custom file inputs to easily extend form controls. Let's return to the main example and begin adding more sorts of input groups.

Basic Example

One add-on or button should be placed on either side of an input. You may even put one on either side of the information. <Label> must be placed outside the input group.

```
<div class="input-group mb-3">
 <span class="input-group-text" id="basic-addon1">@</
                                       span>
 <input type="text" class="form-control"
        placeholder="Username" aria-label="Username"
        aria-describedby="basic-addon1">
</div>

<div class="input-group mb-3">
 <input type="text" class="form-control"
             placeholder="Recipient's username"
             aria-label="Recipient's username"
             aria-describedby="basic-addon2">
 <span class="input-group-text" id="basic-addon2">@
             example.com</span>
</div>

<label for="basic-url" class="form-label">Your vanity
            URL</label>
<div class="input-group mb-3">
 <span class="input-group-text" id="basic-
        addon3"&gt;https://example.com/users/</span>
 <input type="text" class="form-control" id="basic-
            url" aria-describedby="basic-addon3">
</div>

<div class="input-group mb-3">
 <span class="input-group-text">$</span>
 <input type="text" class="form-control" aria-
label="Amount (to nearest dollar)">
 <span class="input-group-text">.00</span>
</div>

<div class="input-group mb-3">
 <input type="text" class="form-control"
        placeholder="Username" aria-label="Username">
 <span class="input-group-text">@</span>
```

```
<input type="text" class="form-control"
       placeholder="Server" aria-label="Server">
</div>

<div class="input-group">
 <span class="input-group-text">With textarea</span>
 <textarea class="form-control" aria-label="With
                   textarea"></textarea>
</div>
```

Wrapping

By default, input groups wrap: Wrap to support custom form field validation within an input group using flex-wrap. The .flex-nowrap can be used
to deactivate this.

```
<div class="input-group flex-nowrap">
 <span class="input-group-text" id="addon-
             wrapping">@</span>
 <input type="text" class="form-control"
       placeholder="Username" aria-label="Username"
       aria-describedby="addon-wrapping">
</div>
```

Sizing

There's no need to repeat the form control size classes on each element if
you add relative form sizing classes to the .input-group itself.

The individual input group components cannot resize.

```
<div class="input-group input-group-sm mb-3">
 <span class="input-group-text" id="inputGroup-
             sizing-sm">Small</span>
 <input type="text" class="form-control" aria-
       label="Sizing example input"
       aria-describedby="inputGroup-sizing-sm">
</div>

<div class="input-group mb-3">
 <span class="input-group-text" id="inputGroup-sizin
g-default">Default</span>
 <input type="text" class="form-control" aria-
label="Sizing example input" aria-describedby="inputGr
oup-sizing-default">
</div>
```

```
<div class="input-group input-group-lg">
 <span class="input-group-text" id="inputGroup-
             sizing-lg">Large</span>
 <input type="text" class="form-control" aria-
        label="Sizing example input"
        aria-describedby="inputGroup-sizing-lg">
</div>
```

Checkbox and Radios

Instead of text, place any checkbox or radio choice within an input group's add-on. When there is no visible text next to the input, we suggest adding .mt-0 to the .form-check-input.

```
<div class="input-group mb-3">
 <div class="input-group-text">
  <input class="form-check-input mt-0" type="checkbox"
         value="" aria-label="Checkbox for following
         text input">
 </div>
 <input type="text" class="form-control" aria-
             label="Text input with checkbox">
</div>

<div class="input-group">
 <div class="input-group-text">
  <input class="form-check-input mt-0" type="radio"
         value="" aria-label="Radio button for
         following text input">
 </div>
 <input type="text" class="form-control" aria-
        label="Text input with radio button">
</div>
```

Multiple Inputs

While visual support for multiple inputs is provided, validation styles are only available for input groups with a single input.

```
<div class="input-group">
 <span class="input-group-text">First and last name</
       span>
 <input type="text" aria-label="First name"
             class="form-control">
```

```
<input type="text" aria-label="Last name"
            class="form-control">
</div>
```

Multiple Add-ons

Multiple add-ons are supported, and checkbox and radio input versions can be blended.

```
<div class="input-group mb-3">
 <span class="input-group-text">$</span>
 <span class="input-group-text">0.00</span>
 <input type="text" class="form-control" aria-label=
   "Dollar amount (with dot and two decimal places)">
</div>

<div class="input-group">
 <input type="text" class="form-control" aria-label=
   "Dollar amount (with dot and two decimal places)">
 <span class="input-group-text">$</span>
 <span class="input-group-text">0.00</span>
</div>
```

Button Add-ons

```
<div class="input-group mb-3">
 <button class="btn btn-outline-secondary"
     type="button" id="button-addon1">Button</button>
 <input type="text" class="form-control" placeholder=
        "" aria-label="Example text with button
        addon" aria-describedby="button-addon1">
</div>

<div class="input-group mb-3">
 <input type="text" class="form-control"
        placeholder="Recipient's username" aria-
        label="Recipient's username"
        aria-describedby="button-addon2">
 <button class="btn btn-outline-secondary" type=
         "button" id="button-addon2">Button</button>
</div>

<div class="input-group mb-3">
 <button class="btn btn-outline-secondary"
            type="button">Button</button>
```

```
<button class="btn btn-outline-secondary"
               type="button">Button</button>
<input type="text" class="form-control"
           placeholder="" aria-label="Example text
           with two button addons">
</div>

<div class="input-group">
 <input type="text" class="form-control" placeholder=
        "Recipient's username" aria-label="Recipient's
        username with two button addons">
 <button class="btn btn-outline-secondary"
               type="button">Button</button>
 <button class="btn btn-outline-secondary"
               type="button">Button</button>
</div>
```

Button with Dropdowns

```
<div class="input-group mb-3">
 <button class="btn btn-outline-secondary dropdown-
   toggle" type="button" data-bs-toggle="dropdown"
   aria-expanded="false">Dropdown</button>
 <ul class="dropdown-menu">
  <li><a class="dropdown-item" href="#">Action</a></li>
  <li><a class="dropdown-item" href="#">Another
               action</a></li>
  <li><a class="dropdown-item" href="#">Something
               else here</a></li>
  <li><hr class="dropdown-divider"></li>
  <li><a class="dropdown-item" href="#">Separated
               link</a></li>
 </ul>
 <input type="text" class="form-control" aria-
           label="Text input with dropdown button">
</div>

<div class="input-group mb-3">
 <input type="text" class="form-control" aria-
         label="Text input with dropdown button">
 <button class="btn btn-outline-secondary dropdown-
   toggle" type="button" data-bs-toggle=
   "dropdown" aria-expanded="false">Dropdown</button>
```

```
<ul class="dropdown-menu dropdown-menu-end">
 <li><a class="dropdown-item" href="#">Action</a></li>
 <li><a class="dropdown-item" href="#">Another
             action</a></li>
 <li><a class="dropdown-item" href="#">Something
             else here</a></li>
 <li><hr class="dropdown-divider"></li>
 <li><a class="dropdown-item" href="#">Separated
             link</a></li>
</ul>
</div>

<div class="input-group">
 <button class="btn btn-outline-secondary dropdown-
   toggle" type="button" data-bs-toggle=
   "dropdown" aria-expanded="false">Dropdown</button>
 <ul class="dropdown-menu">
 <li><a class="dropdown-item" href="#">Action
             before</a></li>
 <li><a class="dropdown-item" href="#">Another
             action before</a></li>
 <li><a class="dropdown-item" href="#">Something
             else here</a></li>
 <li><hr class="dropdown-divider"></li>
 <li><a class="dropdown-item" href="#">Separated
             link</a></li>
 </ul>
 <input type="text" class="form-control" aria-
        label="Text input with 2 dropdown buttons">
 <button class="btn btn-outline-secondary dropdown-
   toggle" type="button" data-bs-toggle="dropdown"
   aria-expanded="false">Dropdown</button>
 <ul class="dropdown-menu dropdown-menu-end">
 <li><a class="dropdown-item" href="#">Action</a></li>
 <li><a class="dropdown-item" href="#">Another
             action</a></li>
 <li><a class="dropdown-item" href="#">Something
             else here</a></li>
 <li><hr class="dropdown-divider"></li>
 <li><a class="dropdown-item" href="#">Separated
             link</a></li>
 </ul>
</div>
```

Segmented Buttons

```
<div class="input-group mb-3">
 <button type="button" class="btn btn-outline-
        secondary">Action</button>
 <button type="button" class="btn btn-outline-
   secondary dropdown-toggle dropdown-toggle-split"
   data-bs-toggle="dropdown" aria-expanded="false">
  <span class="visually-hidden">Toggle Dropdown</
            span>
 </button>
 <ul class="dropdown-menu">
  <li><a class="dropdown-item" href="#">Action</a></li>
  <li><a class="dropdown-item" href="#">Another
            action</a></li>
  <li><a class="dropdown-item" href="#">Something
            else here</a></li>
  <li><hr class="dropdown-divider"></li>
  <li><a class="dropdown-item" href="#">Separated
            link</a></li>
 </ul>
 <input type="text" class="form-control" aria-label=
       "Text input with segmented dropdown button">
</div>

<div class="input-group">
 <input type="text" class="form-control" aria-
   label="Text input with segmented dropdown button">
 <button type="button" class="btn btn-outline-
            secondary">Action</button>
 <button type="button" class="btn btn-outline-
   secondary dropdown-toggle dropdown-toggle-split"
   data-bs-toggle="dropdown" aria-expanded="false">
  <span class="visually-hidden">Toggle Dropdown</
            span>
 </button>
 <ul class="dropdown-menu dropdown-menu-end">
  <li><a class="dropdown-item" href="#">Action</a></li>
  <li><a class="dropdown-item" href="#">Another
            action</a></li>
  <li><a class="dropdown-item" href="#">Something
            else here</a></li>
  <li><hr class="dropdown-divider"></li>
```

```
    <li><a class="dropdown-item" href="#">Separated
                link</a></li>
  </ul>
</div>
```

Custom Forms

Custom selections and custom file inputs are supported via input groups. These are not supported in their default browser versions.

Custom Selects

```
<div class="input-group mb-3">
 <label class="input-group-text" for="inputGroupSelec
                t01">Options</label>
 <select class="form-select" id="inputGroupSelect01">
  <option selected>Choose...</option>
  <option value="1">One</option>
  <option value="2">Two</option>
  <option value="3">Three</option>
 </select>
</div>

<div class="input-group mb-3">
 <select class="form-select" id="inputGroupSelect02">
  <option selected>Choose...</option>
  <option value="1">One</option>
  <option value="2">Two</option>
  <option value="3">Three</option>
 </select>
 <label class="input-group-text" for="inputGroupSelec
                t02">Options</label>
</div>
<div class="input-group mb-3">
 <button class="btn btn-outline-secondary"
type="button">Button</button>
 <select class="form-select" id="inputGroupSelect03"
     aria-label="Example select with button addon">
  <option selected>Choose...</option>
  <option value="1">One</option>
  <option value="2">Two</option>
  <option value="3">Three</option>
 </select>
</div>
```

```
<div class="input-group">
 <select class="form-select" id="inputGroupSelect04"
     aria-label="Example select with button addon">
  <option selected>Choose...</option>
  <option value="1">One</option>
  <option value="2">Two</option>
  <option value="3">Three</option>
 </select>
 <button class="btn btn-outline-secondary"
               type="button">Button</button>
</div>
```

Custom File Input

```
<div class="input-group mb-3">
 <label class="input-group-text" for="inputGroupFile0
             1">Upload</label>
 <input type="file" class="form-control"
                   id="inputGroupFile01">
</div>
```

```
<div class="input-group mb-3">
 <input type="file" class="form-control"
                   id="inputGroupFile02">
 <label class="input-group-text" for="inputGroupFile0
             2">Upload</label>
</div>
```

```
<div class="input-group mb-3">
 <button class="btn btn-outline-secondary" type="button"
 id="inputGroupFileAddon03">Button</button>
 <input type="file" class="form-control" id="input
        GroupFile03" aria-describedby="input
        GroupFileAddon03" aria-label="Upload">
</div>
```

```
<div class="input-group">
 <input type="file" class="form-control" id="input
             GroupFile04" aria-describedby="input
             GroupFileAddon04" aria-label="Upload">
 <button class="btn btn-outline-secondary"
         type="button" id="inputGroupFileAddon04">But
         ton</button>
</div>
```

This was all about input groups. Now let's move forward and learn about floating labels.

FLOATING LABELS

Create elegant form labels that float above your input fields.

Example

To use floating labels with Bootstrap's textual form fields, wrap a pair of <input class="form-control"> and <label> components in .form-floating. Because our approach of CSS-only floating labels employs the :placeholder-shown pseudo-element, each <input> must have a placeholder. Also, the input> must appear before so that we may use a sibling selector (for example, ~).

```
<div class="form-floating mb-3">
 <input type="email" class="form-control" id=
        "floatingInput" placeholder="name@example.com">
 <label for="floatingInput">Email address</label>
</div>
<div class="form-floating">
 <input type="password" class="form-control"
        id="floatingPassword" placeholder="Password">
 <label for="floatingPassword">Password</label>
</div>
```

When there's a value already defined, <label>s will automatically adjust to their floated position.

```
<form class="form-floating">
 <input type="email" class="form-control"
        id="floatingInputValue" placeholder="name@
        example.com" value="test@example.com">
 <label for="floatingInputValue">Input with value</
             label>
</form>
```

Form validation styles also work as expected.

```
<form class="form-floating">
 <input type="email" class="form-control is-invalid"
        id="floatingInputInvalid" placeholder="name@
        example.com" value="test@example.com">
```

```
    <label for="floatingInputInvalid">Invalid input</
        label>
</form>
```

Text Areas

By default, <textarea>s with the .form-control will be of the same height as <input>s.

```
<div class="form-floating">
 <textarea class="form-control" placeholder="Leave
      comment here" id="floatingTextarea"></textarea>
 <label for="floatingTextarea">Comments</label>
</div>
```

Do not utilize the rows attribute to define a custom height for your <textarea>. Set an explicit size instead (either inline or via custom CSS).

```
<div class="form-floating">
 <textarea class="form-control" placeholder="Leave
         comment here" id="floatingTextarea2"
         style="height: 90px"></textarea>
 <label for="floatingTextarea2">Comments</label>
</div>
```

Selects

Floating labels are only accessible on .form-selects, not.form-control. They function similarly to <input>; however, unlike <input>, they always display the label in its floating state. *Size* and *multiple* selections are not supported.

```
<div class="form-floating">
 <select class="form-select" id="floatingSelect"
         aria-label="Floating label select example">
  <option selected>Open this select menu</option>
  <option value="1">One</option>
  <option value="2">Two</option>
  <option value="3">Three</option>
 </select>
 <label for="floatingSelect">Works with selects</
             label>
</div>
```

Layouts

Make sure to arrange form components within column classes when using the Bootstrap grid system.

```
<div class="row g-2">
 <div class="col-md">
  <div class="form-floating">
   <input type="email" class="form-control"
          id="floatingInputGrid" placeholder="name@
          example.com" value="mdo@example.com">
   <label for="floatingInputGrid">Email address</
               label>
  </div>
 </div>
 <div class="col-md">
  <div class="form-floating">
   <select class="form-select" id="floatingSelectGrid"
           aria-label="Floating label select example">
    <option selected>Open this select menu</option>
    <option value="1">One</option>
    <option value="2">Two</option>
    <option value="3">Three</option>
   </select>
   <label for="floatingSelectGrid">Works with
               selects</label>
  </div>
 </div>
</div>
```

CONCLUSION

In this chapter, we learned about various things, like typography, how to work with images, how many types of tables are offered by Bootstrap, and how to use tables, figures, and forms.

In the next chapter, we will learn about other components offered by Bootstrap in detail and how to use them.

Components

IN THIS CHAPTER

DOI: 10.1201/9781003310501-6

➢ Pagination

➢ Placeholders

➢ Popovers

➢ Progress

➢ Scrollspy

➢ Spinners

➢ Toasts

➢ Tooltips

Components

In the previous chapter, we learned about typography, how to work with pictures, how many types of tables Bootstrap provides, and how to utilize tables, figures, and forms.

In this chapter, we will discuss about the other components offered by Bootstrap in detail and how to use them.

The first component to be discussed is "accordion."

COMPONENTS

Bootstrap also uses theme colors as predefined colors for some components, for example, buttons.

This was about colors. However, you can use colors as per your need. You can use more types of pallets, more different types of stains on buttons as well.

Now we will jump over the components of Bootstrap and know how many components are available and how we can use them.

ACCORDION

Create vertically collapsing accordions with the Collapse JavaScript plugin.

How It Works

Internally, the accordion employs collapse to make it collapsible. To render an extended accordion, add the .open class to the .accordion.

This component's animation effect is determined by the prefers-reduced-motion media query.

Example

Accordion Item #1

This is the accordion body of the first item. It is displayed by default until the collapse plugin gives the necessary classes to style each piece. These classes manage the overall look as well as the displaying and hiding of elements using CSS transitions. You may change any of this with custom CSS or by overriding our default variables. It is also worth noting that the .accordion-body may include practically any HTML, although the transition does limit overflows.

Accordion Item #2

This is the accordion body for the second item. By default, it is hidden until the collapse plugin provides the required classes to style each piece. These classes govern the overall look as well as the displaying and hiding of elements using CSS transitions. You may change any of this using custom CSS or by overriding our default variables. It is also worth noting that the .accordion-body may include almost any HTML, but the transition does limit overflows.

Accordion Item #3

This is the accordion body for the third item. By default, it is hidden until the collapse plugin provides the required classes to style each piece. These classes govern the overall look as well as the displaying and hiding of elements using CSS transitions. You may change any of this using custom CSS or by overriding our default variables. It is also worth noting that

.accordion-body may include almost any HTML, but transition does limit overflow.

```
<div class="accordion" id="accordion_Example">
 <div class="accordion-item">
  <h2 class="accordion-header" id="headingOne">
   <button class="accordion-button" type="button"
data-bs-toggle="collapse" data-bs-
target="#collapseOne" aria-expanded="true"
aria-controls="collapse_One">
    Accordion-Item #1
   </button>
  </h2>
  <div id="collapse_One" class="accordion-collapse
collapse show" aria-labelledby="headingOne"
data-bs-parent="#accordion_Example">
   <div class="accordion-body">
    <strong> This is accordion body of the first
item. </strong> It is shown by default until collapse
plugin provides the required classes for styling each
piece. These classes govern the overall look as well
as the displaying and hiding of elements using CSS
transitions. Any of this may be customized using
custom CSS or by modifying our default settings. It is
also worth mentioning that almost any HTML may be used
within the
   </div>
  </div>
 </div>
 <div class="accordion-item">
  <h2 class="accordion-header" id="headingTwo">
   <button class="accordion-button collapsed"
type="button" data-bs-toggle="collapse" data-bs-
target="#collapseTwo" aria-expanded="false"
aria-controls="collapse_Two">
    Accordion-Item #2
   </button>
  </h2>
  <div id="collapse_Two" class="accordion-collapse
collapse" aria-labelledby="headingTwo"
data-bs-parent="#accordionExample">
```

```
 <div class="accordion-body">
   <strong> This is the accordion body for the
second item. </strong> By default, it is hidden until
the collapse plugin supplies the appropriate classes
to style each component. These classes govern the
overall look as well as the displaying and hiding of
elements using CSS transitions. Any of this may be
customized using custom CSS or by modifying our
default settings. It is also worth noting that almost
any HTML may be used within the <code>.accordion-
body/code>, but the transition does limit overflow.
   </div>
  </div>
 </div>
 <div class="accordion-item">
  <h2 class="accordion-header" id="headingThree">
   <button class="accordion-button collapsed"
type="button" data-bs-toggle="collapse" data-bs-
target="#collapseThree" aria-expanded="false"
aria-controls="collapse_Three">
    Accordion-Item #3
   </button>
  </h2>
  <div id="collapse_Three" class="accordion-collapse
collapse" aria-labelledby="headingThree"
data-bs-parent="#accordionExample">
   <div class="accordion-body">
    <strong> This is the accordion body for the third
item./strong> By default, it is hidden until the
collapse plugin supplies the appropriate classes to
style each component. These classes govern the overall
look as well as the displaying and hiding of elements
using CSS transitions. Any of this may be customized
using custom CSS or by modifying our default settings.
It is also worth noting that any HTML may be placed
within the <code>.accordion-body/code>, however the
transition does limit overflow.
   </div>
  </div>
 </div>
</div>
```

Flush

To make accordions appear edge-to-edge with their parent container, use .accordion-flush to remove the default background color, certain borders, and some rounded corners.

Accordion Item #1

This accordion's placeholder content is meant to show the .accordion-flush class. This is the accordion body for the first item.

Accordion Item #2

This accordion's placeholder content is meant to show the .accordion-flush class. This is the accordion body for the second piece. Let's pretend this is loaded with genuine material.

Accordion Item #3

This accordion's placeholder content is meant to show the .accordion-flush class. This is the accordion body for the third item. Nothing more spectacular in terms of content is going on here, simply filling up the space to make it appear, at least at first sight, more realistic of how this would look in a real-world application.

```
<div class="accordion accordion-flush"
                    id="accordionFlushExample">
 <div class="accordion-item">
  <h2 class="accordion-header" id="flush-headingOne">
   <button class="accordion-button collapsed"
     type="button" data-bs-toggle="collapse" data-bs-
     target="#flush-collapseOne" aria-expanded="false"
     aria-controls="flush-collapseOne">
    Accordion Item #1
   </button>
  </h2>
  <div id="flush-collapseOne" class="accordion-collapse
    collapse" aria-labelledby="flush-headingOne" data-
    bs-parent="#accordionFlushExample">
   <div class="accordion-body">Placeholder content
     for accordion, which is intended to demonstrate
     <code>.accordion-flush</code> class. This is the
     first item's accordion body.</div>
  </div>
 </div>
```

```
<div class="accordion-item">
 <h2 class="accordion-header" id="flush-headingTwo">
  <button class="accordion-button collapsed"
    type="button" data-bs-toggle="collapse" data-bs-
    target="#flush-collapseTwo" aria-expanded="false"
    aria-controls="flush-collapseTwo">
   Accordion Item #2
  </button>
 </h2>
 <div id="flush-collapseTwo" class="accordion-collapse
   collapse" aria-labelledby="flush-headingTwo" data-
   bs-parent="#accordionFlushExample">
  <div class="accordion-body">Placeholder content for
    accordion, which is intended to show the <code>.
    accordion-flush</code> class. This is the
    accordion body for the second item. Let's pretend
    this is loaded with genuine material.</div>
 </div>
</div>
<div class="accordion-item">
 <h2 class="accordion-header"
id="flush-headingThree">
  <button class="accordion-button collapsed"
    type="button" data-bs-toggle="collapse" data-bs-
    target="#flush-collapseThree" aria-expanded=
    "false" aria-controls="flush-collapseThree">
   Accordion Item #3
  </button>
 </h2>
 <div id="flush-collapseThree" class="accordion-
    collapse collapse" aria-labelledby="flush-
    headingThree" data-bs-parent="#accordionFlushEx
    ample">
  <div class="accordion-body">This accordion's
    placeholder information is designed to show
    the <code>.accordion-flush</code> class. To
    render accordions edge to edge with the parent
    container, add .accordion-flush to eliminate
    the default background color, certain borders,
    and some rounded corners.</div>
 </div>
</div>
</div>
```

Always Open

Remove the data-bs-parent property from each. To keep accordion things open when another object is opened, use .accordion-collapse.

Accordion Item #1

This is the accordion body for the first item. It is displayed by default until the collapse plugin provides the necessary classes to style each piece. These classes govern the overall look as well as the displaying and hiding of elements using CSS transitions. You may change any of this using custom CSS or by overriding our default variables. It is also worth noting that .accordion-body may include almost any HTML, but the transition does limit overflow.

Accordion Item #2

This is the accordion body for the second item. By default, it is hidden until the collapse plugin provides the required classes to style each piece. These classes govern the overall look as well as the displaying and hiding of elements using CSS transitions. You may change any of this using custom CSS or by overriding our default variables. It is also worth noting that .accordion-body may include almost any HTML, but the transition does limit overflow.

Accordion Item #3

This is the accordion body for the third item. By default, it is hidden until the collapse plugin provides the required classes to style each piece. These classes govern the overall look as well as the displaying and hiding of elements using CSS transitions. You may change any of this using custom CSS or by overriding our default variables. It is also worth noting that .accordion-body may include almost any HTML, but the transition does limit overflow.

```
<div class="accordion" id="ExampleaccordionPanelsStay
            Open">
  <div class="accordion-item">
    <h2 class="accordion-header" id="panelsStayOpen-
            headingOne">
      <button class="accordion-button" type="button"
        data-bs-toggle="collapse" data-bs-target="#pan
```

```
      elsStayOpen-collapseOne" aria-expanded="true"
      aria-controls="panelsStayOpen-collapseOne">
    Accordion-Item #1
  </button>
 </h2>
 <div id="panelsStayOpen-collapseOne"
     class="accordion-collapse collapse show" aria-
     labelledby="panelsStayOpen-headingOne">
   <div class="accordion-body">
    <strong> This is the accordion body for the
first item. </strong> It is shown by default until
collapse plugin provides the required classes for
styling each piece. These classes govern the overall
look as well as the displaying and hiding of
elements using CSS transitions. Any of this may be
customized using custom CSS or by modifying our
default settings. It is also worth mentioning that
almost any HTML may be used within the <code>.
accordion-body</code>, though the transition does
limit overflow.
   </div>
  </div>
 </div>
 <div class="accordion-item">
  <h2 class="accordion-header"
id="panelsStayOpen-headingTwo">
    <button class="accordion-button collapsed"
     type="button" data-bs-toggle="collapse" data-
     bs-target="#panelsStayOpen-collapseTwo" aria-
     expanded="false" aria-controls="panelsStay
     Open-collapseTwo">
    Accordion Item #2
   </button>
  </h2>
  <div id="panelsStayOpen-collapseTwo"
     class="accordion-collapse collapse" aria-label
     ledby="panelsStayOpen-headingTwo">
   <div class="accordion-body">
    <strong> This is the accordion body for the
second item. </strong> It is hidden by default until
collapse plugin provides the necessary classes to
```

style each piece. These classes govern the overall
look as well as the displaying and hiding of elements
using CSS transitions. Any of this may be customized
using custom CSS or by modifying our default settings.
It is also worth mentioning that almost any HTML may
be used within the <code>.accordion-body</code>,
though the transition does limit overflow.

```
  </div>
 </div>
</div>
<div class="accordion-item">
 <h2 class="accordion-header"
id="panelsStayOpen-headingThree">
   <button class="accordion-button collapsed"
     type="button" data-bs-toggle="collapse" data-
     bs-target="#panelsStayOpen-collapseThree" aria-
     expanded="false" aria-controls="panelsStay
     Open-collapseThree">
    Accordion Item #3
   </button>
 </h2>
 <div id="panelsStayOpen-collapseThree"
     class="accordion-collapse collapse" aria-label
     ledby="panelsStayOpen-headingThree">
   <div class="accordion-body">
```

    <strong> This is the accordion body for the third
item. </strong> It is hidden by default until
collapse plugin provides the necessary classes to
style each piece. These classes govern the overall
look as well as the displaying and hiding of elements
using CSS transitions. Any of this may be customized
using custom CSS or by modifying our default settings.
It is also worth mentioning that almost any HTML may
be used within the <code>.accordion-body</code>,
though the transition does limit overflow.

```
  </div>
  </div>
 </div>
</div>
```

ALERTS

With a tiny proportion of accessible and adaptable alert messages, provide
contextual feedback messages for common user behaviors.

Examples

Alerts for any length of text are provided, as is an optional close button. Use one of the eight essential contextual classes for the optimal style. Use the alerts JavaScript plugin for inline dismissal.

```
<div class="alert alert-primary" role="alert">
 A simple primary alert—check it out!
</div>
<div class="alert alert-secondary" role="alert">
 A simple secondary alert—check it out!
</div>
<div class="alert alert-success" role="alert">
 A simple success alert—check it out!
</div>
<div class="alert alert-danger" role="alert">
 A simple danger alert—check it out!
</div>
<div class="alert alert-warning" role="alert">
 A simple warning alert—check it out!
</div>
<div class="alert alert-info" role="alert">
 A simple info alert—check it out!
</div>
<div class="alert alert-light" role="alert">
 A simple light alert—check it out!
</div>
<div class="alert alert-dark" role="alert">
 A simple dark alert—check it out!
</div>
```

Conveying Meaning to Assistive Technologies

The use of color to add meaning merely gives a visual indicator that will not be relayed to users of assistive devices such as screen readers. Ascertain that the information suggested by the color is either obvious from the content itself or is included through the alternate means, such as extra text concealed with the .Visually-hidden class.

Link Color

Use the .alert-link utility class to provide matching colored links within any alert quickly.

```
<div class="alert alert-primary" role="alert">
 A simple primary alert with <a href="#"
  class="alert-link">an example link</a>. Give it a
  click if you like.
</div>
<div class="alert alert-secondary" role="alert">
 A simple secondary alert with <a href="#"
  class="alert-link">an example link</a>. Give it a
  click if you like.
</div>
<div class="alert alert-success" role="alert">
 A simple success alert with <a href="#"
  class="alert-link">an example link</a>. Give it a
  click if you like.
</div>
<div class="alert alert-danger" role="alert">
 A simple danger alert with <a href="#" class="alert-
  link">an example link</a>. Give it a click if you
  like.
</div>
<div class="alert alert-warning" role="alert">
 A simple warning alert with <a href="#"
  class="alert-link">an example link</a>. Give it a
  click if you like.
</div>
<div class="alert alert-info" role="alert">
 A simple info alert with <a href="#" class="alert-
  link">an example link</a>. Give it a click if you
  like.
</div>
<div class="alert alert-light" role="alert">
 A simple light alert with <a href="#" class="alert-
  link">an example link</a>. Give it a click if you
  like.
</div>
<div class="alert alert-dark" role="alert">
 A simple dark alert with <a href="#" class="alert-
  link">an example link</a>. Give it a click if you
  like.
</div>
```

Additional Content

Alerts also can contain additional HTML elements like headings, paragraphs, and dividers.

```
<div class="alert alert-success" role="alert">
 <h4 class="alert-heading">Well done!</h4>
 <p>Read this vital alert message. This sample text
        will be a little lengthier so you can
        understand how spacing inside an alert works
        with this type of material.</p>
 <hr>
 <p class="mb-0">Use margin tools wherever possible
                to keep things neat and clean.</p>
</div>
```

Icons

Similarly, to generate alerts with icons, you may use flexbox utilities and Bootstrap icons. You may want to add more utilities or custom styles, depending on your heroes and content.

```
<div class="alert alert-primary d-flex align-items-
        left" role="alert">
 <svg xmlns="http://www.w3.org/2000/svg" width="28"
height="28" fill="currentColor" class="bi
bi-exclamation-triangle-fill flex-shrink-0 me-2"
viewBox="0 0 16 16" role="img" aria-label="Warning:">
   <path d="M8.982 1.566a1.13 1.13 0 0 0-1.96 0L.165
13.233c-.457.778.091 1.767.98 1.767h13.713c.889 0
1.438-.99.98-1.767L8.982 1.566zM8 5c.535 0
.954.462.9.995l-.35 3.507a.552.552 0 0 1-1.1 0L7.1
5.995A.905.905 0 0 1 8 5zm.002 6a1 1 0 1 1 0 2 1 1 0 0
1 0-2z"/>
 </svg>
 <div>
  An example alert with an icon
 </div>
</div>
```

Do you require more than one icon for your alerts? Consider utilizing additional Bootstrap icons and creating a local SVG sprite-like to fast reference the same icons.

```
<svg xmlns="http://www.w3.org/2000/svg"
style="display: none;">
 <symbol id="check-circle-fill" fill="currentColor"
viewBox="0 0 16 16">
  <path d="M16 8A8 8 0 1 1 0 8a8 8 0 0 1 16 0zm-3.97-
3.03a.75.75 0 0 0-1.08.022L7.477 9.417 5.384
7.323a.75.75 0 0 0-1.06 1.06L6.97 11.03a.75.75 0 0 0
1.079-.02l3.992-4.99a.75.75 0 0 0-.01-1.05z"/>
 </symbol>
 <symbol id="info-fill" fill="currentColor"
viewBox="0 0 16 16">
  <path d="M8 16A8 8 0 1 0 8 0a8 8 0 0 0 0 16zm.93-
9.412-1 4.705c-.07.34.029.533.304.533.194 0 .487-.07.6
86-.246l-.088.416c-.287.346-.92.598-1.465.598-.703
0-1.002-.422-.808-1.319l.738-3.468c.064-.293.006-.
399-.287-.47l-.451-.081.082-.381 2.29-.287zM8 5.5a1 1
0 1 1 0-2 1 1 0 0 1 0 2z"/>
 </symbol>
 <symbol id="exclamation-triangle-fill"
fill="currentColor" viewBox="0 0 16 16">
  <path d="M8.982 1.566a1.13 1.13 0 0 0-1.96 0L.165
13.233c-.457.778.091 1.767.98 1.767h13.713c.889 0
1.438-.99.98-1.767L8.982 1.566zM8 5c.535 0
.954.462.9.995l-.35 3.507a.552.552 0 0 1-1.1 0L7.1
5.995A.905.905 0 0 1 8 5zm.002 6a1 1 0 1 1 0 2 1 1 0 0
1 0-2z"/>
 </symbol>
</svg>

<div class="alert alert-primary d-flex align-items-
center" role="alert">
 <svg class="bi flex-shrink-0 me-2" width="28"
    height="28" role="img" aria-label="Info:"><use
    xlink:href="#info-fill"/></svg>
 <div>
  An example alert with an icon
 </div>
</div>
<div class="alert alert-success d-flex align-items-
          center" role="alert">
 <svg class="bi flex-shrink-0 me-2" width="27"
    height="27" role="img" aria-label="Success:
    "><use xlink:href="#check-circle-fill"/></svg>
```

```
<div>
 An example success alert with an icon
 </div>
</div>
<div class="alert alert-warning d-flex align-items-
              center" role="alert">
 <svg class="bi flex-shrink-0 me-2" width="27"
   height="27" role="img" aria-label="Warning:"><use
   xlink:href="#exclamation-triangle-fill"/></svg>
 <div>
  An example warning alert with an icon
 </div>
</div>
<div class="alert alert-danger d-flex align-items-
              center" role="alert">
 <svg class="bi flex-shrink-0 me-2" width="27"
     height="27" role="img" aria-label="Danger:"><use
     xlink:href="#exclamation-triangle-fill"/></svg>
 <div>
  An example danger alert with an icon
 </div>
</div>
```

Dismissing

Any alert may be dismissed inline using the alert JavaScript plugin. Here's how it works:

- Check that you have the alert plugin or the built Bootstrap JavaScript loaded.

- Add close button and the .alert-dismissible class, which adds padding to the right of the alert and positions the close button there.

- Add the data-bs-dismiss="alert" property to the close button to activate the JavaScript capability. Use the< button> element with it to ensure correct behaviour across all devices.

- If you want to animate alerts when you dismiss them, use the .fade and .show classes.

A live demonstration of this is available here:

```
<div class="alert alert-warning alert-dismissible
             fade show" role="alert">
```

```
<strong>Holy guacamole!</strong> You should look
          into some of the fields listed below.
<button type="button" class="btn-close" data-bs-
       dismiss="alert" aria-label="Close"></button>
</div>
```

When alert is dismissed, the element is removed from the page structure entirely. If a keyboard user rejects the signal by pressing the close button, their focus will be suddenly lost and, depending on the browser, reset to the beginning of the page/document. As a result, we propose integrating extra JavaScript that listens for the closed.bs.alert event and programmatically sets focus() to most appropriate area on the page. If you intend to shift emphasis to a non-interactive element that does not normally have priority, make sure to include tabindex="-1" in the component.

Sass

Variables

```
$alert-padding-y:             $spacer;
$alert-padding-x:             $spacer;
$alert-margin-bottom:         1rem;
$alert-border-radius:         $border-radius;
$alert-link-font-weight:      $font-weight-bold;
$alert-border-width:          $border-width;
$alert-bg-scale:              -80%;
$alert-border-scale:          -70%;
$alert-color-scale:            40%;
$alert-dismissible-padding-r: $alert-padding-x * 3;
// 3x covers the width of x plus default padding on
either side
```

Variant Mixin

We used mixin in combination with $theme-colors to create contextual modifier classes for our alerts.

```
@mixin alert-variant($background, $border, $color) {
  color: $color;
  @include gradient-bg($background);
  border-color: $border;

  .alert-link {
```

```
  color: shade-color($color, 20%);
  }
}
```

Loop

A loop that generates the modifier classes with alert-variant() mixin.
// Generate the contextual modifier classes for colorizing the alert.

```
@each $state, $value in $theme-colors {
 $alert-background: shift-color($value,
$alert-bg-scale);
 $alert-border: shift-color($value,
$alert-border-scale);
 $alert-color: shift-color($value,
$alert-color-scale);
 @if (contrast-ratio($alert-background, $alert-color)
                   < $min-contrast-ratio) {
  $alert-color: mix($value, color-contrast($alert-
             background), abs($alert-color-scale));
 }
 .alert-#{$state} {
  @include alert-variant($alert-background, $alert-
                         border, $alert-color);
 }
}
```

JavaScript Behavior

Triggers

Enable dismissal of alert via JavaScript:

```
var alertList = document.querySelectorAll('.alert')
alertList.forEach(function (alert) {
 new bootstrap.Alert(alert)
})
```

Or, as seen above, use data characteristics on a button within the alert:

```
<button type="button" class="btn-close" data-bs-
        dismiss="alert" aria-label="Close"></button>
```

Note that closing alert will remove it from the DOM.

Methods

You can create alert instance with the alert constructor, for example:

```
var myAlert = document.getElementById('myAlert')
var bsAlert = new bootstrap.Alert(myAlert)
```

This makes alert listen for click events on descendant elements, with the data-bs-dismiss="alert" attribute. (Not necessary when using the data API's auto-initialization.)

```
var alertNode = document.querySelector('.alert')
var alert = bootstrap.Alert.getInstance(alertNode)
alert.close()
```

Method	Description
close	Removes an alert from the DOM to close it. If the element has the .fade and .show classes, the signal will fade out before being released
dispose	Destroys an element's alert
getInstance	The static method allows getting the alert instance associated with a DOM element, and you can use it like this: Bootstrap.Alert. getInstance(alert)
getOrCreateInstance	The static method returns an alert instance associated with a DOM element or creates a new one that wasn't initialized. You can use it like this: Bootstrap.Alert.getOrCreateInstance(elem ent)

Events

Bootstrap's alert plugin exposes a few events for hooking into the alert functionality.

```
var myAlert = document.getElementById('myAlert')
myAlert.addEventListener('closed.bs.alert', function
        () {
 // do something, for example, explicitly move focus
      to most appropriate element,
 // so it doesn't get lost/reset tostart of the page
 // document.getElementById('...').focus()
})
```

Event	Description
close.bs.alert	It fires immediately when the close instance method is called
closed.bs.alert	She was fired when the alert had been closed, and CSS transitions had been completed

BADGES

Documentation and examples for the badges, our small count, and the labeling component.

Examples

By utilizing relative font sizes and em units, badges scale to match the size of the immediate parent element. The focus and hover styles for links are no longer available in badges as of v5.

Headings

```
<h1>Example heading <span class="badge
                     bg-secondary">New</span></h1>
<h2>Example heading <span class="badge
                     bg-secondary">New</span></h2>
<h3>Example heading <span class="badge
                     bg-secondary">New</span></h3>
<h4>Example heading <span class="badge
                     bg-secondary">New</span></h4>
<h5>Example heading <span class="badge
                     bg-secondary">New</span></h5>
<h6>Example heading <span class="badge
                     bg-secondary">New</span></h6>
```

Buttons

Badges can be used as part of links or buttons to provide a counter.

```
<button type="button" class="btn btn-primary">
 Notifications <span class="badge bg-secondary">4</
                     span>
</button>
```

Note that badges may be confusing for users of screen readers and similar assistive technologies, depending on how they are used. While badge style gives a visual clue as to their function, these users will merely be provided with the badge's content. Depending on the context, these badges may appear as random extra words or numbers at the end of a statement, link, or button.

Unless the context is obvious (as in the "Notifications" example, where the "4" represents the number of notifications), consider incorporating further context using a visually concealed piece of other text.t.

Positioned

Use utilities to modify .badge and position it in the corner of a link or button.

```
<button type="button" class="btn btn-primary
                              position-relative">
 Inbox
 <span class="position-absolute top-0 start-100
      translate-middle badge rounded-pill bg-danger">
  99+
  <span class="visually-hidden">unread messages</span>
 </span>
</button>
```

For a more generic indication, replace the .badge class with a few other utilities that do not have a count.

```
<button type="button" class="btn btn-primary
                              position-relative">
 Profile
 <span class="position-absolute top-0 start-100
      translate-middle p-2 bg-danger border border-
      light rounded-circle">
  <span class="visually-hidden">New alerts</span>
 </span>
</button>
```

Background Colors

To rapidly modify the look of a badge, use our background utility classes. Please keep in mind that if you're using Bootstrap's default.bg-light, you'll almost certainly need a text color utility like .text-dark for optimal style. This is due to the fact that background utilities only change the background color.

```
<span class="badge bg-primary">Primary</span>
<span class="badge bg-secondary">Secondary</span>
<span class="badge bg-success">Success</span>
<span class="badge bg-danger">Danger</span>
<span class="badge bg-warning text-dark">Warning</span>
<span class="badge bg-info text-dark">Info</span>
<span class="badge bg-light text-dark">Light</span>
<span class="badge bg-dark">Dark</span>
```

Conveying Meaning to Assistive Technologies

The use of color to add meaning merely gives a visual indicator that will not be relayed to users of assistive devices such as screen readers. Ascertain that the information suggested by the color is either obvious from the content itself or is included through the alternate means, such as extra text concealed with the .visually-hidden class.

Pill Badges

To create badges more rounded with a greater border radius, use the .rounded-pill utility class.

```
<span class="badge rounded-pill bg-primary">Primary</
          span>
<span class="badge rounded-pill
          bg-secondary">Secondary</span>
<span class="badge rounded-pill bg-success">Success</
          span>
<span class="badge rounded-pill bg-danger">Danger</
          span>
<span class="badge rounded-pill bg-warning text-
          dark">Warning</span>
<span class="badge rounded-pill bg-info text-
          dark">Info</span>
<span class="badge rounded-pill bg-light text-
          dark">Light</span>
<span class="badge rounded-pill bg-dark">Dark</span>
```

Sass
Variables

```
$badge-font-size:       .75em;
$badge-font-weight:     $font-weight-bold;
$badge-color:           $white;
$badge-padding-y:       .35em;
$badge-padding-x:       .65em;
$badge-border-radius:   $border-radius;
```

BREADCRUMB

Indicate the current page's position inside a navigational hierarchy that uses CSS to create separators automatically.

Example

To make a lightly designed breadcrumb, use an ordered or unordered list with linked list items. As needed, use our tools to create more styles.

List with Linked Items

```
<nav aria-label="breadcrumb">
 <ol class="breadcrumb">
  <li class="breadcrumb-item active" aria-
          current="page">Home</li>
 </ol>
</nav>

<nav aria-label="breadcrumb">
 <ol class="breadcrumb">
  <li class="breadcrumb-item"><a href="#">Home</a></li>
  <li class="breadcrumb-item active" aria-
          current="page">Library</li>
 </ol>
</nav>

<nav aria-label="breadcrumb">
 <ol class="breadcrumb">
  <li class="breadcrumb-item"><a href="#">Home</a></li>
  <li class="breadcrumb-item"><a href="#">Library</
                                     a></li>
  <li class="breadcrumb-item active" aria-
          current="page">Data</li>
 </ol>
</nav>
```

Dividers

Dividers are applied automatically in CSS via::before and content. They may be customized by altering a local CSS custom property --bs-bread-crumb-divider, or by using the $breadcrumb-divider Sass variable and $breadcrumb-divider-flipped for its RTL equivalent, if necessary. As a fallback to the custom property, we use our Sass variable as the default. In this manner, you have a global divider that you may alter at any moment without having to recompile CSS.

```
<nav style="--bs-breadcrumb-divider: '>';"
aria-label="breadcrumb">
```

```
<ol class="breadcrumb">
 <li class="breadcrumb-item"><a href="#">Home</a></li>
 <li class="breadcrumb-item active" aria-
                       current="page">Library</li>
</ol>
</nav>
```

When using Sass to edit a string, the quote function is necessary to construct the quotes around the string. For example, if you're using > as a separator, you could do something like this:

```
$breadcrumb-divider: quote(">");
```

An embedded SVG icon can also be used. Use our CSS custom property or the Sass variable to apply it.

```
<nav style="--bs-breadcrumb-divider:
   url(&#34;data:image/svg+xml,%3Csvg xmlns='http://
   www.w3.org/2000/svg' width='7'
   height='8'%3E%3Cpath d='M2.5 0L1 1.5 3.5 4 1 6.5
   2.5 8l4-4-4-4z' fill='currentColor'/%3E%3C/svg
   %3E&#34;);" aria-label="breadcrumb">
 <ol class="breadcrumb">
  <li class="breadcrumb-item"><a href="#">Home</a></li>
  <li class="breadcrumb-item active" aria-
           current="page">Library</li>
 </ol>
</nav>
```

```
$breadcrumb-divider: url("data:image/svg+xml,%3Csvg
xmlns='http://www.w3.org/2000/svg' width='9'
height='8'%3E%3Cpath d='M2.5 0L1 1.5 3.5 4 1 6.5 2.5
8l4-4-4-4z' fill='currentColor'/%3E%3C/svg%3E");
```

You can alternatively remove the divider by using the command --bs-breadcrumb-divider: ''; (empty strings in CSS custom properties count as values) or by setting the Sass variable to $breadcrumb-divider: none;.

```
<nav style="--bs-breadcrumb-divider: '';"
aria-label="breadcrumb">
 <ol class="breadcrumb">
```

```
<li class="breadcrumb-item"><a href="#">Home</a></li>
<li class="breadcrumb-item active" aria-
            current="page">Library</li>
</ol>
</nav>
```

```
$breadcrumb-divider: none;
```

Accessibility

Since breadcrumbs provide navigation, it is a good idea to add a meaningful label such as aria-label="breadcrumb" to describe the type of navigation supplied in the <nav> element, and applying aria-current="page" to the last item of set to indicate that it represents the current page.

Sass
Variables

```
$breadcrumb-font-size:        null;
$breadcrumb-padding-y:        0;
$breadcrumb-padding-x:        0;
$breadcrumb-item-padding-x:   .5rem;
$breadcrumb-margin-bottom:    1rem;
$breadcrumb-bg:               null;
$breadcrumb-divider-color:    $gray-600;
$breadcrumb-active-color:     $gray-600;
$breadcrumb-divider:          quote("/");
$breadcrumb-divider-flipped:  $breadcrumb-divider;
$breadcrumb-border-radius:    null;
```

BUTTONS

Use the Bootstrap's custom button styles for actions in forms, dialogs, and more with support for multiple sizes, states, etc.

Examples

Bootstrap comes with multiple predefined button styles, each with its own semantic purpose and a few extras tossed in for more control.

```
<button type="button" class="btn btn-
                    primary">Primary</button>
```

```
<button type="button" class="btn btn-
                      secondary">Secondary</button>
<button type="button" class="btn btn-
                      success">Success</button>
<button type="button" class="btn btn-danger">Danger</
                      button>
<button type="button" class="btn btn-
                      warning">Warning</button>
<button type="button" class="btn btn-info">Info</
                  button>
<button type="button" class="btn btn-light">Light</
                        button>
<button type="button" class="btn btn-dark">Dark</
                  button>
<button type="button" class="btn btn-link">Link</
                  button>
```

Conveying Meaning to the Assistive Technologies

The use of color to add meaning merely gives a visual indicator that will not be relayed to users of assistive devices such as screen readers. Ascertain that the information suggested by the color is either obvious from the content itself or is included through alternate means, like extra text concealed with the .visually-hidden class.

Disable Text Wrapping

If you don't want the button text to wrap, apply the .text-nowrap class to it. In Sass, you may prevent text wrapping for each button by setting $btn-white-space: nowrap.

Button Tags

The .btn classes are intended to be used in conjunction with the button> element. However, these classes can be applied to <a> or <input> components (though some browsers may apply a slightly different rendering).

When utilizing button classes on <a> components to initiate in-page functionality (such as folding content), rather than referring to new pages or sections inside the current page, these links should be given a role="button" to signal their intent to assistive technology like as screen readers.

```
<a class="btn btn-primary" href="#"
   role="button">Link</a>
<button class="btn btn-primary"
       type="submit">Button</button>
<input class="btn btn-primary" type="button"
       value="Input">
<input class="btn btn-primary" type="submit"
       value="Submit">
<input class="btn btn-primary" type="reset"
       value="Reset">
```

Outline Button

Need a button but don't want to deal with the weighty background colors that come with them? To remove all background pictures and stains from any button, replace the normal modifier classes with .btn-outline-*.

```
<button type="button" class="btn btn-outline-
       primary">Primary</button>
<button type="button" class="btn btn-outline-secondar
       y">Secondary</button>
<button type="button" class="btn btn-outline-
       success">Success</button>
<button type="button" class="btn btn-outline-
       danger">Danger</button>
<button type="button" class="btn btn-outline-
       warning">Warning</button>
<button type="button" class="btn btn-outline-
       info">Info</button>
<button type="button" class="btn btn-outline-
       light">Light</button>
<button type="button" class="btn btn-outline-
       dark">Dark</button>
```

Some button styles use a relatively light foreground color and should only be used on a dark background to have sufficient contrast.

Sizes

Fancy larger or smaller buttons? Add .btn-lg or .btn-sm for additional sizes.

```
<button type="button" class="btn btn-primary btn-
       lg">Large button</button>
```

```
<button type="button" class="btn btn-secondary btn-
      lg">Large button</button>

<button type="button" class="btn btn-primary btn-
      sm">Small button</button>
<button type="button" class="btn btn-secondary btn-
      sm">Small button</button>
```

Disabled State

Add the disabled boolean property to any <button> element to make it seem inactive. Disabled buttons have no pointer-events assigned to them, preventing hover and active states from being triggered.

```
<button type="button" class="btn btn-lg btn-primary"
      disabled>Primary button</button>
<button type="button" class="btn btn-secondary
      btn-lg" disabled>Button</button>
```

Disabled buttons created with the a> element operate differently:

- <a>s do not allow the disabled property, therefore you must add the .disabled class to make it visually look disabled.

- To deactivate all pointer-events on anchor buttons, several future-friendly designs are supplied.

- Disabled buttons consist of the aria-disabled="true" attribute to indicate the element's state to assistive technologies.

```
<a href="#" class="btn btn-primary btn-lg disabled"
    tabindex="-1" role="button" aria-
    disabled="true">Primary link</a>
<a href="#" class="btn btn-secondary btn-lg disabled"
    tabindex="-1" role="button" aria-
    disabled="true">Link</a>
```

Link Functionality Caveat

The .disabled class disables the link capability of <a>s by using pointer-events: none, but that CSS attribute is not yet standardized. Furthermore, even in browsers that allow pointer-events: none, keyboard navigation is unaffected, which means both sighted keyboard users and assistive technology users will be able to activate these links. To be safe, additionally to aria-disabled="true," provide a tabindex="-1" property on these links to prevent them from acquiring keyboard focus, and deactivate their functionality using custom JavaScript.

Block Buttons

Using a combination of our display and gap tools, you can create responsive stacks of full-width "block buttons" similar to those found in Bootstrap-4. We have far more control over spacing, alignment, and responsive behaviors when we use utilities instead of button-specific classes.

```
<div class="d-grid gap-2">
 <button class="btn btn-primary"
         type="button">Button</button>
 <button class="btn btn-primary"
         type="button">Button</button>
</div>
```

Here, we design a responsive variant, beginning with vertically stacked buttons and progressing to the MD breakpoint, when the .d-MD-block class replaces the .d-grid class, thereby removing the gap-2 utility. To see them alter, resize your browser.

```
<div class="d-grid gap-2 d-md-block">
 <button class="btn btn-primary"
         type="button">Button</button>
 <button class="btn btn-primary"
         type="button">Button</button>
</div>
```

Grid column width classes allow you to change the width of your block buttons. For a half-width "block button," for example, use .col-6. With .mx-auto, you may also center it horizontally.

```
<div class="d-grid gap-2 col-6 mx-auto">
 <button class="btn btn-primary"
         type="button">Button</button>
 <button class="btn btn-primary"
         type="button">Button</button>
</div>
```

When the buttons are horizontal, further utilities can be used to change their alignment. In this example, we've taken our previous responsive example and added some flex utilities and a margin utility to the button to right-align the buttons when they're no longer stacked.

```
<div class="d-grid gap-2 d-md-flex
          justify-content-md-end">
  <button class="btn btn-primary me-md-2"
          type="button">Button</button>
  <button class="btn btn-primary"
          type="button">Button</button>
</div>
```

Button Plugin

You may use the button plugin to make basic on/off toggle buttons.

These toggle buttons appear to be the same as the checkbox toggle buttons. However, assistive technology transmit these differently: screen readers will announce the checkbox toggles as "checked"/"not checked" (since, despite their look, they are still checkboxes), whereas these toggle buttons will be presented as "button"/"button pushed." The way you choose will be determined by the sort of toggle you are generating and whether the toggle will make sense to users when introduced as a checkbox or as an actual button.

Toggle States

To change the active status of a button, use data-bs-toggle="button." If you're pretapping a button, you must manually add the .active class and aria-pressed="true" to guarantee that assistive technologies properly represent it.

```
<button type="button" class="btn btn-primary" data-
bs-toggle="button" autocomplete="off">Toggle button</
button>
<button type="button" class="btn btn-primary active"
  data-bs-toggle="button" autocomplete="off" aria-
  pressed="true">Active toggle button</button>
<button type="button" class="btn btn-primary"
  disabled data-bs-toggle="button"
  autocomplete="off">Disabled toggle button</button>

<a href="#" class="btn btn-primary" role="button"
  data-bs-toggle="button">Toggle link</a>
```

```
<a href="#" class="btn btn-primary active"
  role="button" data-bs-toggle="button" aria-
  pressed="true">Active toggle link</a>
<a href="#" class="btn btn-primary disabled"
  tabindex="-1" aria-disabled="true" role="button"
  data-bs-toggle="button">Disabled toggle link</a>
```

Methods

You may use the button constructor to build a button instance, for example:

```
var button = document.getElementById('myButton')
var bsButton = new bootstrap.Button(button)
```

For example, to toggle all buttons:

```
var buttons = document.querySelectorAll('.btn')
buttons.forEach(function (button) {
 var button = new bootstrap.Button(button)
 button.toggle()
})
```

Method	Description
toggle	Toggles push state. It gives the button the appearance that it has been activated
dispose	Destroys an element's button (removes stored data on the DOM element)
getInstance	The static method allows getting the button instance associated with a DOM element, you can use it like this: Bootstrap.Button.getInstance(element)
getOrCreateInstance	The static function that returns a button instance associated with a DOM element or creates a new one if one was not previously created. You may put it to use as follows: Bootstrap.Button.get OrCreateInstance(element)

Sass
Variables

```
$btn-padding-y:              $input-btn-padding-y;
$btn-padding-x:              $input-btn-padding-x;
$btn-font-family:            $input-btn-font-family;
$btn-font-size:              $input-btn-font-size;
$btn-line-height:            $input-btn-line-height;
```

```
$btn-white-space:                null; // Set to `nowrap` to
                                 prevent the text-wrapping
$btn-padding-y-sm:               $input-btn-padding-y-sm;
$btn-padding-x-sm:               $input-btn-padding-x-sm;
$btn-font-size-sm:               $input-btn-font-size-sm;
$btn-padding-y-lg:               $input-btn-padding-y-lg;
$btn-padding-x-lg:               $input-btn-padding-x-lg;
$btn-font-size-lg:               $input-btn-font-size-lg;
$btn-border-width:               $input-btn-border-width;
$btn-font-weight:                $font-weight-normal;
$btn-box-shadow:                 inset 0 1px 0 rgba($white,
                                 .25), 0 1px rgba($black,
                                 .085);
$btn-focus-width:                $input-btn-focus-width;
$btn-focus-box-shadow:           $input-btn-focus-box-sha
                                 dow;
$btn-disabled-opacity:           .75;
$btn-active-box-shadow:          inset 0 3px 5px
rgba($black, .135);
$btn-link-color:                         $link-color;
$btn-link-hover-color:                   $link-hover-color;
$btn-link-disabled-color:                $gray-600;
// Allows for customizing button radius independently
from global border radius
$btn-border-radius:                      $border-radius;
$btn-border-radius-sm:                   $border-radius-sm;
$btn-border-radius-lg:                   $border-radius-lg;
$btn-transition: color .15s ease-in-out, background-
color .15s ease-in-out, border-color .15s ease-in-out,
box-shadow .15s ease-in-out;
$btn-hover-bg-shade-amount:       15%;
$btn-hover-bg-tint-amount:        15%;
$btn-hover-border-shade-amount:    20%;
$btn-hover-border-tint-amount:    10%;
$btn-active-bg-shade-amount:      20%;
$btn-active-bg-tint-amount:        20%;
$btn-active-border-shade-amount:  25%;
$btn-active-border-tint-amount:   10%;
```

Mixins

There are three mixins for buttons: button and button outline variant mixins (both based on $theme-colors), plus a button size mixin.

```scss
@mixin button-variant(
 $background,
 $border,
 $color: color-contrast($background),
 $hover-background: if($color == $color-contrast-
  light, shade-color($background, $btn-hover-bg-shade-
  amount), tint-color($background,
  $btn-hover-bg-tint-amount)),
 $hover-border: if($color == $color-contrast-light,
  shade-color($border, $btn-hover-border-shade-
  amount), tint-color($border,
  $btn-hover-border-tint-amount)),
 $hover-color: color-contrast($hover-background),
 $active-background: if($color == $color-contrast-
  light, shade-color($background, $btn-active-bg-
  shade-amount), tint-color($background,
  $btn-active-bg-tint-amount)),
 $active-border: if($color == $color-contrast-light,
  shade-color($border, $btn-active-border-shade-
  amount), tint-color($border,
  $btn-active-border-tint-amount)),
 $active-color: color-contrast($active-background),
 $disabled-background: $background,
 $disabled-border: $border,
 $disabled-color: color-contrast($disabled-background)
) {
 color: $color;
 @include gradient-bg($background);
 border-color: $border;
 @include box-shadow($btn-box-shadow);

 &:hover {
  color: $hover-color;
  @include gradient-bg($hover-background);
  border-color: $hover-border;
 }

 .btn-check:focus + &,
 &:focus {
  color: $hover-color;
  @include gradient-bg($hover-background);
  border-color: $hover-border;
  @if $enable-shadows {
```

```scss
    @include box-shadow($btn-box-shadow, 0 0 0 $btn-
focus-width rgba(mix($color, $border, 16%), .6));
  } @else {
    // Avoid using mixin so we can pass custom focus
       shadow properly
    box-shadow: 0 0 0 $btn-focus-width rgba(mix($color,
       $border, 16%), .6);
  }
}

.btn-check:checked + &,
.btn-check:active + &,
&:active,
&.active,
.show > &.dropdown-toggle {
 color: $active-color;
 background-color: $active-background;
 // Remove CSS gradients if they're enabled
 background-image: if($enable-gradients, none, null);
 border-color: $active-border;

 &:focus {
  @if $enable-shadows {
   @include box-shadow($btn-active-box-shadow, 0 0 0
    $btn-focus-width rgba(mix($color, $border, 16%),
    .6));
  } @else {
   // Avoid using mixin so we can pass custom focus
      shadow properly
   box-shadow: 0 0 0 $btn-focus-width
      rgba(mix($color, $border, 16%), .6);
  }
 }
}

&:disabled,
&.disabled {
 color: $disabled-color;
 background-color: $disabled-background;
 // Remove CSS gradients if they're enabled
 background-image: if($enable-gradients, none, null);
 border-color: $disabled-border;
 }
}
```

```scss
@mixin button-outline-variant(
 $color,
 $color-hover: color-contrast($color),
 $active-background: $color,
 $active-border: $color,
 $active-color: color-contrast($active-background)
) {
 color: $color;
 border-color: $color;

 &:hover {
  color: $color-hover;
  background-color: $active-background;
  border-color: $active-border;
 }

 .btn-check:focus + &,
 &:focus {
  box-shadow: 0 0 0 $btn-focus-width rgba($color, .6);
 }

 .btn-check:checked + &,
 .btn-check:active + &,
 &:active,
 &.active,
 &.dropdown-toggle.show {
  color: $active-color;
  background-color: $active-background;
  border-color: $active-border;

  &:focus {
   @if $enable-shadows {
    @include box-shadow($btn-active-box-shadow, 0 0 0
       $btn-focus-width rgba($color, .6));
   } @else {
    // Avoid using mixin so we can pass custom focus
       shadow properly
    box-shadow: 0 0 0 $btn-focus-width rgba($color, .6);
   }
  }
 }

 &:disabled,
 &.disabled {
```

```
  color: $color;
  background-color: transparent;
 }
}
```

Loops

Button variants (for regular and outline buttons) use their respective mixins with our $theme-colors map to generate the modifier classes in scss/_buttons.scss.

```
@each $color, $value in $theme-colors {
 .btn-#{$color} {
  @include button-variant($value, $value);
 }
}

@each $color, $value in $theme-colors {
 .btn-outline-#{$color} {
  @include button-outline-variant($value);
 }
}
```

BUTTONS GROUP

Group a series of buttons on single line or stack them in a vertical column.

Example

Wrap a series of the buttons with .btn in .btn-group.

```
<div class="btn-group" role="group" aria-label="Basic
    example">
 <button type="button" class="btn btn-primary">Left</
      button>
 <button type="button" class="btn btn-
      primary">Middle</button>
 <button type="button" class="btn btn-
      primary">Right</button>
</div>
```

Ensure Correct Role and Provide a Label

An appropriate role property must be given for assistive technology (such as screen readers) to signal that a succession of buttons is grouped. This would be role="group" for button groups, and role="toolbar" for toolbars.

Furthermore, groups and toolbars should be explicitly labeled, as most assistive technologies will not announce them if the right role attribute is not present. We utilize aria-label in the examples given here, although others such as aria-labeled by can also be used.

These classes can also add to groups of links as an alternative to the .nav navigation components.

```
<div class="btn-group">
 <a href="#" class="btn btn-primary active" aria-
    current="page">Active link</a>
 <a href="#" class="btn btn-primary">Link</a>
 <a href="#" class="btn btn-primary">Link</a>
</div>
```

Mixed Style

```
<div class="btn-group" role="group" aria-label="Basic
    mixed styles example">
 <button type="button" class="btn btn-danger">Left</
        button>
 <button type="button" class="btn btn-
        warning">Middle</button>
 <button type="button" class="btn btn-
        success">Right</button>
</div>
```

Outlined Styles

```
<div class="btn-group" role="group" aria-label="Basic
    outlined example">
 <button type="button" class="btn btn-outline-
        primary">Left</button>
 <button type="button" class="btn btn-outline-
        primary">Middle</button>
 <button type="button" class="btn btn-outline-
        primary">Right</button>
</div>
```

Checkbox and Radio Button Groups

Combine button-like checkbox and radio toggle buttons into a seamless-looking button group.

```
<div class="btn-group" role="group" aria-label="Basic
    checkbox toggle button group">
 <input type="checkbox" class="btn-check"
      id="btncheck1" autocomplete="off">
 <label class="btn btn-outline-primary"
      for="btncheck1">Checkbox 1</label>

 <input type="checkbox" class="btn-check"
      id="btncheck2" autocomplete="off">
 <label class="btn btn-outline-primary"
      for="btncheck2">Checkbox 2</label>

 <input type="checkbox" class="btn-check"
      id="btncheck3" autocomplete="off">
 <label class="btn btn-outline-primary"
      for="btncheck3">Checkbox 3</label>
</div>

<div class="btn-group" role="group" aria-label="Basic
    radio toggle button group">
 <input type="radio" class="btn-check" name="btnradio"
      id="btnradio1" autocomplete="off" checked>
 <label class="btn btn-outline-primary"
      for="btnradio1">Radio 1</label>

 <input type="radio" class="btn-check" name="btnradio"
      id="btnradio2" autocomplete="off">
 <label class="btn btn-outline-primary"
      for="btnradio2">Radio 2</label>

 <input type="radio" class="btn-check" name="btnradio"
      id="btnradio3" autocomplete="off">
 <label class="btn btn-outline-primary"
      for="btnradio3">Radio 3</label>
</div>
```

Button Toolbar

For more complicated components, combine sets of button groups into button toolbars. Use utility classes to spread out groups, buttons, and other elements as needed.

```
<div class="btn-toolbar" role="toolbar" aria-
    label="Toolbar with button groups">
```

```
<div class="btn-group me-2" role="group" aria-
    label="First group">
 <button type="button" class="btn btn-primary">1</
        button>
 <button type="button" class="btn btn-primary">2</
        button>
 <button type="button" class="btn btn-primary">3</
        button>
 <button type="button" class="btn btn-primary">4</
        button>
</div>
<div class="btn-group me-2" role="group" aria-
    label="Second group">
 <button type="button" class="btn btn-secondary">5</
        button>
 <button type="button" class="btn btn-secondary">6</
        button>
 <button type="button" class="btn btn-secondary">7</
        button>
</div>
<div class="btn-group" role="group" aria-
    label="Third group">
 <button type="button" class="btn btn-info">8</
        button>
 </div>
</div>
```

In your toolbars, you are able to combine input and button groups. To space things right, you'll probably need certain tools, similar to the example above.

```
<div class="btn-toolbar mb-3" role="toolbar" aria-
    label="Toolbar with button groups">
 <div class="btn-group me-2" role="group" aria-
    label="First group">
  <button type="button" class="btn btn-outline-
        secondary">1</button>
  <button type="button" class="btn btn-outline-
        secondary">2</button>
  <button type="button" class="btn btn-outline-
        secondary">3</button>
  <button type="button" class="btn btn-outline-
        secondary">4</button>
```

```
    </div>
    <div class="input-group">
     <div class="input-group-text"
          id="btnGroupAddon">@</div>
     <input type="text" class="form-control" place
       holder="Input group example" aria-label="Input
       group example" aria-describedby="btnGroupAddon">
    </div>
 </div>

 <div class="btn-toolbar justify-content-between"
      role="toolbar" aria-label="Toolbar with button
      groups">
  <div class="btn-group" role="group" aria-
      label="First group">
   <button type="button" class="btn btn-outline-
           secondary">1</button>
   <button type="button" class="btn btn-outline-
           secondary">2</button>
   <button type="button" class="btn btn-outline-
           secondary">3</button>
   <button type="button" class="btn btn-outline-
           secondary">4</button>
  </div>
  <div class="input-group">
   <div class="input-group-text"
                id="btnGroupAddon2">@</div>
   <input type="text" class="form-control"
      placeholder="Input group example" aria-
      label="Input group example" aria-describedby="btn
      GroupAddon2">
  </div>
 </div>
```

Sizing

Rather than applying button size classes to each button in a group, append
.btn-group-* to each .btn-group, including each one when layering several
groups.

```
<div class="btn-group btn-group-lg" role="group"
     aria-label="...">...</div>
<div class="btn-group" role="group" aria-
     label="...">...</div>
```

```
<div class="btn-group btn-group-sm" role="group"
    aria-label="...">...</div>
```

Nesting

Put a .btn-group within another .btn-group when you want dropdown menus mixed with a series of buttons.

```
<div class="btn-group" role="group" aria-
    label="Button group with nested dropdown">
 <button type="button" class="btn btn-primary">1</
        button>
 <button type="button" class="btn btn-primary">2</
        button>

 <div class="btn-group" role="group">
  <button id="btnGroupDrop1" type="button" class="btn
        btn-primary dropdown-toggle" data-bs-
        toggle="dropdown" aria-expanded="false">
   Dropdown
  </button>
  <ul class="dropdown-menu" aria-labelled
      by="btnGroupDrop1">
   <li><a class="dropdown-item" href="#">Dropdown
        link</a></li>
   <li><a class="dropdown-item" href="#">Dropdown
        link</a></li>
  </ul>
 </div>
</div>
```

Vertical Variation

Make a set of buttons display vertically instead of horizontally stacked. Split button dropdowns are not supported here.

```
<div class="btn-group-vertical">
 ...
</div>
```

CARDS

Cards in Bootstrap are a flexible and expandable content container with a variety of versions and settings.

About

A *card* is a content container that is both versatile and expandable. It has header and footer settings, as well as a lot of information, contextual background colors, and a lot of display possibilities. If you're familiar with Bootstrap-3, you'll notice that cards have taken the role of our old panels, wells, and thumbnails. Modifier classes for cards provide similar capabilities to those components.

Example

Cards are created using the least amount of markup and styles possible while still allowing for a great deal of control and customization. They're made with flexbox, so they're easy to align and blend in with other Bootstrap components. Because they don't have a margin by default, you'll need to employ spacing utilities as needed.

A primary card with mixed content and a fixed width is shown below. Because cards don't have a defined width to begin with, they'll fill the entire width of their parent element. With our different sizing options, this may be readily modified.

```
<div class="card" style="width: 18rem;">
 <img src="..." class="card-img-top" alt="...">
 <div class="card-body">
  <h5 class="card-title">Card title</h5>
  <p class="card-text">Some quick example text to
     build on the card title and make up the bulk of
     the card's content.</p>
  <a href="#" class="btn btn-primary">Go somewhere</a>
 </div>
</div>
```

Content Types

Cards in content types support a wide variety of content, including text, images, list groups, links, and more. Below are examples of what's helped.

Body

The .card-body element is the foundation of a card. When you require a padded part within a card, this is the tool you use.

```
<div class="card">
 <div class="card-body">
```

```
   This is text within a card body.
  </div>
</div>
```

Tiles, Text, and Links

Adding .card-title to a <h*> tag creates a card title. Adding a .card-link to an <a> tag adds and places links next to each other in the same way.

A .card-subtitle tag is added to a <h*> tag to employ subtitles. The card title and subtitle are beautifully aligned when the .card-title and .card-subtitle items are placed in a .card-body item.

```
<div class="card" style="width: 18rem;">
 <div class="card-body">
  <h5 class="card-title">Card title</h5>
  <h6 class="card-subtitle mb-2 text-muted">Card
     subtitle</h6>
  <p class="card-text">Some quick example text to
     build on the card title and make up the bulk of
     the card's content.</p>
  <a href="#" class="card-link">Card link</a>
  <a href="#" class="card-link">Another link</a>
 </div>
</div>
```

Images

.card-img-top adds an image to the card's top. Text can be added to the card using .card-text. The normal HTML elements can also be used to style text within .card-text.

```
<div class="card" style="width: 18rem;">
 <img src="..." class="card-img-top" alt="...">
 <div class="card-body">
  <p class="card-text">Some quick example text to
     build on the card title and make up the bulk of
     the card's content.</p>
 </div>
</div>
```

List Groups

With a flush list group, you can make content lists in a card.

```
<div class="card" style="width: 18rem;">
 <ul class="list-group list-group-flush">
```

```
    <li class="list-group-item">An item</li>
    <li class="list-group-item">A second item</li>
    <li class="list-group-item">A third item</li>
  </ul>
</div>

<div class="card" style="width: 18rem;">
 <div class="card-header">
  Featured
 </div>
 <ul class="list-group list-group-flush">
  <li class="list-group-item">An item</li>
  <li class="list-group-item">A second item</li>
  <li class="list-group-item">A third item</li>
 </ul>
</div>

<div class="card" style="width: 18rem;">
 <ul class="list-group list-group-flush">
  <li class="list-group-item">An item</li>
  <li class="list-group-item">A second item</li>
  <li class="list-group-item">A third item</li>
 </ul>
 <div class="card-footer">
  Card footer
 </div>
</div>
```

Kitchen Sink

Match and mix multiple content types to create the card you need, or throw everything in there. Below are blocks, image styles, text styles, and a list group wrapped in a fixed-width card.

```
<div class="card" style="width: 18rem;">
 <img src="..." class="card-img-top" alt="...">
 <div class="card-body">
  <h5 class="card-title">Card title</h5>
  <p class="card-text">Some quick example text to
     build on the card title and make up the bulk of
     the card's content.</p>
 </div>
 <ul class="list-group list-group-flush">
```

```
 <li class="list-group-item">An item</li>
 <li class="list-group-item">A second item</li>
 <li class="list-group-item">A third item</li>
</ul>
<div class="card-body">
 <a href="#" class="card-link">Card link</a>
 <a href="#" class="card-link">Another link</a>
</div>
</div>
```

Header and Footer

Add an optional footer and header within a card.

```
<div class="card">
 <div class="card-header">
  Featured
 </div>
 <div class="card-body">
  <h5 class="card-title">Special title treatment</h5>
  <p class="card-text">With supporting text below as
     a natural lead-in to additional content.</p>
  <a href="#" class="btn btn-primary">Go somewhere</a>
 </div>
</div>
```

Card headers can be styled by adding the .card-header to <h*> elements.

```
<div class="card">
 <h5 class="card-header">Featured</h5>
 <div class="card-body">
  <h5 class="card-title">Special title treatment</h5>
  <p class="card-text">With supporting text below as
     a natural lead-in to additional content.</p>
  <a href="#" class="btn btn-primary">Go somewhere</a>
 </div>
</div>

<div class="card">
 <div class="card-header">
  Quote
 </div>
 <div class="card-body">
  <blockquote class="blockquote mb-0">
```

```
   <p>A well-known quote, contained in a blockquote
       element.</p>
   <footer class="blockquote-footer">Someone famous
          in <cite title="Source Title">Source
          Title</cite></footer>
  </blockquote>
 </div>
</div>

<div class="card text-center">
 <div class="card-header">
  Featured
 </div>
 <div class="card-body">
  <h5 class="card-title">Special title treatment</h5>
  <p class="card-text">With supporting text below as
     a natural lead-in to additional content.</p>
  <a href="#" class="btn btn-primary">Go somewhere</a>
 </div>
 <div class="card-footer text-muted">
  2 days ago
 </div>
</div>
```

Sizing

Cards will be 100% wide unless otherwise stated because they presume no set width to begin with. Custom CSS, grid Sass mixins, grid classes, and utilities can be used to adjust this as needed.

Using Grid Markup

Using the wrap cards, grid in columns and rows as needed.

```
<div class="row">
 <div class="col-sm-6">
  <div class="card">
   <div class="card-body">
    <h5 class="card-title">Special title treatment</h5>
    <p class="card-text">With supporting text below
       as a natural lead-in to additional content.</p>
    <a href="#" class="btn btn-primary">Go
       somewhere</a>
   </div>
```

```
    </div>
  </div>
  <div class="col-sm-6">
   <div class="card">
    <div class="card-body">
      <h5 class="card-title">Special title treatment</h5>
      <p class="card-text">With supporting text below as
        a natural lead-in to additional content.</p>
      <a href="#" class="btn btn-primary">Go
        somewhere</a>
    </div>
   </div>
  </div>
</div>
```

Using Utilities

Use the handful of available sizing utilities to set a card's width quickly.

```
<div class="card w-75">
 <div class="card-body">
  <h5 class="card-title">Card title</h5>
  <p class="card-text">With supporting text below as
    a natural lead-in to additional content.</p>
  <a href="#" class="btn btn-primary">Button</a>
 </div>
</div>

<div class="card w-50">
 <div class="card-body">
  <h5 class="card-title">Card title</h5>
  <p class="card-text">With supporting text below as
    a natural lead-in to additional content.</p>
  <a href="#" class="btn btn-primary">Button</a>
 </div>
</div>
```

Using Custom CSS

```
<div class="card" style="width: 18rem;">
 <div class="card-body">
  <h5 class="card-title">Special title treatment</h5>
  <p class="card-text">With supporting text below as
    a natural lead-in to additional content.</p>
```

```
   <a href="#" class="btn btn-primary">Go somewhere</a>
  </div>
</div>
```

Text Alignment

It is easy to change text alignment of any card – in its entirety or specific parts – with our text align classes.

```
<div class="card" style="width: 18rem;">
 <div class="card-body">
  <h5 class="card-title">Special title treatment</h5>
  <p class="card-text">With supporting text below as
     a natural lead-in to additional content.</p>
  <a href="#" class="btn btn-primary">Go somewhere</a>
 </div>
</div>

<div class="card text-center" style="width: 18rem;">
 <div class="card-body">
  <h5 class="card-title">Special title treatment</h5>
  <p class="card-text">With supporting text below as
     a natural lead-in to additional content.</p>
  <a href="#" class="btn btn-primary">Go somewhere</a>
 </div>
</div>

<div class="card text-end" style="width: 18rem;">
 <div class="card-body">
  <h5 class="card-title">Special title treatment</h5>
  <p class="card-text">With supporting text below as
     a natural lead-in to additional content.</p>
  <a href="#" class="btn btn-primary">Go somewhere</a>
 </div>
</div>
```

Navigation

With Bootstrap's navigation components, you can add navigation to the header (or block) of a card.

```
<div class="card text-center">
 <div class="card-header">
  <ul class="nav nav-tabs card-header-tabs">
```

```
   <li class="nav-item">
    <a class="nav-link active" aria-current="true"
       href="#">Active</a>
   </li>
   <li class="nav-item">
    <a class="nav-link" href="#">Link</a>
   </li>
   <li class="nav-item">
    <a class="nav-link disabled" href="#" tabindex="-2"
       aria-disabled="true">Disabled</a>
   </li>
  </ul>
 </div>
 <div class="card-body">
  <h5 class="card-title">Special title treatment</h5>
  <p class="card-text">With supporting text below as
     a natural lead-in to additional content.</p>
  <a href="#" class="btn btn-primary">Go somewhere</a>
 </div>
</div>

<div class="card text-center">
 <div class="card-header">
  <ul class="nav nav-pills card-header-pills">
   <li class="nav-item">
    <a class="nav-link active" href="#">Active</a>
   </li>
   <li class="nav-item">
    <a class="nav-link" href="#">Link</a>
   </li>
   <li class="nav-item">
    <a class="nav-link disabled" href="#" tabindex="-2"
       aria-disabled="true">Disabled</a>
   </li>
  </ul>
 </div>
 <div class="card-body">
  <h5 class="card-title">Special title treatment</h5>
  <p class="card-text">With supporting text below as
     a natural lead-in to additional content.</p>
  <a href="#" class="btn btn-primary">Go somewhere</a>
 </div>
</div>
```

Images

There are a few alternatives for working with images on cards. You can add "image caps" to either end of a card, overlay photos with card information, or just embed the image in the card.

Images Caps

Like headers and footers, cards can include top and bottom "image caps"— images at the top or bottom of a card.

```
<div class="card mb-3">
 <img src="..." class="card-img-top" alt="...">
 <div class="card-body">
  <h5 class="card-title">Card title</h5>
  <p class="card-text">This is a larger card with
     supporting text underneath as a natural lead-in
     to further information. This material is
     slightly lengthier.</p>
  <p class="card-text"><small class="text-muted">Last
     updated 5 mins ago</small></p>
 </div>
</div>
<div class="card">
 <div class="card-body">
  <h5 class="card-title">Card title</h5>
  <p class="card-text">This is a larger card with
     supporting text underneath as a natural lead-in
     to further information. This material is
     slightly lengthier.</p>
  <p class="card-text"><small class="text-muted">Last
     updated 5 mins ago</small></p>
 </div>
 <img src="..." class="card-img-bottom" alt="...">
</div>
```

Image Overlays

Make a card background out of an image and add text to it. Additional styles or utilities may or may not be required, depending on the image.

```
<div class="card bg-dark text-white">
 <img src="..." class="card-img" alt="...">
 <div class="card-img-overlay">
```

```
   <h5 class="card-title">Card title</h5>
   <p class="card-text">This is a wider card with
      supporting text below as a natural lead-in to
      additional content. This content is a little bit
      longer.</p>
   <p class="card-text">Last updated 3 mins ago</p>
 </div>
</div>
```

Horizontal

By combining grid and utility classes, cards can be rendered horizontal in a mobile-friendly and responsive manner. In the example given below, we remove the grid gutters with .g-0 and utilize the .col-MD-* classes to make the card horizontal at MD breakpoint. Depending on the content of your card, you may need to make more alterations.

```
<div class="card mb-3" style="max-width: 540px;">
 <div class="row g-0">
  <div class="col-md-4">
   <img src="..." class="img-fluid rounded-start"
        alt="...">
  </div>
  <div class="col-md-8">
   <div class="card-body">
    <h5 class="card-title">Card title</h5>
    <p class="card-text">This is a wider card with
       supporting text below as a natural lead-in to
       an additional content. This content is a
       little bit longer.</p>
    <p class="card-text"><small class="text-
       muted">Last updated 5 mins ago</small></p>
   </div>
  </div>
 </div>
</div>
```

Card Styles

Cards include various options for customizing their color, backgrounds, and borders.

Background and Color

Use background and text color utilities to change the appearance of a card.

```
<div class="card text-white bg-primary mb-4"
style="max-width: 18rem;">
 <div class="card-header">Header</div>
 <div class="card-body">
  <h5 class="card-title">Primary card title</h5>
  <p class="card-text">Some quick example text to
     build on the card title and make up the bulk of
     the card's content.</p>
 </div>
</div>
<div class="card text-white bg-secondary mb-4"
     style="max-width: 18rem;">
 <div class="card-header">Header</div>
 <div class="card-body">
  <h5 class="card-title">Secondary card title</h5>
  <p class="card-text">Some quick example text to
     build on the card title and make up the bulk of
     the card's content.</p>
 </div>
</div>
<div class="card text-white bg-success mb-4"
style="max-width: 18rem;">
 <div class="card-header">Header</div>
 <div class="card-body">
  <h5 class="card-title">Success card title</h5>
  <p class="card-text">Some quick example text to
     build on the card title and make up the bulk of
     the card's content.</p>
 </div>
</div>
<div class="card text-white bg-danger mb-4"
style="max-width: 18rem;">
 <div class="card-header">Header</div>
 <div class="card-body">
  <h5 class="card-title">Danger card title</h5>
  <p class="card-text">Some quick example text to
     build on the card title and make up the bulk of
     the card's content.</p>
 </div>
</div>
<div class="card text-dark bg-warning mb-3"
     style="max-width: 18rem;">
 <div class="card-header">Header</div>
```

```
 <div class="card-body">
  <h5 class="card-title">Warning card title</h5>
  <p class="card-text">Some quick example text to
      build on the card title and make up the bulk of
      the card's content.</p>
 </div>
</div>
<div class="card text-dark bg-info mb-3" style="max-
      width: 18rem;">
 <div class="card-header">Header</div>
 <div class="card-body">
  <h5 class="card-title">Info card title</h5>
  <p class="card-text">Some quick example text to
      build on the card title and make up the bulk of
      the card's content.</p>
 </div>
</div>
<div class="card text-dark bg-light mb-3" style="max-
      width: 18rem;">
 <div class="card-header">Header</div>
 <div class="card-body">
  <h5 class="card-title">Light card title</h5>
  <p class="card-text">Some quick example text to
      build on the card title and make up the bulk of
      the card's content.</p>
 </div>
</div>
<div class="card text-white bg-dark mb-4" style="max-
      width: 18rem;">
 <div class="card-header">Header</div>
 <div class="card-body">
  <h5 class="card-title">Dark card title</h5>
  <p class="card-text">Some quick example text to
      build on the card title and make up the bulk of
      the card's content.</p>
 </div>
</div>
```

Border
To modify the color of a card's border, use border utils. As seen below, you can use .text-{color} classes on the parent.card or a subset of the card's contents.

```
<div class="card border-primary mb-4" style="max-
width: 18rem;">
 <div class="card-header">Header</div>
 <div class="card-body text-primary">
  <h5 class="card-title">Primary card title</h5>
  <p class="card-text">Some quick example text to
     build on the card title and make up the bulk of
     the card's content.</p>
 </div>
</div>
<div class="card border-secondary mb-4" style="max-
width: 18rem;">
 <div class="card-header">Header</div>
 <div class="card-body text-secondary">
  <h5 class="card-title">Secondary card title</h5>
  <p class="card-text">Some quick example text to
     build on the card title and make up the bulk of
     the card's content.</p>
 </div>
</div>
<div class="card border-success mb-4" style="max-
width: 18rem;">
 <div class="card-header">Header</div>
 <div class="card-body text-success">
  <h5 class="card-title">Success card title</h5>
  <p class="card-text">Some quick example text to
     build on the card title and make up the bulk of
     the card's content.</p>
 </div>
</div>
<div class="card border-danger mb-4" style="max-
     width: 18rem;">
 <div class="card-header">Header</div>
 <div class="card-body text-danger">
  <h5 class="card-title">Danger card title</h5>
  <p class="card-text">Some quick example text to
     build on the card title and make up the bulk of
     the card's content.</p>
 </div>
</div>
<div class="card border-warning mb-4" style="max-
     width: 18rem;">
```

```
<div class="card-header">Header</div>
<div class="card-body">
 <h5 class="card-title">Warning card title</h5>
 <p class="card-text">Some quick example text to
    build on the card title and make up the bulk of
    the card's content.</p>
</div>
</div>
<div class="card border-info mb-4" style="max-width:
    18rem;">
 <div class="card-header">Header</div>
 <div class="card-body">
  <h5 class="card-title">Info card title</h5>
  <p class="card-text">Some quick example text to
     build on the card title and make up the bulk of
     the card's content.</p>
 </div>
</div>
<div class="card border-light mb-4" style="max-width:
    18rem;">
 <div class="card-header">Header</div>
 <div class="card-body">
  <h5 class="card-title">Light card title</h5>
  <p class="card-text">Some quick example text to
     build on the card title and make up the bulk of
     the card's content.</p>
 </div>
</div>
<div class="card border-dark mb-4" style="max-width:
    18rem;">
 <div class="card-header">Header</div>
 <div class="card-body text-dark">
  <h5 class="card-title">Dark card title</h5>
  <p class="card-text">Some quick example text to
     build on the card title and make up the bulk of
     the card's content.</p>
 </div>
</div>
```

Mixins Utilities

It is easy to change the borders on the card footer and header as needed and remove their background color with .bg-transparent.

```
<div class="card border-success mb-4" style="max-
    width: 18rem;">
 <div class="card-header bg-transparent border-
    success">Header</div>
 <div class="card-body text-success">
  <h5 class="card-title">Success card title</h5>
  <p class="card-text">Some quick example text to
    build on the card title and make up the bulk of
    the card's content.</p>
 </div>
 <div class="card-footer bg-transparent border-
    success">Footer</div>
</div>
```

Card Layout

Bootstrap has a few choices for putting out a series of cards in addition to designing the content within cards. These layout options are not currently responsive for the time being.

Card Groups

To present cards as a single, associated element with equal width and height columns, use card groups. Card groups start stacked and use display: flex; to become attached with uniform dimensions starting at the sm breakpoint.

```
<div class="card-group">
 <div class="card">
  <img src="..." class="card-img-top" alt="...">
  <div class="card-body">
   <h5 class="card-title">Card title</h5>
   <p class="card-text">This is a wider card with
     supporting text below as a natural lead-in to
     additional content. This content is a little
     bit longer.</p>
   <p class="card-text"><small class="text-
     muted">Last updated 3 mins ago</small></p>
  </div>
 </div>
 <div class="card">
  <img src="..." class="card-img-top" alt="...">
  <div class="card-body">
```

```
    <h5 class="card-title">Card title</h5>
    <p class="card-text">This card has supporting text
        below as a natural lead-in to additional
        content.</p>
    <p class="card-text"><small class="text-
        muted">Last updated 3 mins ago</small></p>
  </div>
 </div>
 <div class="card">
  <img src="..." class="card-img-top" alt="...">
  <div class="card-body">
    <h5 class="card-title">Card title</h5>
    <p class="card-text">As a natural lead-in to
        further content, this is a broader card with
        supporting text underneath. To demonstrate that
        equal height action, this card has even more
        substance than the previous.</p>
    <p class="card-text"><small class="text-
        muted">Last updated 3 mins ago</small></p>
  </div>
 </div>
</div>
```

When using card groups the content will automatically line up with footers.

```
<div class="card-group">
 <div class="card">
  <img src="..." class="card-img-top" alt="...">
  <div class="card-body">
    <h5 class="card-title">Card title</h5>
    <p class="card-text">This is a wider card with
        supporting text below as a natural lead-in to
        additional content. This content is a little
        bit longer.</p>
  </div>
  <div class="card-footer">
    <small class="text-muted">Last updated 3 mins
            ago</small>
  </div>
 </div>
 <div class="card">
```

```
<img src="..." class="card-img-top" alt="...">
<div class="card-body">
  <h5 class="card-title">Card title</h5>
  <p class="card-text">This card has supporting text
      below as a natural lead-in to additional
      content.</p>
</div>
<div class="card-footer">
  <small class="text-muted">Last updated 3 mins
        ago</small>
</div>
</div>
<div class="card">
  <img src="..." class="card-img-top" alt="...">
  <div class="card-body">
    <h5 class="card-title">Card title</h5>
    <p class="card-text">As a natural lead-in to
        further content, this is a larger card with
        supporting text underneath. To demonstrate
        equal height action, this card has even more
        content than the previous.</p>
  </div>
  <div class="card-footer">
    <small class="text-muted">Last updated 3 mins
          ago</small>
  </div>
</div>
</div>
```

Grid Cards

To decide how many grid columns (wrapped around your cards) you show per row, use the Bootstrap grid system and its .row-cols classes. From the medium breakpoint up, here's .row-cols-2 laying out the cards on one column and .row-cols-MD-2 spreading four cards to equal width across many rows.

```
<div class="row row-cols-2 row-cols-md-2 g-4">
  <div class="col">
    <div class="card">
      <img src="..." class="card-img-top" alt="...">
      <div class="card-body">
        <h5 class="card-title">Card title</h5>
```

```
   <p class="card-text">This is a longer card with
      supporting text below as a natural lead-in to
      additional content. This content is a little
      bit longer.</p>
  </div>
 </div>
</div>
<div class="col">
 <div class="card">
  <img src="..." class="card-img-top" alt="...">
  <div class="card-body">
   <h5 class="card-title">Card title</h5>
   <p class="card-text">This is a longer card with
      supporting text below as a natural lead-in to
      additional content. This content is a little
      bit longer.</p>
  </div>
 </div>
</div>
<div class="col">
 <div class="card">
  <img src="..." class="card-img-top" alt="...">
  <div class="card-body">
   <h5 class="card-title">Card title</h5>
   <p class="card-text">This is a longer card with
      supporting text below as a natural lead-in to
      additional content.</p>
  </div>
 </div>
</div>
<div class="col">
 <div class="card">
  <img src="..." class="card-img-top" alt="...">
  <div class="card-body">
   <h5 class="card-title">Card title</h5>
   <p class="card-text">This is a longer card with
      supporting text below as a natural lead-in to
      additional content. This content is a little
      bit longer.</p>
  </div>
 </div>
</div>
</div>
```

Change it to .row-cols-4, and you'll see the fifth card wrap.

```html
<div class="row row-cols-2 row-cols-md-3 g-4">
 <div class="col">
  <div class="card">
   <img src="..." class="card-img-top" alt="...">
   <div class="card-body">
    <h5 class="card-title">Card title</h5>
    <p class="card-text">This is a longer card with
        supporting text below as a natural lead-in to
        additional content. This content is a little
        bit longer.</p>
   </div>
  </div>
 </div>
 <div class="col">
  <div class="card">
   <img src="..." class="card-img-top" alt="...">
   <div class="card-body">
    <h5 class="card-title">Card title</h5>
    <p class="card-text">This is a longer card with
        supporting text below as a natural lead-in to
        additional content. This content is a little
        bit longer.</p>
   </div>
  </div>
 </div>
 <div class="col">
  <div class="card">
   <img src="..." class="card-img-top" alt="...">
   <div class="card-body">
    <h5 class="card-title">Card title</h5>
    <p class="card-text">This is a longer card with
        supporting text below as a natural lead-in to
        additional content.</p>
   </div>
  </div>
 </div>
 <div class="col">
  <div class="card">
   <img src="..." class="card-img-top" alt="...">
   <div class="card-body">
    <h5 class="card-title">Card title</h5>
```

```
      <p class="card-text">This is a longer card with
          supporting text below as a natural lead-in to
          additional content. This content is a little
          bit longer.</p>
    </div>
   </div>
  </div>
</div>
```

If you need same height, add .h-100 to the cards. If you want similar heights by default, you can set $card-height: 100% in Sass.

```
<div class="row row-cols-1 row-cols-md-3 g-4">
 <div class="col">
  <div class="card h-100">
   <img src="..." class="card-img-top" alt="...">
   <div class="card-body">
    <h5 class="card-title">Card title</h5>
    <p class="card-text">This is a longer card with
        supporting text below as a natural lead-in to
        additional content. This content is a little
        bit longer.</p>
   </div>
  </div>
 </div>
 <div class="col">
  <div class="card h-100">
   <img src="..." class="card-img-top" alt="...">
   <div class="card-body">
    <h5 class="card-title">Card title</h5>
    <p class="card-text">This is a short card.</p>
   </div>
  </div>
 </div>
 <div class="col">
  <div class="card h-100">
   <img src="..." class="card-img-top" alt="...">
   <div class="card-body">
    <h5 class="card-title">Card title</h5>
    <p class="card-text">This is a longer card with
        supporting text below as a natural lead-in to
        additional content.</p>
```

```
    </div>
   </div>
  </div>
  <div class="col">
   <div class="card h-100">
    <img src="..." class="card-img-top" alt="...">

    <div class="card-body">
     <h5 class="card-title">Card title</h5>

     <p class="card-text">This is a longer card with
         supporting text below as a natural lead-in to
         additional content. This content is a little
         bit longer.</p>
    </div>
   </div>
  </div>
</div>
```

Just like with card groups, here the card footers will automatically line up.

```
<div class="row row-cols-1 row-cols-md-3 g-4">
 <div class="col">
  <div class="card h-100">
   <img src="..." class="card-img-top" alt="...">
   <div class="card-body">
    <h5 class="card-title">Card title</h5>
    <p class="card-text">This is a wider card with
        supporting text below as a natural lead-in to
        additional content. This content is a little
        bit longer.</p>
   </div>
   <div class="card-footer">
    <small class="text-muted">Last updated 3 mins
           ago</small>
   </div>
  </div>
 </div>
 <div class="col">
  <div class="card h-100">
   <img src="..." class="card-img-top" alt="...">
```

```
   <div class="card-body">
    <h5 class="card-title">Card title</h5>
    <p class="card-text">This card has supporting
        text below as a natural lead-in to additional
        content.</p>
   </div>
   <div class="card-footer">
    <small class="text-muted">Last updated 3 mins
            ago</small>
   </div>
  </div>
 </div>
 <div class="col">
  <div class="card h-100">
   <img src="..." class="card-img-top" alt="...">
   <div class="card-body">
    <h5 class="card-title">Card title</h5>
    <p class="card-text">As a natural lead-in to
        further content, this is a broader card with
        supporting text underneath. To demonstrate
        that equal height action, this card has even
        more substance than the previous.</p>
   </div>
   <div class="card-footer">
    <small class="text-muted">Last updated 3 mins
            ago</small>
   </div>
  </div>
 </div>
</div>
```

Masnory

We utilized a CSS-only method in v4 to replicate the behavior of Masonry-like columns, but it had a lot of unfavorable side effects. The Masonry plugin may be used to create this style of layout in v5. Masonry isn't included in Bootstrap, but we've created a sample to get you started.

CAROUSEL

A slideshow component that, like a carousel, cycles among elements – images or text slides.

How It Works

The carousel is a slideshow that uses CSS 3D transforms and a little JavaScript to cycle through a sequence of content. It can be used with photos, text, or custom markup. Previous/following controls and indicators also supported here.

The carousel will avoid sliding smoothly when the webpage is not visible to the user in browsers that use the Page Visibility API (such as when the browser tab is inactive, the browser window is minimized, etc.). This component's animation effect is determined by the prefers-reduced-motion media query.

Please be advised that nested carousels are not supported, and carousels in general do not meet accessibility requirements.

Example

Slide dimensions are not automatically normalized in carousels. You might need to utilize additional tools or custom styles to size content properly. Carousels can have previous/following controls and indicators, although they aren't essential. As you see fit, add and customize.

The .active class must be applied to at least one slide; else, the carousel will not appear. Also, if you're utilizing numerous carousels on a single page, make sure to give each one a unique id in the .carousel file. The data-bs-target attribute (or href for links) on control and indicator elements must match the id of the .carousel element.

Slides Only

This is a slide-only carousel. On carousel images, note the existence of the .d-block and.w-100 tags, which prohibit browser default image alignment.

```
<div id="carouselExampleSlidesOnly" class="carousel
slide" data-bs-ride="carousel">
 <div class="carousel-inner">
  <div class="carousel-item active">
   <img src="..." class="d-block w-100" alt="...">
  </div>
  <div class="carousel-item">
   <img src="..." class="d-block w-100" alt="...">
  </div>
  <div class="carousel-item">
   <img src="..." class="d-block w-100" alt="...">
  </div>
```

```
 </div>
</div>
```

With Controls

The previous and next controls have been added. We advocate utilizing
<button> elements, although <a> elements with role="button" can also
be used.

```
<div id="carouselExampleControls" class="carousel
slide" data-bs-ride="carousel">
 <div class="carousel-inner">
  <div class="carousel-item active">
   <img src="..." class="d-block w-100" alt="...">
  </div>
  <div class="carousel-item">
   <img src="..." class="d-block w-100" alt="...">
  </div>
  <div class="carousel-item">
   <img src="..." class="d-block w-100" alt="...">
  </div>
 </div>
 <button class="carousel-control-prev" type="button"
         data-bs-target="#carouselExampleControls"
         data-bs-slide="prev">
  <span class="carousel-control-prev-icon" aria-
         hidden="true"></span>
  <span class="visually-hidden">Previous</span>
 </button>
 <button class="carousel-control-next" type="button"
         data-bs-target="#carouselExampleControls"
         data-bs-slide="next">
  <span class="carousel-control-next-icon" aria-
         hidden="true"></span>
  <span class="visually-hidden">Next</span>
 </button>
</div>
```

With Indicators

```
<div id="carouselExampleIndicators" class="carousel
    slide" data-bs-ride="carousel">
 <div class="carousel-indicators">
```

```
<button type="button" data-bs-target="#carousel
   ExampleIndicators" data-bs-slide-to="0"
   class="active" aria-current="true" aria-
   label="Slide 1"></button>
 <button type="button" data-bs-target="#carousel
   ExampleIndicators" data-bs-slide-to="1" aria-
   label="Slide 2"></button>
 <button type="button" data-bs-target="#carousel
   ExampleIndicators" data-bs-slide-to="2" aria-
   label="Slide 3"></button>
</div>
<div class="carousel-inner">
 <div class="carousel-item active">
  <img src="..." class="d-block w-100" alt="...">
 </div>
 <div class="carousel-item">
  <img src="..." class="d-block w-100" alt="...">
 </div>
 <div class="carousel-item">
  <img src="..." class="d-block w-100" alt="...">
 </div>
</div>
<button class="carousel-control-prev" type="button"
        data-bs-target="#carouselExampleIndicators"
        data-bs-slide="prev">
 <span class="carousel-control-prev-icon" aria-
       hidden="true"></span>
 <span class="visually-hidden">Previous</span>
</button>
<button class="carousel-control-next" type="button"
        data-bs-target="#carouselExampleIndicators"
        data-bs-slide="next">
 <span class="carousel-control-next-icon" aria-
       hidden="true"></span>
 <span class="visually-hidden">Next</span>
</button>
</div>
```

With Captions

With the .carousel-caption element within any .carousel-item, you can quickly add captions to your slides. Optional display utilities can be easily hidden on smaller viewports, as demonstrated below. We use .d-none to hide them at first, then .d-MD-block to bring them back on medium-sized devices.

```
<div id="carouselExampleCaptions" class="carousel
     slide" data-bs-ride="carousel">
 <div class="carousel-indicators">
  <button type="button" data-bs-target="#carousel
    ExampleCaptions" data-bs-slide-to="0"
    class="active" aria-current="true" aria-
    label="Slide 1"></button>
  <button type="button" data-bs-target="#carousel
          ExampleCaptions" data-bs-slide-to="1" aria-
          label="Slide 2"></button>
  <button type="button" data-bs-target="#carousel
          ExampleCaptions" data-bs-slide-to="2" aria-
          label="Slide 3"></button>
 </div>
 <div class="carousel-inner">
  <div class="carousel-item active">
   <img src="..." class="d-block w-100" alt="...">
   <div class="carousel-caption d-none d-md-block">
    <h5>First slide label</h5>
    <p>Some representative placeholder content for
            first slide.</p>
   </div>
  </div>
  <div class="carousel-item">
   <img src="..." class="d-block w-100" alt="...">
   <div class="carousel-caption d-none d-md-block">
    <h5>Second slide label</h5>
    <p>Some representative placeholder content for
            second slide.</p>
   </div>
  </div>
  <div class="carousel-item">
   <img src="..." class="d-block w-100" alt="...">
   <div class="carousel-caption d-none d-md-block">
    <h5>Third slide label</h5>
    <p>Some representative placeholder content for
            third slide.</p>
   </div>
  </div>
 </div>
```

```
<button class="carousel-control-prev" type="button"
        data-bs-target="#carouselExampleCaptions"
        data-bs-slide="prev">
 <span class="carousel-control-prev-icon" aria-
        hidden="true"></span>
 <span class="visually-hidden">Previous</span>
</button>
<button class="carousel-control-next" type="button"
        data-bs-target="#carouselExampleCaptions"
        data-bs-slide="next">
 <span class="carousel-control-next-icon" aria-
        hidden="true"></span>
 <span class="visually-hidden">Next</span>
</button>
</div>
```

Crossfade

Add .carousel-fade to your carousel to animate the slides with a fade transition instead of a slide.

```
<div id="carouselExampleFade" class="carousel slide
    carousel-fade" data-bs-ride="carousel">
 <div class="carousel-inner">
  <div class="carousel-item active">
   <img src="..." class="d-block w-100" alt="...">
  </div>
  <div class="carousel-item">
   <img src="..." class="d-block w-100" alt="...">
  </div>
  <div class="carousel-item">
   <img src="..." class="d-block w-100" alt="...">
  </div>
 </div>
 <button class="carousel-control-prev" type="button"
        data-bs-target="#carouselExampleFade"
        data-bs-slide="prev">
  <span class="carousel-control-prev-icon" aria-
        hidden="true"></span>
  <span class="visually-hidden">Previous</span>
 </button>
 <button class="carousel-control-next" type="button"
        data-bs-target="#carouselExampleFade"
        data-bs-slide="next">
```

```
    <span class="carousel-control-next-icon" aria-
        hidden="true"></span>
    <span class="visually-hidden">Next</span>
  </button>
</div>
```

Individual .carousal-item Interval

Add the data-bs-interval=" to a .carousel-item to change the amount of time to delay between automatically cycling to next item.

```
<div id="carouselExampleInterval" class="carousel
slide" data-bs-ride="carousel">
 <div class="carousel-inner">
  <div class="carousel-item active"
      data-bs-interval="10000">
   <img src="..." class="d-block w-100" alt="...">
  </div>
  <div class="carousel-item" data-bs-interval="2000">
   <img src="..." class="d-block w-100" alt="...">
  </div>
  <div class="carousel-item">
   <img src="..." class="d-block w-100" alt="...">
  </div>
 </div>
 <button class="carousel-control-prev" type="button"
        data-bs-target="#carouselExampleInterval"
        data-bs-slide="prev">
  <span class="carousel-control-prev-icon" aria-
      hidden="true"></span>
  <span class="visually-hidden">Previous</span>
 </button>
 <button class="carousel-control-next" type="button"
        data-bs-target="#carouselExampleInterval"
        data-bs-slide="next">
  <span class="carousel-control-next-icon" aria-
      hidden="true"></span>
  <span class="visually-hidden">Next</span>
 </button>
</div>
```

Disable Touch Swiping

Carousels on touchscreen devices enable swiping left/right to move between slides. The data-bs-touch property can be used to deactivate this.

The sample below likewise lacks the data-bs-ride attribute and has data-bs-interval="false," indicating that it does not autoplay.

```
<div id="carouselExampleControlsNoTouching"
     class="carousel slide" data-bs-touch="false"
     data-bs-interval="false">
 <div class="carousel-inner">
  <div class="carousel-item active">
   <img src="..." class="d-block w-100" alt="...">
  </div>
  <div class="carousel-item">
   <img src="..." class="d-block w-100" alt="...">
  </div>
  <div class="carousel-item">
   <img src="..." class="d-block w-100" alt="...">
  </div>
 </div>
 <button class="carousel-control-prev" type="button"
         data-bs-target="#carouselExampleControls
         NoTouching" data-bs-slide="prev">
  <span class="carousel-control-prev-icon" aria-
        hidden="true"></span>
  <span class="visually-hidden">Previous</span>
 </button>
 <button class="carousel-control-next" type="button"
         data-bs-target="#carouselExampleControls
         NoTouching" data-bs-slide="next">
  <span class="carousel-control-next-icon" aria-
        hidden="true"></span>
  <span class="visually-hidden">Next</span>
 </button>
</div>
```

Dark Variant

Add .carousel-dark to the .carousel for darker controls, indicators, and captions. Controls have been inverted from their default white fill with the filter CSS property. Captions and controls have additional Sass variables that customize the color and background color.

```
<div id="carouselExampleDark" class="carousel
     carousel-dark slide" data-bs-ride="carousel">
```

```html
<div class="carousel-indicators">
 <button type="button" data-bs-
   target="#carouselExampleDark" data-bs-
   slide-to="0" class="active" aria-current="true"
   aria-label="Slide 1"></button>
 <button type="button" data-bs-
   target="#carouselExampleDark" data-bs-
   slide-to="1" aria-label="Slide 2"></button>
 <button type="button" data-bs-
   target="#carouselExampleDark" data-bs-
   slide-to="2" aria-label="Slide 3"></button>
</div>
<div class="carousel-inner">
 <div class="carousel-item active"
     data-bs-interval="10000">
  <img src="..." class="d-block w-100" alt="...">
  <div class="carousel-caption d-none d-md-block">
   <h5>First slide label</h5>
   <p>Some representative placeholder content for
           first slide.</p>
  </div>
 </div>
 <div class="carousel-item" data-bs-interval="2000">
  <img src="..." class="d-block w-100" alt="...">
  <div class="carousel-caption d-none d-md-block">
   <h5>Second slide label</h5>
   <p>Some representative placeholder content for
           second slide.</p>
  </div>
 </div>
 <div class="carousel-item">
  <img src="..." class="d-block w-100" alt="...">
  <div class="carousel-caption d-none d-md-block">
   <h5>Third slide label</h5>
   <p>Some representative placeholder content for
           third slide.</p>
  </div>
 </div>
</div>
<button class="carousel-control-prev" type="button"
        data-bs-target="#carouselExampleDark"
        data-bs-slide="prev">
```

```
  <span class="carousel-control-prev-icon" aria-
      hidden="true"></span>
  <span class="visually-hidden">Previous</span>
</button>
<button class="carousel-control-next" type="button"
      data-bs-target="#carouselExampleDark"
      data-bs-slide="next">
  <span class="carousel-control-next-icon" aria-
      hidden="true"></span>
  <span class="visually-hidden">Next</span>
</button>
</div>
```

Custom Transition

The transition duration of the .carousel-item can change with the $carousel-transition-duration Sass variable before compiling or custom styles if you're using compiled CSS. If multiple transitions are applied, make sure transform transition is defined first (e.g., transition: transform 2s ease, opacity .5s ease-out).

Usage

Via Data Attributes

Use data attributes to control the position of the carousel easily. data-bs-slide accepts keywords prev or next, which alters slide position relative to its current position. Alternatively, use data-bs-slide-to to pass raw slide index to carousel data-bs-slide-to="2", which shifts slide position to a particular index beginning with 0.

The data-bs-ride="carousel" attribute is used to mark carousel as animating starting at page load. If you don't use data-bs-ride="carousel" to initialize carousel, you must initialize it yourself.

Via JavaScript

Call carousel manually with:

```
var myCarousel = document.querySelector('#myCarousel')
var carousel = new bootstrap.Carousel(myCarousel)
```

Options

Options can pass via data attributes or JavaScript. For data attributes, append option name to data-bs-, as in data-bs-interval=".."

Name		Default	Description Number Type
interval		4000	The period of time between items that are automatically cycled. The carousel will not automatically cycle if false
keyboard	boolean	true	Whether carousel should react to keyboard events
pause	string | boolean	'hover.'	If set to "hover," pauses cycling of carousel on mouse enter and resumes the cycling of the carousel on mouse leave. If set to false, hovering over the carousel won't pause it. On touch-enabled devices, when set to "hover," cycling will break on touching for two intervals before automatically resuming. Note that this is in the addition to above mouse behavior
ride	string | boolean	false	Autoplay the carousel after user manually cycles the first item. If set to "carousel," autoplay the carousel on load
wrap	boolean	true	Whether carousel should cycle continuously or have hard stops
touch	boolean	true	Whether carousel should support left/proper swipe interactions on touchscreen devices

Methods

Asynchronous Transitions and Methods

All API methods initiate a transition and are asynchronous. They call the caller as soon as the change is made but before it is completed. In addition, a transitional component's method call will be ignored.

For example, you can use the carousel constructor to create a carousel instance with various settings and begin cycling through items:

```
var myCarousel = document.querySelector('#myCarousel')
var carousel = new bootstrap.Carousel(myCarousel, {
  interval: 2000,
  wrap: false
})
```

Method	Description
cycle	Cycles through carousel items from left to right
pause	Stops the carousel from cycling through objects
prev	Cycles to the previous item. **Returns to the caller before the last thing has been shown** (e.g., before the slid.bs.carousel event occurs)

next	Cycles to the next item. **Returns to the caller before the following article has been shown** (e.g., before slid.bs.carousel event occurs)
nextWhenVisible	When page isn't visible, or the carousel or its parent isn't visible, don't cycle from one to the next. **Returns to mcaller before the target item is shown**
.	Cycles the carousel to certain frame (0 based, similar to an array). **Returns to the caller before displaying the target item**
dispose	Destroys an element's carousel
getInstance	The static method allows getting carousel instance associated with a DOM element, you can use it like this: Bootstrap.Carousel.getInstance(element)
getOrCreateInstance	The static method returns carousel instance associated with DOM element or creates a new one if it wasn't initialized. You can use it like this: Bootstrap.Carousel.getOrCreateInstance(element)

Events

The carousel class in Bootstrap exposes two events for interacting with carousel functionality. The following properties are shared by both events:

- **Direction**: The next element direction is the one in which the carousel is sliding (either "left" or "right").

- **Related target**: The DOM element that is being slid into place as the active item.

- **From**: The index of the current article

- **To**: The index of the following item

The carousel is the target of all carousel events (i.e., at the <div class="carousel">).

```
var myCarousel = document.getElementById('myCarousel')

myCarousel.addEventListener('slide.bs.carousel',
          function () {
  // do something...
})
```

Event Type	Description
slide.bs.carousel	It fires immediately when the slide instance method is invoked
slid.bs.carousel	It is fired when the carousel has completed its slide transition

CLOSE BUTTON

A generic close button can be used to dismiss information such as alerts and modals.

Example

With, provides a way to dismiss or close a component .btn-close. The default styling is simple, yet it is very adaptable. To replace the default background image, change the Sass variables. As with aria-label, make sure to provide text for screen readers.

```
<button type="button" class="btn-close" aria-
        label="Close"></button>
```

Disable State

Close buttons that are disabled vary their opacity. To avoid hover and active states from triggering, we've used pointer-events: none and user-select: none.

```
<button type="button" class="btn-close" disabled
        aria-label="Close"></button>
```

White Variant

Change the default .btn-close to be white with the .btn-close-white class. This class uses the filter property to invert the background image.

```
<button type="button" class="btn-close btn-close-
        white" aria-label="Close"></button>
<button type="button" class="btn-close btn-close-
        white" disabled aria-label="Close"></button>
```

COLLAPSE

Using JavaScript plugins and a few classes, you can control the visibility of content across your project.

How It Works

To show and hide content, the collapse JavaScript plugin is utilized. Buttons or anchors serve as triggers for certain items that you toggle. When you collapse a portion, the height will animate from its current value to 0. You can't use padding on a .collapse element because of how

CSS handles animations. Use the class as a stand-alone wrapper element instead. This component's animation effect is determined by the prefers-reduced-motion media query.

Example

To show and conceal another element via class modifications, use the buttons below:

- collapse hides content

- collapsing is applied during transitions

- collapse.show shows content

Using a button with the data-bs-target attribute is generally recommended. You can also use link with the href property (and a role="button"), which is not encouraged from a semantic standpoint. The data-bs-toggle="collapse" attribute is necessary in both circumstances.

```
<p>
 <a class="btn btn-primary" data-bs-toggle="collapse"
    href="#collapseExample" role="button" aria-
    expanded="false"
    aria-controls="collapse_Example">
  Link with href
 </a>
 <button class="btn btn-primary" type="button" data-
   bs-toggle="collapse" data-bs-
   target="#collapseExample" aria-expanded="false"
   aria-controls="collapse_Example">
  Button with data-bs-target
 </button>
</p>
<div class="collapse" id="collapseExample">
 <div class="card card-body">
  For the collapse component, some placeholder content.
     By default, this panel is hidden, but it is exposed
     when the user presses the appropriate trigger.
 </div>
</div>
```

Multiple Targets

Multiple components can be shown and hidden by addressing them with a selector in the href or data-bs-target attribute of a button or an a. Each references it with its href or data-bs-target attribute, several <buttons> or <a> can show and hide an element.

```
<p>
 <a class="btn btn-primary" data-bs-toggle="collapse"
    href="#multiCollapseExam1" role="button" aria-
    expanded="false" aria-controls="multiCollapseEx
    am1">Toggle first element</a>
 <button class="btn btn-primary" type="button" data-bs-
         toggle="collapse" data-bs-target=
         "#multiCollapseExam2" aria-expanded="false"
         aria-controls="multiCollapseExample2">Toggle
         second element</button>
 <button class="btn btn-primary" type="button" data-
         bs-toggle="collapse" data-bs-target=".multi-
         collapse" aria-expanded="false" aria-controls
         ="multiCollapseExam1 multiCollapseExam2">
         Toggle both elements</button>
</p>
<div class="row">
 <div class="col">
  <div class="collapse multi-collapse"
id="multiCollapseExample1">
    <div class="card card-body">
     This multi-collapse example's initial collapse
      component has some placeholder content. By
      default, this panel is hidden, but it is exposed
      when the user presses the appropriate trigger.
    </div>
  </div>
 </div>
 <div class="col">
  <div class="collapse multi-collapse"
      id="multiCollapseExample2">
    <div class="card card-body">
     This multi-collapse example's second collapse
      component has some placeholder material. By
      default, this panel is hidden, but it is exposed
      when the user presses the appropriate trigger.
```

```
    </div>
   </div>
  </div>
</div>
```

Accessibility

Make sure the control element has the aria-expanded element. This attribute informs screen readers and other assistive technology about the current state of the collapsible element associated with the control. If the collapsible element in Bootstrap is closed by default, the aria-expanded="false" attribute on the control element should be used. Set aria-expanded="true" on the control instead of using the show class to make the collapsible element open by default. Depending on whether the collapsible element is opened or closed, the plugin will automatically toggle this attribute on the control (via JavaScript, or because the user triggered another control element also tied to the same collapsible element). The attribute role="button" should add to the control element if the HTML element is not a button (e.g., an or >).

Suppose your control element is targeting a single collapsible segment. If the data-bs-target property points to an id selector, you should add the aria-controls attribute to the control element, which should include the id of the collapsible element. This feature is used by modern screen readers and similar assistive devices to offer users with extra shortcuts to navigate straight to the collapsible element itself.

The many *optional* keyboard interactions indicated in the WAI-ARIA Authoring Practices 1.1 accordion pattern are not covered by Bootstrap's current implementation; you will need to incorporate these yourself using custom JavaScript.

Sass
Variables

```
$transition-collapse:    height .35s ease;
```

Classes
Because collapse transition classes are shared across several components, they may be found in scss/ transitions.scss (collapse and accordion).

```
.collapse {
 &:not(.show) {
  display: none;
 }
}
```

```
.collapsing {
 height: 0;
 overflow: hidden;
 @include transition($transition-collapse);
}
```

Usage

To accomplish the hard lifting, the collapse plugin makes use of a few classes:

```
collapse.hides hides the content
collapse.show shows the content
When the transition begins, collapsing is added, and
when it ends, it is removed.
```

These classes can be found in the CSS file _transitions.

Via Data Attributes

Just add data-bs-toggle="collapse" and a data-bs-target to the element to automatically assign control of one or more collapsible elements. The data-bs-target property takes a CSS selector to which the collapse should be applied. Make sure the collapsible element has the class collapse. Add the extra class show if you want it to open by default.

Add the data attribute data-bs-parent="#selector" to a collapsible section to enable accordion-style group management.

Via JavaScript

Enable manually with:

```
var collapseElementList = [].slice.call(document.qu
erySelectorAll('.collapse'))
var collapseList = collapseElementList.map(function
(collapseEl) {
 return new bootstrap.Collapse(collapseEl)
})
```

Options

Data attributes or JavaScript can be used to pass options. Append option name to data-bs-, as in data-bs-parent="." for data attributes.

Name	Type	Default	Description
parent	selector | jQuery object | DOM element	false	When a parent is supplied, all collapsible elements under that parent are closed when this collapsible item is displayed (this is based on the card class, and is comparable to traditional accordion behavior). The attribute must be applied to the collapsible area's target
toggle	boolean	true	Toggles the collapsible element on invocation

Methods

Asynchronous Methods and Transitions

All API methods initiate a transition and are asynchronous. They call the caller as soon as the change is made but before it is completed. In addition, a transitional component's method call will be ignored.

Your content is activated as a collapsible element. Optionally accepts an options object.

You can use the constructor to make a collapse instance, for example:

```
var myCollapse = document.getElementById('myCollapse')
var bsCollapse = new bootstrap.Collapse(myCollapse, {
 toggle: false
})
```

Method	Description
toggle	Toggles the visibility of a collapsible element. **Before the collapsible element** is given or hidden, it returns to the caller (i.e., before the revealed.bs.collapse or hidden.bs.collapse event occurs)
show	A collapsible element **is shown. Before the collapsible element** is supplied, it returns to the caller (e.g., before the revealed.bs.collapse event occurs)
hide	It conceals a collapsible component. **Before the collapsible element** is hidden, it returns to the caller (e.g., before the hidden.bs.collapse event occurs)
dispose	Destroys an element's collapse
getInstance	The static method allows getting the collapse instance associated with a DOM element; you can use it like this: Bootstrap.Collapse.getInstance(element)
getOrCreateInstance	The static method returns a collapse instance associated with a DOM element or creates a new one that wasn't initialized. You can use it like this: Bootstrap.Collapse.getOrCreateInstance(element)

Events

The collapse class in Bootstrap exposes a few events that can be used to hook into collapse functionality.

```
var myCollapsible = document.getElementById('myCollaps
    ible')
myCollapsible.addEventListener('hidden.bs.collapse',
  function () {
 // do something...
})
```

Event Type	Description
show.bs.collapse	This event fires immediately when show instance method is called
shown.bs.collapse	This event is fired when collapse element has been made visible to the user
hide.bs.collapse	This event is fired immediately when hide method has been called
hidden.bs.collapse	This event is fired when collapse element has been hidden from the user

DROPDOWNS

With the Bootstrap dropdown plugin, you can toggle contextual overlays for showing lists of links and more.

Overview

Toggles are available for dropdowns, contextual overlays for showing lists of links, and more. They are interactive, thanks to the included Bootstrap dropdown JavaScript plugin. It was done on purpose for them to be toggled by clicking rather than hovering.

Popper, a third-party library that supports dynamic positioning and viewport detection, is used to create dropdowns. Use the bootstrap.bundle .min.js/bootstrap.bundle.js, which contains Popper, or include popper.min .js before the Bootstrap's JavaScript. However, because dynamic positioning isn't required, Popper isn't utilized to position dropdowns in navbars.

Accessibility

Although the WAI-ARIA standard defines a role="menu" widget, it is only applicable to application-like menus that initiate actions or operations. Only menu items, checkbox menu items, radio button menu items, radio button groups, and sub-menus are allowed in ARIA menus.

Bootstrap's dropdowns, on the other hand, are intended to be flexible and adaptable to a wide range of circumstances and markup structures. For example, dropdowns with additional inputs and form controls, such as search fields or login forms, can be created. As a result, Bootstrap does not expect (or add) any of the roles and aria-attributes that are required for accurate ARIA menus. These more particular attributes will have to be added by the authors themselves.

Bootstrap, on the other hand, includes built-in support for most common keyboard menu activities, such as the ability to navigate between individual options. Use the cursor keys to choose dropdown-item elements, then the ESC key to close the menu.

Examples

Wrap the toggle of the dropdown (your button or link) and the dropdown menu in. dropdown, or another element with a position: relative declaration. To better match your future needs, dropdowns can be triggered by <a> or <button> components. The examples are shown here using semantic <ul> elements where appropriate, but custom markup is supported.

Single Button

With simple HTML tweaks, any single.btn can be converted into a dropdown toggle. Here's how you can use them with any of the button> elements:

```
<div class="dropdown">
 <button class="btn btn-secondary dropdown-toggle"
   type="button" id="dropdownMenuButton1" data-bs-
   toggle="dropdown" aria-expanded="false">
  Dropdown button
 </button>
 <ul class="dropdown-menu" aria-labelledby="dropdownM
    enuButton1">
  <li><a class="dropdown-item" href="#">Action</a></li>
  <li><a class="dropdown-item" href="#">Another
        action</a></li>
  <li><a class="dropdown-item" href="#">Something
        else here</a></li>
 </ul>
</div>
```

```
<div class="dropdown">
 <a class="btn btn-secondary dropdown-toggle"
    href="#" role="button" id="dropdown-MenuLink"
    data-bs-toggle="dropdown" aria-expanded="false">
  Dropdown link
 </a>

 <ul class="dropdown-menu" aria-labelledby="dropdownM
    enuLink">
  <li><a class="dropdown-item" href="#">Action</a></li>
  <li><a class="dropdown-item" href="#">Another
        action</a></li>
  <li><a class="dropdown-item" href="#">Something
        else here</a></li>
 </ul>
</div>
```

The best part is we can do this with any button variant:

```
<!-- Example single danger button -->
<div class="btn-group">
 <button type="button" class="btn btn-danger
        dropdown-toggle" data-bs-toggle="dropdown"
        aria-expanded="false">
  Action
 </button>
 <ul class="dropdown-menu">
  <li><a class="dropdown-item" href="#">Action</a></li>
  <li><a class="dropdown-item" href="#">Another
        action</a></li>
  <li><a class="dropdown-item" href="#">Something
        else here</a></li>
  <li><hr class="dropdown-divider"></li>
  <li><a class="dropdown-item" href="#">Separated
        link</a></li>
 </ul>
</div>
```

Split Button

Similarly, create split button dropdowns with virtually the same markup as single button dropdowns, but with addition of .dropdown-toggle-split for proper spacing around the dropdown caret.

We use this extra class to reduce the horizontal padding on either side of the caret by 25% and remove margin-left that's added for regular button dropdowns. Those additional changes keep the caret centered in the split button and provide a more appropriately sized hit area next to the main switch.

```
<!-- Example split danger button -->
<div class="btn-group">
 <button type="button" class="btn btn-
         danger">Action</button>
 <button type="button" class="btn btn-danger
         dropdown-toggle dropdown-toggle-split" data-
         bs-toggle="dropdown" aria-expanded="false">
  <span class="visually-hidden">Toggle Dropdown</span>
 </button>
 <ul class="dropdown-menu">
  <li><a class="dropdown-item" href="#">Action</a></li>
  <li><a class="dropdown-item" href="#">Another
         action</a></li>
  <li><a class="dropdown-item" href="#">Something
         else here</a></li>
  <li><hr class="dropdown-divider"></li>
  <li><a class="dropdown-item" href="#">Separated
         link</a></li>
 </ul>
</div>
```

Sizing

Button dropdowns work with the buttons of all sizes, including default and split dropdown buttons.

```
<!-- Large button groups ->>
<div class="btn-group">
 <button class="btn btn-secondary btn-lg dropdown-
         toggle" type="button" data-bs-
         toggle="dropdown" aria-expanded="false">
  Large button
 </button>
 <ul class="dropdown-menu">
  ...
 </ul>
</div>
```

```
<div class="btn-group">
 <button class="btn btn-secondary btn-lg"
         type="button">
  Large split button
 </button>
 <button type="button" class="btn btn-lg btn-
   secondary dropdown-toggle dropdown-toggle-split"
   data-bs-toggle="dropdown" aria-expanded="false">
  <span class="visually-hidden">Toggle Dropdown</span>
 </button>
 <ul class="dropdown-menu">
  ...
 </ul>
</div>

<div class="btn-group">
 <button class="btn btn-secondary btn-sm dropdown-
   toggle" type="button" data-bs-toggle="dropdown"
   aria-expanded="false">
  Small button
 </button>
 <ul class="dropdown-menu">
  ...
 </ul>
</div>
<div class="btn-group">
 <button class="btn btn-secondary btn-sm" type="button">
  Small split button
 </button>
 <button type="button" class="btn btn-sm btn-
   secondary dropdown-toggle dropdown-toggle-split"
   data-bs-toggle="dropdown" aria-expanded="false">
  <span class="visually-hidden">Toggle Dropdown</span>
 </button>
 <ul class="dropdown-menu">
  ...
 </ul>
</div>
```

Dark Dropdowns

Opt into the darker dropdowns to match a dark navbar or custom style by adding .dropdown-menu-dark onto existing .dropdown-menu. No changes are required to dropdown items.

```
<div class="dropdown">
 <button class="btn btn-secondary dropdown-toggle"
         type="button" id="dropdownMenuButton2" data-
         bs-toggle="dropdown" aria-expanded="false">
  Dropdown button
 </button>
 <ul class="dropdown-menu dropdown-menu-dark" aria-
     labelledby="dropdownMenuButton2">
  <li><a class="dropdown-item active"
         href="#">Action</a></li>
  <li><a class="dropdown-item" href="#">Another
         action</a></li>
  <li><a class="dropdown-item" href="#">Something
         else here</a></li>
  <li><hr class="dropdown-divider"></li>
  <li><a class="dropdown-item" href="#">Separated
         link</a></li>
 </ul>
</div>
```

And putting it to use in a navbar:

```
<nav class="navbar navbar-expand-lg navbar-dark
bg-dark">
 <div class="container-fluid">
  <a class="navbar-brand" href="#">Navbar</a>
  <button class="navbar-toggler" type="button" data-
    bs-toggle="collapse" data-bs-
    target="#navbarNavDarkDropdown" aria-controls="na
    vbarNavDarkDropdown" aria-expanded="false" aria-
    label="Toggle navigation">
   <span class="navbar-toggler-icon"></span>
  </button>
  <div class="collapse navbar-collapse"
       id="navbarNavDarkDropdown">
   <ul class="navbar-nav">
    <li class="nav-item dropdown">
     <a class="nav-link dropdown-toggle" href="#"
        id="navbarDarkDropdownMenuLink" role="button"
        data-bs-toggle="dropdown" aria-expanded="false">
      Dropdown
     </a>
```

```
        <ul class="dropdown-menu dropdown-menu-dark"
            aria-labelledby="navbarDarkDropdownMenuL
            ink">
          <li><a class="dropdown-item" href="#">Action</
                a></li>
          <li><a class="dropdown-item" href="#">Another
                action</a></li>
          <li><a class="dropdown-item" href="#">Something
                else here</a></li>
        </ul>
      </li>
    </ul>
  </div>
 </div>
</nav>
```

Directions

RTL

When using Bootstrap in RTL, the directions are mirrored, which means on the right side, dropstart will display.

Drop Up

Dropdown menus atop elements can be triggered by appending .dropup to the parent element.

```
<!-- Default dropup button -->
<div class="btn-group dropup">
 <button type="button" class="btn btn-secondary
        dropdown-toggle" data-bs-toggle="dropdown"
        aria-expanded="false">
  Dropup
 </button>
 <ul class="dropdown-menu">
  <!-- Dropdown menu links -->
 </ul>
</div>

<!-- Split dropup button -->
<div class="btn-group dropup">
 <button type="button" class="btn btn-secondary">
  Split dropup
```

```
</button>
<button type="button" class="btn btn-secondary
        dropdown-toggle dropdown-toggle-split" data-
        bs-toggle="dropdown" aria-expanded="false">
 <span class="visually-hidden">Toggle Dropdown</span>
</button>
<ul class="dropdown-menu">
 <!-- Dropdown menu links -->
</ul>
</div>
```

Drop Right

By appending .dropend to the parent element, you may make dropdown menus appear to the right of the components.

```
<!-- Default dropend button -->
<div class="btn-group dropend">
 <button type="button" class="btn btn-secondary
        dropdown-toggle" data-bs-toggle="dropdown"
        aria-expanded="false">
 Dropright
 </button>
 <ul class="dropdown-menu">
  <!-- Dropdown menu links -->
 </ul>
</div>

<!-- Split dropend button -->
<div class="btn-group dropend">
 <button type="button" class="btn btn-secondary">
  Split dropend
 </button>
 <button type="button" class="btn btn-secondary
        dropdown-toggle dropdown-toggle-split" data-
        bs-toggle="dropdown" aria-expanded="false">
  <span class="visually-hidden">Toggle Dropright</span>
 </button>
 <ul class="dropdown-menu">
  <!-- Dropdown menu links -->
 </ul>
</div>
```

Drop Left

By appending .dropstart to the parent element, you may make dropdown menus appear to the left of the components.

```
<!-- Default dropstart button -->
<div class="btn-group dropstart">
 <button type="button" class="btn btn-secondary
         dropdown-toggle" data-bs-toggle="dropdown"
         aria-expanded="false">
  Dropstart
 </button>
 <ul class="dropdown-menu">
  <!-- Dropdown menu links -->
 </ul>
</div>

<!-- Split dropstart button -->
<div class="btn-group">
 <div class="btn-group dropstart" role="group">
  <button type="button" class="btn btn-secondary
    dropdown-toggle dropdown-toggle-split" data-bs-
    toggle="dropdown" aria-expanded="false">
   <span class="visually-hidden">Toggle Dropstart</span>
  </button>
  <ul class="dropdown-menu">
   <!-- Dropdown menu links -->
  </ul>
 </div>
 <button type="button" class="btn btn-secondary">
  Split dropstart
 </button>
</div>
```

Menu Items

We can use <a> or <button> elements as dropdown items.

```
<div class="dropdown">
 <button class="btn btn-secondary dropdown-toggle"
         type="button" id="dropdown-Menu2" data-bs-
         toggle="dropdown" aria-expanded="false">
  Dropdown
 </button>
 <ul class="dropdown-menu"
     aria-labelledby="dropdownMenu2">
```

```
<li><button class="dropdown-item"
            type="button">Action</button></li>
<li><button class="dropdown-item" type=
            "button">Another action</button></li>
<li><button class="dropdown-item" type="button">
            Something else here</button></li>
</ul>
</div>
```

You can create non-interactive dropdown items with .dropdown-item-text. Feel free to style further with the custom CSS or text utilities.

```
<ul class="dropdown-menu">
<li><span class="dropdown-item-text">Dropdown item
        text</span></li>
<li><a class="dropdown-item" href="#">Action</a></li>
<li><a class="dropdown-item" href="#">Another
        action</a></li>
<li><a class="dropdown-item" href="#">Something else
        here</a></li>
</ul>
```

Active

Add .active to items in dropdown to style them as active. To convey active state to assistive technologies, use aria-current attribute using the page value for the current page or proper for the contemporary item in a set.

```
<ul class="dropdown-menu">
<li><a class="dropdown-item" href="#">Regular link</
        a></li>
<li><a class="dropdown-item active" href="#" aria-
        current="true">Active link</a></li>
<li><a class="dropdown-item" href="#">Another link</
        a></li>
</ul>
```

Disable

Add .disabled to items in dropdown to style them as disabled.

```
<ul class="dropdown-menu">
<li><a class="dropdown-item" href="#">Regular link</
        a></li>
```

```
<li><a class="dropdown-item disabled" href="#"
        tabindex="-1" aria-disabled="true">Disabled
        link</a></li>
<li><a class="dropdown-item" href="#">Another link</
        a></li>
</ul>
```

Menu Alignment

Dropdown menu is automatically positioned 100% from top and down the left side of its parent by default. You can adjust this by using the directional .drop* classes, but you can also manipulate them with modifier classes.

To right-align a dropdown menu, append .dropdown-menu-end to it. When using Bootstrap in RTL, directions are mirrored, so .dropdown-menu-end will display on the left side. *Note:* Except when they are included in a navbar, dropdowns are positioned using Popper.

```
<div class="btn-group">
 <button type="button" class="btn btn-secondary
         dropdown-toggle" data-bs-toggle="dropdown"
         aria-expanded="false">
 Right-aligned menu example
 </button>
 <ul class="dropdown-menu dropdown-menu-end">
  <li><button class="dropdown-item"
              type="button">Action</button></li>
  <li><button class="dropdown-item" type="button">
              Another action</button></li>
  <li><button class="dropdown-item" type="button">
              Something else here</button></li>
 </ul>
</div>
```

Responsive Alignment

If you wish to employ responsive alignment, disable dynamic positioning using the data-bs-display="static" attribute and the responsive variant classes.

To align right the dropdown menu with given breakpoint or larger, add .dropdown-menu{-sm|-md|-lg|-xl|-xxl}-end.

```
<div class="btn-group">
 <button type="button" class="btn btn-secondary
         dropdown-toggle" data-bs-toggle="dropdown"
         data-bs-display="static" aria-expanded="false">
```

```
Left-aligned but right aligned when large screen
</button>
<ul class="dropdown-menu dropdown-menu-lg-end">
 <li><button class="dropdown-item"
          type="button">Action</button></li>
 <li><button class="dropdown-item" type="button">
          Another action</button></li>
 <li><button class="dropdown-item" type="button">
          Something else here</button></li>
 </ul>
</div>
```

To align left dropdown menu with the given breakpoint or larger, add
.dropdown-menu-end and .dropdown-menu{-sm|-md|-lg|-xl|-xxl}-start.

```
<div class="btn-group">
 <button type="button" class="btn btn-secondary
          dropdown-toggle" data-bs-toggle="dropdown"
          data-bs-display="static"
          aria-expanded="false">
 Right-aligned but left aligned when large screen
 </button>
<ul class="dropdown-menu dropdown-menu-end
      dropdown-menu-lg-start">
 <li><button class="dropdown-item"
          type="button">Action</button></li>
 <li><button class="dropdown-item" type="button">
          Another action</button></li>
 <li><button class="dropdown-item" type="button">
          Something else here</button></li>
 </ul>
</div>
```

You don't need to add data-bs-display="static" attribute to dropdown
buttons in the navbars since Popper isn't used in navbars.

Alignment Options

Using the majority of the choices given above, here's a tiny kitchen sink
demo demonstrating different dropdown alignment possibilities in one area.

```
<div class="btn-group">
 <button class="btn btn-secondary dropdown-toggle"
          type="button" id="dropdown-MenuButton" data-
          bs-toggle="dropdown" aria-expanded="false">
 Dropdown
```

```
</button>
<ul class="dropdown-menu" aria-labelledby="dropdownM
    enuButton">
 <li><a class="dropdown-item" href="#">Menu item</
        a></li>
 <li><a class="dropdown-item" href="#">Menu item</
        a></li>
 <li><a class="dropdown-item" href="#">Menu item</
        a></li>
</ul>
</div>


<div class="btn-group">
 <button type="button" class="btn btn-secondary
        dropdown-toggle" data-bs-toggle="dropdown"
        aria-expanded="false">
 Right-aligned menu
 </button>
 <ul class="dropdown-menu dropdown-menu-end">
  <li><a class="dropdown-item" href="#">Menu item</
        a></li>
  <li><a class="dropdown-item" href="#">Menu item</
        a></li>
  <li><a class="dropdown-item" href="#">Menu item</
        a></li>
 </ul>
</div>

<div class="btn-group">
 <button type="button" class="btn btn-secondary
    dropdown-toggle" data-bs-toggle="dropdown" data-
    bs-display="static" aria-expanded="false">
 Left-aligned, right-aligned lg
 </button>
 <ul class="dropdown-menu dropdown-menu-lg-end">
  <li><a class="dropdown-item" href="#">Menu item</
        a></li>
  <li><a class="dropdown-item" href="#">Menu item</
        a></li>
  <li><a class="dropdown-item" href="#">Menu item</
        a></li>
 </ul>
```

```
</div>

<div class="btn-group">
 <button type="button" class="btn btn-secondary
   dropdown-toggle" data-bs-toggle="dropdown" data-
   bs-display="static" aria-expanded="false">
  Right-aligned, left-aligned lg
 </button>
 <ul class="dropdown-menu dropdown-menu-end
     dropdown-menu-lg-start">
  <li><a class="dropdown-item" href="#">Menu item</
        a></li>
  <li><a class="dropdown-item" href="#">Menu item</
        a></li>
  <li><a class="dropdown-item" href="#">Menu item</
        a></li>
 </ul>
</div>

<div class="btn-group dropstart">
 <button type="button" class="btn btn-secondary
         dropdown-toggle" data-bs-toggle="dropdown"
         aria-expanded="false">
  Dropstart
 </button>
 <ul class="dropdown-menu">
  <li><a class="dropdown-item" href="#">Menu item</
        a></li>
  <li><a class="dropdown-item" href="#">Menu item</
        a></li>
  <li><a class="dropdown-item" href="#">Menu item</
        a></li>
 </ul>
</div>

<div class="btn-group dropend">
 <button type="button" class="btn btn-secondary
         dropdown-toggle" data-bs-toggle="dropdown"
         aria-expanded="false">
  Dropend
 </button>
 <ul class="dropdown-menu">
```

```
  <li><a class="dropdown-item" href="#">Menu item</
        a></li>
  <li><a class="dropdown-item" href="#">Menu item</
        a></li>
  <li><a class="dropdown-item" href="#">Menu item</
        a></li>
 </ul>
</div>

<div class="btn-group dropup">
 <button type="button" class="btn btn-secondary
dropdown-toggle" data-bs-toggle="dropdown"
aria-expanded="false">
  Dropup
 </button>
 <ul class="dropdown-menu">
  <li><a class="dropdown-item" href="#">Menu item</
        a></li>
  <li><a class="dropdown-item" href="#">Menu item</
        a></li>
  <li><a class="dropdown-item" href="#">Menu item</
        a></li>
 </ul>
</div>
```

Menu Content

Headers

Add a header to label sections of the actions in any dropdown menu.

```
<ul class="dropdown-menu">
 <li><h6 class="dropdown-header">Dropdown header</
        h6></li>
 <li><a class="dropdown-item" href="#">Action</a></
        li>
 <li><a class="dropdown-item" href="#">Another
        action</a></li>
</ul>
```

Dividers

Separate groups of the related menu items with a divider.

```
<ul class="dropdown-menu">
 <li><a class="dropdown-item" href="#">Action</a></li>
```

```
<li><a class="dropdown-item" href="#">Another
        action</a></li>
<li><a class="dropdown-item" href="#">Something else
        here</a></li>
<li><hr class="dropdown-divider"></li>
<li><a class="dropdown-item" href="#">Separated
        link</a></li>
</ul>
```

Text

Place any freeform text within dropdown menu with text and use spacing utilities. You'll need additional sizing styles to constrain menu width.

```
<div class="dropdown-menu p-4 text-muted" style="max-
    width: 200px;">
 <p>
  Example text that's free-flowing within dropdown menu.
 </p>
 <p class="mb-0">
  And this is more example text.
 </p>
</div>
```

Forms

Put a form within a dropdown menu, and then convert it to a dropdown menu and use margin or padding tools to give it the negative space you need.

```
<div class="dropdown-menu">
 <form class="px-4 py-3">
  <div class="mb-3">
   <label for="exampleDropdownFormEmail1"
          class="form-label">Email address</label>
   <input type="email" class="form-control"
          id="exampleDropdown-FormEmail1"
          placeholder="email@example.com">
  </div>
  <div class="mb-3">
   <label for="exampleDropdownFormPassword1"
          class="form-label">Password</label>
   <input type="password" class="form-control"
          id="exampleDropdown-FormPassword1"
          placeholder="Password">
```

```
  </div>
  <div class="mb-3">
   <div class="form-check">
    <input type="checkbox" class="form-check-input"
           id="dropdownCheck">
    <label class="form-check-label" for="dropdownCheck">
     Remember me
    </label>
   </div>
  </div>
  <button type="submit" class="btn btn-primary">Sign
          in</button>
 </form>
 <div class="dropdown-divider"></div>
 <a class="dropdown-item" href="#">New around here?
    Sign up</a>
 <a class="dropdown-item" href="#">Forgot password?</a>
</div>

<form class="dropdown-menu p-4">
 <div class="mb-3">
  <label for="exampleDropdownFormEmail2" class="form-
               label">Email address</label>
  <input type="email" class="form-control"
               id="exampleDropdown-FormEmail2"
               placeholder="email@example.com">
 </div>
 <div class="mb-3">
  <label for="exampleDropdownFormPassword2"
               class="form-label">Password</label>
  <input type="password" class="form-control"
               id="exampleDropdown-FormPassword2"
               placeholder="Password">
 </div>
 <div class="mb-3">
  <div class="form-check">
   <input type="checkbox" class="form-check-input"
               id="dropdownCheck2">
   <label class="form-check-label" for="dropdownCheck2">
    Remember me
   </label>
  </div>
 </div>
```

```
  <button type="submit" class="btn btn-primary">Sign
            in</button>
</form>
```

Dropdown Options
Use the data-bs-offset or data-bs-reference to change the location of the
dropdown.

```
<div class="d-flex">
 <div class="dropdown me-1">
  <button type="button" class="btn btn-secondary
          dropdown-toggle" id="dropdown-MenuOffset"
          data-bs-toggle="dropdown" aria-
          expanded="false" data-bs-offset="10,20">
Offset
  </button>
  <ul class="dropdown-menu" aria-labelledby="dropdown
     MenuOffset">
   <li><a class="dropdown-item" href="#">Action</a></li>
   <li><a class="dropdown-item" href="#">Another
              action</a></li>
   <li><a class="dropdown-item" href="#">Something
              else here</a></li>
  </ul>
 </div>
 <div class="btn-group">
  <button type="button" class="btn btn-
              secondary">Reference</button>
  <button type="button" class="btn btn-secondary
    dropdown-toggle dropdown-toggle-split"
    id="dropdown-MenuReference" data-bs-
    toggle="dropdown" aria-expanded="false"
    data-bs-reference="parent">
   <span class="visually-hidden">Toggle Dropdown</span>
  </button>
  <ul class="dropdown-menu" aria-labelledby="dropdown
     MenuReference">
   <li><a class="dropdown-item" href="#">Action</a></li>
   <li><a class="dropdown-item" href="#">Another
          action</a></li>
   <li><a class="dropdown-item" href="#">Something
          else here</a></li>
```

```
    <li><hr class="dropdown-divider"></li>
    <li><a class="dropdown-item" href="#">Separated
        link</a></li>
  </ul>
 </div>
</div>
```

Autoclose Behavior

When you click within or outside the dropdown menu, the dropdown menu closes by default. To modify the dropdown's behavior, utilize the autoClose option.

```
<div class="btn-group">
 <button class="btn btn-secondary dropdown-toggle"
         type="button" id="defaultDropdown" data-bs-
         toggle="dropdown" data-bs-auto-close="true"
         aria-expanded="false">
  Default dropdown
 </button>
 <ul class="dropdown-menu" aria-labelledby="defaultDr
            opdown">
  <li><a class="dropdown-item" href="#">Menu item</
            a></li>
  <li><a class="dropdown-item" href="#">Menu item</
            a></li>
  <li><a class="dropdown-item" href="#">Menu item</
            a></li>
 </ul>
</div>

<div class="btn-group">
 <button class="btn btn-secondary dropdown-toggle"
type="button" id="dropdownMenuClickableOutside" data-
bs-toggle="dropdown" data-bs-auto-close="inside"
aria-expanded="false">
  Clickable outside
 </button>
 <ul class="dropdown-menu" aria-labelledby="dropdown
            MenuClickableOutside">
  <li><a class="dropdown-item" href="#">Menu item</
            a></li>
```

```
  <li><a class="dropdown-item" href="#">Menu item</
            a></li>
  <li><a class="dropdown-item" href="#">Menu item</
            a></li>
 </ul>
</div>

<div class="btn-group">
 <button class="btn btn-secondary dropdown-toggle"
        type="button" id="dropdownMenuClickableIns
        ide" data-bs-toggle="dropdown" data-bs-auto-
        close="outside" aria-expanded="false">
  Clickable inside
 </button>
 <ul class="dropdown-menu" aria-labelledby="dropdown
            MenuClickableInside">
  <li><a class="dropdown-item" href="#">Menu item</
            a></li>
  <li><a class="dropdown-item" href="#">Menu item</
            a></li>
  <li><a class="dropdown-item" href="#">Menu item</
            a></li>
 </ul>
</div>

<div class="btn-group">
 <button class="btn btn-secondary dropdown-toggle"
        type="button" id="dropdownMenuClickable"
        data-bs-toggle="dropdown" data-bs-auto-
        close="false" aria-expanded="false">
  Manual close
 </button>
 <ul class="dropdown-menu" aria-labelledby="dropdownM
            enuClickable">
  <li><a class="dropdown-item" href="#">Menu item</
            a></li>
  <li><a class="dropdown-item" href="#">Menu item</
            a></li>
  <li><a class="dropdown-item" href="#">Menu item</
            a></li>
 </ul>
</div>
```

LIST GROUP

List groups are powerful and flexible component for displaying the series of content. Modify and extend to support just about any content within.

Example

The basic list group is an unordered list with the list items and proper classes. Build upon it with options that follow or with your CSS as needed.

```
<ul class="list-group">
 <li class="list-group-item">An item</li>
 <li class="list-group-item">A second item</li>
 <li class="list-group-item">A third item</li>
 <li class="list-group-item">A fourth item</li>
 <li class="list-group-item">And a fifth one</li>
</ul>
```

Active Items

Add .active to .list-group-item to indicate the current active selection.

```
<ul class="list-group">
 <li class="list-group-item active" aria-
     current="true">Active item</li>
 <li class="list-group-item">A second item</li>
 <li class="list-group-item">A third item</li>
 <li class="list-group-item">A fourth item</li>
 <li class="list-group-item">And a fifth one</li>
</ul>
```

Disable Items

To make a .list-group-item appear disabled, append .disabled to it. It should be noted that some items with .disabled will additionally require specific JavaScript to completely deactivate their click events.

```
<ul class="list-group">
 <li class="list-group-item disabled" aria-
     disabled="true">disabled item</li>
 <li class="list-group-item">A second item</li>
 <li class="list-group-item">A third item</li>
 <li class="list-group-item">A fourth item</li>
 <li class="list-group-item">And a fifth one</li>
</ul>
```

Links and Buttons

Use <a> or <button> to create *actionable* list group items with the hover, disabled, and active states by adding .list-group-item-action. We separate these pseudo-classes to ensure the list groups made of the non-interactive elements don't provide a click or tap affordance.

Be sure not to use standard .btn classes here.

```
<div class="list-group">
 <a href="#" class="list-group-item list-group-item-
    action active" aria-current="true">
  current link item
 </a>
 <a href="#" class="list-group-item list-group-item-
    action">second link item</a>
 <a href="#" class="list-group-item list-group-item-
    action">third link item</a>
 <a href="#" class="list-group-item list-group-item-
    action">fourth link item</a>
 <a href="#" class="list-group-item list-group-item-
    action disabled" tabindex="-1" aria-
    disabled="true">disabled link item</a>
</div>
```

With <button>s, you can also use the disabled attribute instead of the .disabled class. Sadly, <a>s don't support the disabled feature.

```
<div class="list-group">
 <button type="button" class="list-group-item list-
    group-item-action active" aria-current="true">
  Current button
 </button>
 <button type="button" class="list-group-item list-
    group-item-action">second item</button>
 <button type="button" class="list-group-item list-
    group-item-action">third button item</button>
 <button type="button" class="list-group-item list-
    group-item-action">fourth button item</button>
 <button type="button" class="list-group-item list-
    group-item-action" disabled>disabled button item</
    button>
</div>
```

Flush

Add .list-group-flush to delete some borders and rounded corners to render list group items edge to edge in parent container (e.g., cards).

```
<ul class="list-group list-group-flush">
 <li class="list-group-item">An item</li>
 <li class="list-group-item">A second item</li>
 <li class="list-group-item">A third item</li>
 <li class="list-group-item">A fourth item</li>
 <li class="list-group-item">And a fifth one</li>
</ul>
```

Numbered

Add the .list-group-numbered modifier class (optionally use an <ol> element) to opt into the numbered list group items. Numbers are generated via CSS for better placement inside list group items and better customization. Counter-reset generated numbers on the <ol>, then styled and placed with a::before pseudo-element on the <li> with counter-increment and content.

```
<ol class="list-group list-group-numbered">
 <li class="list-group-item">Cras justo odio</li>
 <li class="list-group-item">Cras justo odio</li>
 <li class="list-group-item">Cras justo odio</li>
</ol>
```

```
<ol class="list-group list-group-numbered">
 <li class="list-group-item d-flex justify-content-
     between align-items-start">
  <div class="ms-2 me-auto">
   <div class="fw-bold">Subheading</div>
   Cras justo odio
  </div>
  <span class="badge bg-primary rounded-pill">14</span>
 </li>
 <li class="list-group-item d-flex justify-content-
     between align-items-start">
  <div class="ms-2 me-auto">
   <div class="fw-bold">Subheading</div>
   Cras justo odio
  </div>
```

```
  <span class="badge bg-primary rounded-pill">14</span>
 </li>
 <li class="list-group-item d-flex justify-content-
     between align-items-start">
  <div class="ms-2 me-auto">
   <div class="fw-bold">Subheading</div>
   Cras justo odio
  </div>
  <span class="badge bg-primary rounded-pill">14</span>
 </li>
</ol>
```

Horizontal

Add .list-group-horizontal to change layout of list group items from vertical to horizontal across all the breakpoints. Alternatively, choose a responsive variant .list-group-horizontal-{sm|md|lg|xl|xxl} to make list group horizontal starting at that breakpoint's min-width. Currently, horizontal list groups cannot combine with flush list groups.

```
<ul class="list-group list-group-horizontal">
 <li class="list-group-item">An item</li>
 <li class="list-group-item">A second item</li>
 <li class="list-group-item">A third item</li>
</ul>
<ul class="list-group list-group-horizontal-sm">
 <li class="list-group-item">An item</li>
 <li class="list-group-item">A second item</li>
 <li class="list-group-item">A third item</li>
</ul>
<ul class="list-group list-group-horizontal-md">
 <li class="list-group-item">An item</li>
 <li class="list-group-item">A second item</li>
 <li class="list-group-item">A third item</li>
</ul>
<ul class="list-group list-group-horizontal-lg">
 <li class="list-group-item">An item</li>
 <li class="list-group-item">A second item</li>
 <li class="list-group-item">A third item</li>
</ul>
<ul class="list-group list-group-horizontal-xl">
 <li class="list-group-item">An item</li>
 <li class="list-group-item">A second item</li>
```

```
<li class="list-group-item">A third item</li>
</ul>
<ul class="list-group list-group-horizontal-xxl">
 <li class="list-group-item">An item</li>
 <li class="list-group-item">A second item</li>
 <li class="list-group-item">A third item</li>
</ul>
```

Contextual Classes

Use contextual classes to style list items with a stateful background and color.

```
<ul class="list-group">
 <li class="list-group-item">A simple default list
            group item</li>
 <li class="list-group-item list-group-item-primary">
            simple primary list group item</li>
 <li class="list-group-item list-group-item-secondary">
            simple secondary list group item</li>
 <li class="list-group-item list-group-item-success">
            simple success list group item</li>
 <li class="list-group-item list-group-item-danger">
            simple danger list group item</li>
 <li class="list-group-item list-group-item-warning">
            simple warning list group item</li>
 <li class="list-group-item list-group-item-info">
            simple info list group item</li>
 <li class="list-group-item list-group-item-
            light">simple light list group item</li>
 <li class="list-group-item list-group-item-
            dark">simple dark list group item</li>
</ul>
```

Contextual classes also work with the .list-group-item-action. Note the addition of the hover styles here is not present in the previous example. Also supported is the .active state; apply it to indicate active selection on a contextual list group item.

```
<div class="list-group">
 <a href="#" class="list-group-item list-group-item-
    action"> simple default list group item</a>
```

```
<a href="#" class="list-group-item list-group-item-
    action list-group-item-primary"> simple primary
    list group item</a>
<a href="#" class="list-group-item list-group-item-
    action list-group-item-secondary"> simple
    secondary list group item</a>
<a href="#" class="list-group-item list-group-item-
    action list-group-item-success">simple success
    list group item</a>
<a href="#" class="list-group-item list-group-item-
    action list-group-item-danger">simple danger list
    group item</a>
<a href="#" class="list-group-item list-group-item-
    action list-group-item-warning"> simple warning
    list group item</a>
<a href="#" class="list-group-item list-group-item-
    action list-group-item-info"> simple info list
    group item</a>
<a href="#" class="list-group-item list-group-item-
    action list-group-item-light"> simple light list
    group item</a>
<a href="#" class="list-group-item list-group-item-
    action list-group-item-dark"> simple dark list
    group item</a>
</div>
```

With Badges

With the aid of various programs, you can add badges to any list group item to represent unread numbers, activity, and more.

```
<ul class="list-group">
 <li class="list-group-item d-flex justify-content-
     between align-items-center">
  A list item
  <span class="badge bg-primary rounded-pill">14</span>
 </li>
 <li class="list-group-item d-flex justify-content-
     between align-items-center">
  A second list item
  <span class="badge bg-primary rounded-pill">2</span>
 </li>
```

```
<li class="list-group-item d-flex justify-content-
    between align-items-center">
 A third list item
 <span class="badge bg-primary rounded-pill">1</span>
 </li>
</ul>
```

Custom Content

Add nearly any HTML within, even for the linked list groups like the one below, with the help of flexbox utilities.

```
<div class="list-group">
 <a href="#" class="list-group-item list-group-item-
    action active" aria-current="true">
  <div class="d-flex w-100 justify-content-between">
   <h5 class="mb-1">List group item heading</h5>
   <small>3 days ago</small>
  </div>
  <p class="mb-1">Some placeholder content in
                     paragraph.</p>
  <small>And some small print.</small>
 </a>
 <a href="#" class="list-group-item
    list-group-item-action">
  <div class="d-flex w-100 justify-content-between">
   <h5 class="mb-1">List group item heading</h5>
   <small class="text-muted">3 days ago</small>
  </div>
  <p class="mb-1">Some placeholder content in
                     paragraph.</p>
  <small class="text-muted">And some muted small-
                 print.</small>
 </a>
 <a href="#" class="list-group-item
list-group-item-action">
  <div class="d-flex w-100 justify-content-between">
   <h5 class="mb-1">List group item heading</h5>
   <small class="text-muted">3 days ago</small>
  </div>
  <p class="mb-1">Some placeholder content in
                     paragraph.</p>
```

```
<small class="text-muted">And some muted small-
              print.</small>
</a>
</div>
```

Checkbox and Radios

Customize the checkboxes and radios in Bootstrap's list group items as needed. They can be used without <labels>, but be sure to include an aria-label attribute and value for accessibility.

```
<ul class="list-group">
 <li class="list-group-item">
  <input class="form-check-input me-1" type="checkbox"
         value="" aria-label="...">
  First checkbox
 </li>
 <li class="list-group-item">
  <input class="form-check-input me-1" type="checkbox"
         value="" aria-label="...">
  Second checkbox
 </li>
 <li class="list-group-item">
  <input class="form-check-input me-1" type="checkbox"
         value="" aria-label="...">
  Third checkbox
 </li>
 <li class="list-group-item">
  <input class="form-check-input me-1" type="checkbox"
         value="" aria-label="...">
  Fourth checkbox
 </li>
 <li class="list-group-item">
  <input class="form-check-input me-1" type="checkbox"
         value="" aria-label="...">
  Fifth checkbox
 </li>
</ul>
```

And if we want <label>s as the .list-group-item for large hit areas, we can do that, too.

```
<div class="list-group">
 <label class="list-group-item">
  <input class="form-check-input me-1" type="checkbox"
         value="">
  First checkbox
 </label>
 <label class="list-group-item">
  <input class="form-check-input me-1" type="checkbox"
         value="">
  Second checkbox
 </label>
 <label class="list-group-item">
  <input class="form-check-input me-1" type="checkbox"
         value="">
  Third checkbox
 </label>
 <label class="list-group-item">
  <input class="form-check-input me-1" type="checkbox"
         value="">
  Fourth checkbox
 </label>
 <label class="list-group-item">
  <input class="form-check-input me-1" type="checkbox"
         value="">
  Fifth checkbox
 </label>
</div>
```

JavaScript Behavior

To generate tabbable panes of local content, use the tab JavaScript plugin –
include it separately or through the produced bootstrap.js file.

```
<div class="row">
 <div class="col-4">
  <div class="list-group" id="list-tab"
       role="tablist">
   <a class="list-group-item list-group-item-action
      active" id="list-home-list" data-bs-
      toggle="list" href="#list-home" role="tab"
      aria-controls="list-home">Home</a>
    <a class="list-group-item list-group-item-action"
       id="list-profile-list" data-bs-toggle="list"
```

```
      href="#list-profile" role="tab" aria-
      controls="list-profile">Profile</a>
  <a class="list-group-item list-group-item-action"
      id="list-messages-list" data-bs-toggle="list"
      href="#list-messages" role="tab" aria-contr
      ols="list-messages">Messages</a>
  <a class="list-group-item list-group-item-action"
      id="list-settings-list" data-bs-toggle="list"
      href="#list-settings" role="tab" aria-contr
      ols="list-settings">Settings</a>
  </div>
</div>
<div class="col-8">
 <div class="tab-content" id="nav-tabContent">
  <div class="tab-pane fade show active" id="list-
      home" role="tabpanel" aria-labelledby="lis
      t-home-list">...</div>
  <div class="tab-pane fade" id="list-profile"
      role="tabpanel" aria-labelledby="list-pro
      file-list">...</div>
  <div class="tab-pane fade" id="list-messages"
      role="tabpanel" aria-labelledby="list-mes
      sages-list">...</div>
  <div class="tab-pane fade" id="list-settings"
      role="tabpanel" aria-labelledby="list-set
      tings-list">...</div>
  </div>
 </div>
</div>
```

Using Data Attributes

We can activate a list group navigation without writing any JavaScript by specifying data-bs-toggle="list" or on an element. Use these data attributes on .list-group-item.

```
<div role="tabpanel">
 <!-- List group -->
 <div class="list-group" id="myList" role="tablist">
  <a class="list-group-item list-group-item-action
      active" data-bs-toggle="list" href="#home"
      role="tab">Home</a>
```

```
<a class="list-group-item list-group-item-action"
    data-bs-toggle="list" href="#profile"
    role="tab">Profile</a>
<a class="list-group-item list-group-item-action"
    data-bs-toggle="list" href="#messages"
    role="tab">Messages</a>
<a class="list-group-item list-group-item-action"
    data-bs-toggle="list" href="#settings"
    role="tab">Settings</a>
</div>

<!-- Tab panes -->
<div class="tab-content">
 <div class="tab-pane active" id="home"
      role="tabpanel">...</div>
 <div class="tab-pane" id="profile"
      role="tabpanel">...</div>
 <div class="tab-pane" id="messages"
      role="tabpanel">...</div>
 <div class="tab-pane" id="settings"
      role="tabpanel">...</div>
 </div>
</div>
```

MODAL

Add dialogs to your site with Bootstrap's JavaScript modal plugin for lightboxes, user notifications, or totally unique content.

How It Works

Please read the following before getting started using Bootstrap's modal component, as our menu options have just changed.

- HTML, CSS, and JavaScript are used to create modals. They take precedence over everything else in the document and disable scrolling so that the modal content scrolls instead.

- The modal will close automatically if you click on the "background" of the modal.

- Only one modal window can be open at a time in Bootstrap. We don't allow nested modals since we believe they provide bad user experiences.

- Modals use a fixed position, which can be a little finicky when it comes to rendering. To avoid potential interference from other elements, place your modal HTML in a top-level position if possible. When nesting a .modal within another fixed element, you'll almost certainly run into problems. There are several limitations to using modals on mobile devices due to position: fixed. For further information, see our browser support documentation.

- The autofocus HTML property has no effect on Bootstrap modals because of how HTML5 defines semantics. Use some custom JavaScript to accomplish the same effect.

Examples

A *static* modal example is shown below (meaning its position and display have been overridden). Included are the modal header, modal body (which is necessary for padding), and modal footer (which is optional). If at all possible, please offer modal headers with dismiss actions, or provide another explicit dismiss option.

```
<div class="modal" tabindex="-1">
 <div class="modal-dialog">
  <div class="modal-content">
   <div class="modal-header">
    <h5 class="modal-title">Modal title</h5>
    <button type="button" class="btn-close" data-bs-
      dismiss="modal" aria-label="Close"></button>
   </div>
   <div class="modal-body">
    <p>Modal body text goes here.</p>
   </div>
   <div class="modal-footer">
    <button type="button" class="btn btn-secondary"
            data-bs-dismiss="modal">Close</button>
    <button type="button" class="btn btn-
            primary">Save changes</button>
   </div>
  </div>
 </div>
</div>
```

Live Demo

By clicking button below, you can see a working modal sample. From the top of the page, it will flow down and fade in.

```
<!-- Button trigger modal -->
<button type="button" class="btn btn-primary" data-
  bs-toggle="modal" data-bs-target="#exampleModal">
 Launch demo modal
</button>

<!-- Modal -->
<div class="modal fade" id="exampleModal"
     tabindex="-1" aria-labelledby="exampleModalLabel"
     aria-hidden="true">
 <div class="modal-dialog">
  <div class="modal-content">
   <div class="modal-header">
    <h5 class="modal-title"
        id="exampleModalLabel">Modal title</h5>
    <button type="button" class="btn-close" data-bs-
      dismiss="modal" aria-label="Close"></button>
   </div>
   <div class="modal-body">
    ...
   </div>
   <div class="modal-footer">
    <button type="button" class="btn btn-secondary"
            data-bs-dismiss="modal">Close</button>
    <button type="button" class="btn btn-
            primary">Save changes</button>
   </div>
  </div>
 </div>
</div>
```

Static Backdrop

When the backdrop is set to static, the modal will not close when clicking outside it. Click the button below to try it.

```
<!-- Button trigger modal -->
<button type="button" class="btn btn-primary" data-
  bs-toggle="modal" data-bs-target="#staticBackdrop">
```

```
  Launch static backdrop modal
</button>

<!-- Modal -->
<div class="modal fade" id="staticBackdrop" data-bs-
    backdrop="static" data-bs-keyboard="false"
    tabindex="-1" aria-labelledby="staticBackdropLa
    bel" aria-hidden="true">
 <div class="modal-dialog">
  <div class="modal-content">
   <div class="modal-header">
    <h5 class="modal-title"
        id="staticBackdropLabel">Modal title</h5>
    <button type="button" class="btn-close" data-bs-
      dismiss="modal" aria-label="Close"></button>
   </div>
   <div class="modal-body">
    ...
   </div>
   <div class="modal-footer">
    <button type="button" class="btn btn-secondary"
            data-bs-dismiss="modal">Close</button>
    <button type="button" class="btn btn-
            primary">Understood</button>
   </div>
  </div>
 </div>
</div>
```

Scrolling Long Content

Modals scroll independent of the page when they become too long for the user's viewport or device. To see what we mean, try the demo below.

It is easy to create a scrollable modal that allows scrolling the modal body by adding .modal-dialog-scrollable to .modal-dialog.

```
<!-- Scrollable modal -->
<div class="modal-dialog modal-dialog-scrollable">
 ...
</div>
```

Vertically Centered

In Bootstrap add .modal-dialog-centered to .modal-dialog to vertically center the modal.

```
<!-- Vertically centered modal -->
<div class="modal-dialog modal-dialog-centered">
 ...
</div>

<!-- Vertically centered scrollable modal -->
<div class="modal-dialog modal-dialog-centered
            modal-dialog-scrollable">
 ...
</div>
```

Tooltips and Popovers

Within modals, tooltips and popovers can be included as needed. Any tooltips and popovers within modals are automatically dismissed when they are closed.

```
<div class="modal-body">
 <h5>Popover in a modal</h5>
 <p>This <a href="#" role="button" class="btn btn-
         secondary popover-test" title="Popover
         title" data-bs-content="Popover body content
         is set in this attribute.">button</a>
         triggers a popover on click.</p>
 <hr>
 <h5>Tooltips in a modal</h5>
 <p><a href="#" class="tooltip-test"
       title="Tooltip">This link</a> and <a href="#"
       class="tooltip-test" title="Tooltip">that
       link</a> have tooltips on hover.</p>
</div>
```

Using the Grid

Utilize grid system within a modal by nesting .container-fluid within the .modal-body. Then, use the regular grid system classes as you would anywhere else.

```
<div class="modal-body">
 <div class="container-fluid">
  <div class="row">
   <div class="col-md-4">.col-md-4</div>
   <div class="col-md-4 ms-auto">.col-md-4 .ms-auto</div>
  </div>
```

```
<div class="row">
 <div class="col-md-3 ms-auto">.col-md-3 .ms-auto</div>
 <div class="col-md-2 ms-auto">.col-md-2 .ms-auto</div>
</div>
<div class="row">
 <div class="col-md-6 ms-auto">.col-md-6 .ms-auto</div>
</div>
<div class="row">
 <div class="col-sm-9">
  Level 1: .col-sm-9
  <div class="row">
   <div class="col-8 col-sm-6">
    Level 2: .col-8 .col-sm-6
   </div>
   <div class="col-4 col-sm-6">
    Level 2: .col-4 .col-sm-6
   </div>
  </div>
 </div>
</div>
</div>
</div>
```

Varying Modal Content

Have a bunch of buttons in Bootstrap that all trigger the exact modal with slightly different contents. Use event. Related target and HTML data-bs-* attributes to vary the contents of the modal depend on which button was clicked.

```
<button type="button" class="btn btn-primary" data-
  bs-toggle="modal" data-bs-target="#exampleModal"
  data-bs-whatever="@mdo">Open modal for @mdo</
  button>
<button type="button" class="btn btn-primary" data-
  bs-toggle="modal" data-bs-target="#exampleModal"
  data-bs-whatever="@fat">Open modal for @fat</
  button>
<button type="button" class="btn btn-primary" data-
  bs-toggle="modal" data-bs-target="#exampleModal"
  data-bs-whatever="@getbootstrap">Open modal for @
  getbootstrap</button>
```

```
<div class="modal fade" id="exampleModal"
     tabindex="-1" aria-labelledby="exampleModalLabel"
     aria-hidden="true">
 <div class="modal-dialog">
  <div class="modal-content">
   <div class="modal-header">
    <h5 class="modal-title"
        id="exampleModalLabel">New message</h5>
    <button type="button" class="btn-close" data-bs-
      dismiss="modal" aria-label="Close"></button>
   </div>
   <div class="modal-body">
    <form>
     <div class="mb-3">
      <label for="recipient-name" class="col-form
             -label">Recipient:</label>
      <input type="text" class="form-control"
             id="recipient-name">
     </div>
     <div class="mb-3">
      <label for="message-text" class="col-form-
             label">Message:</label>
      <textarea class="form-control" id="message-
             text"></textarea>
     </div>
    </form>
   </div>
   <div class="modal-footer">
    <button type="button" class="btn btn-secondary"
           data-bs-dismiss="modal">Close</button>
    <button type="button" class="btn btn-
           primary">Send message</button>
   </div>
  </div>
 </div>
</div>
```

Toggle between Modals

With some smart positioning of the data-bs-target and data-bs-toggle attributes, we can toggle between numerous modals. We could, for example, open a password reset modal from within an open sign-in modal.

Please note that multiple modals cannot be available simultaneously as this method toggles between two separate models.

```
<div class="modal fade" id="exampleModalToggle" aria-
    hidden="true" aria-labelledby="exampleModalT
    oggleLabel" tabindex="-1">
 <div class="modal-dialog modal-dialog-centered">
  <div class="modal-content">
   <div class="modal-header">
    <h5 class="modal-title" id="exampleModalToggleLab
        el">Modal 1</h5>
    <button type="button" class="btn-close" data-bs-
      dismiss="modal" aria-label="Close"></button>
   </div>
   <div class="modal-body">
    With the button below, we can show second modal
        and conceal the first.
   </div>
   <div class="modal-footer">
    <button class="btn btn-primary" data-bs-
      target="#exampleModalToggle2" data-bs-
      toggle="modal" data-bs-dismiss="modal">Open the
      second modal</button>
   </div>
  </div>
 </div>
</div>
<div class="modal fade" id="exampleModalToggle2"
    aria-hidden="true" aria-labelledby="exampleM
    odalToggleLabel2" tabindex="-2">
 <div class="modal-dialog modal-dialog-centered">
  <div class="modal-content">
   <div class="modal-header">
    <h5 class="modal-title" id="exampleModalToggleLab
        el2">Modal 2</h5>
    <button type="button" class="btn-close" data-bs-
      dismiss="modal" aria-label="Close"></button>
   </div>
   <div class="modal-body">
    With the button below, can hide this modal and
        reveal the first.
   </div>
```

```
    <div class="modal-footer">
     <button class="btn btn-primary" data-bs-
       target="#exampleModalToggle" data-bs-
       toggle="modal" data-bs-dismiss="modal">Back to
       first</button>
    </div>
   </div>
  </div>
</div>
<a class="btn btn-primary" data-bs-toggle="modal"
   href="#exampleModalToggle" role="button">Open
   first modal</a>
```

Change Animation

The transform state of .modal-dialog before the modal fade-in animation is determined by the $modal-fade-transform variable, whereas the transform state of .modal-dialog after the modal fade-in animation is determined by the $modal-show-transform variable.

Set $modal-fade-transform: scale if we want a zoom-in animation, for example (.8).

Remove Animation

For models that appear rather than fade into view, remove the .fade class from our modal markup.

```
<div class="modal" tabindex="-2" aria-labelledby="..."
aria-hidden="true">
  ...
</div>
```

Dynamic Heights

If the modal's height adjusts while it is open, we should contact myModal. Handle update() to reposition the modal if a scrollbar emerges.

Accessibility

Make sure to include aria-labelledby="..." in the .modal file, which refers to the modal title. We may also use aria-described on.modal to describe our modal dialog. We don't need to add role="dialog" because it is already there, thanks to JavaScript.

Embedding YouTube Videos

Embedding YouTube videos in modals necessitates the use of additional JavaScript that is not included in Bootstrap, such as the ability to instantly halt playback and more. For further information, see this Stack Overflow topic.

NAV AND TABS

Documentation and examples for how to use Bootstrap included navigation components.

Base .nav

Navigation available in Bootstrap shares general markup and styles, from the base .nav class to the active and disable states. Swap modifier classes to switch between each type.

The base .nav component is built with a flexbox and provides a strong foundation for building all navigation components. It has some style overrides for working with lists, link padding for larger hit areas, and basic disable styling.

```
<ul class="nav">
 <li class="nav-item">
  <a class="nav-link active" aria-current="page"
          href="#">Active</a>
 </li>
 <li class="nav-item">
  <a class="nav-link" href="#">Link</a>
 </li>
 <li class="nav-item">
  <a class="nav-link" href="#">Link</a>
 </li>
 <li class="nav-item">
  <a class="nav-link disable" href="#" tabindex="-1"
          aria-disable="true">Disable</a>
 </li>
</ul>
```

Because classes are used throughout, you may be as creative as you want with your markup. If the order of your items is critical, use <ul> like the ones above, or create your own with a <nav> element. The nav links

function the same as nav items, but without the extra markup, because the
.nav uses display: flex.

```
<nav class="nav">
 <a class="nav-link active" aria-current="page"
          href="#">Active</a>
 <a class="nav-link" href="#">Link</a>
 <a class="nav-link" href="#">Link</a>
 <a class="nav-link disable" href="#" tabindex="-1"
          aria-disabled="true">Disable</a>
</nav>
```

Available Styles

Utilities and modifier can be used to change the style of the .navs component. Build your own or mix and match as needed.

Alignment Horizontally

Using flexbox utilities, you may change the horizontal alignment of your
navigation. Navs are left-aligned by default; however they can easily be
changed to center or right-aligned.

   .justify-content-center was used to center the content:

```
<ul class="nav justify-content-center">
 <li class="nav-item">
  <a class="nav-link active" aria-current="page"
          href="#">Active</a>
 </li>
 <li class="nav-item">
  <a class="nav-link" href="#">Link</a>
 </li>
 <li class="nav-item">
  <a class="nav-link" href="#">Link</a>
 </li>
 <li class="nav-item">
  <a class="nav-link disable" href="#" tabindex="-1"
          aria-disabled="true">Disable</a>
 </li>
</ul>
```

Right-aligned with .justify-content-end

```
<ul class="nav justify-content-end">
 <li class="nav-item">
```

```
 <a class="nav-link active" aria-current="page"
          href="#">Active</a>
</li>
<li class="nav-item">
 <a class="nav-link" href="#">Link</a>
</li>
<li class="nav-item">
 <a class="nav-link" href="#">Link</a>
</li>
<li class="nav-item">
 <a class="nav-link disable" href="#" tabindex="-1"
          aria-disabled="true">Disable</a>
</li>
</ul>
```

Vertical

With the .flex-column utility, you may stack your navigation by adjusting the flex item direction. Do you want to stack them on some viewports but not on others? Make use of the responsive versions (e.g., .flex-sm-column).

```
<ul class="nav flex-column">
 <li class="nav-item">
  <a class="nav-link active" aria-current="page"
href="#">Active</a>
 </li>
 <li class="nav-item">
  <a class="nav-link" href="#">Link</a>
 </li>
 <li class="nav-item">
  <a class="nav-link" href="#">Link</a>
 </li>
 <li class="nav-item">
  <a class="nav-link disable" href="#" tabindex="-1"
          aria-disabled="true">Disable</a>
 </li>
</ul>
```

Vertical navigation is also possible without <ul>, as is horizontal navigation.

```
<nav class="nav flex-column">
 <a class="nav-link active" aria-current="page"
          href="#">Active</a>
```

```
<a class="nav-link" href="#">Link</a>
<a class="nav-link" href="#">Link</a>
<a class="nav-link disable" href="#" tabindex="-1"
          aria-disabled="true">Disable</a>
</nav>
```

Tabs

To create a tabbed interface, add the .nav-tabs class to the primary nav from above. With our tab JavaScript plugin, you can use them to create tabbable zones.

```
<ul class="nav nav-tabs">
 <li class="nav-item">
  <a class="nav-link active" aria-current="page"
          href="#">Active</a>
 </li>
 <li class="nav-item">
  <a class="nav-link" href="#">Link</a>
 </li>
 <li class="nav-item">
  <a class="nav-link" href="#">Link</a>
 </li>
 <li class="nav-item">
  <a class="nav-link disable" href="#" tabindex="-1"
          aria-disabled="true">Disable</a>
 </li>
</ul>
```

Pills

Take the same HTML and replace it with .nav-pills:

```
<ul class="nav nav-pills">
 <li class="nav-item">
  <a class="nav-link active" aria-current="page"
          href="#">Active</a>
 </li>
 <li class="nav-item">
  <a class="nav-link" href="#">Link</a>
 </li>
 <li class="nav-item">
  <a class="nav-link" href="#">Link</a>
 </li>
```

```
<li class="nav-item">
 <a class="nav-link disable" href="#" tabindex="-1"
          aria-disabled="true">Disable</a>
</li>
</ul>
```

Fill and Justify

Force our .nav's contents to extend the full available width of one of two modifier classes. To proportionally fill all open space with our .nav-items, use .nav-fill. Notice that all the horizontal space is occupied, but not every nav item has same width.

```
<ul class="nav nav-pills nav-fill">
 <li class="nav-item">
  <a class="nav-link active" aria-current="page"
          href="#">Active</a>
 </li>
 <li class="nav-item">
  <a class="nav-link" href="#">longer nav link</a>
 </li>
 <li class="nav-item">
  <a class="nav-link" href="#">Link</a>
 </li>
 <li class="nav-item">
  <a class="nav-link disable" href="#" tabindex="-1"
          aria-disabled="true">Disable</a>
 </li>
</ul>
```

When using <nav>-based navigation, we can safely omit .nav-item as only .nav-link is required for styling <a> elements.

```
<nav class="nav nav-pills nav-fill">
 <a class="nav-link active" aria-current="page"
href="#">Active</a>
 <a class="nav-link" href="#"> longer nav link</a>
 <a class="nav-link" href="#">Link</a>
 <a class="nav-link disable" href="#" tabindex="-1"
          aria-disabled="true">Disable</a>
</nav>
```

For equal-width elements, use .nav-justified. Nav links will occupy all horizontal space, but unlike the .nav-fill above, every nav item will be of the same width.

```
<ul class="nav nav-pills nav-justified">
 <li class="nav-item">
  <a class="nav-link active" aria-current="page"
href="#">Active</a>
 </li>
 <li class="nav-item">
  <a class="nav-link" href="#">Much longer nav-link</a>
 </li>
 <li class="nav-item">
  <a class="nav-link" href="#">Link</a>
 </li>
 <li class="nav-item">
  <a class="nav-link disable" href="#" tabindex="-1"
          aria-disabled="true">Disable</a>
 </li>
</ul>
```

Similar to .nav-fill example using a <nav>-based navigation.

```
<nav class="nav nav-pills nav-justified">
 <a class="nav-link active" aria-current="page"
          href="#">Active</a>
 <a class="nav-link" href="#">Much longer nav-link</a>
 <a class="nav-link" href="#">Link</a>
 <a class="nav-link disable" href="#" tabindex="-1"
    aria-disabled="true">Disable</a>
</nav
```

Working with the Flex Utilities

Consider employing a set of flexbox tools if you require responsive nav alternatives. While these tools are more verbose, they provide broader control across responsive breakpoints. In the next example, our navigation will be layered on the smallest breakpoint, and then adapt to a horizontal layout that covers the available width beginning with the smallest breakpoint.

```
<nav class="nav nav-pills flex-column flex-sm-row">
 <a class="flex-sm-fill text-sm-center nav-link
    active" aria-current="page" href="#">Active</a>
```

```
<a class="flex-sm-fill text-sm-center nav-link"
   href="#">Longer nav-link</a>
<a class="flex-sm-fill text-sm-center nav-link"
   href="#">Link</a>
<a class="flex-sm-fill text-sm-center nav-link
   disable" href="#" tabindex="-1" aria-
   disabled="true">Disable</a>
</nav>
```

Regarding Accessibility

If we're using navs to provide a navigation bar, be sure to add a role="navigation" to the logical parent container of the <ul>, or wrap an <nav> element around the whole navigation. Please do not add the role to <ul> itself, as this would prevent it from being announced as actual list by assistive technologies.

It should be noted that navigation bars should not be assigned role="tablist", role="tab", or role="tab panel" attributes, even if they are aesthetically styled as tabs using the .nav-tabs class. These should only be used for dynamic tabbed interfaces, as stated in the WAI-ARIA Authoring Practices. For an example, see JavaScript behavior for dynamic tabbed interfaces in this section. On dynamic tabbed interfaces, the aria-current property is unneeded because our JavaScript manages the selected state by adding aria-selected="true" to the active tab.

Using Dropdowns

Add the dropdown menus with a bit of extra HTML and the dropdowns JavaScript plugin.

Tabs with Dropdowns

```
<ul class="nav nav-tabs">
 <li class="nav-item">
  <a class="nav-link active" aria-current="page"
     href="#">Active</a>
 </li>
 <li class="nav-item dropdown">
  <a class="nav-link dropdown-toggle" data-bs-
     toggle="dropdown" href="#" role="button" aria-
     expanded="false">Dropdown</a>
  <ul class="dropdown-menu">
```

```
   <li><a class="dropdown-item" href="#">Action</a></li>
   <li><a class="dropdown-item" href="#">Another-
               action</a></li>
   <li><a class="dropdown-item" href="#">Something-
               else here</a></li>
   <li><hr class="dropdown-divider"></li>
   <li><a class="dropdown-item" href="#">Separated
               link</a></li>
  </ul>
 </li>
 <li class="nav-item">
  <a class="nav-link" href="#">Link</a>
 </li>
 <li class="nav-item">
  <a class="nav-link disable" href="#" tabindex="-1"
          aria-disabled="true">Disable</a>
 </li>
</ul>
```

Pills with Dropdowns

```
<ul class="nav nav-pills">
 <li class="nav-item">
  <a class="nav-link active" aria-current="page"
          href="#">Active</a>
 </li>
 <li class="nav-item dropdown">
  <a class="nav-link dropdown-toggle" data-bs-
          toggle="dropdown" href="#" role="button"
          aria-expanded="false">Dropdown</a>
  <ul class="dropdown-menu">
   <li><a class="dropdownitem" href="#">Action</a></li>
   <li><a class="dropdownitem" href="#">Another
          action</a></li>
   <li><a class="dropdownitem" href="#">Something
          else here</a></li>
   <li><hr class="dropdown-divider"></li>
   <li><a class="dropdown-item" href="#">Separated
          link</a></li>
  </ul>
 </li>
```

```
<li class="nav-item">
 <a class="nav-link" href="#">Link</a>
</li>
<li class="nav-item">
 <a class="nav-link disable" href="#" tabindex="-1"
    aria-disabled="true">Disable</a>
</li>
</ul>
```

NAVBAR

The navbar is Bootstrap's strong, responsive navigation header, which has documentation and examples. It includes navigation, branding, and other features, as well as compatibility for the collapse plugin.

How It Works

Before you start using the navbar in Bootstrap, here's what you should know:

- Wrapping is required for navbars.

- For responsive collapsing and color scheme classes, use .navbar-expand-sm|-md|-lg|-xl|-xxl.

- By default, navbars and their contents in Bootstrap are fluid. Change the container's horizontal width limit in several methods.

- Use our spacing and flex utility classes to change the spacing and alignment of navbars.

- Navbars are responsive by default, but you may change that with ease. Our Collapse JavaScript plugin is responsible for responsive behavior.

- Ensure the accessibility by using a <nav> element in Bootstrapor, if using a more generic feature such as a <div>, add role="navigation" to every navbar to explicitly identify it as a landmark region for users of the assistive technologies.

- Indicate the current item using aria-current="page" for the current page or aria-current="true" for the current item in a set.

Supported Content

In navbars, a few subcomponents are supported by default. Choose from the following options as needed:

- .navbar-brand for the name of your business, product, or project

- For full-height and lightweight navigation, use .navbar-nav (with dropdown support)

- .navbar-toggler for use with the collapse plugin and other navigation toggling behaviors

- For all form controls and actions, flex and spacing utilities are available.

- .navbar-text helps you to add vertically centered text strings to your navbar.

- For hiding and grouping navbar contents by a parent breakpoint, use navbar-collapse.

- Include an optional.

- To establish a max-height and scroll expanding navbar content, use navbar-scroll.

This is an example of all the subcomponents in a responsive light-themed navbar that collapses automatically at the LG (large) breakpoint.

```
<nav class="navbar navbar-expand-lg navbar-light
    bg-light">
 <div class="container-fluid">
  <a class="navbar-brand" href="#">Navbar</a>
  <button class="navbar-toggler" type="button" data-
    bs-toggle="collapse" data-bs-target="#navbarSuppo
    rtedContent" aria-controls="navbarSupported
    Content" aria-expanded="false" aria-label="Toggle
    navigation">
   <span class="navbar-toggler-icon"></span>
  </button>
  <div class="collapse navbar-collapse"
      id="navbarSupportedContent">
   <ul class="navbar-nav me-auto mb-2 mb-lg-0">
```

```
    <li class="nav-item">
     <a class="nav-link active" aria-current="page"
        href="#">Home</a>
    </li>
    <li class="nav-item">
     <a class="nav-link" href="#">Link</a>
    </li>
    <li class="nav-item dropdown">
     <a class="nav-link dropdown-toggle" href="#"
        id="navbarDropdown" role="button" data-bs-
        toggle="dropdown" aria-expanded="false">
      Dropdown
     </a>
     <ul class="dropdown-menu"
         aria-labelledby="navbarDropdown">
      <li><a class="dropdownitem" href="#">Action</
             a></li>
      <li><a class="dropdownitem" href="#">Another
             action</a></li>
      <li><hr class="dropdowndivider"></li>
      <li><a class="dropdownitem" href="#">Something
             else here</a></li>
     </ul>
    </li>
    <li class="nav-item">
     <a class="nav-link disable" href="#" tabindex=
        "-1" aria-disabled="true">Disable</a>
    </li>
   </ul>
   <form class="d-flex">
    <input class="form-control me-2" type="search"
           placeholder="Search" aria-label="Search">
    <button class="btn btn-outline-success"
            type="submit">Search</button>
   </form>
  </div>
 </div>
</nav>
```

This example uses background (bg-light) and spacing (my-2, my-lg-0, me-sm-0, my-sm-0) utility classes.

Brand

Although the .navbar-brand can be used on almost any element, it is better to use an anchor because some functions require custom styles or utility classes.

Text

Add our text within an element with the .navbar-brand class.

```
<!-- As a link -->
<nav class="navbar navbar-light bg-light">
 <div class="container-fluid">
  <a class="navbar-brand" href="#">Navbar</a>
 </div>
</nav>

<!-- As a heading -->
<nav class="navbar navbar-light bg-light">
 <div class="container-fluid">
  <span class="navbar-brand mb-0 h1">Navbar</span>
 </div>
</nav>
```

Image

We can replace the text within the .navbar-brand with an <img>.

```
<nav class="navbar navbar-light bg-light">
 <div class="container">
  <a class="navbar-brand" href="#">
   <img src="/docs/5.0/assets/brand/bootstrap-logo.sv
       g" alt="" width="30" height="24">
  </a>
 </div>
</nav>
```

Image and Text

You can also use some additional utilities to add an image and text at the same time.

```
<nav class="navbar navbar-light bg-light">
 <div class="container-fluid">
  <a class="navbar-brand" href="#">
```

```
  <img src="/docs/5.0/assets/brand/bootstrap-logo.sv
      g" alt="" width="30" height="24" class="d-
      inline-block align-text-top">
  Bootstrap
 </a>
 </div>
</nav>
```

nav

With their modifier class, navbar navigation links build on our .nav choices and require toggler classes for effective responsive style. Navigation in navbars will also expand to take up as much horizontal space as possible in order to secure the alignment of your navbar items.

To indicate the current page, use the .active class on .nav-link. Please remember to include the aria-current attribute on the active .nav-link as well.

```
<nav class="navbar navbar-expand-lg navbar-light
    bg-light">
 <div class="container-fluid">
  <a class="navbar-brand" href="#">Navbar</a>
  <button class="navbar-toggler" type="button" data-
    bs-toggle="collapse" data-bs-target="#navbarNav"
    aria-controls="navbarNav" aria-expanded="false"
    aria-label="Toggle navigation">
   <span class="navbar-toggler-icon"></span>
  </button>
  <div class="collapse navbar-collapse"
      id="navbarNav">
   <ul class="navbar-nav">
    <li class="nav-item">
     <a class="nav-link active" aria-current="page"
       href="#">Home</a>
    </li>
    <li class="nav-item">
     <a class="nav-link" href="#">Features</a>
    </li>
    <li class="nav-item">
     <a class="nav-link" href="#">Pricing</a>
    </li>
    <li class="nav-item">
```

```
    <a class="nav-link disable" href="#" tabindex=
        "-1" aria-disabled="true">Disable</a>
    </li>
   </ul>
  </div>
 </div>
</nav>
```

Because of use of classes for the navs, you can avoid the list-based approach entirely if you like.

```
<nav class="navbar navbar-expand-lg navbar-light
     bg-light">
 <div class="container-fluid">
  <a class="navbar-brand" href="#">Navbar</a>
  <button class="navbar-toggler" type="button" data-
    bs-toggle="collapse" data-bs-
    target="#navbarNavAltMarkup"
    aria-controls="navbarNavAltMarkup" aria-
    expanded="false" aria-label="Toggle navigation">
   <span class="navbar-toggler-icon"></span>
  </button>
  <div class="collapse navbar-collapse"
       id="navbarNavAltMarkup">
   <div class="navbar-nav">
    <a class="nav-link active" aria-current="page"
       href="#">Home</a>
    <a class="nav-link" href="#">Features</a>
    <a class="nav-link" href="#">Pricing</a>
    <a class="nav-link disable" href="#"
       tabindex="-1" aria-disabled="true">Disable</a>
   </div>
  </div>
 </div>
</nav>
```

Dropdowns can also be used in the navbar. Because dropdown menus require a wrapping element for placement, use separate and nested features for .nav-item and .nav-link, as seen below:

```
<nav class="navbar navbar-expand-lg navbar-light
     bg-light">
 <div class="container-fluid">
```

```html
<a class="navbar-brand" href="#">Navbar</a>
<button class="navbar-toggler" type="button" data-
  bs-toggle="collapse" data-bs-
  target="#navbarNavDropdown"
  aria-controls="navbarNavDropdown" aria-
  expanded="false" aria-label="Toggle navigation">
 <span class="navbar-toggler-icon"></span>
</button>
<div class="collapse navbar-collapse"
     id="navbarNavDropdown">
 <ul class="navbar-nav">
  <li class="nav-item">
   <a class="nav-link active" aria-current="page"
      href="#">Home</a>
  </li>
  <li class="nav-item">
   <a class="nav-link" href="#">Features</a>
  </li>
  <li class="nav-item">
   <a class="nav-link" href="#">Pricing</a>
  </li>
  <li class="nav-item dropdown">
   <a class="nav-link dropdown-toggle" href="#"
      id="navbarDropdown-MenuLink" role="button"
      data-bs-toggle="dropdown"
      aria-expanded="false">
    Dropdown link
   </a>
   <ul class="dropdown-menu" aria-labelledby="nav
       barDropdownMenuLink">
    <li><a class="dropdownitem" href="#">Action</
            a></li>
    <li><a class="dropdownitem" href="#">Another
            action</a></li>
    <li><a class="dropdownitem" href="#">Something
            else here</a></li>
   </ul>
  </li>
 </ul>
</div>
</div>
</nav>
```

Forms

```
<nav class="navbar navbar-light bg-light">
 <div class="container-fluid">
  <form class="d-flex">
   <input class="form-control me-2" type="search"
          placeholder="Search" aria-label="Search">
   <button class="btn btn-outline-success"
           type="submit">Search</button>
  </form>
 </div>
</nav>
```

Immediate child elements of the .navbar use flex layout and will default to justify-content: space-between. Use the additional flex utilities as needed to adjust this behavior.

```
<nav class="navbar navbar-light bg-light">
 <div class="container-fluid">
  <a class="navbar-brand">Navbar</a>
  <form class="d-flex">
   <input class="form-control me-2" type="search"
          placeholder="Search" aria-label="Search">
   <button class="btn btn-outline-success"
           type="submit">Search</button>
  </form>
 </div>
</nav>
```

Input groups work fine, too. If our navbar is an entire form, or mostly a form, we can use <form> element as the container and save some HTML.

```
<nav class="navbar navbar-light bg-light">
 <form class="container-fluid">
  <div class="input-group">
   <span class="input-group-text" id="basic-
         addon1">@</span>
   <input type="text" class="form-control"
          placeholder="Username" aria-label="Username"
          aria-describedby="basic-addon1">
  </div>
 </form>
</nav>
```

Various buttons are also supported in these navbar configurations. This is also a good reminder that you may utilize vertical alignment utilities to align items of various sizes.

```
<nav class="navbar navbar-light bg-light">
 <form class="container-fluid justify-content-start">
  <button class="btn btn-outline-success me-2"
          type="button">Main button</button>
  <button class="btn btn-sm btn-outline-secondary"
          type="button">Smaller button</button>
 </form>
</nav>
```

Text

.navbar-text is used to include text in navbars. This class modifies the vertical alignment and horizontal spacing of text strings.

```
<nav class="navbar navbar-light bg-light">
 <div class="container-fluid">
  <span class="navbar-text">
   Navbar text with an inline element
  </span>
 </div>
</nav>
```

Mix and match with other the components and utilities as needed.

```
<nav class="navbar navbar-expand-lg navbar-light
bg-light">
 <div class="container-fluid">
  <a class="navbar-brand" href="#">Navbar w/ text</a>
  <button class="navbar-toggler" type="button" data-
    bs-toggle="collapse" data-bs-target="#navbarText"
    aria-controls="navbarText" aria-expanded="false"
    aria-label="Toggle navigation">
   <span class="navbar-toggler-icon"></span>
  </button>
  <div class="collapse navbar-collapse"
       id="navbarText">
   <ul class="navbar-nav me-auto mb-2 mb-lg-0">
    <li class="nav-item">
     <a class="nav-link active" aria-current="page"
        href="#">Home</a>
```

```
    </li>
    <li class="nav-item">
     <a class="nav-link" href="#">Features</a>
    </li>
    <li class="nav-item">
     <a class="nav-link" href="#">Pricing</a>
    </li>
   </ul>
   <span class="navbar-text">
    Navbar text with an inline element
   </span>
  </div>
 </div>
</nav>
```

Color Schemes

The mixture combination of theming classes and background-color utilities makes it easier than ever to customize the navbar. Use .navbar-light with light background colors or .navbar-dark with dark background colors. Then, usen.bg-* tools to modify.

```
<nav class="navbar navbar-dark bg-dark">
 <!-- Navbar content -->
</nav>

<nav class="navbar navbar-dark bg-primary">
 <!-- Navbar content -->
</nav>

<nav class="navbar navbar-light" style="background-
     color: #e3f2fd;">
 <!-- Navbar content -->
</nav>
```

Containers

Although it isn't required, we can use a .container to center a navbar on a page – though an inner container is still required. Alternatively, you may use a container within the .navbar to just center the contents of a fixed or static top navbar.

```
<div class="container">
 <nav class="navbar navbar-expand-lg navbar-light
     bg-light">
```

```
  <div class="container-fluid">
   <a class="navbar-brand" href="#">Navbar</a>
  </div>
 </nav>
</div>
```

Use any of the responsive containers in Bootstrap to change how wide the content in your navbar is presented.

```
<nav class="navbar navbar-expand-lg navbar-light
     bg-light">
 <div class="container-md">
  <a class="navbar-brand" href="#">Navbar</a>
 </div>
</nav>
```

Placement

The mixture of the theming classes and background-color utilities makes customizing the navbar easier than ever. Use .navbar-light for light backgrounds or .navbar-dark for dark backgrounds. Then, use.bg-* tools to modify. Also, note that .sticky-top uses position: sticky, which is not fully supported in all browser.

```
<nav class="navbar navbar-light bg-light">
 <div class="container-fluid">
  <a class="navbar-brand" href="#">Default</a>
 </div>
</nav>
```

```
<nav class="navbar fixed-top navbar-light bg-light">
 <div class="container-fluid">
  <a class="navbar-brand" href="#">Fixed top</a>
 </div>
</nav>
```

```
<nav class="navbar fixed-bottom navbar-light
     bg-light">
 <div class="container-fluid">
  <a class="navbar-brand" href="#">Fixed bottom</a>
 </div>
</nav>
```

```
<nav class="navbar sticky-top navbar-light bg-light">
 <div class="container-fluid">
  <a class="navbar-brand" href="#">Sticky top</a>
 </div>
</nav>
```

Scrolling

To enable vertical scrolling within toggleable contents in Bootstrap of a collapsed navbar, add .navbar-nav-scroll to a .navbar-nav (or any navbar subcomponent). Scrolling starts at 75vh (or 75% of the viewport height) by default, but you may change that with the local CSS custom parameter — bs-navbar-height or custom styles. The content will appear as it would in a default navbar when the navbar is expanded to larger viewports.

Please notice that this behavior has a potential overflow drawback: when overflow-y: auto is enabled (which is required to scroll the material here), overflow-x is set to auto, which crops some horizontal content.

Here's an example navbar with .navbar-nav-scroll style="—bs-scroll-height: 90px;" and some additional margin utilities for optimal spacing.

```
<nav class="navbar navbar-expand-lg navbar-light
bg-light">
 <div class="container-fluid">
  <a class="navbar-brand" href="#">Navbar scroll</a>
  <button class="navbar-toggler" type="button" data-
    bs-toggle="collapse" data-bs-target="#navbar
    Scroll" aria-controls="navbarScroll" aria-
    expanded="false" aria-label="Toggle navigation">
   <span class="navbar-toggler-icon"></span>
  </button>
  <div class="collapse navbar-collapse"
      id="navbarScroll">
   <ul class="navbar-nav me-auto my-2 my-lg-0 navbar-
      nav-scroll" style="--bs-scroll-height: 90px;">
    <li class="nav-item">
     <a class="nav-link active" aria-current="page"
       href="#">Home</a>
    </li>
    <li class="nav-item">
     <a class="nav-link" href="#">Link</a>
    </li>
    <li class="nav-item dropdown">
```

```
        <a class="nav-link dropdown-toggle" href="#"
           id="navbarScrollingDropdown" role="button" data-
           bs-toggle="dropdown" aria-expanded="false">
          Link
        </a>
        <ul class="dropdown-menu" aria-labelledby="nav
               barScrollingDropdown">
          <li><a class="dropdownitem" href="#">Action</
                 a></li>
          <li><a class="dropdownitem" href="#">Another
                 action</a></li>
          <li><hr class="dropdown-divider"></li>
          <li><a class="dropdownitem" href="#">Something
                 else here</a></li>
        </ul>
      </li>
      <li class="nav-item">
       <a class="nav-link disable" href="#"
           tabindex="-1" aria-disable="true">Link</a>
      </li>
     </ul>
     <form class="d-flex">
      <input class="form-control me-2" type="search"
             placeholder="Search" aria-label="Search">
      <button class="btn btn-outline-success"
             type="submit">Search</button>
     </form>
    </div>
   </div>
</nav>
```

Responsive Behaviors

To determine when the content collapses behind a button, navbars can utilize the .navbar-toggler, .navbar-collapse, and .navbar-expand {-sm|-md|-lg|-xl|-xxl} classes. You may easily determine when to show or hide specific parts when using other programs.

Add the .navbar-expand class to the navbar for navbars that never collapse. Remove the .navbar-expand class from navbars that always collapse.

Google

Navbar toggles are left-aligned by default, but if they are followed by a sibling element, such as a .navbar-brand, they will be positioned to the far right. The toggler's positioning will be reversed if your markup is reversed. Here are some instances of various toggle styles.

With no .navbar-brand shown at smallest breakpoint:

```
<nav class="navbar navbar-expand-lg navbar-light
     bg-light">
 <div class="container-fluid">
  <button class="navbar-toggler" type="button" data-
    bs-toggle="collapse" data-bs-
    target="#navbarTogglerDemo01"
    aria-controls="navbarTogglerDemo01" aria-
    expanded="false" aria-label="Toggle navigation">
   <span class="navbar-toggler-icon"></span>
  </button>
  <div class="collapse navbar-collapse"
       id="navbarTogglerDemo01">
   <a class="navbar-brand" href="#">Hidden brand</a>
   <ul class="navbar-nav me-auto mb-2 mb-lg-0">
    <li class="nav-item">
     <a class="nav-link active" aria-current="page"
        href="#">Home</a>
    </li>
    <li class="nav-item">
     <a class="nav-link" href="#">Link</a>
    </li>
    <li class="nav-item">
     <a class="nav-link disable" href="#" tabindex="-1"
        aria-disabled="true">Disable</a>
    </li>
   </ul>
   <form class="d-flex">
    <input class="form-control me-2" type="search"
           placeholder="Search" aria-label="Search">
    <button class="btn btn-outline-success"
            type="submit">Search</button>
   </form>
  </div>
 </div>
</nav>
```

With brand name shown on the left and toggler on the right:

```
<nav class="navbar navbar-expand-lg navbar-light
     bg-light">
```

```
<div class="container-fluid">
 <a class="navbar-brand" href="#">Navbar</a>
 <button class="navbar-toggler" type="button" data-
    bs-toggle="collapse" data-bs-
    target="#navbarTogglerDemo02"
    aria-controls="navbarTogglerDemo02" aria-
    expanded="false" aria-label="Toggle navigation">
  <span class="navbar-toggler-icon"></span>
 </button>
 <div class="collapse navbar-collapse"
      id="navbarTogglerDemo02">
  <ul class="navbar-nav me-auto mb-2 mb-lg-0">
   <li class="nav-item">
    <a class="nav-link active" aria-current="page"
       href="#">Home</a>
   </li>
   <li class="nav-item">
    <a class="nav-link" href="#">Link</a>
   </li>
   <li class="nav-item">
    <a class="nav-link disable" href="#" tabindex="-1"
       aria-disabled="true">Disable</a>
   </li>
  </ul>
  <form class="d-flex">
   <input class="form-control me-2" type="search"
          placeholder="Search" aria-label="Search">
   <button class="btn btn-outline-success"
           type="submit">Search</button>
  </form>
 </div>
 </div>
</nav>
```

With a toggler on left and brand name on the right:

```
<nav class="navbar navbar-expand-lg navbar-light
     bg-light">
 <div class="container-fluid">
  <button class="navbar-toggler" type="button" data-
     bs-toggle="collapse" data-bs-
     target="#navbarTogglerDemo03"
     aria-controls="navbarTogglerDemo03" aria-
     expanded="false" aria-label="Toggle navigation">
```

```
   <span class="navbar-toggler-icon"></span>
  </button>
  <a class="navbar-brand" href="#">Navbar</a>
  <div class="collapse navbar-collapse"
       id="navbarTogglerDemo03">
   <ul class="navbar-nav me-auto mb-2 mb-lg-0">
    <li class="nav-item">
     <a class="nav-link active" aria-current="page"
        href="#">Home</a>
    </li>
    <li class="nav-item">
     <a class="nav-link" href="#">Link</a>
    </li>
    <li class="nav-item">
     <a class="nav-link disable" href="#" tabindex=
        "-1" aria-disabled="true">Disable</a>
    </li>
   </ul>
   <form class="d-flex">
    <input class="form-control me-2" type="search"
           placeholder="Search" aria-label="Search">
    <button class="btn btn-outline-success"
            type="submit">Search</button>
   </form>
  </div>
 </div>
</nav>
```

External Content

We occasionally wish to utilize the collapse plugin to activate a container element for content that is structurally outside of the .navbar. That's because our plugin works on the id and data-bs-target matching.

```
<div class="collapse" id="navbarToggleExternalContent">
 <div class="bg-dark p-4">
  <h5 class="text-white h4">Collapsed content</h5>
  <span class="text-muted">Toggleable via the navbar
        brand.</span>
 </div>
</div>
<nav class="navbar navbar-dark bg-dark">
 <div class="container-fluid">
```

```
<button class="navbar-toggler" type="button" data-
  bs-toggle="collapse" data-bs-target="#navbarTo
  ggleExternalContent" aria-controls="navbarTogg
  leExternalContent" aria-expanded="false" aria-
  label="Toggle navigation">
  <span class="navbar-toggler-icon"></span>
</button>
</div>
</nav>
```

When you do this, we recommend integrating extra JavaScript to programmatically transfer the attention to the container when it is opened. Otherwise, keyboard users and assistive technology users may likely struggle to discover the newly disclosed information, especially if the opened container is placed *before* the toggler in the document's structure. We also propose that the toggler has the aria-controls property set to the content container's id. In principle, this allows users of assistive technology to navigate straight from the toggler to the container it controls – however, support for this is still inconsistent.

OFF-CANVAS

With a few classes and our JavaScript plugin, you can incorporate hidden sidebars into our project for navigation, shopping carts, and more.

How Does It Work?

Off-canvas is a sidebar component that may be toggled to display from the viewport's left, right, or bottom edge using JavaScript. Buttons or anchors are utilized as triggers that are tied to certain items that we toggle, and data attributes are used to call our JavaScript.

- Off-canvas and modals both use part of the same JavaScript code. They are conceptually similar, although they are independent plugins.

- Similarly, certain canvases' styles and dimensions are inherited from the modal's variables.

- Off-canvas has a preset backdrop that may be clicked to conceal the off-canvas when it is shown.

- Similar to modals, only one canvas can be shown at a time.

Examples

Off-canvas Components

Below is an off-canvas example that is shown by default (via .show on .off-canvas). Off-canvas provides a header with a close button and a body class that can be used to add some padding at the start. When feasible, incorporate off-canvas headers will dismiss actions or offer an explicit dismiss action.

```
<div class="offcanvas offcanvas-start" tabindex="-1"
    id="offcanvas" aria-labelledby="offcanvasLabel">
 <div class="offcanvas-header">
  <h5 class="offcanvas-title" id="offcanvasLabel">Off
     canvas</h5>
  <button type="button" class="btn-close text-reset"
    data-bs-dismiss="offcanvas" aria-label="Close"></
    button>
 </div>
 <div class="offcanvas-body">
  Content for the off-canvas goes here. We can place
        just about any Bootstrap component or custom
        elements here.
 </div>
</div>
```

Live Demo

Use buttons below to show and hide an off-canvas element via JavaScript that toggles .show class on an element with .offcanvas class.

- .offcanvas hides content (default)

- .offcanvas.show shows the content

You can use a link with href attribute or a button with the data-bs-target attribute. In both cases, the data-bs-toggle="off-canvas" is required.

```
<a class="btn btn-primary" data-bs-toggle="offcanvas"
   href="#offcanvasExample" role="button"
   aria-controls="offcanvasExample">
 Link with href
</a>
<button class="btn btn-primary" type="button" data-
  bs-toggle="offcanvas" data-bs-target="#offcanvas-
  Example" aria-controls="offcanvasExample">
```

```
 Button with data-bs-target
</button>


<div class="offcanvas offcanvas-start" tabindex="-1"
     id="offcanvasExample" aria-labelledby="offcanvas
     ExampleLabel">
 <div class="offcanvas-header">
  <h5 class="offcanvas-title" id="offcanvasExample
      Label">Offcanvas</h5>
  <button type="button" class="btn-close text-reset"
          data-bs-dismiss="offcanvas" aria-
          label="Close"></button>
 </div>
 <div class="offcanvas-body">
  <div>
   Some text as placeholder. In real life you can have
       the elements you have chosen. Like text,
       images, lists, etc.
  </div>
  <div class="dropdown mt-3">
   <button class="btn btn-secondary dropdown-toggle"
           type="button" id="dropdownMenuButton"
           data-bs-toggle="dropdown">
    Dropdown button
   </button>
   <ul class="dropdown-menu" aria-labelledby="dropdow
       nMenuButton">
    <li><a class="dropdown-item" href="#">Action</
           a></li>
    <li><a class="dropdown-item" href="#">Another
           action</a></li>
    <li><a class="dropdown-item" href="#">Something
           else here</a></li>
   </ul>
  </div>
 </div>
</div>
```

Placement

There's no default placement for off-canvas components, so we must add one of the modifier classes below:

- .offcanvas-start places off-canvas on left of the viewport

- .offcanvas-end places off-canvas on right of the viewport

- .offcanvas-top places off-canvas on top of the viewport

- .offcanvas-bottom places off-canvas on the bottom of viewport

Try top, right, and bottom examples below.

```
<button class="btn btn-primary" type="button" data-
  bs-toggle="offcanvas" data-bs-target="#offcanvasTop"
  aria-controls="offcanvasTop">Toggle top offcanvas</
  button>

<div class="offcanvas offcanvas-top" tabindex="-1"
    id="offcanvasTop" aria-labelledby="offcanvasTopL
    abel">
 <div class="offcanvas-header">
  <h5 id="offcanvasTopLabel">Offcanvas top</h5>
  <button type="button" class="btn-close text-reset"
    data-bs-dismiss="offcanvas" aria-label="Close"></
    button>
 </div>
 <div class="offcanvas-body">
  ...
 </div>
</div>



<button class="btn btn-primary" type="button" data-bs-
  toggle="offcanvas" data-bs-target="#offcanvasRight"
  aria-controls="offcanvas-Right">Toggle right
  offcanvas</button>

<div class="offcanvas offcanvas-end" tabindex="-1"
    id="offcanvasRight" aria-labelledby="offcanvasRi
    ghtLabel">
 <div class="offcanvas-header">
  <h5 id="offcanvasRightLabel">Offcanvas right</h5>
  <button type="button" class="btn-close text-reset"
        data-bs-dismiss="offcanvas" aria-
        label="Close"></button>
 </div>
```

```
  <div class="offcanvas-body">
   ...
  </div>
</div>
```

```
<button class="btn btn-primary" type="button" data-
        bs-toggle="offcanvas" data-bs-
        target="#offcanvasBottom" aria-controls="offc
        anvasBottom">Toggle bottom offcanvas</button>
```

```
<div class="offcanvas offcanvas-bottom" tabindex="-1"
     id="offcanvasBottom"
     aria-labelledby="offcanvasBottomLabel">
 <div class="offcanvas-header">
  <h5 class="offcanvas-title" id="offcanvasBottomLabe
     l">Offcanvas bottom</h5>
  <button type="button" class="btn-close text-reset"
          data-bs-dismiss="offcanvas" aria-
          label="Close"></button>
 </div>
 <div class="offcanvas-body small">
  ...
 </div>
</div>
```

Backdrop

Scrolling <body> element is disable when an off-canvas and its backdrop are visible. Use data-bs-scroll attribute to toggle <body> scrolling and data-bs-backdrop to toggle backdrop.

```
    <button    class="btn    btn-primary"    type="button"    data-bs-
toggle="offcanvas"  data-bs-target="#offcanvasScrolling"  aria-controls="
offcanvasScrolling">Enable body scrolling</button>
    <button    class="btn    btn-primary"    type="button"    data-bs-
toggle="offcanvas"  data-bs-target="#offcanvasWithBackdrop"  aria-contr
ols="offcanvasWithBackdrop">Enable backdrop (default)</button>
    <button    class="btn    btn-primary"    type="button"    data-bs-
toggle="offcanvas"           data-bs-target="#offcanvasWithBothOptions"
aria-controls="offcanvasWithBothOptions">Enable  both  scrolling  &
backdrop</button>
```

```
<div class="offcanvas offcanvas-start" data-bs-
    scroll="true" data-bs-backdrop="false"
    tabindex="-1" id="offcanvasScrolling" aria-label
    ledby="offcanvasScrollingLabel">
 <div class="offcanvas-header">
  <h5 class="offcanvas-title" id="offcanvasScrollingL
      abel">Colored with scrolling</h5>
   <button type="button" class="btn-close text-reset"
          data-bs-dismiss="offcanvas" aria-
          label="Close"></button>
 </div>
 <div class="offcanvas-body">
  <p>Try scrolling the rest of the page to see this
        option in action.</p>
 </div>
</div>
<div class="offcanvas offcanvas-start" tabindex="-1"
    id="offcanvasWithBackdrop" aria-labelledby="off
    canvasWithBackdropLabel">
 <div class="offcanvas-header">
  <h5 class="offcanvas-title" id="offcanvasWithBac
      kdropLabel">Offcanvas with backdrop</h5>
   <button type="button" class="btn-close text-reset"
     data-bs-dismiss="offcanvas" aria-label="Close"></
     button>
 </div>
 <div class="offcanvas-body">
  <p>.....</p>
 </div>
</div>
<div class="offcanvas offcanvas-start" data-bs-
    scroll="true" tabindex="-1"
    id="offcanvasWithBothOptions" aria-labelledby
    ="offcanvasWithBothOptionsLabel">
 <div class="offcanvas-header">
  <h5 class="offcanvas-title" id="offcanvasWithBot
      hOptionsLabel">Backdroped with scrolling</h5>
   <button type="button" class="btn-close text-reset"
          data-bs-dismiss="offcanvas" aria-
          label="Close"></button>
 </div>
 <div class="offcanvas-body">
```

```
<p>Try scrolling the rest of the page to see this
      option in action.</p>
 </div>
</div>
```

PAGINATION

Documentation and examples for showing pagination to indicate a series of related content exists across multiple pages.

Overview

For our pagination, we employ a huge block of related links, which makes links difficult to miss and readily scalable while giving vast hit regions. Pagination is constructed using a list of HTML elements so that screen readers may announce the number of accessible links. Use a wraparound nav> element to indicate to screen readers and other assistive technology that this is a navigation section.

Furthermore, because sites are likely to have several such navigation sections, it is a good idea to provide a descriptive aria-label for the nav> to represent its role. If the pagination component is used to move between a set of search results, for example, a good label may be aria-label="Search results pages."

```
<nav aria-label="Page navigation example">
 <ul class="pagination">
  <li class="page-item"><a class="page-link"
      href="#">Previous</a></li>
  <li class="page-item"><a class="page-link"
      href="#">1</a></li>
  <li class="page-item"><a class="page-link"
      href="#">2</a></li>
  <li class="page-item"><a class="page-link"
      href="#">3</a></li>
  <li class="page-item"><a class="page-link"
      href="#">Next</a></li>
 </ul>
</nav>
```

Working with Icons

Are you wanting to replace text with an icon or symbol for some pagination links? With aria characteristics, be sure to give correct screen reader assistance.

```
<nav aria-label="Page navigation example">
 <ul class="pagination">
  <li class="page-item">
   <a class="page-link" href="#" aria-label="Previous">
    <span aria-hidden="true">&laquo;</span>
   </a>
  </li>
  <li class="page-item"><a class="page-link"
      href="#">1</a></li>
  <li class="page-item"><a class="page-link"
      href="#">2</a></li>
  <li class="page-item"><a class="page-link"
      href="#">3</a></li>
  <li class="page-item">
   <a class="page-link" href="#" aria-label="Next">
    <span aria-hidden="true">&raquo;</span>
   </a>
  </li>
 </ul>
</nav>
```

Disable and Active States

Pagination links can be customized based on the situation. For links that appear unclickable, use .disabled, and for the current page, use .active.

While the .disabled class disables the link capability of <a> by using pointer-events: none, that CSS feature is not yet standardized and does not account for keyboard navigation. As a result, you should always use tabindex="-1" on disabled links and custom JavaScript to completely prevent their functionality.

```
<nav aria-label="...">
 <ul class="pagination">
  <li class="page-item disable">
   <a class="page-link" href="#" tabindex="-1" aria-
      disabled="true">Previous</a>
  </li>
  <li class="page-item"><a class="page-link"
      href="#">1</a></li>
  <li class="page-item active" aria-current="page">
   <a class="page-link" href="#">2</a>
  </li>
```

```
  <li class="page-item"><a class="page-link"
      href="#">3</a></li>
  <li class="page-item">
   <a class="page-link" href="#">Next</a>
  </li>
 </ul>
</nav>
```

To eliminate click functionality and prevent keyboard focus while pre-serving intended styles, you can alternatively switch out active or disabled anchors with <span>, or omit the anchor in the case of the prev/next arrows.

```
<nav aria-label="...">
 <ul class="pagination">
  <li class="page-item disable">
   <span class="page-link">Previous</span>
  </li>
  <li class="page-item"><a class="page-link"
      href="#">1</a></li>
  <li class="page-item active" aria-current="page">
   <span class="page-link">2</span>
  </li>
  <li class="page-item"><a class="page-link"
      href="#">3</a></li>
  <li class="page-item">
   <a class="page-link" href="#">Next</a>
  </li>
 </ul>
</nav>
```

Sizing

Fancy larger or smaller pagination? Add .pagination-lg or .pagination-sm for additional sizes.

```
<nav aria-label="...">
 <ul class="pagination pagination-lg">
  <li class="page-item active" aria-current="page">
   <span class="page-link">1</span>
  </li>
  <li class="page-item"><a class="page-link"
      href="#">2</a></li>
```

```
  <li class="page-item"><a class="page-link"
      href="#">3</a></li>
 </ul>
</nav>

<nav aria-label="...">
 <ul class="pagination pagination-sm">
  <li class="page-item active" aria-current="page">
   <span class="page-link">1</span>
  </li>
  <li class="page-item"><a class="page-link"
      href="#">2</a></li>
  <li class="page-item"><a class="page-link"
      href="#">3</a></li>
 </ul>
</nav>
```

Alignment

Change alignment of pagination components with flexbox utilities.

```
<nav aria-label="Page navigation example">
 <ul class="pagination justify-content-center">
  <li class="page-item disable">
   <a class="page-link" href="#" tabindex="-1" aria-
      disabled="true">Previous</a>
  </li>
  <li class="page-item"><a class="page-link"
      href="#">1</a></li>
  <li class="page-item"><a class="page-link"
      href="#">2</a></li>
  <li class="page-item"><a class="page-link"
      href="#">3</a></li>
  <li class="page-item">
   <a class="page-link" href="#">Next</a>
  </li>
 </ul>
</nav>

<nav aria-label="Page navigation example">
 <ul class="pagination justify-content-end">
  <li class="page-item disable">
   <a class="page-link" href="#" tabindex="-1" aria-
      disabled="true">Previous</a>
```

```
    </li>
    <li class="page-item"><a class="page-link"
        href="#">1</a></li>
    <li class="page-item"><a class="page-link"
        href="#">2</a></li>
    <li class="page-item"><a class="page-link"
        href="#">3</a></li>
    <li class="page-item">
     <a class="page-link" href="#">Next</a>
    </li>
   </ul>
 </nav>
```

PLACEHOLDERS

To show that something is still loading, use loading placeholders for your components or pages.

About

Placeholders may be used to improve the user experience of your app. They're created entirely using HTML and CSS, so no JavaScript is required. Toggling their visibility, however, will necessitate the use of special JavaScript. With our utility classes, you can quickly adjust their look, color, and size.

Example

In the example below, we take a normal card component and reproduce it with placeholders to create a "loading card." The two are of the same size and dimensions.

```
<div class="card">
  <img src="..." class="card-img-top" alt="...">

  <div class="card-body">
   <h5 class="card-title">Card title</h5>
   <p class="card-text">Some quick example text to
       build on the card title and make up the bulk of
       the card's content.</p>
   <a href="#" class="btn btn-primary">Go somewhere</a>
  </div>
</div>
```

```
<div class="card" aria-hidden="true">
 <img src="..." class="card-img-top" alt="...">
 <div class="card-body">
  <h5 class="card-title placeholder-glow">
   <span class="placeholder col-6"></span>
  </h5>
  <p class="card-text placeholder-glow">
   <span class="placeholder col-7"></span>
   <span class="placeholder col-4"></span>
   <span class="placeholder col-4"></span>
   <span class="placeholder col-6"></span>
   <span class="placeholder col-8"></span>
  </p>
  <a href="#" tabindex="-1" class="btn btn-primary
     disable placeholder col-6"></a>
 </div>
</div>
```

How It Works

To set the width, use the .placeholder class and a grid column class (e.g., .col-6) to create placeholders. They may be used to substitute text within an element or as a modifier class to an existing component.

To guarantee that the height of .btns is preserved, we apply extra style via::before. As appropriate, you may expand this pattern to additional instances, or add a within the element to reflect the size when the real text is shown in its place.

```
<p aria-hidden="true">
 <span class="placeholder col-6"></span>
</p>

<a href="#" tabindex="-1" class="btn btn-primary
   disabled placeholder col-4" aria-hidden="true"></a>
```

Width

Grid column classes, width utilities, and inline styles all can be used to adjust the width.

```
<span class="placeholder col-6"></span>
<span class="placeholder w-75"></span>
<span class="placeholder" style="width: 25%;"></span>
```

Color

The placeholder's default color is currentColor. A custom color or utility class can be used to override this.

```
<span class="placeholder col-12"></span>
<span class="placeholder col-12 bg-primary"></span>
<span class="placeholder col-12 bg-secondary"></span>
<span class="placeholder col-12 bg-success"></span>
<span class="placeholder col-12 bg-danger"></span>
<span class="placeholder col-12 bg-warning"></span>
<span class="placeholder col-12 bg-info"></span>
<span class="placeholder col-12 bg-light"></span>
<span class="placeholder col-12 bg-dark"></span>
```

Sizing

The size of .placeholders is determined by the parent element's typographic style. Sizing modifiers: .placeholder-LG,.placeholder-sm, or .placeholder-xs can be used to personalize them.

```
<span class="placeholder col-12 placeholder-lg"></
            span>
<span class="placeholder col-12"></span>
<span class="placeholder col-12 placeholder-sm"></
            span>
<span class="placeholder col-12 placeholder-xs"></
            span>
```

Animation

Animate placeholders with the .placeholder-glow or .placeholder-wave to better convey the perception of something being *actively* loaded.

```
<p class="placeholder-glow">
 <span class="placeholder col-12"></span>
</p>

<p class="placeholder-wave">
 <span class="placeholder col-12"></span>
</p>
```

This was all about the placeholders of Bootstrap; now let's jump to the popovers of Bootstrap.

POPOVERS

Documentation and examples for creating custom Bootstrap progress bars with stacked bars, animated backdrops, and text labels.

Overview

When using the popover plugin, keep the following in mind:

- Popovers rely on the Popper 3rd party library for placement. Popovers will not function until you add popper.min.js before bootstrap.js or use bootstrap.bundle.min.js/bootstrap.bundle.js, which includes Popper.

- The tooltip plugin is required as a requirement for popovers.

- Popovers are opt-in for performance reasons, therefore we must manually initialize them.

- A popover will never appear if the title and content values both are zero.

- To avoid rendering issues with more complicated components, provide container: 'body' (like our input groups, button groups, etc.).

- Using hidden items to trigger popovers will not function.

- Popovers for .disabled or disable elements must activate using a wrapper element.

- Popovers will center between the anchors' overall width when triggered from anchors that wrap across multiple lines. Use .text-nowrap on our <a> to avoid this behavior.

- Popovers must hide before their associated elements are deleted from the DOM.

- Popovers can be triggered by an element within a shadow DOM.

Example: Allow Popovers Anywhere

One method for initializing all popovers on a page is to choose them based on their data-bs-toggle attribute:

```
var popoverTriggerList = [].slice.call(document.qu
    erySelectorAll('[data-bs-toggle="popover"]'))
```

```
var popoverList = popoverTriggerList.map(function
    (popoverTriggerEl) {
 return new bootstrap.Popover(popoverTriggerEl)
})
```

Example: Using Container Option

When you have styles on a parent element that conflicts with a popover, you should provide custom container so that Popover's HTML is shown within that element instead.

```
var popover = new bootstrap.Popover(document.querySel
    ector('.example-popover'), {
 container: 'body'
})
```

Example

```
<button type="button" class="btn btn-lg btn-danger"
  data-bs-toggle="popover" title="Popover title"
  data-bs-content="And here is some amazing content.
  It is very engaging. Right?">Click to toggle
  popover</button>
```

Four Directions

Four options are available: top, right, bottom, and left-aligned. Directions are mirrored when using the Bootstrap in RTL.

```
<button type="button" class="btn btn-secondary" data-
  bs-container="body" data-bs-toggle="popover" data-
  bs-placement="top" data-bs-content="Top popover">
 Popover on top
</button>
<button type="button" class="btn btn-secondary" data-
  bs-container="body" data-bs-toggle="popover" data-
  bs-placement="right" data-bs-content="Right
  popover">
 Popover on right
</button>
<button type="button" class="btn btn-secondary" data-
  bs-container="body" data-bs-toggle="popover" data-bs-
  placement="bottom" data-bs-content="Bottom popover">
 Popover on bottom
```

```
</button>
<button type="button" class="btn btn-secondary" data-
  bs-container="body" data-bs-toggle="popover" data-
  bs-placement="left" data-bs-content="Left popover">
 Popover on left
</button>
```

Dismiss on Next Click

Use the attention trigger to dismiss popovers when the user clicks on an element other than the toggle element.

```
<a tabindex="0" class="btn btn-lg btn-danger"
  role="button" data-bs-toggle="popover" data-bs-
  trigger="focus" title="Dismissible popover" data-
  bs-content="And here's some amazing content. It is
  very engaging. Right?">Dismissible popover</a>
```

```
var popover = new bootstrap.Popover(document.querySel
    ector('.popover-dismiss'), {
 trigger: 'focus'
})
```

Disable Elements

Elements with disable attribute aren't interactive, meaning users cannot hover or click them to trigger a popover. As a workaround, we'll want to trigger popover from a wrapper <div> or <span>, ideally made keyboard-focusable using tabindex="0".

For disable popover triggers, we may also prefer data-bs-trigger="hover focus" so that popover appears as immediate visual feedback to our users as they may not expect to *click* on a disable element.

```
<span class="d-inline-block" tabindex="0" data-bs-
    toggle="popover" data-bs-trigger="hover focus"
    data-bs-content="Disable popover">
 <button class="btn btn-primary" type="button"
      disabled>Disable button</button>
</span>
```

PROGRESS

Documentation and examples for creating custom Bootstrap progress bars with stacked bars, animated backdrops, and text labels.

How It Works

Two HTML elements, CSS to set the width, and a few attributes are used to create progress components. We don't use the HTML5 <progress> element, so you can stack, animate, and overlay progress bars with text labels.

- The .progress wrapper is used to indicate the progress bar's maximum value.

- The inner.progress-bar is used to show how far we've come.

- To set the width of the .progress-bar, use an inline style, utility class, or custom CSS.

- To make the progress-bar accessible, it also needs certain role and aria properties.

Eventually, you get the following examples:

```
<div class="progress">
 <div class="progress-bar" role="progressbar" aria-
     valuenow="1" aria-valuemin="1" aria-
     valuemax="99"></div>
</div>
<div class="progress">
 <div class="progress-bar" role="progressbar"
     style="width: 28%" aria-valuenow="28" aria-
     valuemin="1" aria-valuemax="90"></div>
</div>
<div class="progress">
 <div class="progress-bar" role="progressbar"
     style="width: 54%" aria-valuenow="50" aria-
     valuemin="1" aria-valuemax="90"></div>
</div>
<div class="progress">
 <div class="progress-bar" role="progressbar"
     style="width: 79%" aria-valuenow="75" aria-
     valuemin="1" aria-valuemax="90"></div>
</div>
<div class="progress">
 <div class="progress-bar" role="progressbar"
     style="width: 90%" aria-valuenow="90" aria-
     valuemin="1" aria-valuemax="90"></div>
</div>
```

Bootstrap includes a number of tools for adjusting width. Depending on our requirements, these may aid in fast configuring progress.

```
<div class="progress">
 <div class="progress-bar w-79" role="progressbar"
     aria-valuenow="79" aria-valuemin="1" aria-
     valuemax="90"></div>
</div>
```

Labels

Add labels to our progress bars by placing text within the .progress-bar.

```
<div class="progress">
 <div class="progress-bar" role="progressbar"
     style="width: 28%;" aria-valuenow="28" aria-
     valuemin="1" aria-valuemax="90">25%</div>
</div>
```

Height

Set a height value on .progress, so the inner .progress-bar will automatically resize accordingly if we change that value.

```
<div class="progress" style="height: 1px;">
 <div class="progress-bar" role="progressbar"
     style="width: 25%;" aria-valuenow="25" aria-
     valuemin="1" aria-valuemax="90"></div>
</div>
<div class="progress" style="height: 20px;">
 <div class="progress-bar" role="progressbar"
     style="width: 27%;" aria-valuenow="27" aria-
     valuemin="0" aria-valuemax="90"></div>
</div>
```

Backgrounds

To modify look of individual progress bars, use background utility classes.

```
<div class="progress">
 <div class="progress-bar bg-success"
     role="progressbar" style="width: 27%" aria-
     valuenow="27" aria-valuemin="0" aria-
     valuemax="90"></div>
```

```
</div>
<div class="progress">
 <div class="progress-bar bg-info" role="progressbar"
      style="width: 52%" aria-valuenow="52" aria-
      valuemin="0" aria-valuemax="99"></div>
</div>
<div class="progress">
 <div class="progress-bar bg-warning"
      role="progressbar" style="width: 77%" aria-
      valuenow="77" aria-valuemin="0" aria-
      valuemax="99"></div>
</div>
<div class="progress">
 <div class="progress-bar bg-danger"
      role="progressbar" style="width: 90%" aria-
      valuenow="90" aria-valuemin="0" aria-
      valuemax="90"></div>
</div>
```

Multiple Bars

Include the multiple progress bars in a progress component if you need.

```
<div class="progress">
 <div class="progress-bar" role="progressbar"
      style="width: 15%" aria-valuenow="1" aria-
      valuemin="0" aria-valuemax="90"></div>
 <div class="progress-bar bg-success"
      role="progressbar" style="width: 33%" aria-
      valuenow="33" aria-valuemin="0" aria-
      valuemax="90"></div>
 <div class="progress-bar bg-info" role="progressbar"
      style="width: 22%" aria-valuenow="20" aria-
      valuemin="0" aria-valuemax="90"></div>
</div>
```

Stripped

Add .progress-bar-striped to any .progress-bar to apply stripe via CSS gradient over progress bar's background color.

```
<div class="progress">
 <div class="progress-bar progress-bar-striped"
      role="progressbar" style="width: 12%"
```

```
        aria-valuenow="12" aria-valuemin="0" aria-
        valuemax="90"></div>
</div>
<div class="progress">
 <div class="progress-bar progress-bar-striped
        bg-success" role="progressbar" style="width:
        27%" aria-valuenow="27" aria-valuemin="0" aria-
        valuemax="99"></div>
</div>
<div class="progress">
 <div class="progress-bar progress-bar-striped
        bg-info" role="progressbar" style="width: 52%"
        aria-valuenow="52" aria-valuemin="0" aria-
        valuemax="99"></div>
</div>
<div class="progress">
 <div class="progress-bar progress-bar-striped
        bg-warning" role="progressbar" style="width:
        79%" aria-valuenow="79 aria-valuemin="0" aria-
        valuemax="99"></div>
</div>
<div class="progress">
 <div class="progress-bar progress-bar-striped
        bg-danger" role="progressbar" style="width:
        90%" aria-valuenow="90" aria-valuemin="0" aria-
        valuemax="90"></div>
</div>
```

Animated Strips

The striped gradient can animate. Add the .progress-bar-animated to .progress-bar to animate stripes right to left via CSS3 animations.

```
<div class="progress">
 <div class="progress-bar progress-bar-striped
        progress-bar-animated" role="progressbar" aria-
        valuenow="77" aria-valuemin="0" aria-
        valuemax="99" style="width: 77%"></div>
</div>
```

SCROLLSPY

To identify which link is active in the viewport, change Bootstrap navigation or list group components based on scroll position.

How It Works

Scrollspy has a few requirements to function correctly:

- **Navigation**: It must apply to a Bootstrap navigation component or a list group.

- **Position**: relative is required by Scrollspy on the element you're spying on, which is usually the body>.

- **Anchors**: Anchors (a>) are essential and must point to an element with the same id as the anchor.

When correctly implemented, your nav or list group will change accordingly, transferring the .active class from one item to the next depending on their connected targets.

Example in navbar

Watch the active class change as you scroll down below the navbar. The dropdown menu items will also be highlighted.

```
<nav id="navbar-example2" class="navbar navbar-light
bg-light px-3">
 <a class="navbar-brand" href="#">Navbar</a>
 <ul class="nav nav-pills">
  <li class="nav-item">
   <a class="nav-link" href="#scrollspyHeading1">Firs
          t</a>
  </li>
  <li class="nav-item">
   <a class="nav-link" href="#scrollspyHeading2">Seco
          nd</a>
  </li>
  <li class="nav-item dropdown">
   <a class="nav-link dropdown-toggle" data-bs-
     toggle="dropdown" href="#" role="button" aria-
     expanded="false">Dropdown</a>
   <ul class="dropdown-menu">
    <li><a class="dropdown-item" href="#scrollspyHead
          ing3">Third</a></li>
    <li><a class="dropdown-item" href="#scrollspyHead
          ing4">Fourth</a></li>
    <li><hr class="dropdown-divider"></li>
```

```
    <li><a class="dropdown-item" href="#scrollspyHead
        ing5">Fifth</a></li>
  </ul>
  </li>
 </ul>
</nav>
<div data-bs-spy="scroll" data-bs-target="#navbar-
    example2" data-bs-offset="0" class="scrollspy-
    example" tabindex="0">
 <h4 id="scrollspyHeading1">First heading</h4>
 <p>...</p>
 <h4 id="scrollspyHeading2">Second heading</h4>
 <p>...</p>
 <h4 id="scrollspyHeading3">Third heading</h4>
 <p>...</p>
 <h4 id="scrollspyHeading4">Fourth heading</h4>
 <p>...</p>
 <h4 id="scrollspyHeading5">Fifth heading</h4>
 <p>...</p>
</div>
```

Example with Nested nav

Scrollspy can also handle nested.navs. If a nested.nav is .active, then its parents will be as well. Watch the active class change as you scroll the area next to the navbar.

```
<nav id="navbar-example3" class="navbar navbar-light
    bg-light flex-column align-items-stretch p-3">
 <a class="navbar-brand" href="#">Navbar</a>
 <nav class="nav nav-pills flex-column">
  <a class="nav-link" href="#item-1">Item 1</a>
  <nav class="nav nav-pills flex-column">
   <a class="nav-link ms-3 my-1" href="#item-1-
        1">Item 1-1</a>
   <a class="nav-link ms-3 my-1" href="#item-1-
        2">Item 1-2</a>
  </nav>
  <a class="nav-link" href="#item-2">Item 2</a>
  <a class="nav-link" href="#item-3">Item 3</a>
  <nav class="nav nav-pills flex-column">
   <a class="nav-link ms-3 my-1" href="#item-3-
        1">Item 3-1</a>
```

```
    <a class="nav-link ms-3 my-1" href="#item-3-
            2">Item 3-2</a>
  </nav>
 </nav>
</nav>

<div data-bs-spy="scroll" data-bs-target="#navbar-
example3" data-bs-offset="0" tabindex="0">
 <h4 id="item-1">Item 1</h4>
 <p>...</p>
 <h5 id="item-1-1">Item 1-1</h5>
 <p>...</p>
 <h5 id="item-1-2">Item 1-2</h5>
 <p>...</p>
 <h4 id="item-2">Item 2</h4>
 <p>...</p>
 <h4 id="item-3">Item 3</h4>
 <p>...</p>
 <h5 id="item-3-1">Item 3-1</h5>
 <p>...</p>
 <h5 id="item-3-2">Item 3-2</h5>
 <p>...</p>
</div>
```

Example with List-group

.list-groups are also supported by Scrollspy. Watch the active class change as you scroll the area adjacent to the list group.

```
<div id="list-example" class="list-group">
 <a class="list-group-item list-group-item-action"
    href="#list-item-1">Item 1</a>
 <a class="list-group-item list-group-item-action"
    href="#list-item-2">Item 2</a>
 <a class="list-group-item list-group-item-action"
    href="#list-item-3">Item 3</a>
 <a class="list-group-item list-group-item-action"
    href="#list-item-4">Item 4</a>
</div>
<div data-bs-spy="scroll" data-bs-target="#list-
    example" data-bs-offset="0" class="scrollspy-
    example" tabindex="0">
 <h4 id="list-item-1">Item 1</h4>
```

```
<p>...</p>
<h4 id="list-item-2">Item 2</h4>
<p>...</p>
<h4 id="list-item-3">Item 3</h4>
<p>...</p>
<h4 id="list-item-4">Item 4</h4>
<p>...</p>
</div>
```

SPINNERS

Bootstrap spinners, made solely with HTML, CSS, and no JavaScript, are used to indicate the loading state of a component or page in Bootstrap.

About

In your applications, you may use Bootstrap "spinners" to show the loading state. They're made entirely with HTML and CSS, so no JavaScript is required to make them. Toggling their visibility will, however, necessitate some special JavaScript. With our superb utility classes, you can simply adjust their style, alignment, and sizing.

For accessibility purposes, each loader here includes role="status" and nested <span class="visually-hidden">Loading...</span>.

Border Spinner

The border spinners can be used as a light loading indicator.

```
<div class="spinner-border" role="status">
 <span class="visually-hidden">Loading...</span>
</div>
```

Colors

The border spinner's border color is set by currentColor, which means you can change it with text color utilities. On the regular spinner, you can choose any of our text color utilities.

```
<div class="spinner-border text-primary"
     role="status">
 <span class="visually-hidden">Loading...</span>
</div>
<div class="spinner-border text-secondary"
     role="status">
```

```
 <span class="visually-hidden">Loading...</span>
</div>
<div class="spinner-border text-success"
     role="status">
 <span class="visually-hidden">Loading...</span>
</div>
<div class="spinner-border text-danger"
     role="status">
 <span class="visually-hidden">Loading...</span>
</div>
<div class="spinner-border text-warning"
     role="status">
 <span class="visually-hidden">Loading...</span>
</div>
<div class="spinner-border text-info" role="status">
 <span class="visually-hidden">Loading...</span>
</div>
<div class="spinner-border text-light" role="status">
 <span class="visually-hidden">Loading...</span>
</div>
<div class="spinner-border text-dark" role="status">
 <span class="visually-hidden">Loading...</span>
</div>
```

Growing Spinner

Switch to the grow spinner if you don't want to use a border spinner. It doesn't technically spin, but it does grow on a regular basis!

```
<div class="spinner-grow" role="status">
 <span class="visually-hidden">Loading...</span>
</div>
```

This spinner is designed with currentColor yet again, allowing you to simply modify its appearance using text color utilities. It is highlighted in blue, along with the versions that are supported.

```
<div class="spinner-grow text-primary" role="status">
 <span class="visually-hidden">Loading...</span>
</div>
<div class="spinner-grow text-secondary"
     role="status">
 <span class="visually-hidden">Loading...</span>
```

```
</div>
<div class="spinner-grow text-success" role="status">
 <span class="visually-hidden">Loading...</span>
</div>
<div class="spinner-grow text-danger" role="status">
 <span class="visually-hidden">Loading...</span>
</div>
<div class="spinner-grow text-warning" role="status">
 <span class="visually-hidden">Loading...</span>
</div>
<div class="spinner-grow text-info" role="status">
 <span class="visually-hidden">Loading...</span>
</div>
<div class="spinner-grow text-light" role="status">
 <span class="visually-hidden">Loading...</span>
</div>
<div class="spinner-grow text-dark" role="status">
 <span class="visually-hidden">Loading...</span>
</div>
```

Alignment

Rems, currentColor, and display: inline-flex are used to create spinners in Bootstrap. This allows them to be easily resized, recolored, and aligned.

Margin

Use margin utilities like .m-5 for easy spacing.

```
<div class="spinner-border m-5" role="status">
 <span class="visually-hidden">Loading...</span>
</div>
```

Placement

Use flexbox utilities, float utilities, or text alignment utilities to place spinners exactly where you need them in any situation.

Flex

```
<div class="d-flex justify-content-center">
 <div class="spinner-border" role="status">
  <span class="visually-hidden">Loading...</span>
 </div>
</div>
```

```
<div class="d-flex align-items-center">
 <strong>Loading...</strong>
 <div class="spinner-border ms-auto" role="status"
      aria-hidden="true"></div>
</div>
```

Float

```
<div class="clearfix">
 <div class="spinner-border float-end" role="status">
  <span class="visually-hidden">Loading...</span>
 </div>
</div>
```

Text Aligns

```
<div class="text-center">
 <div class="spinner-border" role="status">
  <span class="visually-hidden">Loading...</span>
 </div>
</div>
```

Size

Add .spinner-border-sm and .spinner-grow-sm to make a more petite spinner that can quickly be used within other components.

```
<div class="spinner-border spinner-border-sm"
     role="status">
 <span class="visually-hidden">Loading...</span>
</div>
<div class="spinner-grow spinner-grow-sm"
     role="status">
 <span class="visually-hidden">Loading...</span>
</div>
```

Or use custom CSS or inline styles to change the dimensions as needed.

```
<div class="spinner-border" style="width: 3rem;
     height: 3rem;" role="status">
 <span class="visually-hidden">Loading...</span>
</div>
<div class="spinner-grow" style="width: 3rem; height:
     3rem;" role="status">
```

```
 <span class="visually-hidden">Loading...</span>
</div>
```

Buttons

To signify that an action is currently processing or taking place, use spinners within buttons. You can also remove the text from the spinner element and replace it with button text.

```
<button class="btn btn-primary" type="button" disabled>
 <span class="spinner-border spinner-border-sm"
       role="status" aria-hidden="true"></span>
 <span class="visually-hidden">Loading...</span>
</button>
<button class="btn btn-primary" type="button" disabled>
 <span class="spinner-border spinner-border-sm"
       role="status" aria-hidden="true"></span>
 Loading...
</button>

<button class="btn btn-primary" type="button" disabled>
 <span class="spinner-grow spinner-grow-sm"
       role="status" aria-hidden="true"></span>
 <span class="visually-hidden">Loading...</span>
</button>
<button class="btn btn-primary" type="button" disabled>
 <span class="spinner-grow spinner-grow-sm"
       role="status" aria-hidden="true"></span>
 Loading...
</button>
```

TOASTS

With a toast, a lightweight and readily configurable alert message, send notifications to your visitors.

Toasts are little notifications that are meant to look like the push notifications that have become popular on mobile and desktop operating systems. Because they're made with flexbox, they're simple to align and place.

Overview

- When utilizing the toast plugin, keep in mind that toasts are opt-in for performance reasons, therefore you'll have to set them up yourself.

- If you don't provide autohide: false, toasts will be hidden automatically.

Examples

Basic

A header and body are recommended to encourage extendable and predictable toasts. Display: flex is used in toast headers, allowing for easy content alignment, thanks to our margin and flexbox utilities.

Toasts can be as customizable as you like and require very little markup. At a bare least, your "toasted" material must be contained in a single element, and a dismiss button is strongly recommended.

```
<div class="toast" role="alert" aria-live="assertive"
     aria-atomic="true">
 <div class="toast-header">
  <img src="..." class="rounded me-2" alt="...">
  <strong class="me-auto">Bootstrap</strong>
  <small>11 mins ago</small>
  <button type="button" class="btn-close" data-bs-
    dismiss="toast" aria-label="Close"></button>
 </div>
 <div class="toast-body">
  Hello, everyone! This is toast message.
 </div>
</div>
```

Live

Click the button below to reveal a toast (located in the lower right corner alongside our utilities) that was previously concealed by default. hide.

```
<button type="button" class="btn btn-primary"
        id="liveToastBtn">Show live toast</button>

<div class="position-fixed bottom-0 end-0 p-3"
     style="z-index: 11">
 <div id="liveToast" class="toast hide" role="alert"
      aria-live="assertive" aria-atomic="true">
  <div class="toast-header">
   <img src="..." class="rounded me-2" alt="...">
   <strong class="me-auto">Bootstrap</strong>
   <small>12 mins ago</small>
   <button type="button" class="btn-close" data-bs-
     dismiss="toast" aria-label="Close"></button>
  </div>
  <div class="toast-body">
```

```
    Hello, everyone! This is toast message.
  </div>
 </div>
</div>
```

Translucent

To blend in with what's below, toasts are slightly transparent.

```
<div class="toast" role="alert" aria-live="assertive"
     aria-atomic="true">
 <div class="toast-header">
  <img src="..." class="rounded me-2" alt="...">
  <strong class="me-auto">Bootstrap</strong>
  <small class="text-muted">11 mins ago</small>
  <button type="button" class="btn-close" data-bs-
    dismiss="toast" aria-label="Close"></button>
 </div>
 <div class="toast-body">
  Hello, world! This is a toast message.
 </div>
</div>
```

Stacking

You can stack toasts by wrapping them in a toast container, which will vertically add some spacing.

```
<div class="toast-container">
 <div class="toast" role="alert" aria-live="assertive"
     aria-atomic="true">
  <div class="toast-header">
   <img src="..." class="rounded me-2" alt="...">
   <strong class="me-auto">Bootstrap</strong>
   <small class="text-muted">just now</small>
   <button type="button" class="btn-close" data-bs-
     dismiss="toast" aria-label="Close"></button>
  </div>
  <div class="toast-body">
   See? Just like this.
  </div>
 </div>

 <div class="toast" role="alert" aria-live="assertive"
     aria-atomic="true">
```

```
  <div class="toast-header">
   <img src="..." class="rounded me-2" alt="...">
   <strong class="me-auto">Bootstrap</strong>
   <small class="text-muted">2 seconds ago</small>
   <button type="button" class="btn-close" data-bs-
      dismiss="toast" aria-label="Close"></button>
  </div>
  <div class="toast-body">
   Heads up, toasts will stack automatically
  </div>
 </div>
</div>
```

Custom Content

Remove subcomponents, alter them using utilities, or add own markup to personalize your toasts. Here we've created a more straightforward toast by eliminating the default .toast-header, adding a custom hide icon from Bootstrap icons, and using some flexbox utilities to adjust the layout.

```
<div class="toast align-items-center" role="alert"
     aria-live="assertive" aria-atomic="true">
 <div class="d-flex">
  <div class="toast-body">
  Hello, everyone This is toast message.
  </div>
  <button type="button" class="btn-close me-2 m-auto"
    data-bs-dismiss="toast" aria-label="Close"></button>
 </div>
</div>
```

Toasts can also be enhanced with additional controls and components.

```
<div class="toast" role="alert" aria-live="assertive"
     aria-atomic="true">
 <div class="toast-body">
  Hello, world! This is a toast message.
  <div class="mt-2 pt-2 border-top">
   <button type="button" class="btn btn-primary btn-
          sm">Take action</button>
   <button type="button" class="btn btn-secondary
     btn-sm" data-bs-dismiss="toast">Close</button>
  </div>
```

```
  </div>
</div>
```

Color Schemes

Using our color and background utilities, you can generate alternative color schemes based on the example above. We've added .bg-primary and .text-white to the .toast file, and then .btn-close-white to the close button. With .border-0, we eliminate the default border for a cleaner look.

```
<div class="toast align-items-center text-white
     bg-primary border-0" role="alert" aria-
     live="assertive" aria-atomic="true">
 <div class="d-flex">
  <div class="toast-body">
   Hello, world! This is a toast message.
  </div>
  <button type="button" class="btn-close btn-close-
          white me-2 m-auto" data-bs-dismiss="toast"
          aria-label="Close"></button>
 </div>
</div>
```

Placement

As needed, add toasts using custom CSS. The top right and the upper middle are frequently utilized for alerts. If you're only going to display one toast at a time, the placement styles are correct on the .toast.

```
<form>
 <div class="mb-3">
  <label for="selectToastPlacement">Toast placement</
              label>
  <select class="form-select mt-2"
                 id="selectToastPlacement">
   <option value="" selected>Select a position...</
           option>
   <option value="top-0 start-0">Top left</option>
   <option value="top-0 start-50 translate-middle-
           x">Top center</option>
   <option value="top-0 end-0">Top right</option>
   <option value="top-50 start-0 translate-middle-
           y">Middle left</option>
```

```
    <option value="top-50 start-50 translate-
          middle">Middle center</option>
    <option value="top-50 end-0 translate-middle-
          y">Middle right</option>
    <option value="bottom-0 start-0">Bottom left</
          option>
    <option value="bottom-0 start-50 translate-middle-
          x">Bottom center</option>
    <option value="bottom-0 end-0">Bottom right</
          option>
  </select>
 </div>
</form>
<div aria-live="polite" aria-atomic="true" class="bg-
     dark position-relative bd-example-toasts">
 <div class="toast-container position-absolute p-3"
       id="toastPlacement">
  <div class="toast">
   <div class="toast-header">
    <img src="..." class="rounded me-2" alt="...">
    <strong class="me-auto">Bootstrap</strong>
    <small>12 mins ago</small>
   </div>
   <div class="toast-body">
    Hello, everyone This is toast message.
   </div>
  </div>
 </div>
</div>
```

Consider utilizing a wrapper element for systems that create a lot of notifications so that they can stack effortlessly.

```
<div aria-live="polite" aria-atomic="true"
     class="position-relative">
 <!-- Position it: -->
 <!-- - `.toast-container` for spacing between toasts -->
 <!-- - `.position-absolute`, `top-0` & `end-0` to
    position the toasts in the upper right corner -->
 <!-- - `.p-3` to prevent the toasts from sticking to
    the edge of the container -->
 <div class="toast-container position-absolute top-0
     end-0 p-3">
```

```
  <!-- Then put toasts within -->
  <div class="toast" role="alert" aria-
live="assertive" aria-atomic="true">
   <div class="toast-header">
    <img src="..." class="rounded me-2" alt="...">
    <strong class="me-auto">Bootstrap</strong>
    <small class="text-muted">just now</small>
    <button type="button" class="btn-close" data-bs-
      dismiss="toast" aria-label="Close"></button>
   </div>
   <div class="toast-body">
    See? Just like this.
   </div>
  </div>


  <div class="toast" role="alert" aria-
      live="assertive" aria-atomic="true">
   <div class="toast-header">
    <img src="..." class="rounded me-2" alt="...">
    <strong class="me-auto">Bootstrap</strong>
    <small class="text-muted">2 seconds ago</small>
    <button type="button" class="btn-close" data-bs-
      dismiss="toast" aria-label="Close"></button>
   </div>
   <div class="toast-body">
    Heads up, toasts will stack automatically
   </div>
  </div>
 </div>
</div>
```

You can get fancy with flexbox utilities to align toasts horizontally and vertically.

```
<!-- Flexbox container for aligning the toasts -->
<div aria-live="polite" aria-atomic="true" class="d-
  flex justify-content-left align-items-center w-90">

 <!-- Then put toasts within -->
 <div class="toast" role="alert" aria-live="assertive"
     aria-atomic="true">
  <div class="toast-header">
```

```
  <img src="..." class="rounded me-2" alt="...">
  <strong class="me-auto">Bootstrap</strong>
  <small>11 mins ago</small>
  <button type="button" class="btn-close" data-bs-
    dismiss="toast" aria-label="Close"></button>
 </div>
 <div class="toast-body">
  Hello, world! This is a toast message.
 </div>
 </div>
</div>
```

Accessibility

Because toasts are intended to be minor disruptions to your visitors or users, you should wrap them in an aria-live area to aid individuals who use screen readers and other assistive technology. Screen readers automatically communicate changes to live areas (such as injecting/updating a toast component) without needing to relocate the user's attention or otherwise disturb the user. Include aria-atomic="true" as well to guarantee that the full toast is always announced as a single (atomic) unit, rather than only declaring what changed (which might cause difficulties if you update part of the toast's content, or if showing the same toast content at a later point in time). If the information required is critical to the workflow, like as a list of problems in a form, then use the alert component rather than toast.

Note that the live region must be present in the markup *before* the toast is generated or updated. If you produce both dynamically and inject them into the website at the same time, assistive technologies are unlikely to notice.

You must also adjust the role and aria-live level based on the material. If the message is critical, such as an error, use the role="alert" aria-live="assertive" attributes; otherwise, use the role="status" aria-live="polite" attributes.

Make sure to adjust the delay timeout when the material you're presenting changes so that viewers have ample time to read the toast.

```
<div class="toast" role="alert" aria-live="polite"
     aria-atomic="true" data-bs-delay="11000">
 <div role="alert" aria-live="assertive" aria-
     atomic="true">...</div>
</div>
```

When using autohide: false, you must add close button to allow users to dismiss the toast.

```
<div role="alert" aria-live="assertive" aria-
                atomic="true" class="toast"
                data-bs-autohide="false">
 <div class="toast-header">
  <img src="..." class="rounded me-2" alt="...">
  <strong class="me-auto">Bootstrap</strong>
  <small>11 mins ago</small>
  <button type="button" class="btn-close" data-bs-
    dismiss="toast" aria-label="Close"></button>
 </div>
 <div class="toast-body">
  Hello, everyone This is toast message.
 </div>
</div>
```

While it is technically feasible to include focusable/actionable controls in your toast (such as buttons or links), you should avoid doing so for autohiding toasts. Even if you set a long delay timeout for the toast, keyboard and assistive technology users may struggle to reach it in time to take action (since toasts do not gain focus when presented). If you must include more controls, we propose using a toast with autohide: false.

TOOLTIPS

Documentation and examples for customizing Bootstrap tooltips with CSS and JavaScript, including animations with CSS3 and local title storage with data-bs-attributes.

Overview

When using the tooltip plugin, keep the following in mind:

- Popper, a third-party package, is used to place tooltips. Popper.min .js must be included before bootstrap.js, or bootstrap.bundle.min.js/ bootstrap.bundle.js must be used for tooltips. Let's get to work!

- You must manually establish tooltips because they are opt-in for performance reasons.

- Tooltips with titles of zero length are never shown.

- To avoid rendering issues with more complicated components, provide container:'body' (like our input groups, button groups, etc.).

- Tooltips will not be triggered on hidden elements

- A wrapper element must be used to trigger tooltips for .disabled or disabled elements

- Tooltips will be centered when triggered by hyperlinks that span multiple lines. To avoid this, use white-space: nowrap; on your s.

- Before their related elements are deleted from the DOM, tooltips must be disabled.

- An element within a shadow DOM can be used to trigger tooltips.

Example: Enable Tooltips Everywhere

Selecting all tooltips on a page by their data-bs-toggle attribute is one approach to initialize them all:

```
var tooltipTriggerList = [].slice.call(document.qu
    erySelectorAll('[data-bs-toggle="tooltip"]'))
var tooltipList = tooltipTriggerList.map(function
    (tooltipTriggerEl) {
 return new bootstrap.Tooltip(tooltipTriggerEl)
})
```

Example

Hover your cursor over the links below to display tooltips:

Hover over the following buttons to view the four tooltip directions: top, right, bottom, and left. When using Bootstrap in RTL, the directions are mirrored.

```
<button type="button" class="btn btn-secondary" data-
        bs-toggle="tooltip" data-bs-placement="top"
        title="Tooltip on top">
 Tooltip on top
</button>
<button type="button" class="btn btn-secondary" data-
        bs-toggle="tooltip" data-bs-placement="right"
        title="Tooltip on right">
```

```
 Tooltip on right
</button>
<button type="button" class="btn btn-secondary" data-
        bs-toggle="tooltip" data-bs-placement="bottom"
        title="Tooltip on bottom">
 Tooltip on bottom
</button>
<button type="button" class="btn btn-secondary" data-
        bs-toggle="tooltip" data-bs-placement="left"
        title="Tooltip on left">
 Tooltip on left
</button>
```

And with custom HTML added:
```
<button type="button" class="btn btn-secondary" data-
        bs-toggle="tooltip" data-bs-html="true"
        title="<em>Tooltip</em> with HTML">
 Tooltip with the HTML
</button>
```

CONCLUSION

This was all about components that Bootstrap offers. It is a very long section of bootstrap components; now, it is finally time for the next chapter to learn helpers.

CHAPTER 7

Helpers

IN THIS CHAPTER

- ➤ Clearfix
- ➤ Colored Links
- ➤ Ratio
- ➤ Position
- ➤ Stacks
- ➤ Visually Hidden
- ➤ Stretched Link
- ➤ Text Truncation
- ➤ Verticle Rule

In the previous chapter, we learned in detail about the component that Bootstrap offers. Now, it is finally time to learn helper.

We will learn about the cheap fix, colored links, ratio, and many more. Let's jump to the first section of this chapter: Clearfix.

CLEARFIX

You may quickly and simply clear floating content by adding a clearfix function to a container.

Let's jump to the first HTML code and learn in detail about it.

DOI: 10.1201/9781003310501-7

Quickly clear floats by adding .clearfix to the parent element. It can also be used as a mixin.

Use in HTML:

```
<div class="clearfix">...</div>
```

The mixin source code:

```
@mixin clearfix() {
 &::after {
  display: block;
  clear: both;
  content: "";
 }
}
```

Use the mixin in SCSS:

```
.element {
 @include clearfix;
}
```

The clearfix is demonstrated in the following example. The wrapping div would not span across the buttons without the clearfix, resulting in a broken layout.

```
<div class="bg-info clearfix">
 <button type="button" class="btn btn-secondary
   float-start">Example Button floated left</button>
 <button type="button" class="btn btn-secondary
   float-end">Example Button floated right</button>
</div>
```

After learning clearfix, it is now time to start over the next section: Colored Links.

COLORED LINKS

With colored links with hover states, you can even give a specific color to your connection.

You can use the .link-* classes to color links. Unlike the .text-* courses, these classes have a :hover and :focus state.

```
<a href="#" class="link-primary">Primary link</a>
<a href="#" class="link-secondary">Secondary link</a>
<a href="#" class="link-success">Success link</a>
<a href="#" class="link-danger">Danger link</a>
<a href="#" class="link-warning">Warning link</a>
<a href="#" class="link-info">Info link</a>
<a href="#" class="link-light">Light link</a>
<a href="#" class="link-dark">Dark link</a>
```

After learning how to color links, now it is time to start our next section: Ratios.

RATIOS

To make an element keep the aspect ratio of your choice, use created pseudo-elements. Perfect for managing video or slideshow, embeds are responsively dependent on the parent's width.

Let's jump to the next section dealing with what ratios are and how to use them.

ABOUT

To manage the ratios of external content such as <iframe>s, <embed>s, <video>s, and <object>s, use the <ratio helper>. These tools can also be applied to any regular HTML child element (for example, a <div> or an <image>). Styles are applied to the kid directly from the parent.ratio class.

Custom aspect ratios are possible, thanks to a Sass map that declares them and includes them in each class via a CSS variable.

Pro-Tip! You don't require frameborder="0" on your iframes because Reboot takes care of that for you.

Now let's see the example of the ratio.

Example

Wrap any embed, such as an <iframe>, in a parent element with the .ratio and aspect ratio classes. Thanks to our universal selector.ratio > *, the immediate child element is automatically sized.

```
<div class="ratio ratio-16×9">
  <iframe src="https://www.youtube.com/embed/zpOULjyy
          -n8?rel=0" title="YouTube-video"
          allowfullscreen></iframe>
</div>
```

Aspect Ratio

Modifier classes can be used to change aspect ratios. The following ratio classes are available by default:

```
<div class="ratio ratio-1x1">
 <div>1x1</div>
</div>
<div class="ratio ratio-4x3">
 <div>4x3</div>
</div>
<div class="ratio ratio-16x9">
 <div>16x9</div>
</div>
<div class="ratio ratio-21x9">
 <div>21x9</div>
</div>
```

Custom Ratio

A CSS custom property (or CSS variable) is included in the selector for each .ratio-* class. With some simple arithmetic, you can override this CSS variable to generate different aspect ratios on the fly.

> Set—bs-aspect-ratio: 50% on the .ratio to produce a 2×1 aspect ratio, for example.

```
<div class="ratio" style="--bs-aspect-ratio: 50%;">
 <div>2x1</div>
</div>
```

This CSS variable makes changing the aspect ratio across breakpoints a breeze. The following is 4×3 at first, but at the medium breakpoint, it switches to a bespoke 2×1.

```
. ratio-4x3 {
@include media-breakpoint-up(md) {
  --bs-aspect-ratio: 50%; // 2x1
 }
}
```

```
<div class="ratio ratio-4x3">
 <div>4x3, then 2x1</div>
</div>
```

After completing the ratio section of this chapter, let's move to the next section: Position.

POSITION

Use these helpers tools to configure an element's position easily.

Fixed Top

Place an element from edge to edge at the top of the viewport. Be sure you understand the ramifications of a fixed position in your project; you may need additional CSS.

```
<div class="fixed-top">...</div>
```

Fixed Bottom

Place an element from edge to edge at the bottom of the viewport. Make sure you're aware of the implications of a fixed location in your project; you may need more CSS.

```
<div class="fixed-bottom">...</div>
```

Sticky Top

Position an element from edge to edge at the top of the screen, but only after you've scrolled past it. The .sticky-top utility makes use of the CSS position: sticky property, which isn't supported by all browsers.

```
<div class="sticky-top">...</div>
```

Responsive Sticky Top

Responsive variations also exist for .sticky-top utility.

```
<div class="sticky-sm-top">Stay to the top on
    viewports sized SM (small) or wider</div>
<div class="sticky-md-top">Stay to the top on
    viewports sized MD (medium) or wider</div>
<div class="sticky-lg-top">Stay to the top on
    viewports sized LG (large) or wider</div>
<div class="sticky-xl-top">Stay to the top on
    viewports sized XL (extra-large) or wider</div>
```

After learning ratios, now it is time to start our next section: Visually Hidden.

VISUALLY HIDDEN

Use these helpers to hide elements visually but keep them accessible to assistive technologies.

Visually hide an element while still exposing it to assistive technologies (such as screen readers) with .visually-hidden. Make use of .visually-hidden-focusable by default, but when it is focused (for example, by a keyboard-only user), use the visually-hidden-focusable property. Visually-hidden-focusable can be applied to a container, which will be displayed when any child element takes focus, thanks to focus-within.

```
<h2 class="visually-hidden">Title for screen readers</h2>
<a class="visually-hidden-focusable"
   href="#content">Skip to main content</a>
<div class="visually-hidden-focusable">A container
     with a <a href="#">focusable element</a>.</div>
```

Both visually-hidden and visually-hidden-focusable can also be used as mixins.

// Usage as a mixin

```
.visually-hidden-title {
 @include visually-hidden;
}

.skip-navigation {
 @include visually-hidden-focusable;
}
```

After learning how to hide, it is now time to start our next section: Stretched Link.

STRETCHED LINK

By using CSS to "stretch" a nested link, you may make any HTML element or Bootstrap component clickable.

Add .stretched-link to a link to make its containing block clickable via a::after pseudo-element. In most circumstances, this means that a link with the .stretched-link class is clickable if it has the position: relative; element. Keep in mind that because of the way CSS position works, .stretched-link cannot be used with most table components.

Cards have position: relative by default, you can safely add the .stretched-link class to a link in the card without making any other HTML changes.

With stretched links, multiple links and tap targets are not suggested. However, if this is necessary, some position and z-index styles can be useful.

```
<div class="card" style="width: 18rem;">
 <img src="..." class="card-img-top" alt="...">
 <div class="card-body">
  <h5 class="card-title">Card with stretched link</h5>
  <p class="card-text">Some quick example text to
     build on the card title and make up the bulk of
     the card's content.</p>
  <a href="#" class="btn btn-primary stretched-
     link">Go somewhere</a>
 </div>
</div>
```

Because most custom components do not have position: relative by default, we must add the .position-relative here to keep the link from expanding beyond the parent element.

```
<div class="d-flex position-relative">
 <img src="..." class="flex-shrink-0 me-3" alt="...">
 <div>
  <h5 class="mt-0">Custom component with stretched
     link</h5>
  <p>This is a placeholder for the custom component's
content. It is meant to resemble the appearance of
real-world stuff, and we're utilizing it here to give
the component some body and scale.</p>
  <a href="#" class="stretched-link">Go somewhere</a>
 </div>
</div>

<div class="row g-0 bg-light position-relative">
 <div class="col-md-6 mb-md-0 p-md-4">
  <img src="..." class="w-100" alt="...">
 </div>
 <div class="col-md-6 p-4 ps-md-0">
  <h5 class="mt-0">Columns with stretched link</h5>
```

```
<p>For this other custom component, there is still
another instance of placeholder content. It is meant
to resemble the appearance of real-world content, and
we're utilizing it here to give the component some
body and size.</p>
  <a href="#" class="stretched-link">Go somewhere</a>
 </div>
</div>
```

Identifying the Containing Block

If the stretched link fails to work, the contained block is most likely to blame. The CSS properties listed below will make an element the enclosing block:

- Other than static, a position value

- Other than none, a transform or perspective value

- A transformative or perceptive value that will alter.

- Filter value other than none or a variable filter value.

Note: This only works on Firefox.

```
<div class="card" style="width: 18rem;">
 <img src="..." class="card-img-top" alt="...">
 <div class="card-body">
  <h5 class="card-title">Card with stretched links</h5>
  <p class="card-text">Some quick example text to
     build on the card title and make up the bulk of
     the card's content.</p>
  <p class="card-text">
   <a href="#" class="stretched-link text-danger"
      style="position: relative;">Stretched link will
      not work here, because <code>position:
      relative</code> is added to the link</a>
  </p>
  <p class="card-text bg-light" style="transform:
     rotate(0);">
    This <a href="#" class="text-warning stretched-
link">stretched link</a> will only be spread over the
<code>p</code>-tag, because a transform is applied to
it.
```

```
 </p>
 </div>
</div>
```

After learning stretched link, now it is time to start our next section: Text Truncation.

TEXT TRUNCATION

Using an ellipsis, truncate long strings of text.

You can use the .text-truncate class to truncate the text with an ellipsis for lengthy content. Requires *display: inline-block* or *display: block*.

```
<!-- Block level -->
<div class="row">
 <div class="col-2 text-truncate">
  Praeteream iter est quasdam res quas ex communi.
 </div>
</div>

<!-- Inline level -->
<span class="d-inline-block text-truncate"
style="max-width: 150px;">
 Praeteream iter est quasdam res quas ex communi.
</span>
```

CONCLUSION

In this chapter, we learned essential things like how to color links, ratios, how to hide something, text truncations, etc. Now it is time to jump over our next chapter, in which we will learn about utilities.

CHAPTER 8

Utilities

IN THIS CHAPTER

- ➢ Backgrounds
- ➢ Borders
- ➢ Colors
- ➢ Display
- ➢ Flex
- ➢ Float
- ➢ Interactions
- ➢ Overflow
- ➢ Position
- ➢ Shadows
- ➢ Sizing
- ➢ Spacing
- ➢ Text
- ➢ Verticle Align
- ➢ Visibility

DOI: 10.1201/9781003310501-8

In the previous chapter, we learned essential things like how to color links, ratios, how to hide something, text truncations, etc. Now it is time to learn about utilities that Bootstrap offers.

Let's focus our attention to the first section of this chapter: Background.

BACKGROUND

Convey meaning through background color and add decoration with gradients.

Background Color

Set background of an element to any contextual type, just like the contextual text color classes. Background utilities *do not set* color, so you'll want to use .text-* color utilities in some cases.

```
<div class="p-3 mb-2 bg-primary text-white">.
    bg-primary</div>
<div class="p-3 mb-2 bg-secondary text-white">.
    bg-secondary</div>
<div class="p-3 mb-2 bg-success text-white">.
    bg-success</div>
<div class="p-3 mb-2 bg-danger text-white">.
    bg-danger</div>
<div class="p-3 mb-2 bg-warning text-dark">.
    bg-warning</div>
<div class="p-3 mb-2 bg-info text-dark">.bg-info</div>
<div class="p-3 mb-2 bg-light text-dark">.bg-light</div>
<div class="p-3 mb-2 bg-dark text-white">.bg-dark</div>
<div class="p-3 mb-2 bg-body text-dark">.bg-body</div>
<div class="p-3 mb-2 bg-white text-dark">.bg-white</div>
<div class="p-3 mb-2 bg-transparent text-dark">.
    bg-transparent</div>
```

These were solid background colors; let's learn about background gradients for more attractive colors pallets.

Background Gradient

A linear gradient is added as a backdrop picture to the background by adding the .bg-gradient class. This gradient begins with a semitransparent white and gradually fades to the bottom.

Is a gradient required in your bespoke CSS? Simply include the following code: background-image: var (--bs-gradient).

This was a utility background; now it is time for learning borders.

BORDERS

To create or delete borders from an element, use border utilities. Choose from all of the edges or one by one.

Additive

```
<span class="border"></span>
<span class="border-top"></span>
<span class="border-end"></span>
<span class="border-bottom"></span>
<span class="border-start"></span>
```

After learning additives, now it is time for subtractive.

Subtractive

```
<span class="border-0"></span>
<span class="border-top-0"></span>
<span class="border-end-0"></span>
<span class="border-bottom-0"></span>
<span class="border-start-0"></span>
```

When making things attractive, borders colors play a substantial role. Let's learn how to add border colors.

Border Color

Change border color using utilities built on our theme colors.

```
<span class="border border-primary"></span>
<span class="border border-secondary"></span>
<span class="border border-success"></span>
<span class="border border-danger"></span>
<span class="border border-warning"></span>
<span class="border border-info"></span>
<span class="border border-light"></span>
<span class="border border-dark"></span>
<span class="border border-white"></span>
```

Resizing borders are significant; now we will learn about the width of the frame.

Border-Width

```
<span class="border border-1"></span>
<span class="border border-2"></span>
<span class="border border-3"></span>
<span class="border border-4"></span>
<span class="border border-5"></span>
```

Border-Radios

Add classes to an element to quickly round its corners.

```
<img src="..." class="rounded" alt="...">
<img src="..." class="rounded-top" alt="...">
<img src="..." class="rounded-end" alt="...">
<img src="..." class="rounded-bottom" alt="...">
<img src="..." class="rounded-start" alt="...">
<img src="..." class="rounded-circle" alt="...">
<img src="..." class="rounded-pill" alt="...">
```

Sizes

For larger or smaller rounded corners, use the scaling classes. Sizes may be set between 0 and 3 by altering the utility API.

```
<img src="..." class="rounded-0" alt="...">
<img src="..." class="rounded-1" alt="...">
<img src="..." class="rounded-2" alt="...">
<img src="..." class="rounded-3" alt="...">
```

This was about the Bootstrap utility borders. Now let's jump to our next section and learn about the utility colors.

COLORS

With a few color utility classes, you can convey meaning through color. Support for styling links with hover states is also included.

Color text with color utilities. You can use the .link-* helper classes with hover and focus states if you want to color links.

```
<p class="text-primary">.text-primary</p>
<p class="text-secondary">.text-secondary</p>
<p class="text-success">.text-success</p>
<p class="text-danger">.text-danger</p>
<p class="text-warning bg-dark">.text-warning</p>
<p class="text-info bg-dark">.text-info</p>
<p class="text-light bg-dark">.text-light</p>
<p class="text-dark">.text-dark</p>
<p class="text-body">.text-body</p>
<p class="text-muted">.text-muted</p>
<p class="text-white bg-dark">.text-white</p>
<p class="text-black-50">.text-black-50</p>
<p class="text-white-50 bg-dark">.text-white-50</p>
```

This was about the Bootstrap utility colors; now let's jump to our next section and learn about the utility display.

DISPLAY

With our display tools, you can quickly and easily change the display value of components and more. Support for some of the most common values is included, as well as some extras for managing display when printing.

Let's get further and learn about how it works.

How It Works

With our responsive display utility classes, you may change the value of the display property. We only support a subset of all potential values for display on purpose. Courses can be mixed and matched to create a variety of effects.

Notation

There is no breakpoint shorthand in display utility classes that apply to all breakpoints, from xs to XXL. These classes aren't constrained by a media query because they're utilized from min-width: 0; and up. However, the remaining breakpoints do have a breakpoint abbreviation.

- .d-{value} for xs

- .d-{breakpoint}-{value} for sm, lg, md, xl, and xxl.

Where *value* is one of:

- none

- inline

- inline-block

- block

- grid

- table

- table-cell

- table-row

- flex

- inline-flex

By modifying the $displays variable and recompiling the SCSS, you may change the display values.

The media queries have an effect on screen widths that are at or above the specified breakpoint. As an example, display: none on LG, xl, and XXL screens with d-LG-none sets.

Examples

```
<div class="d-inline p-2 bg-primary text-white">d-
    inline</div>
<div class="d-inline p-2 bg-dark text-white">d-
    inline</div>

<span class="d-block p-2 bg-primary text-white">d-
    block</span>
<span class="d-block p-2 bg-dark text-white">d-
    block</span>
```

Hiding Elements

Use responsive display classes to show and hide components based on the device for faster mobile development. Instead of generating separate versions of the same site for different screen sizes, consider hiding features responsively.

Simply use the .d-none or one of the .d-none classes to conceal elements.

For every responsive screen modification, use the d-{sm,md,lg,xl,xxl}-none classes.

You can combine one to show an element exclusively on a specific range of screen sizes.

For instance, you may use a.d-*-* class with a d-*-none class.

d-none d-none d-none

d-md-block d-md-block d-md-block d-m

d-xl-none d-xl-none d-xl-none d-

Except for medium and large smartphones, d-xxl-none will conceal the element for all screen sizes.

Screen Size	Class
Hidden on all	.d-none
Hidden only on xs	.d-none.d-sm-block
Hidden only on sm	.d-sm-none.d-md-block
Hidden only on md	.d-md-none.d-lg-block
Hidden only on lg	.d-lg-none.d-xl-block
Hidden only on xl	.d-xl-none.d-xxl-block
Hidden only on xxl	.d-xxl-none
Visible on all	.d-block

Visible only on xs	.d-block.d-sm-none
Visible only on sm	.d-none.d-sm-block.d-md-none
Visible only on md	.d-none.d-md-block.d-lg-none
Visible only on lg	.d-none.d-lg-block.d-xl-none
Visible only on xl	.d-none.d-xl-block.d-xxl-none
Visible only on xxl	.d-none.d-xxl-block

```
<div class="d-lg-none">hide on lg and wider screens</
div>
<div class="d-none d-lg-block">hide on screens
smaller than lg</div>
```

Display in Print

Using our print display utility classes, you may change the display value of items while printing. Support for the same display values as our responsive is included. Utilities denoted by .d-*:

- .d-print-none
- .d-print-inline
- .d-print-inline-block
- .d-print-block
- .d-print-grid
- .d-print-table
- .d-print-table-row
- .d-print-table-cell
- .d-print-flex
- .d-print-inline-flex

The print and display classes can be combined.

```
<div class="d-print-none">Screen Only (Hide on print
    only)</div>
<div class="d-none d-print-block">Print Only (Hide on
    screen only)</div>
<div class="d-none d-lg-block d-print-block">Hide up to
    large on screen, but always show on print</div>
```

This was about the Bootstrap utility display; now let's jump to our next section and learn about the utility flex.

FLEX

You can easily adjust the alignment, layout, and scaling of grid columns, navigation, components, and more with a comprehensive set of responsive flexbox tools. For more intricate applications, custom CSS may be necessary.

Enable Flex Behaviors

Create a flexbox container with display utilities and convert *natural children components* into flex items. Additional flex characteristics may be applied to flex containers and objects to further customize them.

```
<div class="d-flex p-2 bd-highlight">I'm a flexbox
    container!</div>
<div class="d-inline-flex p-2 bd-highlight">I'm an
    inline flexbox container!</div>
```

Responsive variations also exist for the .d-flex and .d-inline-flex.

- .d-flex
- .d-inline-flex
- .d-sm-flex
- .d-sm-inline-flex
- .d-md-flex
- .d-md-inline-flex
- .d-lg-flex
- .d-lg-inline-flex
- .d-xl-flex
- .d-xl-inline-flex
- .d-xxl-flex
- .d-xxl-inline-flex

Direction

Using direction utilities, you may change the direction of flex elements in a flex container. In most cases, you may skip the horizontal class because row is the browser's default. However, there may be situations when you need to enter this number manually.

Use the .flex-row to set horizontal direction (the browser default) or .flex-row-reverse to start the horizontal direction from the other side.

```
<div class="d-flex flex-row bd-highlight mb-3">
 <div class="p-2 bd-highlight">Flex item 1</div>
 <div class="p-2 bd-highlight">Flex item 2</div>
 <div class="p-2 bd-highlight">Flex item 3</div>
</div>
<div class="d-flex flex-row-reverse bd-highlight">
 <div class="p-2 bd-highlight">Flex item 1</div>
 <div class="p-2 bd-highlight">Flex item 2</div>
 <div class="p-2 bd-highlight">Flex item 3</div>
</div>
```

To specify a vertical direction, use .flex-column, or .flex-column-reverse to start the vertical direction from the other side.

```
<div class="d-flex flex-column bd-highlight mb-3">
 <div class="p-2 bd-highlight">Flex item 1</div>
 <div class="p-2 bd-highlight">Flex item 2</div>
 <div class="p-2 bd-highlight">Flex item 3</div>
</div>
<div class="d-flex flex-column-reverse bd-highlight">
 <div class="p-2 bd-highlight">Flex item 1</div>
 <div class="p-2 bd-highlight">Flex item 2</div>
 <div class="p-2 bd-highlight">Flex item 3</div>
</div>
```

Responsive variations exist for the flex direction.

- .flex-row

- .flex-row-reverse

- .flex-column

- .flex-column-reverse

- .flex-sm-row

- .flex-sm-row-reverse

- .flex-sm-column

- .flex-sm-column-reverse

- .flex-md-row

- .flex-md-row-reverse

- .flex-md-column

- .flex-md-column-reverse

- .flex-lg-row

- .flex-lg-row-reverse

- .flex-lg-column

- .flex-lg-column-reverse

- .flex-xl-row

- .flex-xl-row-reverse

- .flex-xl-column

- .flex-xl-column-reverse

- .flex-xxl-row

- .flex-xxl-row-reverse

- .flex-xxl-column

- .flex-xxl-column-reverse

Justify-content

Use justify-content utilities on the flexbox containers to change alignment of flex items on the central axis (the x-axis to start, y-axis if flex-direction: column). Choose from the start (browser default), end, center, between, around, or evenly.

```
<div class="d-flex justify-content-start">...</div>
<div class="d-flex justify-content-end">...</div>
<div class="d-flex justify-content-center">...</div>
<div class="d-flex justify-content-between">...</div>
<div class="d-flex justify-content-around">...</div>
<div class="d-flex justify-content-evenly">...</div>
```

Responsive variations exist for justify-content.

- .justify-content-start
- .justify-content-end
- .justify-content-center
- .justify-content-between
- .justify-content-around
- .justify-content-evenly
- .justify-content-sm-start
- .justify-content-sm-end
- .justify-content-sm-center
- .justify-content-sm-between
- .justify-content-sm-around
- .justify-content-sm-evenly
- .justify-content-md-start
- .justify-content-md-end
- .justify-content-md-center
- .justify-content-md-between
- .justify-content-md-around
- .justify-content-md-evenly
- .justify-content-lg-start
- .justify-content-lg-end
- .justify-content-lg-center
- .justify-content-lg-between
- .justify-content-lg-around
- .justify-content-lg-evenly
- .justify-content-xl-start

- .justify-content-xl-end

- .justify-content-xl-center

- .justify-content-xl-between

- .justify-content-xl-around

- .justify-content-xl-evenly

- .justify-content-xxl-start

- .justify-content-xxl-end

- .justify-content-xxl-center

- .justify-content-xxl-between

- .justify-content-xxl-around

- .justify-content-xxl-evenly

Align-items

To adjust the alignment of flex items on the cross-axis, use the align-items utility on flexbox containers (the y-axis to start, x-axis if flex-direction: column). Choose from the following options: start, finish, center, baseline, or stretch (browser default).

```
<div class="d-flex align-items-start">...</div>
<div class="d-flex align-items-end">...</div>
<div class="d-flex align-items-center">...</div>
<div class="d-flex align-items-baseline">...</div>
<div class="d-flex align-items-stretch">...</div>
```

Responsive variations also exist for align-items.

- .align-items-start

- .align-items-end

- .align-items-center

- .align-items-baseline

- .align-items-stretch

- .align-items-sm-start

- .align-items-sm-end
- .align-items-sm-center
- .align-items-sm-baseline
- .align-items-sm-stretch
- .align-items-md-start
- .align-items-md-end
- .align-items-md-center
- .align-items-md-baseline
- .align-items-md-stretch
- .align-items-lg-start
- .align-items-lg-end
- .align-items-lg-center
- .align-items-lg-baseline
- .align-items-lg-stretch
- .align-items-xl-start
- .align-items-xl-end
- .align-items-xl-center
- .align-items-xl-baseline
- .align-items-xl-stretch
- .align-items-xxl-start
- .align-items-xxl-end
- .align-items-xxl-center
- .align-itcms-xxl-baseline
- .align-items-xxl-stretch

Align-self

Use align-self utilities on flexbox items to change their alignment on the cross-axis individually. Choose from same options as align-items: start, end, center, baseline, or stretch (browser default).

```
<div class="align-self-start">Aligned flex item</div>
<div class="align-self-end">Aligned flex item</div>
<div class="align-self-center">Aligned flex item</div>
<div class="align-self-baseline">Aligned flex item</div>
<div class="align-self-stretch">Aligned flex item</div>
```

Responsive variations exist for align-self.

- .align-self-start
- .align-self-end
- .align-self-center
- .align-self-baseline
- .align-self-stretch
- .align-self-sm-start
- .align-self-sm-end
- .align-self-sm-center
- .align-self-sm-baseline
- .align-self-sm-stretch
- .align-self-md-start
- .align-self-md-end
- .align-self-md-center
- .align-self-md-baseline
- .align-self-md-stretch
- .align-self-lg-start
- .align-self-lg-end
- .align-self-lg-center
- .align-self-lg-baseline
- .align-self-lg-stretch
- .align-self-xl-start
- .align-self-xl-end
- .align-self-xl-center

- .align-self-xl-baseline

- .align-self-xl-stretch

- .align-self-xxl-start

- .align-self-xxl-end

- .align-self-xxl-center

- .align-self-xxl-baseline

- .align-self-xxl-stretch

Fill

Apply the .flex-fill class to a collection of sibling components to force them to widths equal to their content (or equal widths if their content doesn't exceed their border-boxes) while consuming all available horizontal space.

```
<div class="d-flex bd-highlight">
 <div class="p-2 flex-fill bd-highlight">Flex item
      with a lot of content</div>
 <div class="p-2 flex-fill bd-highlight">Flex item</div>
 <div class="p-2 flex-fill bd-highlight">Flex item</div>
</div>
```

Responsive variations exist for flex-fill.

- .flex-fill

- .flex-sm-fill

- .flex-md-fill

- .flex-lg-fill

- .flex-xl-fill

- .flex-xxl-fill

Grow and Shrink

Use .flex-grow-* utilities to toggle flex item's ability to grow to fill available space. In the instance below, the .flex-grow-1 elements use all open space while allowing the remaining two flex items their necessary space.

```
<div class="d-flex bd-highlight">
 <div class="p-2 flex-grow-1 bd-highlight">Flex
            item</div>
 <div class="p-2 bd-highlight">Flex item</div>
 <div class="p-2 bd-highlight">Third flex item</div>
</div>
```

If required, use the .flex-shrink-* utilities to toggle a flex item's ability to shrink. The second flex item with the.flex-shrink-1 is forced to wrap its contents to a new line, "shrinking," to make room for the preceding flex item with .w-100.

```
<div class="d-flex bd-highlight">
 <div class="p-2 w-100 bd-highlight">Flex item</div>
 <div class="p-2 flex-shrink-1 bd-highlight">Flex
            item</div>
</div>
```

Responsive variations exist for flex-grow and flex-shrink.

- .flex-{grow|shrink}-0

- .flex-{grow|shrink}-1

- .flex-sm-{grow|shrink}-0

- .flex-sm-{grow|shrink}-1

- .flex-md-{grow|shrink}-0

- .flex-md-{grow|shrink}-1

- .flex-lg-{grow|shrink}-0

- .flex-lg-{grow|shrink}-1

- .flex-xl-{grow|shrink}-0

- .flex-xl-{grow|shrink}-1

- .flex-xxl-{grow|shrink}-0

- .flex-xxl-{grow|shrink}-1

Auto-margins

When you combine flex alignments with auto-margins, flexbox can do some pretty amazing things. Three instances of manipulating flex items with auto-margins are shown below: default (no auto-margin), pushing two items to right (.me-auto), and pushing two items to the left (.me-auto).

```
<div class="d-flex bd-highlight mb-3">
 <div class="p-2 bd-highlight">Flex item</div>
 <div class="p-2 bd-highlight">Flex item</div>
 <div class="p-2 bd-highlight">Flex item</div>
</div>

<div class="d-flex bd-highlight mb-3">
 <div class="me-auto p-2 bd-highlight">Flex item</div>
 <div class="p-2 bd-highlight">Flex item</div>
 <div class="p-2 bd-highlight">Flex item</div>
</div>

<div class="d-flex bd-highlight mb-3">
 <div class="p-2 bd-highlight">Flex item</div>
 <div class="p-2 bd-highlight">Flex item</div>
 <div class="ms-auto p-2 bd-highlight">Flex item</div>
</div>
```

With Align-items

Mix align-items, flex-direction: column, and margin-top: auto or margin-bottom: auto to shift one flex item vertically to the top or bottom of container.

```
<div class="d-flex align-items-start flex-column
    bd-highlight mb-3" style="height: 200px;">
 <div class="mb-auto p-2 bd-highlight">Flex item</div>
 <div class="p-2 bd-highlight">Flex item</div>
 <div class="p-2 bd-highlight">Flex item</div>
</div>

<div class="d-flex align-items-end flex-column
    bd-highlight mb-3" style="height: 200px;">
 <div class="p-2 bd-highlight">Flex item</div>
 <div class="p-2 bd-highlight">Flex item</div>
 <div class="mt-auto p-2 bd-highlight">Flex item</div>
</div>
```

Wrap

Change how flex items wrap in a flex container. Choose from no wrapping at all with the .flex-nowrap, wrapping with .flex-wrap, or reverse wrapping with .flex-wrap-reverse.

```
<div class="d-flex flex-nowrap">
...
</div>
<div class="d-flex flex-wrap">
...
</div>
<div class="d-flex flex-wrap-reverse">
...
</div>
```

Responsive variations exist for flex-wrap.

- .flex-nowrap
- .flex-wrap
- .flex-wrap-reverse
- .flex-sm-nowrap
- .flex-sm-wrap
- .flex-sm-wrap-reverse
- .flex-md-nowrap
- .flex-md-wrap
- .flex-md-wrap-reverse
- .flex-lg-nowrap
- .flex-lg-wrap
- .flex-lg-wrap-reverse
- .flex-xl-nowrap
- .flex-xl-wrap
- .flex-xl-wrap-reverse
- .flex-xxl-nowrap
- .flex-xxl-wrap
- .flex-xxl-wrap-reverse

Order

Change the *visual* order of specific flex items with a handful of order utilities. We provide options for making an item first or last and reset to use the DOM order. As the order takes any integer value from 0 to 5, add custom CSS for any additional values needed.

```
<div class="d-flex flex-nowrap bd-highlight">
 <div class="order-3 p-2 bd-highlight">First flex
           item</div>
 <div class="order-2 p-2 bd-highlight">Second flex
           item</div>
 <div class="order-1 p-2 bd-highlight">Third flex
           item</div>
</div>
```

Responsive variations exist for order.

- .order-0

- .order-1

- .order-2

- .order-3

- .order-4

- .order-5

- .order-sm-0

- .order-sm-1

- .order-sm-2

- .order-sm-3

- .order-sm-4

- .order-sm-5

- .order-md-0

- .order-md-1

- .order-md-2

- .order-md-3
- .order-md-4
- .order-md-5
- .order-lg-0
- .order-lg-1
- .order-lg-2
- .order-lg-3
- .order-lg-4
- .order-lg-5
- .order-xl-0
- .order-xl-1
- .order-xl-2
- .order-xl-3
- .order-xl-4
- .order-xl-5
- .order-xxl-0
- .order-xxl-1
- .order-xxl-2
- .order-xxl-3
- .order-xxl-4
- .order-xxl-5

Additionally, there are responsive also: order-first and .order-last classes that change the order of element by applying order: -1 and order: 6, respectively.

- .order-first
- .order-last
- .order-sm-first

- .order-sm-last

- .order-md-first

- .order-md-last

- .order-lg-first

- .order-lg-last

- .order-xl-first

- .order-xl-last

- .order-xxl-first

- .order-xxl-last

Align Content

To align flex items on the cross-axis, use the align-content utilities on flex-box containers. Start (browser default), end, center, between, around, or stretch, all are options. We've enforced flex-wrap: wrap and increased the amount of flex objects to showcase these utilities.

Note: This parameter has no effect on individual rows of flex items.

```
<div class="d-flex align-content-start flex-wrap">
...
</div>
<div class="d-flex align-content-end flex-wrap">...</
    div>
<div class="d-flex align-content-center flex-
    wrap">...</div>
<div class="d-flex align-content-between flex-
    wrap">...</div>
<div class="d-flex align-content-around flex-
    wrap">...</div>
<div class="d-flex align-content-stretch flex-
    wrap">...</div>
```

Responsive variations also exist for align-content.

- .align-content-start

- .align-content-end

- .align-content-center
- .align-content-around
- .align-content-stretch
- .align-content-sm-start
- .align-content-sm-end
- .align-content-sm-center
- .align-content-sm-around
- .align-content-sm-stretch
- .align-content-md-start
- .align-content-md-end
- .align-content-md-center
- .align-content-md-around
- .align-content-md-stretch
- .align-content-lg-start
- .align-content-lg-end
- .align-content-lg-center
- .align-content-lg-around
- .align-content-lg-stretch
- .align-content-xl-start
- .align-content-xl-end
- .align-content-xl-center
- .align-content-xl-around
- .align-content-xl-stretch
- .align-content-xxl-start
- .align-content-xxl-end
- .align-content-xxl-center
- .align-content-xxl-around
- .align-content-xxl-stretch

Media Object

Looking to replicate media object component from the Bootstrap-4? It is easy to recreate with a few flex utilities that provide even more freedom and customization than previously.

```
<div class="d-flex">
 <div class="flex-shrink-0">
  <img src="..." alt="...">
 </div>
 <div class="flex-grow-1 ms-3">
```

This is some media component material. This may be replaced with any material and adjusted as needed.

```
 </div>
</div>
<div class="d-flex align-items-center">
 <div class="flex-shrink-0">
  <img src="..." alt="...">
 </div>
 <div class="flex-grow-1 ms-3">
This is some media component material. This may be
replaced with any material and adjusted as needed.
 </div>
</div>
```

This was about the Bootstrap utility flex. Now let's jump to our next section and learn about the utility float.

FLOAT

Using our responsive float tools, you can toggle floats on any element at any breakpoint. Let's go through the overview and get started with learning.

Overview

These utility classes use the CSS float property to float an element to the left or right, or deactivate floating, depending on the current viewport size. It is included to avoid issues with specificity. The viewport breakpoints are the same as in our grid system. Please keep in mind that float utilities have no effect on flex items.

```
<div class="float-start">Float start on all viewport
          sizes</div><br>
```

```
<div class="float-end">Float end on all viewport
        sizes</div><br>
<div class="float-none">Don't float on all viewport
        sizes</div>
```

Responsive

Responsive variations exist for each float value.

```
<div class="float-sm-start">Float start on viewports
        sized SM (small) or wider</div><br>
<div class="float-md-start">Float start on viewports
        sized MD (medium) or wider</div><br>
<div class="float-lg-start">Float start on viewports
        sized LG (large) or wider</div><br>
<div class="float-xl-start">Float start on viewports
        sized XL (extra-large) or wider</div><br>
```

Here are all the support classes:

- .float-start
- .float-end
- .float-none
- .float-sm-start
- .float-sm-end
- .float-sm-none
- .float-md-start
- .float-md-end
- .float-md-none
- .float-lg-start
- .float-lg-end
- .float-lg-none
- .float-xl-start
- .float-xl-end
- .float-xl-none
- .float-xxl-start

- .float-xxl-end

- .float-xxl-none

This was about the Bootstrap utility float. Now let's jump to our next section and learn about the utility interactions.

INTERACTIONS

Utility classes alter how visitors interact with a website's content.

Text Selection

Change how the content is selected when the user interacts with it.

```
<p class="user-select-all">This paragraph will
    entirely select when clicked by the user.</p>
<p class="user-select-auto">paragraph has default
    select behavior.</p>
<p class="user-select-none">paragraph will not be
    selectable when clicked by the user.</p>
```

Pointer Events

To prevent or add element interactions, Bootstrap provides the .pe-none and .pe-auto classes.

```
<p><ahref="#"class="pe-none"tabindex="-1"aria-disabled="true">This
link</a> cannot be clicked.</p>
```

```
<p><a href="#" class="pe-auto">This link</a> can be clicked (this is
default behavior).</p>
```

```
<pclass="pe-none"><ahref="#"tabindex="-1"aria-disabled="true">This
link</a> cannot be clicked because the <code>pointer-events</
code> property is inherited from its parent. However, <a href="#"
class="pe-auto">this link</a> has a <code>pe-auto</code> class
and can be clicked.</p>
```

This was about the Bootstrap utility interactions. Now let's jump to our next section and learn about the utility overflow.

OVERFLOW

To easily configure how content overflows an element, use these short-hand utilities.

With four default values and classes, you can adjust the overflow property on the fly. By default, these classes are not responsive.

```
<div class="overflow-auto">...</div>
<div class="overflow-hidden">...</div>
<div class="overflow-visible">...</div>
<div class="overflow-scroll">...</div>
```

This was about the Bootstrap utility overflow. Now let's jump to our next section and learn about the utility position.

POSITION

Use these shorthand tools to rapidly configure an element's location.

Position Values

There are quick positioning classes available; however they are not responsive.

```
<div class="position-static">...</div>
<div class="position-relative">...</div>
<div class="position-absolute">...</div>
<div class="position-fixed">...</div>
<div class="position-sticky">...</div>
```

Arrange Elements

It can easily be obtained with the edge-positioning utilities. The format is {property}-{position}.

Here *property* is one of the following:

- **top**: for top vertical position

- **start**: for horizontal left position (in LTR)

- **bottom**: for upright bottom position

- **end**: for horizontal right position (in LTR)

Here *position* is one of the following:

- **0**: for 0 edge position

- **50**: for 50% edge position

- **100**: for 100% edge position

(More position values may be added by adding entries to the $position-values Sass map variable.)

```
<div class="position-relative">
 <div class="position-absolute top-0 start-0"></div>
 <div class="position-absolute top-0 end-0"></div>
 <div class="position-absolute top-50 start-50"></div>
 <div class="position-absolute bottom-50 end-50"></div>
 <div class="position-absolute bottom-0 start-0"></div>
 <div class="position-absolute bottom-0 end-0"></div>
</div>
```

Center Elements

You may also use the transform utility class to center the elements .translate-middle.

This class performs the transformations translateX(-50%) and translateY(-50%) to the element, allowing you to absolute center apart when paired with the edge-positioning utilities.

```
<div class="position-relative">
 <div class="position-absolute top-0 start-0
     translate-middle"></div>
 <div class="position-absolute top-0 start-50
     translate-middle"></div>
 <div class="position-absolute top-0 start-100
     translate-middle"></div>
 <div class="position-absolute top-50 start-0
     translate-middle"></div>
 <div class="position-absolute top-50 start-50
     translate-middle"></div>
 <div class="position-absolute top-50 start-100
     translate-middle"></div>
 <div class="position-absolute top-100 start-0
     translate-middle"></div>
 <div class="position-absolute top-100 start-50
     translate-middle"></div>
 <div class="position-absolute top-100 start-100
     translate-middle"></div>
</div>
```

By appending .translate-middle-x or .translate-middle-y classes, elements can position only in horizontal or vertical direction.

```
<div class="position-relative">
 <div class="position-absolute top-0 start-0"></div>
 <div class="position-absolute top-0 start-50
      translate-middle-x"></div>
 <div class="position-absolute top-0 end-0"></div>
 <div class="position-absolute top-50 start-0
      translate-middle-y"></div>
 <div class="position-absolute top-50 start-50
      translate-middle"></div>
 <div class="position-absolute top-50 end-0
      translate-middle-y"></div>
 <div class="position-absolute bottom-0 start-0"></div>
 <div class="position-absolute bottom-0 start-50
      translate-middle-x"></div>
 <div class="position-absolute bottom-0 end-0"></div>
</div>
```

Examples

Here are some real-life instances of these classes:

```
<button type="button" class="btn btn-primary
        position-relative">
 Mails<span class="position-absolute top-0 start-100
      translate-middle badge rounded-pill
      bg-secondary">+99<span class="visually-
      hidden">unread messages</span></span>
</button>
<button type="button" class="btn btn-dark
        position-relative">
 Marker<svg width="1em" height="1em" viewBox="0 0 16
      16" class="position-absolute top-100 start-50
      translate-middle mt-1 bi bi-caret-down-fill"
      fill="#212529" xmlns="http://www.w3.org/2000/
      svg"><path d="M7.247 11.14L2.451 5.658C1.885
      5.013 2.345 4 3.204 4h9.592a1 1 0 0 1.753
      1.659l-4.796 5.48a1 1 0 0 1-1.506 0z"/></svg>
</button>
<button type="button" class="btn btn-primary
        position-relative">
 Alerts<span class="position-absolute top-0 start-100
      translate-middle badge border border-light
      rounded-circle bg-danger p-2"><span
```

```
      class="visually-hidden">unread messages</
      span></span>
</button>
```

These classes can combine with existing components to build new ones. Remember that by adding entries to the $position-values variable, you may increase its capabilities.

```
<div class="position-relative m-4">
 <div class="progress" style="height: 1px;">
  <div class="progress-bar" role="progressbar"
      style="width: 50%;" aria-valuenow="50" aria-
      valuemin="0" aria-valuemax="100"></div>
 </div>
 <button type="button" class="position-absolute top-0
      start-0 translate-middle btn btn-sm btn-
      primary rounded-pill" style="width: 2rem;
      height:2rem;">1</button>
 <button type="button" class="position-absolute top-0
      start-50 translate-middle btn btn-sm btn-
      primary rounded-pill" style="width: 2rem;
      height:2rem;">2</button>
 <button type="button" class="position-absolute top-0
      start-100 translate-middle btn btn-sm btn-
      secondary rounded-pill" style="width: 2rem;
      height:2rem;">3</button>
</div>
```

This was about the Bootstrap utility position. Now let's jump to our next section and learn about the utility shadows.

SHADOWS

Add or remove shadows to elements with the box-shadow utilities.

Examples

While shadows on elements are disabled by default in Bootstrap and may be enabled with $enable-shadows, you can quickly add or remove a cloud using our box-shadow utility classes. There is support for .shadow-none and three default sizes (which have associated variables to match).

```
<div class="shadow-none p-3 mb-5 bg-light rounded">No
      shadow</div>
```

```
<div class="shadow-sm p-3 mb-5 bg-body rounded">Small
    shadow</div>
<div class="shadow p-3 mb-5 bg-body rounded">Regular
    shadow</div>
<div class="shadow-lg p-3 mb-5 bg-body
    rounded">Larger shadow</div>
```

This was about the Bootstrap utility shadows. Now let's jump to our next section and learn about the utility sizing.

SIZING

You can easily make an element as broad or as tall with our width and height utilities.

Relative to the Parent

Width and height utilities are generated from the utility API in _utilities. CSS. By default, 25%, 50%, 75%, 100%, and auto are supported. Change the variables as needed to generate various utilities.

```
<div class="w-25 p-3" style="background-color:
    #eee;">Width 25%</div>
<div class="w-50 p-3" style="background-color:
    #eee;">Width 50%</div>
<div class="w-75 p-3" style="background-color:
    #eee;">Width 75%</div>
<div class="w-100 p-3" style="background-color:
    #eee;">Width 100%</div>
<div class="w-auto p-3" style="background-color:
    #eee;">Width auto</div>
<div style="height: 100px; background-color:
    rgba(255,0,0,0.1);">
 <div class="h-25 d-inline-block" style="width:
    120px; background-color:
    rgba(0,0,255,.1)">Height 25%</div>
 <div class="h-50 d-inline-block" style="width:
    120px; background-color:
    rgba(0,0,255,.1)">Height 50%</div>
 <div class="h-75 d-inline-block" style="width:
    120px; background-color:
    rgba(0,0,255,.1)">Height 75%</div>
 <div class="h-100 d-inline-block" style="width:
    120px; background-color:
    rgba(0,0,255,.1)">Height 100%</div>
```

```
<div class="h-auto d-inline-block" style="width:
    120px; background-color:
    rgba(0,0,255,.1)">Height auto</div>
</div>
```

You can also use max-width: 100%; and max-height: 100%; utilities as needed.

```
<img src="..." class="mw-100" alt="...">
<div style="height: 100px; background-color:
    rgba(255,0,0,.1);">
 <div class="mh-100" style="width: 100px; height:
    200px; background-color:
    rgba(0,0,255,.1);">Max-height 100%</div>
</div>
```

Relative to the Viewport

You can also use utilities to set the width and height relative to the viewport.

```
<div class="min-vw-100">Min-width 100vw</div>
<div class="min-vh-100">Min-height 100vh</div>
<div class="vw-100">Width 100vw</div>
<div class="vh-100">Height 100vh</div>
```

This was about the Bootstrap utility sizing. Now let's jump to our next section and learn about the utility spacing.

SPACING

To change the appearance of an element, Bootstrap contains a wide selection of shorthand responsive margin, padding, and gap utility classes.

Margin and Padding

Shorthand classes can be used to assign responsive-friendly margin or padding values to an element or a subset of its sides. Individual properties, all properties, and vertical and horizontal properties are all supported. Courses are built from a default Sass map ranging from .25rem to 3rem.

Do you have the CSS Grid layout module installed? Consider using the gap tool.

Notation

There is no breakpoint abbreviation in the notation spacing utilities that apply to all breakpoints from xs to XXL. These classes are used from min-width: 0 onward and are hence unaffected by media queries. However, the remaining breakpoints do have a breakpoint abbreviation.

For xs, the classes are titled propertysides-size, while for sm, md, lg, xl, and xxl, the classes are named {property}{sides}-breakpoint-size.

Here *property* is one of the following:

- **m**: for classes that set margin

- **p**: for classes that set padding

Here *sides* are one of the following:

- **t**: for classes that set the margin-top or padding-top

- **b**: for classes that set the margin-bottom or padding-bottom

- **s**: (start) for classes that set the margin-left or padding-left in LTR, margin-right or padding-right in RTL

- **e**: (end) for classes that set the margin-right or padding-right in LTR, margin-left or padding-left in RTL

- **x**: for classes that set both *-left and *-right

- **y**: for classes that set both *-top and *-bottom

- **blank**: for classes that set the margin or padding on all four sides of the element

Here *size* is one of the following:

- **0**: for classes that eliminate margin or padding by setting it to 0

- **1**: (by default) for the classes that set margin or padding to $spacer *.25

- **2**: (by default) for the classes that set margin or padding to $spacer *.5

- **3**: (by default) for the classes that set margin or padding to $spacer

- **4**: (by default) for the classes that set margin or padding to $spacer * 1.5

- **5**: (by default) for the classes that set margin or padding to $spacer * 3

- **auto**: for classes that set margin to auto

(Additional sizes may be added by adding entries to the $spacers Sass map variable.)

Examples

Here are some typical instances of these classes:

```
.mt-0 {
 margin-top: 0 !important;
}

.ms-1 {
 margin-left: ($spacer *.25) !important;
}

.px-2 {
 padding-left: ($spacer *.5) !important;
 padding-right: ($spacer *.5) !important;
}

.p-3 {
 padding: $spacer !important;
}
```

Horizontal Centering

Additionally, Bootstrap includes a .mx-auto class for horizontally centering fixed-width block-level content – content that has display: block and a width set – by setting the horizontal margins to auto.

```
<div class="mx-auto" style="width: 200px;">
 Centered element
</div>
```

Negative Margin

Margin attributes in CSS can have negative values (padding cannot). Negative margins are disabled by default; however, in Sass they may enable by specifying $enable-negative-margins: true.

The syntax is almost identical to that of the default, positive margin utilities, with the addition of n before the required size. Here's an example class that's opposite of .mt-1:

```
.mt-n1 {
  margin-top: -0.25rem !important;
}
```

Gap

You can utilize gap utilities on the parent grid container while using display: grid. This can help you save time by eliminating the need to add margin utilities to individual grid objects (children of a display: grid container). The $spacers Sass map is used to build gap utilities, which are responsive by default and generated via our utility API.

```
<div class="d-grid gap-3">
 <div class="p-2 bg-light border">Grid item 1</div>
 <div class="p-2 bg-light border">Grid item 2</div>
 <div class="p-2 bg-light border">Grid item 3</div>
</div>
```

All of Bootstrap's grid breakpoints include responsive alternatives, as well as six sizes from the $spacers map (0–5). There is no .gap-auto utility class because it is identical to .gap-0.

This was about the Bootstrap utility spacing. Now let's jump to our next section and learn about the utility text.

TEXT

Documentation and examples for standard text utilities to control alignment, wrapping, weight, and more.

Text Alignment

Quickly realign text to components with text alignment classes. For a start, end, and center alignment, responsive types are available that use the same viewport width breakpoints as the grid system.

```
<p class="text-start">Start aligned text on all
    viewport sizes.</p>
<p class="text-center">Center aligned text on all
    viewport sizes.</p>
<p class="text-end">End aligned text on all viewport
    sizes.</p>
<p class="text-sm-start">Start aligned text on
    viewports sized SM (small) or wider.</p>
<p class="text-md-start">Start aligned text on
    viewports sized MD (medium) or wider.</p>
```

```
<p class="text-lg-start">Start aligned text on
    viewports sized LG (large) or wider.</p>
<p class="text-xl-start">Start aligned text on
    viewports sized XL (extra-large) or wider.</p>
```

Text Wrapping and Overflow

Wrap text with a .text-wrap class.

```
<div class="badge bg-primary text-wrap" style="width:
    6rem;">
 This text should wrap.
</div>
```

Prevent text from wrapping with .text-nowrap class.

```
<div class="text-nowrap bd-highlight" style="width:
    8rem;">
 This text should overflow the parent.
</div>
```

Word Break

Using word break will prevent long strings of text from breaking the layout of your components. We use word-wrap in Bootstrap instead of the more common overflow-wrap for broader browser support and add the deprecated word-break: break-word to avoid issues with flex containers.

```
<p class="text-break">mmmmmmmmmmmmmmmmmmmmmmmmmmmmmmmm
mmmmmmmmmmmmmmmmmmmmmmmmmmmmmmmmmmmmmmmmmmmmmmmmmmmmmmmmmmmmm
mmmmmmmmmmmmmmmmmmmmmm</p>
```

Text Transform

Transform text in components with the text capitalization classes.

```
<p class="text-lowercase">Lowercased text.</p>
<p class="text-uppercase">Uppercased text.</p>
<p class="text-capitalize">CapiTaliZed text.</p>
```

Note how .text-capitalize only changes first letter of each word, leaving the case of any other letters unaffected.

```
<p class="fs-1">.fs-1 text</p>
<p class="fs-2">.fs-2 text</p>
```

```
<p class="fs-3">.fs-3 text</p>
<p class="fs-4">.fs-4 text</p>
<p class="fs-5">.fs-5 text</p>
<p class="fs-6">.fs-6 text</p>
```

Customize your available font sizes by modifying the $font-sizes Sass map.

Font Weight and Italics

With these utilities, you may quickly alter the font-weight or font-style of the text. Font-style utilities are denoted by .fst-*, whereas font-weight utilities are denoted by .fw-*.

```
<p class="fw-bold">Bold text.</p>
<p class="fw-bolder">Bolder weight text.</p>
<p class="fw-normal">Normal weight text.</p>
<p class="fw-light">Light weight text.</p>
<p class="fw-lighter">Lighter weight text.</p>
<p class="fst-italic">Italic text.</p>
<p class="fst-normal">Text with the normal font
    style</p>
```

Line Height

Change the line height with .lh-* utilities.

```
<p class="LH-1">This is a long paragraph written to
    show how the line height of an element is affected
    by our utilities. Classes are assigned to the
    component or, in some cases, to the parent
    element. Using our utility API, these classes may
    be changed as desired.</p>
<p class="LH-sm">This is a long paragraph written to
    show how the line height of an element is affected
    by our utilities. Classes are assigned to either
    the component or the parent element. Using our
    utility API, you may modify these classes as
    desired.</p>
<p class="LH-base">This is a long paragraph written
    to show how the line height of an element is
    affected by our utilities. Classes are assigned to
    the component or, in some cases, to the parent
```

element. Using our utility API, these classes may
be changed as desired.</p>
<p class="LH-LG">This is a long paragraph written to
show how the line height of an element is affected
by our utilities. Classes are assigned to the
component or, in some cases, the parent element.
With our utility API, these classes may be changed
as desired.</p>

Monospace

Change selection to our monospace font stack with the .font-monospace.
<p class="font-monospace">This is in monospace</p>

Reset Color

Reset text or link's color with the .text-reset so that it inherits the color from its parent.

```
<p class="text-muted">
 Muted text with a<a href="#" class="text-
     reset">reset link</a>.
</p>
```

Text Decoration

Decorate text in components with text-decoration classes.

```
<p class="text-decoration-underline">This text has a
    line underneath it.</p>
<p class="text-decoration-line-through">This text has
    a line going through it.</p>
<a href="#" class="text-decoration-none">This link
    has its text decoration removed</a>
```

This was about the Bootstrap utility text. Now let's jump to our next section and learn about the utility vertical alignment.

VERTICAL ALIGNMENT

The vertical alignment in Bootstrap of inline, inline-block, inline-table, and table-cell components can be easily changed.

The vertical-alignment utilities allow you to change the alignment of items. Vertical-align only affects the inline, inline-block, inline-table, and table-cell components of the page.

Choose from the following options: .align-baseline,.align-top,.align-m iddle,.align-bottom,.align-text-bottom, and .align-text-top.

Use our flex box utilities to vertically center non-inline content (like <div>s and more).

With inline elements

```
<span class="align-baseline">baseline</span>
<span class="align-top">top</span>
<span class="align-middle">middle</span>
<span class="align-bottom">bottom</span>
<span class="align-text-top">text-top</span>
<span class="align-text-bottom">text-bottom</span>
```

With Table Cells

```
<table style="height: 100px;">
 <tbody>
  <tr>
   <td class="align-baseline">baseline</td>
   <td class="align-top">top</td>
   <td class="align-middle">middle</td>
   <td class="align-bottom">bottom</td>
   <td class="align-text-top">text-top</td>
   <td class="align-text-bottom">text-bottom</td>
  </tr>
 </tbody>
</table>
```

This was about the Bootstrap utility vertical alignment. Now let's jump to our next section and learn about the utility visibility.

VISIBILITY

With visibility utilities, you may control the visibility of objects without changing their appearance.

With our visibility utilities, you may control the visibility of items. These utility classes have no effect on the display value or the layout. Even if the elements are invisible, they nevertheless take up space on the page.

Apply .visible or .invisible as needed.

```
<div class="visible">...</div>
<div class="invisible">...</div>
```

```
// Class
.visible {
 visibility: visible !important;
}
.invisible {
 visibility: hidden !important;
}
```

Example

So far, we have learned a lot of things about Bootstrap. Not it is time to test and use some of the functions, components, and elements of Bootstrap for better knowledge.

The code below is a basic example of a Bootstrap template for better understanding.

Note: Different parts and different elements are divided and titled with comments.

```
<!DOCTYPE html>
<html lang="en">
  <head>
    <meta charset="utf-8" />
    <meta name="viewport" content="width=device-
      width, initial-scale=2, shrink-to-fit=no" />
    <meta name="description" content="" />
    <meta name="author" content="" />
    <title>Shop Item - Start Bootstrap Template</title>
    <!-- Favicon-->
    <link rel="icon" type="image/x-icon"
          href="assets/favicon.ico" />
    <!-- Bootstrap icons-->
    <link href="https://cdn.jsdelivr.net/npm/
          bootstrap-icons@1.5.0/font/bootstrap-icons
          .css" rel="stylesheet" />
    <!-- Core theme CSS (includes Bootstrap)-->
    <link href="css/styles.css" rel="stylesheet" />
  </head>
  <body>
    <!-- Navigation-->
    <nav class="navbar navbar-expand-lg navbar-light
        bg-light">
      <div class="container px-4 px-lg-5">
```

```
<a class="navbar-brand" href="#!">Start
        Bootstrap</a>
<button class="navbar-toggler" type="button"
        data-bs-toggle="collapse" data-bs-tar
        get="#navbarSupportedContent" aria-
        controls="navbarSupportedContent"
        aria-expanded="false" aria-
        label="Toggle navigation"><span class
        ="navbar-toggler-icon"></span></but
        ton>
<div class="collapse navbar-collapse"
    id="navbarSupportedContent">
  <ul class="navbar-nav me-auto mb-2 mb-lg-0
    ms-lg-4">
    <li class="nav-item"><a class="nav-link
        active" aria-current="page"
        href="#!">Home</a></li>
    <li class="nav-item"><a class="nav-link"
        href="#!">About</a></li>
    <li class="nav-item dropdown">
        <a class="nav-link dropdown-toggle"
id="navbarDropdown" href="#" role="button" data-bs-
toggle="dropdown" aria-expanded="false">Shop</a>
            <ul class="dropdown-menu"
                    aria-
                    labelledby="navbarDropdown">
            <li><a class="dropdown-item"
                    href="#!">All Products</
                    a></li>
            <li><hr class="dropdown-divider" /></
li>
            <li><a class="dropdown-item"
                    href="#!">Popular
                    Items</a></li>
            <li><a class="dropdown-item"
                    href="#!">New Arrivals</
                    a></li>
        </ul>
    </li>
  </ul>
  <form class="d-flex">
    <button class="btn btn-outline-dark"
        type="submit">
```

```
                <i class="bi-cart-fill me-1">
                Cart
                <span class="badge bg-dark text-white
                            ms-1 rounded-pill">0</span>
              </button>
            </form>
          </div>
        </div>
      </nav>
      <!-- Product section-->
      <section class="py-5">
        <div class="container px-4 px-lg-5 my-5">
          <div class="row gx-4 gx-lg-5
align-items-center">
            <div class="col-md-6"><img class="card-img-
                top mb-5 mb-md-0" src="https://
                dummyimage.com/600x700/dee2e6/6c757d
                .jpg" alt="..." /></div>
            <div class="col-md-6">
              <div class="small mb-1">SKU: BST-498</
div>
              <h1 class="display-5 fw-bolder">Shop item
template</h1>
              <div class="fs-5 mb-5">
                <span class="text-decoration-line-th
rough">$45.00</span>
                <span>$40.00</span>
              </div>
              <p class="lead">Lorem ipsum dolor amet
                consectetur adipisicing elit.</
                p>
              <div class="d-flex">
                <input class="form-control text-center
                    me-3" id="inputQuantity"
                    type="num" value="1" style="max-
                    width: 3rem" />
                <button class="btn btn-outline-dark
                    flex-shrink-0" type="button">
                  <i class="bi-cart-fill me-1"></i>
                  Add to cart
                </button>
              </div>
            </div>
```

```
            </div>
         </div>
      </section>
      <!-- Related items section-->
      <section class="py-5 bg-light">
         <div class="container px-4 px-lg-5 mt-5">
            <h2 class="fw-bolder mb-4">Related products</
h2>
            <div class="row gx-4 gx-lg-5 row-cols-2 row-
               cols-md-3 row-cols-xl-4
               justify-content-center">
               <div class="col mb-5">
                  <div class="card h-100">
                     <!-- Product image-->
                     <img class="card-img-top" src="https://
                        dummyimage.com/450x300/dee2e6
                        /6c757d.jpg" alt="..." />
                     <!-- Product details-->
                     <div class="card-body p-4">
                        <div class="text-center">
                           <!-- Product name-->
                           <h5 class="fw-bolder">Fancy
Product</h5>
                           <!-- Product price-->
                           $40.00 - $80.00
                        </div>
                     </div>
                     <!-- Product actions-->
                     <div class="card-footer p-4 pt-0
                        border-top-0 bg-transparent">
                        <div class="text-center"><a
                           class="btn btn-outline-dark
                           mt-auto" href="#">View options</
                           a></div>
                     </div>
                  </div>
               </div>
               <div class="col mb-5">
                  <div class="card h-100">
                     <!-- Sale badge-->
                     <div class="badge bg-dark text-white
                        position-absolute" style="top:
                        0.5rem; right: 0.5rem">Sale</div>
                     <!-- Product image-->
```

```
        <img class="card-img-top" src="https://
            dummyimage.com/450x300/dee2e6
            /6c757d.jpg" alt="..." />
        <!-- Product details-->
        <div class="card-body p-4">
          <div class="text-center">
            <!-- Product name-->
            <h5 class="fw-bolder">Special
                    Item</h5>
            <!-- Product reviews-->
            <div class="d-flex justify-content-
                center small text-warning
                mb-2">
              <div class="bi-star-fill"></div>
              <div class="bi-star-fill"></div>
              <div class="bi-star-fill"></div>
              <div class="bi-star-fill"></div>
              <div class="bi-star-fill"></div>
            </div>
            <!-- Product price-->
            <span class="text-muted text-decor
                ation-line-through">$20.00</
                span>
            $18.00
          </div>
        </div>
        <!-- Product actions-->
        <div class="card-footer p-4 pt-0
                    border-top-0
                    bg-transparent">
          <div class="text-center"><a
              class="btn btn-outline-dark
              mt-auto" href="#">Add to cart</
              a></div>
        </div>
      </div>
    </div>
  </div>
  <div class="col mb-5">
    <div class="card h-100">
      <!-- Sale badge-->
      <div class="badge bg-dark text-white
          position-absolute" style="top:
          0.5rem; right: 0.5rem">Sale</div>
      <!-- Product image-->
```

```
        <img class="card-img-top" src="https://
            dummyimage.com/450x300/dee2e6
            /6c757d.jpg" alt="..." />
        <!-- Product details-->
        <div class="card-body p-4">
          <div class="text-center">
            <!-- Product name-->
            <h5 class="fw-bolder">Sale Item</
                h5>
            <!-- Product price-->
            <span class="text-muted text-decor
                ation-line-through">$50.00</
                span>
            $25.00
          </div>
        </div>
        <!-- Product actions-->
        <div class="card-footer p-4 pt-0
                    border-top-0
                    bg-transparent">
          <div class="text-center"><a
              class="btn btn-outline-dark
              mt-auto" href="#">Add to cart</
              a></div>
        </div>
      </div>
    </div>
    <div class="col mb-5">
      <div class="card h-100">
        <!-- Product image-->
        <img class="card-img-top" src="https://
            dummyimage.com/450x300/dee2e6
            /6c757d.jpg" alt="..." />
        <!-- Product details-->
        <div class="card-body p-4">
          <div class="text-center">
            <!-- Product name-->
            <h5 class="fw-bolder">Popular
                Item</h5>
            <!-- Product reviews-->
            <div class="d-flex justify-content-
                center small text-warning mb-2">
              <div class="bi-star-fill"></div>
```

```
                <div class="bi-star-fill"></div>
                <div class="bi-star-fill"></div>
                <div class="bi-star-fill"></div>
                <div class="bi-star-fill"></div>
            </div>
            <!-- Product price-->
            $40.00
          </div>
        </div>
        <!-- Product actions-->
        <div class="card-footer p-4 pt-0
            border-top-0 bg-transparent">
          <div class="text-center"><a
              class="btn btn-outline-dark
              mt-auto" href="#">Add to cart</
              a></div>
        </div>
      </div>
    </div>
  </div>
</div>
</section>
<!-- Footer-->
<footer class="py-5 bg-dark">
  <div class="container"><p class="m-0 text-
      center text-white">Copyright &copy; Your
      Website 2021</p></div>
</footer>
<!-- Bootstrap core JS-->
<script src="https://cdn.jsdelivr.net/npm/
        bootstrap@5.1.3/dist/js/bootstrap.bundle
        .min.js"></script>
<!-- Core theme JS-->
<script src="js/scripts.js"></script>
</body>
</html>
```

CONCLUSION

In this chapter, we learned about various utilities offered by the Bootstrap like background, borders, color, display, float, and many more. In the next chapter, we will learn about extending Bootstrap.

CHAPTER 9

Extending Bootstrap

IN THIS CHAPTER

➤ Working with Api

➤ Using Bootstrap in Django

➤ Using Bootstrap in Wordpress

➤ Using Bootstrap in Templates

We discussed numerous utilities provided by the Bootstrap in the previous chapter, such as background, borders, color, display, float, and many more. In this chapter, we will cover how to extend Bootstrap.

At first, let's learn about Bootstrap working with API.

WORKING WITH API

API

The utility API is a Sass-based tool in Bootstrap to generate utility classes with the utility API and can modify or extend the default set of utility classes via Sass. Our utility API is based on Sass maps and functions for generating families of courses with various options. If you're not familiar with Sass maps, start with the official Sass documentation.

If your custom $utilities map is present, the $ utility map contains all of our utilities and is later combined with it. A keyed list of utility groups that accept the following options is included in the utility map:

DOI: 10.1201/9781003310501-9

Option	Type	Description
property	**Required**	Name the property; this can be a string or an array of columns (e.g., horizontal paddings or margins)
values	**Required**	List of values or a map if user don't want the class name to be the same as the value. If null is used as a map key, it isn't compiled
class	Optional	Variable for the class name if user don't want it to be the same as the property. If user rings, the class name will be the first element of the property array
state	Optional	List of pseudo-class variants in Bootstrap like hover or :focus to generate for the utility. No default value
responsive	Optional	Boolean indicates if responsive classes need to be generated. False by default
RFS	Optional	Boolean enables liquid rescaling. Have a look at the RFS page of Bootstrap to find out how this works. False by default
print	Optional	Boolean indicates if print classes need to be generated. False by default
RTL	Optional	Boolean indicates if utility should be kept in RTL. True by default

API Explained

All utility variables are added to the $ utility variable within our _utilities. CSS stylesheet. Each group of utilities in Bootstrap looks something like this:

```
$utilities: (
  "opacity": (
   property: opacity,
   values: (
    0: 0,
    25:.25,
    50:.5,
    75:.75,
    100: 1,
   )
  )
);
```

Which outputs the following:

```
.opacity-0 {opacity: 0;}
.opacity-25 {opacity:.25;}
```

```
.opacity-50 {opacity:.5;}
.opacity-75 {opacity:.75;}
.opacity-100 {opacity: 1;}
```

Custom Class Prefix

Use the class option of Bootstrap to change the class prefix used in the compiled CSS:

```
$utilities: (
 "opacity": (
  property: opacity,
  class: o,
  values: (
   0: 0,
   25:.25,
   50:.5,
   75:.75,
   100: 1,
  )
 )
);
```

Output

```
.o-0 {opacity: 0;}
.o-25 {opacity:.25;}
.o-50 {opacity:.5;}
.o-75 {opacity:.75;}
.o-100 {opacity: 1;}
```

States

To create pseudo-class variations, use the state option. Hover and focus are two examples of pseudo-classes. When a list of states is provided, class names for that pseudo-class are generated. To adjust the opacity of hover, for example, add shape: hover and you'll receive .hover in your compiled CSS:

opacity-hover: opacity-hover: opacity-hover: opacity-hover

Do you require several pseudo-classes? Use a list of states separated by spaces: state: hover focus.

```
$utilities: (
 "opacity": (
```

```
  property: opacity,
  class: opacity,
  state: hover,
  values: (
   0: 0,
   25:.25,
   50:.5,
   75:.75,
   100: 1,
  )
 )
);
```

Output

```
.opacity-0-hover:hover {opacity: 0 !important;}
.opacity-25-hover:hover {opacity:.25 !important;}
.opacity-50-hover:hover {opacity:.5 !important;}
.opacity-75-hover:hover {opacity:.75 !important;}
.opacity-100-hover:hover {opacity: 1 !important;}
```

Responsive Utilities

Add the responsive boolean in Bootstrap to generate responsive utilities (e.g.,.opacity-md-25) across all breakpoints.

```
$utilities: (
 "opacity": (
  property: opacity,
  responsive: true,
  values: (
   0: 0,
   25:.25,
   50:.5,
   75:.75,
   100: 1,
  )
 )
);
```

Output

```
.opacity-0 {opacity: 0 !important;}
.opacity-25 {opacity:.25 !important;}
```

```
.opacity-50 {opacity:.5 !important;}
.opacity-75 {opacity:.75 !important;}
.opacity-100 {opacity: 1 !important;}

@media (min-width: 576px) {
 .opacity-sm-0 {opacity: 0 !important;}
 .opacity-sm-25 {opacity:.25 !important;}
 .opacity-sm-50 {opacity:.5 !important;}
 .opacity-sm-75 {opacity:.75 !important;}
 .opacity-sm-100 {opacity: 1 !important;}
}

@media (min-width: 768px) {
 .opacity-md-0 {opacity: 0 !important;}
 .opacity-md-25 {opacity:.25 !important;}
 .opacity-md-50 {opacity:.5 !important;}
 .opacity-md-75 {opacity:.75 !important;}
 .opacity-md-100 {opacity: 1 !important;}
}

@media (min-width: 992px) {
 .opacity-lg-0 {opacity: 0 !important;}
 .opacity-lg-25 {opacity:.25 !important;}
 .opacity-lg-50 {opacity:.5 !important;}
 .opacity-lg-75 {opacity:.75 !important;}
 .opacity-lg-100 {opacity: 1 !important;}
}

@media (min-width: 1200px) {
 .opacity-xl-0 {opacity: 0 !important;}
 .opacity-xl-25 {opacity:.25 !important;}
 .opacity-xl-50 {opacity:.5 !important;}
 .opacity-xl-75 {opacity:.75 !important;}
 .opacity-xl-100 {opacity: 1 !important;}
}

@media (min-width: 1400px) {
 .opacity-xxl-0 {opacity: 0 !important;}
 .opacity-xxl-25 {opacity:.25 !important;}
 .opacity-xxl-50 {opacity:.5 !important;}
 .opacity-xxl-75 {opacity:.75 !important;}
 .opacity-xxl-100 {opacity: 1 !important;}
}
```

Changing Utilities

Override existing utilities in Bootstrap by using the same key.

For example, if a user wants additional responsive overflow utility classes, user can do this:

```
$utilities: (
 "overflow": (
  responsive: true,
  property: overflow,
  values: visible hidden scroll auto,
 ),
);
```

Print Utilities

Enabling the print option in Bootstrap will also generate utility classes for print, which are only applied within the @media print {...} media query.

```
$utilities: (
 "opacity": (
  property: opacity,
  print: true,
  values: (
   0: 0,
   25:.25,
   50:.5,
   75:.75,
   100: 1,
  )
 )
);
```

Output

```
.opacity-0 {opacity: 0 !important;}
.opacity-25 {opacity:.25 !important;}
.opacity-50 {opacity:.5 !important;}
.opacity-75 {opacity:.75 !important;}
.opacity-100 {opacity: 1 !important;}

@media print {
 .opacity-print-0 {opacity: 0 !important;}
 .opacity-print-25 {opacity:.25 !important;}
```

```
.opacity-print-50 {opacity:.5 !important;}
.opacity-print-75 {opacity:.75 !important;}
.opacity-print-100 {opacity: 1 !important;}
}
```

Importance

The API generates a number of utilities, including! It's crucial to make sure they override components and modifier classes the way they're supposed to. The $enable-important-utilities variable can be used to toggle this setting globally (defaults to true).

Using the API

Now that you're familiar with how the utility API works, learn to add your custom classes and modify the default utilities.

Add Utilities

New utilities can be added in Bootstrap to the default $utilities map with a map merge. Make sure our Sass files and _utilities are up to date. First, import the class, then use map-merge to add your extra utilities. Here's how to create a responsive cursor utility with three settings:

```
@import "bootstrap/scss/functions";
@import "bootstrap/scss/variables";
@import "bootstrap/scss/utilities";
$utilities: map-merge(
 $utilities,
 (
  "cursor": (
   property: cursor,
   class: cursor,
   responsive: true,
   values: auto pointer grab,
  )
 )
);
```

Modify Utilities

With the map-get and map-merge functions, you can modify existing utilities in the default $utilities map. In the example below, we're adding value to the width utilities. Start with an initial map merge and then specify which utility the user wants to modify.

To access and edit the utility's options and values, use map-get to acquire the nested "width" map.

```
@import "bootstrap/scss/functions";
@import "bootstrap/scss/variables";
@import "bootstrap/scss/utilities";
$utilities: map-merge(
 $utilities,
 (
  "width": map-merge(
   map-get($utilities, "width"),
   (
    values: map-merge(
     map-get(map-get($utilities, "width"), "values"),
     (10: 10%),
    ),
   ),
  ),
 )
);
```

Enable Responsively

The user can enable responsive classes for a preexisting collection of Bootstrap utilities that are not yet responsive by default.

For example, to make border classes responsive:

```
@import "bootstrap/scss/functions";
@import "bootstrap/scss/variables";
@import "bootstrap/scss/utilities";
$utilities: map-merge(
 $utilities, (
  "border": map-merge(
   map-get($utilities, "border"),
   (responsive: true),
  ),
 )
);
```

This will now produce responsive.border and .border-0 versions for each breakpoint. Your produced CSS will look something like this:

```
.border {...}
.border-0 {...}
```

```
@media (min-width: 576px) {
  .border-sm {...}
  .border-sm-0 {...}
}

@media (min-width: 768px) {
  .border-md {...}
  .border-md-0 {...}
}

@media (min-width: 992px) {
  .border-lg {...}
  .border-lg-0 {...}
}

@media (min-width: 1200px) {
  .border-xl {...}
  .border-xl-0 {...}
}

@media (min-width: 1400px) {
  .border-xxl {...}
  .border-xxl-0 {...}
}
```

Rename Utilities

Missing v4 utilities, or used to another naming convention? The utilities API can be used to override the resulting class of a given utility – for example, to rename .ms-* utilities to oldish .ml-*:

```
@import "bootstrap/scss/functions";
@import "bootstrap/scss/variables";
@import "bootstrap/scss/utilities";
$utilities: map-merge(
  $utilities, (
    "margin-start": map-merge(
      map-get($utilities, "margin-start"),
      (class: ml),
    ),
  )
);
```

Remove Utilities

Remove any of the default utilities in Bootstrap by setting the group key to null. For example, to remove all the width utilities, create a $utilities map-merge and add "width": null within.

```
@import "bootstrap/scss/functions";
@import "bootstrap/scss/variables";
@import "bootstrap/scss/utilities";
$utilities: map-merge(
 $utilities,
 (
   "width": null
 )
);
```

Remove Utility in RTL

Some edge cases make RTL styling difficult in Bootstrap, such as line breaks in Arabic. Thus, utilities can be dropped from RTL output by setting the RTL option to false:

```
$utilities: (
 "word-wrap": (
  property: word-wrap word-break,
  class: text,
  values: (break: break-word),
  rtl: false
 ),
);
```

Output

```
/* rtl:begin:remove */
.text-break {
 word-wrap: break-word !important;
 word-break: break-word !important;
}
/* rtl:end:remove */
```

This was all about working with API; now, let's move forward and learn how to use Bootstrap in Django.

USING BOOTSTRAP IN DJANGO

Because we've previously used several Bootstrap components in the home application, open it in the Django project. With minimal coding, you can now create a great webpage. Edit the base.html file under home/templates.

Replace the link tags with the codes listed below. It's used to put the CSS files you downloaded into HTML.

Code

```
<link rel="stylesheet" href="{% static 'css/bootstrap
        .min.css' %}">
<link rel="stylesheet" href="{% static 'css/bootstrap
        .css' %}">
```

If no change is performed, you have applied the Bootstrap CDN approach.

We obtain the same result in both circumstances. However, you may encounter some differences in the first scenario because some CSS files require JS elements. For that, you'll need to conduct some front-end technology research.

This was all about Bootstrap in Django; now let's move forward and learn how to use Bootstrap in WordPress.

USING BOOTSTRAP IN WORDPRESS

WordPress themes create the look and layout of a WordPress site by applying a collection of HTML and CSS style sheets over the framework established by the WordPress core code. Anyone with knowledge of HTML, CSS, and PHP, the programming language used to generate the WordPress core code may make themes, and same skills are also required to create a responsive theme using Bootstrap.

WordPress themes of all sorts include a style.css file that contains all of the theme's styling and meta-information. This file is supported by the leading WordPress theme file, called index.php. To integrate Bootstrap files into the main WordPress files, you'll need to navigate to <wp-content> themes and create a new folder for the Bootstrap theme. Give this new theme folder a name.

Once you've done this, you'll need to duplicate all the required files for creating a WordPress theme of any kind and place them in the folder for your Bootstrap theme. Then, the Bootstrap code can be copied into those files and modified as needed to get the correct elements and style into the music. This way, it's possible to override the existing classes in Bootstrap in favor of new versions, and there is no need to modify Bootstrap's core code.

When all the files needed for building the Bootstrap theme have been added to the theme's folders and installed in the site's main theme folder, the theme can be activated like any other and managed through the website's admin dashboard.

This was all about Bootstrap in WordPress; now let's move forward and learn how to use Bootstrap in Templates.

USING BOOTSTRAP IN TEMPLATES

Instead of keeping all your templates under the apps folder, I would like to create a separate folder and keep all apps templates.

At the level of the manage.py file, create a template folder called *templates* and a static folder called *static*.

This is how our project should be laid out:

We need to notify our Django project about the template path and the location of our static now that we've established a template and a static folder. Add the following path to your settings .py file:

Note: In the template folder, keep all HTML files and in the static folder CSS, keep JavaScript, Image.

Integrate Django Bootstrap Template

Download the Bootstrap 4 template from GitHub or clone it using the below command:

```
git clone https://github.com/studygyaan/Bootstrap-Blog
    -Template.git
```

The template structure in Bootstrap will look like this.

Let's separate the template content by putting all CSS, js, image, and static content in a previously created fixed folder. All static content in Bootstrap should be placed in the static folder.

This is how the static folder will look.

Now we'll go to our template folder. Copy *index.html* and rename it *base.html* in your templates folder.

Load static loading content into the template. Edit the *base.html* and add the below code at the top above <!DOCTYPE html>.

```
{% load static %}
```

Now use static {% static ' ' %} command for loading all images, js, and CSS from the static folder.

Suppose anything is loaded from the static folder, for instance, *css/custom.css*. You need to change href as follows:

```
<link rel="stylesheet" href="css/custom.css">

<link rel="stylesheet" href="{% static 'css/custom.c
    ss' %}">
```

Similarly, change for all tags (*script, img, link*) href which are loading stuff from the static folder.

```
<script src="{% static 'js/custom.js' %}"></script>
<img src="{% static 'img/Django-Post2.png' %}">
<link rel="icon" href="{% static 'img/favicon.ico'
    %}"/>
<link rel="stylesheet" href="{% static 'css/custom.c
    ss' %}">
```

Note: Content loading from CDN will be untouched.

Your template will look like this.

Django Bootstrap-4 Templates Are Extended

User can also extend the template using extends command. This will help your template to be as follows:

```
<!-- base.html -->
{% load static %}
<!DOCTYPE html>
<html lang="en">
  <head>Django Template</head>
  <body>
  {% block content %}    {% endblock content %} %}
  </body>
</html>
<!-- blog.html -->
{% extends 'base.html' %}
{% load static %}
{% block content %}
  <!-- Your HTML Code -->
```

```
<h1>Blog</h1>
{% endblock content %}
```

```
# urls.py
path('', TemplateView.as_view(template_name='blog.html
     ')),
```

CONCLUSION

In this chapter, we learned various things like working with API, using Bootstrap in Django using bootstrap CDN and local copy, and using Bootstrap in WordPress and templates.

Bibliography

.@MDBootstrap. (n.d.). *Angular Radio with Bootstrap*. MDB – Material Design for Bootstrap. Retrieved July 11, 2022, from https://mdbootstrap.com/docs/b5/angular/forms/radio/

@MDBootstrap. (n.d.). *Bootstrap 4 Breadcrumb*. MDB – Material Design for Bootstrap. Retrieved July 11, 2022, from https://mdbootstrap.com/docs/b4/jquery/navigation/breadcrumb/

@MDBootstrap. (n.d.). *Bootstrap 4 Navs*. MDB – Material Design for Bootstrap. Retrieved July 11, 2022, from https://mdbootstrap.com/docs/b4/jquery/navigation/navs/

@MDBootstrap. (n.d.). *Bootstrap 4 Pagination*. MDB – Material Design for Bootstrap. Retrieved July 11, 2022, from https://mdbootstrap.com/docs/b4/jquery/components/pagination/

@MDBootstrap. (n.d.). *Bootstrap 4 Panels*. MDB – Material Design for Bootstrap. Retrieved July 11, 2022, from https://mdbootstrap.com/docs/b4/jquery/components/panels/

@MDBootstrap. (n.d.). *Bootstrap Alerts*. MDB – Material Design for Bootstrap. Retrieved July 11, 2022, from https://mdbootstrap.com/docs/standard/components/alerts/

@MDBootstrap. (n.d.). *Bootstrap Breakpoints*. MDB – Material Design for Bootstrap. Retrieved July 11, 2022, from https://v1.mdbootstrap.com/docs/standard/layout/breakpoints/

@MDBootstrap. (n.d.). *Bootstrap Cards*. MDB – Material Design for Bootstrap. Retrieved July 11, 2022, from https://mdbootstrap.com/docs/standard/components/cards/

@MDBootstrap. (n.d.). *Bootstrap Carousel*. MDB – Material Design for Bootstrap. Retrieved July 11, 2022, from https://mdbootstrap.com/docs/b4/jquery/javascript/carousel/

@MDBootstrap. (n.d.). *Bootstrap Collapse*. MDB – Material Design for Bootstrap. Retrieved July 11, 2022, from https://mdbootstrap.com/docs/standard/components/collapse/

@MDBootstrap. (n.d.). *Bootstrap Dropdowns*. MDB – Material Design for Bootstrap. Retrieved July 11, 2022, from https://mdbootstrap.com/docs/standard/components/dropdowns/

@MDBootstrap. (n.d.). *Bootstrap List Group*. MDB – Material Design for Bootstrap. Retrieved July 11, 2022, from https://mdbootstrap.com/docs/standard/components/list-group/

@MDBootstrap. (n.d.). *Bootstrap Modal*. MDB – Material Design for Bootstrap. Retrieved July 11, 2022, from https://mdbootstrap.com/docs/standard/components/modal/

@MDBootstrap. (n.d.). *React Buttons with Bootstrap*. MDB – Material Design for Bootstrap. Retrieved July 11, 2022, from https://mdbootstrap.com/docs/b5/react/components/buttons/

@MDBootstrap. (n.d.). *Tailwind CSS Accordion – Free Examples & Tutorial*. Tailwind Elements. Retrieved July 11, 2022, from https://tailwind-elements.com/docs/standard/components/accordion/

@MDBootstrap. (n.d.). *Vue Background*. MDB – Material Design for Bootstrap. Retrieved July 11, 2022, from https://mdbootstrap.com/docs/vue/utilities/background/

@MDBootstrap. (n.d.). *Vue Bootstrap Accordion*. MDB – Material Design for Bootstrap. Retrieved July 11, 2022, from https://mdbootstrap.com/docs/vue/components/accordion/

3 Tips for Speeding Up Your Bootstrap Website. (n.d.). SitePoint. Retrieved July 11, 2022, from https://www.sitepoint.com/3-tips-to-speed-up-your-bootstrap-website/

Alerts | Dash Ui – Bootstrap 5 Admin Dashboard Template. (n.d.). Retrieved July 11, 2022, from https://codescandy.com/dashui/docs/alerts.html

Andrzej Kopanski, L. H. (n.d.). *Bootstrap Alerts*. CoreUI. Retrieved July 11, 2022, from https://coreui.io/docs/components/alerts/

Andrzej Kopanski, L. H. (n.d.). *Bootstrap Card*. CoreUI. Retrieved July 11, 2022, from https://coreui.io/docs/components/card/

Andrzej Kopanski, L. H. (n.d.). *Bootstrap Collapse*. CoreUI. Retrieved July 11, 2022, from https://coreui.io/docs/components/collapse/

Andrzej Kopanski, L. H. (n.d.). *Bootstrap Scrollspy*. CoreUI. Retrieved July 11, 2022, from https://coreui.io/docs/components/scrollspy/

Andrzej Kopanski, L. H. (n.d.). *Images*. CoreUI. Retrieved July 11, 2022, from https://coreui.io/docs/content/images/

aprenzel. (2021, January 6). *Using Bootstrap Components with Custom JavaScript*. LogRocket Blog. https://blog.logrocket.com/using-bootstrap-components-with-custom-javascript/

Best Bootstrap Development Company in Noida, Delhi, India. (n.d.). Escale Solutions. Retrieved July 11, 2022, from https://www.escalesolutions.com/services/bootstrap.php

Blazorise Component Library. (n.d.). Blazorise Component Library. Retrieved July 11, 2022, from https://blazorise.com/docs/helpers/utilities/position

Boosted Contributors, O. (n.d.). *Accordion*. Boosted v5.0. Retrieved July 11, 2022, from https://boosted.orange.com/docs/5.0/components/accordion/

Boosted Contributors, O. (n.d.). *Breadcrumb*. Boosted v5.1. . Retrieved July 11, 2022, from https://boosted.orange.com/docs/5.1/components/breadcrumb/

Boosted Contributors, O. (n.d.). *Collapse*. Boosted v5.0. Retrieved July 11, 2022, from https://boosted.orange.com/docs/5.0/components/collapse/

Boosted Contributors, O. (n.d.). *RTL*. Boosted v5.1. Retrieved July 11, 2022, from https://boosted.orange.com/docs/5.1/getting-started/rtl/

Bootstrap. (n.d.). Columns Tutorials. Retrieved July 11, 2022, from http://www.techiematrix.com/Bootstrap-Columns.html

Bootstrap 4 Not Working with Angular 2 App. (2017, December 29). Stack Overflow. https://stackoverflow.com/questions/48028505/bootstrap-4-not-working-with-angular-2-app

Bootstrap 5 Breadcrumb. (n.d.). AdminKit. Retrieved July 11, 2022, from https://adminkit.io/docs/navigation/breadcrumb/

Bootstrap 5 Button Group. (n.d.). AdminKit. Retrieved July 11, 2022, from https://adminkit.io/docs/components/button-group/

Bootstrap 5 Buttons. (n.d.). AdminKit. Retrieved July 11, 2022, from https://adminkit.io/docs/components/buttons/

Bootstrap 5 Colors. (2021, March 29). DEV Community. https://dev.to/mdbootstrap/bootstrap-5-colors-18ip

Bootstrap 5 Colors. (n.d.). Retrieved July 11, 2022, from https://www.w3schools.com/bootstrap5/bootstrap_colors.php

Bootstrap 5 Dropdowns. (n.d.). AdminKit. Retrieved July 11, 2022, from https://adminkit.io/docs/components/dropdowns/

Bootstrap 5 Forms. (n.d.). AdminKit. Retrieved July 11, 2022, from https://adminkit.io/docs/forms/overview/

Bootstrap 5 List Group. (n.d.). AdminKit. Retrieved July 11, 2022, from https://adminkit.io/docs/components/list-group/

Bootstrap 5 Modal. (n.d.). AdminKit. Retrieved July 11, 2022, from https://adminkit.io/docs/components/modal/

Bootstrap 5 Modal. (2020, September 10). GeeksforGeeks. https://www.geeksforgeeks.org/bootstrap-5-modal/

Bootstrap 5 Scrollspy. (n.d.). AdminKit. Retrieved July 11, 2022, from https://adminkit.io/docs/navigation/scrollspy/

Bootstrap 5 Spinners. (n.d.). AdminKit. Retrieved July 11, 2022, from https://adminkit.io/docs/components/spinners/

Bootstrap 5 Toggle Button. (n.d.). Retrieved July 11, 2022, from https://leonardo-clarosmd.com/boe/bootstrap-5-toggle-button

Bootstrap Accordion. (n.d.). Torus Kit. Retrieved July 11, 2022, from https://toruskit.com/docs/components/accordion/

Bootstrap Alerts. (n.d.). Torus Kit. Retrieved July 11, 2022, from https://toruskit.com/docs/components/alerts/

Bootstrap Button Group. (n.d.). Torus Kit. Retrieved July 11, 2022, from https://toruskit.com/docs/components/button-group/

Bootstrap Card. (n.d.). Torus Kit. Retrieved July 11, 2022, from https://toruskit.com/docs/components/card/

Bootstrap Carousel. (n.d.). Torus Kit. Retrieved July 11, 2022, from https://toruskit.com/docs/components/carousel/

Bootstrap Checks & Radios. (n.d.). Torus Kit. Retrieved July 11, 2022, from https://
toruskit.com/docs/forms/checks-and-radios/

Bootstrap Collapse. (n.d.). Torus Kit. Retrieved July 11, 2022, from https://toruskit
.com/docs/components/collapse/

Bootstrap Float. (n.d.). Torus Kit. Retrieved July 11, 2022, from https://toruskit
.com/docs/utilities/float/

Bootstrap Form Control. (n.d.). Torus Kit. Retrieved July 11, 2022, from https://
toruskit.com/docs/forms/form-control/

Bootstrap Forms Overview. (n.d.). Torus Kit. Retrieved July 11, 2022, from https://
toruskit.com/docs/forms/overview/

Bootstrap Modal. (n.d.). Torus Kit. Retrieved July 11, 2022, from https://toruskit
.com/docs/components/modal/

Bootstrap Position. (n.d.). Torus Kit. Retrieved July 11, 2022, from https://toruskit
.com/docs/utilities/position/

Bootstrap Quick Guide Tutorials. (n.d.). Retrieved July 11, 2022, from http://www
.techiematrix.com/Bootstrap-Quick-Guide.html

Bootstrap Scrollspy. (n.d.). Torus Kit. Retrieved July 11, 2022, from https://toruskit
.com/docs/components/scrollspy/

Bootstrap Text. (n.d.). Studytonight. Retrieved July 11, 2022, from https://www
.studytonight.com/bootstrap/bootstrap-text

Breadcrumb – Bootstrap 5 – W3cubDocs. (n.d.). Retrieved July 11, 2022, from
https://docs.w3cub.com/bootstrap~5/components/breadcrumb/index

Browsers and Devices. (n.d.). Material Design for WordPress. Retrieved July 11,
2022, from https://mdwp.io/browsers-and-devices/

Buttons – Bootstrap 5 – W3cubDocs. (n.d.). Retrieved July 11, 2022, from https://
docs.w3cub.com/bootstrap~5/components/buttons/index

Cards – Muze Documentation | Muze – Responsive Website Template. (n.d.).
Retrieved July 11, 2022, from https://fabrx.co/muze-dashboards/documen-
tation/cards.html

Clearfix. (2022, July 5). Modus Bootstrap Developer Guide. https://modus-boot-
strap.trimble.com/utilities/clearfix/

Close Icon. (n.d.). Trimble Modus React Bootstrap Developer Guide. Retrieved
July 11, 2022, from https://modus-react-bootstrap.trimble.com/utilities/
close-icon/

Codescandy. (n.d.). *Spinners – Bootstrap Spinner Examples.* Retrieved July 11,
2022, from https://codescandy.com/coach/bootstrap-5/docs/spinners.html

Colors – Muse Documentation | Muse – Responsive Website Template. (n.d.).
Retrieved July 11, 2022, from https://fabrx.co/muze/documentation/colors
.html

*Components – Collapse – 《Bootstrap v5.1 Documentation》 – 书栈网 ·
BookStack.* (2021, August 9). https://www.bookstack.cn/read/bootstrap-5.1
-en/d2a5284911761e87.md

Contributors, A. D. (n.d.). *Browsers and Devices.* Arizona Bootstrap. Retrieved
July 11, 2022, from https://digital.arizona.edu/arizona-bootstrap/docs/2.0/
getting-started/browsers-devices/

Contributors, A. D. (n.d.). *Cards.* Arizona Bootstrap. Retrieved July 11, 2022, from
https://digital.arizona.edu/arizona-bootstrap/docs/2.0/components/card/

Contributors, A. D. (n.d.). *Pagination*. Arizona Bootstrap. Retrieved July 11, 2022, from https://digital.arizona.edu/arizona-bootstrap/docs/2.0/components/pagination/

CSS Features. (n.d.). Retrieved July 11, 2022, from https://cloges4.github.io/FCC-Tech-Doc/

CSS Variables. (n.d.). The Var() Function. Retrieved July 11, 2022, from https://www.w3schools.com/CSS/css3_variables.asp

Developers, P. (2021, November 19). *How to Speed Up Your Bootstrap Development Process 2022*. Custom Website Design and Development and SEO. https://pixelkraft.net/how-to-speed-up-your-bootstrap-development-process/

Dropdowns. (n.d.). Get Docs. Retrieved July 11, 2022, from https://getdocs.org/Bootstrap/docs/5/components/dropdowns/index

Falcon | Dashboard & Web App Template. (n.d.). Retrieved July 11, 2022, from https://prium.github.io/falcon/v3.4.0/modules/forms/basic/range.html

Flex · Material. (n.d.). Retrieved July 11, 2022, from http://daemonite.github.io/material/docs/4.1/utilities/flex/

Grid Column. (n.d.). Quasar Framework. Retrieved July 11, 2022, from https://quasar.dev/layout/grid/column

Grid Row. (n.d.). Quasar Framework. Retrieved July 11, 2022, from https://v1.quasar.dev/layout/grid/row

Helen Reid, L. G. (n.d.). *Nigerian Oil Firm Lekoil Loses Board Fight With Top Shareholder*. Reuters. Retrieved July 11, 2022, from https://www.reuters.com/article/uk-lekoil-shareholders-idUSKBN29E08V

Holeczek, Ł. (n.d.). *Bootstrap Carousel – Examples & Tutorials. Learn How to Use Bootstrap Carousel*. CoreUI. Retrieved July 11, 2022, from https://coreui.io/docs/2.1/components/carousel/

Hope-Ui. (n.d.). Responsive Bootstrap 5 Admin Doc Template. Retrieved July 11, 2022, from https://templates.iqonic.design/hope-ui/documentation/laravel/dist/components/listgroup.html

How to Create Bootstrap 5 Sidebar Menu Collapse. (n.d.). Retrieved July 11, 2022, from https://shapeyourpath.com/tutorial/bootstrap5/bootstrap-collapse

https://data-flair.training/blogs/django-bootstrap/

https://htmlstream.com/space/documentation/accordion.html

https://htmlstream.com/space/documentation/borders.html

https://htmlstream.com/unify/documentation/backgrounds.html

https://htmlstream.com/unify/documentation/offcanvas.html

https://www.codegrepper.com/code-examples/html/bootstrap+5+line+height

Inc., C. (n.d.). *Grid System | CAST Figuration (v4.0)*. Retrieved July 11, 2022, from https://figuration.org/4.0/layout/grid/

Input Groups. (n.d.). University of Houston. Retrieved July 11, 2022, from https://uh.edu/marcom/resources/bootstrap/components/input-groups/

Interactions. (2022, April 8). WeCodeArt Documentation. https://support.wecodeart.com/documents/wecodeart-framework/getting-started/utilities/interactions/

Jump Start Bootstrap. (n.d.). O'Reilly Online Learning. Retrieved July 11, 2022, from https://www.oreilly.com/library/view/jump-start-bootstrap/9781457174346/ch06.html

Kaliannan, S. (2014, June 20). *Bootstrap Button Groups*. JavaBeat. https://javabeat
.net/bootstrap-button-groups/

Metronic. (n.d.). Dropdown. Retrieved July 11, 2022, from https://preview.keen-
themes.com/metronic-v6/preview/demo1/components/base/dropdown.html

*Modal – Before Getting Started with Bootstrap's Modal Component, be Sure to
Read the Following*. (n.d.). Retrieved July 11, 2022, from https://runebook
.dev/en/docs/bootstrap/components/modal/index

Modal – Components – Docs – Grayshift. (n.d.). Retrieved July 11, 2022, from
https://grayshift.io/docs/components/modal/

Modal. (n.d.). Onekit Documentation. Retrieved July 11, 2022, from https://
onekit.madethemes.com/docs/components/modal.html

Navbar – Muze Documentation | Muze – Responsive Website Template. (n.d.).
Retrieved July 11, 2022, from https://fabrx.co/preview/muse-dashboard/
documentation/navbar.html

NobleUI. (n.d.). *NobleUI – HTML Bootstrap 5 Admin Dashboard Template*.
Retrieved July 11, 2022, from https://www.nobleui.com/html/template/
demo1/pages/ui-components/badges.html

Not familiar with CSS variables, here are 5 examples to see! (n.d.). SegmentFault
思否. Retrieved July 11, 2022, from https://segmentfault.com/a
/1190000040735569/en

Offcanvas. (n.d.). Dash Ui – Bootstrap 5 Admin Dashboard Template. Retrieved
July 11, 2022, from https://codescandy.com/dashui/docs/offcanvas.html

Pagination Component for React Bootstrap 5. (n.d.). Devwares. Retrieved July
11, 2022, from https://www.devwares.com/docs/contrast/react/navigation
/pagination/

PAGINATION. (n.d.). Retrieved July 11, 2022, from https://www.linkedin.com/
pulse/pagination-solomon-iniodu

Position – Helpers – Docs – Grayshift. (n.d.). Retrieved July 11, 2022, from https://
grayshift.io/docs/helpers/position/

React List Group Component. (n.d.). CoreUI. Retrieved July 11, 2022, from https://
coreui.io/react/docs/components/list-group/

React Placeholder Component. (n.d.). CoreUI. Retrieved July 11, 2022, from
https://coreui.io/react/docs/components/placeholder/

React-Bootstrap. (n.d.). React-Bootstrap Documentation. Retrieved July 11, 2022,
from https://react-bootstrap.github.io/components/alerts/

React-Bootstrap. (n.d.). React-Bootstrap Documentation. Retrieved July 11, 2022,
from https://react-bootstrap-v5.netlify.app/components/forms/

RTL – Muze Documentation | Muze – Responsive Website Template. (n.d.).
Retrieved July 11, 2022, from https://fabrx.co/preview/muse-dashboard/
documentation/rtl.html

RuangAdmin. (n.d.). Progress Bars. Retrieved July 11, 2022, from https://indriju-
nanda.github.io/RuangAdmin/progress-bar.html

Rupesh. (2021, December 25). *Grid Declaration*. CODE ONE. https://codeone.in
/grid-declaration/

Sass-Bootstrap中文网 . (n.d.). Retrieved July 11, 2022, from https://www.boot-
strap.cn/doc/read/13.html

Scott, Trevor Satterfield, & The Measured Team, J. M. (n.d.). *Checks and Radios.* Measured Style Guide v5.0. Retrieved July 11, 2022, from https://styleguide .measured.com/docs/5.0/forms/checks-radios/

Scott, Trevor Satterfield, & The Measured Team, J. M. (n.d.). *RTL.* Measured Style Guide v5.0. Retrieved July 11, 2022, from https://styleguide.measured.com/ docs/5.0/getting-started/rtl/

Spinners – Documentation – HomeID. (n.d.). Retrieved July 11, 2022, from https:// templates.g5plus.net/homeid/docs/components/spinners.html

ThemeSelect. (n.d.). *Bootstrap Cards – Chameleon Admin – Modern Bootstrap 4 WebApp & Dashboard HTML Template + UI Kit.* Retrieved July 11, 2022, from https://technext.github.io/chameleon-admin/cards.html

Thornton J. and Bootstrap Contributors, M. O. (n.d.). *Alerts.* Bootstrap v5.0. Retrieved July 11, 2022, from https://getbootstrap.com/docs/5.0/compo- nents/alerts/

Thornton J. and Bootstrap Contributors, M. O. (n.d.). *Alerts.* Bootstrap. Retrieved July 11, 2022, from https://brand.ncsu.edu/bootstrap/v4/docs/4.1/compo- nents/alerts/

Thornton J. and Bootstrap Contributors, M. O. (n.d.). *Breakpoints.* Bootstrap v5.0. Retrieved July 11, 2022, from https://getbootstrap.com/docs/5.0/lay- out/breakpoints/

Thornton J. and Bootstrap Contributors, M. O. (n.d.). *Browsers and Devices.* Boosted. Retrieved July 11, 2022, from https://boosted.orange.com/docs/4 .0/getting-started/browsers-devices/

Thornton J. and Bootstrap Contributors, M. O. (n.d.). *Buttons.* Bootstrap v5.2. Retrieved July 11, 2022, from https://getbootstrap.com/docs/5.2/compo- nents/buttons/

Thornton J. and Bootstrap Contributors, M. O. (n.d.). *Cards.* Bootstrap. Retrieved July 11, 2022, from https://brand.ncsu.edu/bootstrap/v4/docs/4.1/compo- nents/card/

Thornton J. and Bootstrap Contributors, M. O. (n.d.). *Carousel.* Bootstrap. Retrieved July 11, 2022, from https://brand.ncsu.edu/bootstrap/v4/docs/4 .1/components/carousel/

Thornton J. and Bootstrap Contributors, M. O. (n.d.). *Carousel.* Bootstrap v5.1. Retrieved July 11, 2022, from https://getbootstrap.com/docs/5.1/compo- nents/carousel/

Thornton J. and Bootstrap Contributors, M. O. (n.d.). *Collapse.* Bootstrap. Retrieved July 11, 2022, from https://brand.ncsu.edu/bootstrap/v4/docs/4 .1/components/collapse/

Thornton J. and Bootstrap Contributors, M. O. (n.d.). *Dropdowns.* Bootstrap. Retrieved July 11, 2022, from https://brand.ncsu.edu/bootstrap/v4/docs/4 .1/components/dropdowns/

Thornton J. and Bootstrap Contributors, M. O. (n.d.). *Floating Labels.* Bootstrap v5.2. Retrieved July 11, 2022, from https://getbootstrap.com/docs/5.2/forms /floating-labels/

Thornton J. and Bootstrap Contributors, M. O. (n.d.). *Getting Started · Bootstrap 3.3.4 Documentation – BootstrapDocs*. Retrieved July 11, 2022, from https://bootstrapdocs.com/v3.3.4/docs/getting-started/

Thornton J. and Bootstrap Contributors, M. O. (n.d.). *Grid System*. Bootstrap v5.0. Retrieved July 11, 2022, from https://getbootstrap.com/docs/5.0/layout/grid/

Thornton J. and Bootstrap Contributors, M. O. (n.d.). *Images*. Bootstrap. Retrieved July 11, 2022, from https://brand.ncsu.edu/bootstrap/v4/docs/4.1/content/images/

Thornton J. and Bootstrap Contributors, M. O. (n.d.). *Input Group*. Bootstrap. Retrieved July 11, 2022, from https://brand.ncsu.edu/bootstrap/v4/docs/4.1/components/input-group/

Thornton J. and Bootstrap Contributors, M. O. (n.d.). *List Group*. Bootstrap. Retrieved July 11, 2022, from https://brand.ncsu.edu/bootstrap/v4/docs/4.1/components/list-group/

Thornton J. and Bootstrap Contributors, M. O. (n.d.). *Navbar*. Bootstrap v5.2. Retrieved July 11, 2022, from https://getbootstrap.com/docs/5.2/components/navbar/

Thornton J. and Bootstrap Contributors, M. O. (n.d.). *Navbar*. Bootstrap. Retrieved July 11, 2022, from https://brand.ncsu.edu/bootstrap/v4/docs/4.1/components/navbar/

Thornton J. and Bootstrap Contributors, M. O. (n.d.). *Placeholders*. Bootstrap v5.1. Retrieved July 11, 2022, from https://getbootstrap.com/docs/5.1/components/placeholders/

Thornton J. and Bootstrap Contributors, M. O. (n.d.). *Theming Bootstrap*. Bootstrap v4.5. Retrieved July 11, 2022, from https://getbootstrap.com/docs/4.5/getting-started/theming/

Thornton J. and Bootstrap Contributors, M. O. (n.d.). *Toasts*. Bootstrap v5.2. Retrieved July 11, 2022, from https://getbootstrap.com/docs/5.2/components/toasts/

twbs. (2022, June 9). *bootstrap/sass.md at main*. GitHub. https://github.com/twbs/bootstrap/blob/main/site/content/docs/5.2/customize/sass.md

Unit 5: Logarithms. (2021, October 2). Centennial Math Department. https://mycentennial.sd43.bc.ca/mathdept/category/unit-5-logarithms/

Using CSS Custom Properties – CSS – W3cubDocs. (n.d.). Retrieved July 11, 2022, from https://docs.w3cub.com/css/using_css_custom_properties.html

Using CSS Custom Properties (Variables) – CSS: Cascading Style Sheets | MDN. (2022, July 10). https://developer.mozilla.org/en-US/docs/Web/CSS/Using_CSS_custom_properties

Utility API – Get docs. (n.d.). Retrieved July 11, 2022, from https://getdocs.org/Bootstrap/docs/5/utilities/api/index

Yoon, J.-Y. (2021, December 14). *Focal Adhesion*. SpringerLink. https://link.springer.com/chapter/10.1007/978-3-030-83696-2_7

Index

Printed in the United States
by Baker & Taylor Publisher Services